DATE DUE

FEB 2 0 2003		
FEB 0 5 2004		
DEC 2 0 2004		

Demco, Inc. 38-293

Third Edition

An Introduction to Object-Oriented Programming

Third Edition

An Introduction to Object-Oriented Programming

Timothy A. Budd

Oregon State University

Boston San Francisco New York
London Toronto Sydney Tokyo Singapore Madrid
Mexico City Munich Paris Cape Town Hong Kong Montreal

Executive Editor: Susan Hartman Sullivan
Associate Editor: Elinor Actipis
Executive Marketing Manager: Michael Hirsch
Production Supervisor: Diane Freed
Composition: Windfall Software, using ZzTEX
Copyeditor: Debbie Prato
Technical Art: LM Graphics
Proofreader: Brooke Albright
Text Design: Windfall Software
Cover Designer: Gina Hagen Kolenda
Cover Illustration: Susan Cyr
Design Manager: Gina Hagen
Prepress and Manufacturing: Caroline Fell

Access the latest information about Addison-Wesley titles from our World Wide Web site: www.aw.com/cs

Many of the designations used by manufacturers and sellers to distinguish their products are claimed as trademarks. Where those designations appear in this book, and Addison-Wesley was aware of a trademark claim, the designations have been printed in initial caps or all caps.

The programs and applications presented in this book have been included for their instructional value. They have been tested with care, but are not guaranteed for any particular purpose. The publisher does not offer any warranties or representations, nor does it accept any liabilities with respect to the programs or applications.

Library of Congress Cataloging-in-Publication Data

Budd, Timothy.
  An introduction to object-oriented programming / Timothy A. Budd.—3rd ed.
    p. cm.
  Includes index.
  ISBN 0-201-76031-2(pbk.)
  1. Object-oriented programming (Computer science) I. Title.

QA76.64B83 2002
005.1'17–dc21

2001045060
CIP

1 2 3 4 5 6 7 8 9 10—HP—04030201

Preface

When I began writing my first book on Smalltalk in 1983, I distinctly remember thinking that I must write quickly so as to not miss the crest of the object-oriented programming wave. Who would have thought that two decades later object-oriented programming would still be going strong? And what a long, strange trip it has been.

In the two decades that object-oriented programming has been studied, it has become *the* dominant programming paradigm. In the process, it has changed almost every facet of computer science. And yet I find that my goal for the third edition of this book has remained unchanged from the first. It is still my hope to impart to my students and, by extension, my readers an understanding of object-oriented programming based on general principles and not specific to any particular language.

Languages come and go in this field with dizzying rapidity. In the first edition I discussed Objective-C and Apple's version of Object Pascal, both widely used at that time. Although both languages still exist, neither can at present be considered a dominant language. (However, I talk about Objective-C in the third edition because from a language point of view it has many interesting and unique features.) Between the first edition and the third many languages seem to have disappeared (such as Actor and Turing), while others have come into existence (such as Java, Eiffel, and Self). Many existing languages have acquired object extensions (such as Common Lisp and Object Perl), and many have burst onto the scene for a short while and then just as suddenly disappeared (for example, Sather and Dylan). Then there is Beta, a language that hints at wonderful ideas behind an incomprehensible syntax. Prediction is difficult, particularly about the future. Will languages that are just now appearing, such as Ruby, have staying power, or will they go the way of Dylan? What about C#? It is difficult to imagine that any language with Microsoft behind it will fail to be successful, but stranger things have happened. (Personally, I think that C# will last because it presents a route for Visual Basic programmers to finally progress to a better language, but that

v

few Java or C++ programmers will migrate to the new language. Time will tell if my powers of foresight are any better than anybody else's.)

For the present edition I have expanded the number of languages that I use for examples, but I have eliminated many long narratives on a single language. Descriptions of techniques are often given in the form of tables or shorter explanations. As with the first two editions, I make no pretenses of being a reference manual for any language, and students producing anything more than trivial programs in any of the languages I discuss would do well to avail themselves of a language-specific source.

Nevertheless, in this third edition I have attempted to retain the overall structure I used in the first two editions. This can be described as a series of themes.

I. Introduction and Design. Chapter 1 introduces in an informal setting the basic concepts of object-oriented programming. Chapter 2 continues this by discussing the tools used by computer scientists to deal with complexity and how object-oriented techniques fit into this framework. Chapter 3 introduces the principle of designing by responsibility. These three chapters are fundamental, and their study should not be given short shrift. In particular, I strongly encourage at least one, if not several, group exercises in which CRC cards, introduced in Chapter 3, are used in problem solving. The manipulation of physical index cards in a group setting is one of the best techniques I have encountered for developing and reinforcing the notions of behavior, responsibility, and encapsulation.

In the past decade the field of object-oriented design has expanded considerably. And for many readers Chapter 3 may either be too little or too much—too much if they already have extensive experience with object-oriented modeling languages and design, and too little if they have never heard of these topics. Nevertheless, I have tried to strike a balance. I have continued to discuss responsibility-driven design, although it is now only one of many alternative object-oriented design techniques, because I think it is the simplest approach for beginning students to understand.

II. Classes, Methods, and Messages. Chapters 4 and 5 introduce the basic syntax used by our example languages (Smalltalk, C++, Java, Objective-C, Object and Delphi Pascal, and several others) to create classes and methods and to send messages. Chapter 4 concentrates on the compile-time features (classes and methods), and Chapter 5 describes the dynamic aspects (creating objects and sending messages). Chapters 6 and 7 reinforce these ideas with the first of a series of *case studies*—example programs developed in an object-oriented fashion and illustrating various features of the technique.

III. Inheritance and Software Reuse. Although inheritance is introduced in Chapter 1, it does not play a prominent role again until Chapter 8. Inheritance and polymorphic substitution is discussed as a primary technique for software reuse. The case study in Chapter 9, written in the newly introduced language C#, both illustrates the application of inheritance and the use of a standard API (application programming interface).

IV. Inheritance in More Detail.   Chapters 10 through 13 delve into the concepts of inheritance and substitution in greater detail. The introduction of inheritance into a programming language has an impact on almost every other aspect of the language, and this impact is often not initially obvious to the student (or programmer). Chapter 10 discusses the sometimes subtle distinction between *subclasses* and *subtypes*. Chapter 11 investigates how different languages approach the use of static and dynamic features. Chapter 12 examines some of the surprising implications that result from the introduction of inheritance and polymorphic substitution into a language. Chapter 13 discusses the often misunderstood topic of multiple inheritance.

V. Polymorphism.   Much of the power of object-oriented programming comes through the application of various forms of polymorphism. Chapter 14 introduces the basic mechanisms used for attaining polymorphism in object-oriented languages and is followed by four chapters that explore the principal forms of polymorphism in great detail.

VI. Applications of Polymorphism.   Chapter 19 examines one of the most common applications of polymorphism, the development of classes for common data structure abstractions. Chapter 20 is a case study that examines a recent addition to the language C++, the STL. Chapter 21 presents the idea of *frameworks*, a popular and very successful approach to software reuse that builds on the mechanisms provided by polymorphism. Chapter 22 describes one well-known framework, the Java Abstract Windowing Toolkit.

VII. Object Interactions.   Starting in Chapter 23 we move up a level of abstraction and consider classes in more general relationships and not just the parent/child relationship. Chapter 23 discusses the ways two or more classes (or objects) can interact with each other. Many of these interactions have been captured and defined in a formalism called a *design pattern*. The concept of design patterns and a description of the most common design patterns are presented in Chapter 24.

VIII. Advanced Topics.   The final three chapters discuss topics that can be considered advanced for an introductory text such as this one. These include the idea of reflection and introspection (Chapter 25), network programming (Chapter 26), and the implementation techniques used in the execution of object-oriented languages (Chapter 27).

In the ten-week course I teach at Oregon State University I devote approximately one week to each of the major areas just described. Students in this course are upper-division undergraduate and first-year graduate students. In conjunction with the lectures, students work on moderate-sized projects, using an object-oriented language of their choice, and the term ends with student presentations of project designs and outcomes.

Any attempt to force a complex and multifaceted topic into a linear narrative will run into issues of ordering, and this book is no exception. In general my approach has been to introduce an idea as early as possible and then in later chapters explore the idea in more detail, bringing out aspects or issues that might not be obvious on first encounter. Despite my opinion that my ordering makes sense, I am aware that others may find it convenient to select a different approach. In particular, some instructors find it useful to bring forward some of the software engineering issues that I postpone until Chapter 23, thereby bringing them closer to the design chapter (Chapter 3). Similarly, while multiple inheritance is a form of inheritance and therefore rightly belongs in Section IV, the features that make multiple inheritance difficult to work with derive from interactions with polymorphism and hence might make more sense after students have had time to read Section V. For these reasons and many more, instructors should feel free to adapt the material and the order of presentation to their own particular circumstance.

Assumed Background ◻

I have presented the material in this book assuming only that the reader is knowledgeable in some conventional programming language, such as Pascal or C. In my courses, the material has been used successfully at the upper-division (junior or senior) undergraduate level and at the first-year graduate level. In some cases (particularly in the last quarter of the book), further knowledge may be helpful but is not assumed. For example, a student who has taken a course in software engineering may find some of the material in Chapter 23 more relevant, and one who has had a course in compiler construction will find Chapter 27 more intelligible. Both chapters can be simplified in presentation if necessary.

Many sections have been marked with an asterisk (*). These represent optional material. Such sections may be interesting but are not central to the ideas being presented. Often they cover a topic that is relevant only to a particular object-oriented language and not to object-oriented programming in general. This material can be included or omitted at the discretion of the instructor, depending on the interests and backgrounds of the students and the instructor or on the dictates of time.

Obtaining the Source ⊡

Source code for the case studies presented in the book can be accessed via the mechanism of anonymous ftp from the machine `ftp.cs.orst.edu` in the directory `/pub/budd/oopintro`. This directory will also be used to maintain a number of other items, such as an errata list, study questions for each chapter, and copies of the overhead slides I use in my course. This information can also be accessed via the World Wide Web from my personal home pages at `http://www.cs.orst.edu/~budd`. Requests for further information can be forwarded to the electronic mail address `budd@cs.orst.edu` or to Professor Timothy A. Budd, Department of Computer Science, Oregon State University, Corvallis, Oregon 97331.

Acknowledgments ⊡

I am certainly grateful to the 65 students in my course, CS589, at Oregon State University, who in the fall of 1989 suffered through the development of the first draft of the first edition of this text. They received one chapter at a time, often only a day or two before I lectured on the material. Their patience in this regard is appreciated. Their specific comments, corrections, critiques, and criticisms were most helpful. In particular, I wish to acknowledge the detailed comments provided by Thomas Amoth, Kim Drongesen, Frank Griswold, Rajeev Pandey, and Phil Ruder.

The solitaire game developed in Chapter 9 was inspired by the project completed by Kim Drongesen, and the billiards game in Chapter 7 was based on the project by Guenter Mamier and Dietrich Wettschereck. In both cases, however, the code itself has been entirely rewritten and is my own. In fact, in both cases my code is considerably stripped down for the purposes of exposition and is in no way comparable to the greatly superior projects completed by those students.

For an author, it is always useful to have others provide an independent perspective on one's work, and I admit to gaining useful insights into the first edition from a study guide prepared by Arina Brintz, Louise Leenen, Tommie Meyer, Helene Rosenblatt, and Anel Viljoen of the Department of Computer Science and Information Systems at the University of South Africa in Pretoria.

Countless people have provided assistance by pointing out errors or omissions in the first two editions and by offering improvements. I am grateful to them all and sorry that I cannot list them by name.

I benefitted greatly from comments provided by several readers of an early manuscript draft of this third edition. These reviewers included Ali Behforooz (Towson University), Hang Lau (Concordia University, Canada), Blayne Mayfield (Oklahoma State University), Robert Morse (University of Evansville), Roberto

Ordóñez (Andrews University), Shon Vick (University of Maryland, Baltimore County), and Conrad Weisert (Information Disciplines, Inc.). I have made extensive revisions in response to their comments, and therefore any remaining errors are mine alone and no reflection on their efforts.

For the third edition my capable, competent, and patient editor at Addison-Wesley has been Susan Hartman-Sullivan, assisted by Elinor Actipis. Final copy was coordinated by Diane Freed. Layout and production were performed by Paul Anagnostopoulos and Jacqui Scarlott of Windfall Software. I have worked with Paul and Jacqui on several books now, and I'm continually amazed by the results they are able to achieve from my meager words.

Contents

5   ▫   Messages, Instances, and Initialization   101

6   ▫   A Case Study: The Eight-Queens Puzzle 125

7 ◻ A Case Study: A Billiards Game   147

8 ◻ Inheritance and Substitution   161

10 ▫ Subclasses and Subtypes   207

11 ▫ Static and Dynamic Behavior   221

12 ▫ Implications of Substitution   235

13 ▫ Multiple Inheritance   253

23 ▫ Object Interconnections   441

24 ▫ Design Patterns   463

25 ▫ Reflection and Introspection   479

Third Edition

An Introduction to Object-Oriented Programming

CHAPTER 1

Thinking Object-Oriented

Although the fundamental features of what we now call object-oriented programming were invented in the 1960s, object-oriented languages really caught the attention of the computing public-at-large in the 1980s. Two seminal events were the publication of a widely read issue of *Byte* (August 1981) that described the programming language Smalltalk, and the first international conference on object-oriented programming languages and applications, held in Portland, Oregon in 1986.

Now, almost 20 years later, the situation noted in the first edition of this book (1991) still exists.

Object-oriented programming (OOP) has become exceedingly popular in the past few years. Software producers rush to release object-oriented versions of their products. Countless books and special issues of academic and trade journals have appeared on the subject. Students strive to list "experience in object-oriented programming" on their résumés. To judge from this frantic activity, object-oriented programming is being greeted with even more enthusiasm than we saw heralding earlier revolutionary ideas, such as "structured programming" or "expert systems."

My intent in these first two chapters is to investigate and explain the basic principles of object-oriented programming and, in so doing to illustrate the following two propositions.

- OOP is a revolutionary idea, totally unlike anything that has come before in programming.

- OOP is an evolutionary step, following naturally on the heels of earlier programming abstractions.

1.1 ▢ Why Is OOP Popular?

There are a number of important reasons why in the past two decades object-oriented programming has become the dominant programming paradigm. Object-oriented programming scales very well, from the most trivial of problems to the most complex tasks. It provides a form of abstraction that resonates with techniques people use to solve problems in their everyday lives. And for most of the dominant object-oriented languages there are an increasingly large number of libraries that assist in the development of applications for many domains.

Object-oriented programming is just the latest in a long series of solutions that has been proposed to help solve the "software crisis." At heart, the software crisis simply means that our imaginations, and the tasks we would like to solve with the help of computers, almost always outstrip our abilities.

But while object-oriented techniques *do* facilitate the creation of complex software systems, it is important to remember that OOP is not a panacea. Programming a computer is still one of the most difficult tasks people undertake. Becoming proficient in programming requires talent, creativity, intelligence, logic, the ability to build and use abstractions, and experience—even when the best of tools are available.

I suspect another reason for the particular popularity of languages such as C++ and Delphi (as opposed to languages such as Smalltalk and Beta) is that managers and programmers alike hope that a C or Pascal programmer can be changed into a C++ or Delphi programmer with no more effort than the addition of a few characters to their job title. Unfortunately, this hope is a long way from being realized. Object-oriented programming is a new way of thinking about what it means to compute, about how we can structure information and communicate our intentions both to each other and to the machine. To become proficient in object-oriented techniques requires a complete reevaluation of traditional software development.

1.2 ▢ Language and Thought

In his book *Language, Thought & Reality*, Benjamin Lee Whorf discusses the ideas of linguist Edward Sapir.

> Human beings do not live in the objective world alone, nor alone in the world of social activity as ordinarily understood, but are very much at the mercy of the particular language which has become the medium of expression for their society. It is quite an illusion to imagine that one adjusts

to reality essentially without the use of language and that language is merely an incidental means of solving specific problems of communication or reflection. The fact of the matter is that the "real world" is to a large extent unconsciously built up on the language habits of the group . . . . We see and hear and otherwise experience very largely as we do because the language habits of our community predispose certain choices of interpretation.

This quote emphasizes the fact that the languages we speak directly influence the way in which we view the world. This is true not only for natural languages, such as the kind studied by early-twentieth-century American linguists Edward Sapir and Benjamin Lee Whorf, but also for artificial languages, such as those we use in programming computers.

1.2.1 Eskimos and snow

An almost universally cited example of the phenomenon of language influencing thought, although also perhaps an erroneous one, is that Eskimo (or Inuit) languages have different words to describe different types of snow—wet, fluffy, heavy, icy, and so on. This is not surprising. Any community with common interests will naturally develop a specialized vocabulary for concepts they wish to discuss. (Meteorologists, despite working in English, face similar problems of communication and have also developed their own extensive vocabulary.)

What is important is to not overgeneralize the conclusion we can draw from this simple observation. It is not that the Eskimo eye is in any significant respect different from my own or that Eskimos can see things I cannot perceive. With time and training I could do just as well at differentiating types of snow. But the language I speak (English) does not *force* me into doing so, and so it is not natural to me. Thus, a different language (such as Inuktitut) can *lead* one (but does not *require* one) to view the world in a different fashion.

Making effective use of object-oriented principles requires one to view the world in a new way. But simply using an object-oriented language (such as Java or C++) does not, by itself, force one to become an object-oriented programmer. While the use of an object-oriented language will simplify the development of object-oriented solutions, it is true, as it has been quipped, that "FORTRAN programs can be written in any language."

1.2.2 An example from computer languages

The relationship we noted between language and thought for natural languages is even more pronounced in artificial computer languages. That is, the language in which a programmer thinks a problem will be solved will fundamentally color and alter the way an algorithm is developed.

Here is an example that illustrates this relationship between computer language and problem solution. Several years ago a student working in genetic research was faced with a task in the analysis of DNA sequences. The problem could be reduced to relatively simple form. The DNA is represented as a vector of N integer values, where N is very large (on the order of tens of thousands). The problem was to discover whether any pattern of length M, where M was a fixed and small constant (say 5 or 10), is ever repeated in the array of values.

The programmer dutifully sat down and wrote a simple and straightforward FORTRAN program something like the following.

```
      DO 10 I = 1, N-M
      DO 10 J = 1, N-M
      FOUND = .TRUE.
      DO 20 K = 1, M
   20 IF X[I+K-1] .NE. X[J+K-1] THEN FOUND = .FALSE.
      IF FOUND THEN ...
   10 CONTINUE
```

He was somewhat disappointed when trial runs indicated his program would need many hours to complete. He discussed his problem with a second student who happened to be proficient in the programming language APL. She offered to try to write a program for this problem. The first student was dubious. After all, FORTRAN was known to be one of the most "efficient" programming languages. It was compiled; APL was only interpreted. So it was with a certain amount of incredulity that he discovered that the APL programmer was able to write an algorithm that worked in a matter of minutes, not hours.

What the APL programmer had done was to rearrange the problem. Rather than working with a vector of N elements, she reorganized the data into a matrix with roughly N rows and M columns.

$$
\begin{array}{cccc}
x_1 & x_2 & \cdots & x_m \\
x_2 & x_3 & \cdots & x_{m+1} \\
\vdots & \vdots & \cdots \vdots & \vdots \\
x_{n-m} & & \cdots & x_{n-1} \\
x_{n-(m-1)} & & \cdots x_{n-1} & x_n
\end{array}
$$

She then ordered this matrix by rows (that is, treated each row as a unit, moving entire rows during the process of sorting). If any pattern was repeated, then two adjacent rows in the ordered matrix would have identical values.

```
  .   .   .
T  G  G  A  C  C
T  G  G  A  C  C
  .   .   .
```

It was a trivial matter to check for this condition. The reason the APL program was faster had nothing to do with the speed of APL versus FORTRAN; it was simply that the FORTRAN program employed an algorithm that was $O(M \times N^2)$, whereas the sorting solution used by the APL programmer required approximately $O(M \times N \log N)$ operations.

The point of this story is not that APL is in any way a "better" programming language than FORTRAN but that the APL programmer was naturally led to discover an entirely different form of solution. The reason, in this case, is that loops are very difficult to write in APL, whereas sorting is trivial—it is a built-in operator defined as part of the language. Thus, because the sorting operation is so easy to perform, good APL programmers tend to look for novel applications for it. This is how the programming language in which the solution is to be written directs the programmer's mind to view the problem in a certain way.

*1.2.3   Church's conjecture and the Whorf hypothesis

The assertion that the language in which an idea is expressed can influence or direct a line of thought is relatively easy to believe. However, a stronger conjecture, known in linguistics as the Sapir-Whorf hypothesis, goes much further and remains controversial.

The Sapir-Whorf hypothesis asserts that it may be possible for an individual working in one language to imagine thoughts or to utter ideas that cannot in any way be translated, or even understood by individuals operating in a different linguistic framework. According to advocates of the hypothesis, this can occur when the language of the second individual has no equivalent words and lacks even concepts or categories for the ideas involved in the thought. It is interesting to compare this possibility with an almost directly opposite concept from computer science—namely, Church's conjecture.

Starting in the 1930s and continuing through the 1940s and 1950s there was a great deal of interest within the mathematical and nascent computing community in a variety of formalisms that could be used for the calculation of functions. Examples are the notations proposed by Church [Church 1936], Post [Post 1936], Markov [Markov 1951], Turing [Turing 1936], Kleene [Kleene 1936], and others. Over time a number of arguments were put forth to demonstrate that many of these systems could be used in the simulation of other systems. Often, such arguments for a pair of systems could be made in both directions, effectively showing that the systems were identical in computation power. The sheer number of such arguments led the logician Alonzo Church to pronounce a conjecture that is now associated with his name.

Church's Conjecture: Any computation for which there is an effective procedure can be realized by a Turing machine.

By nature this conjecture must remain unproven and unprovable, since we have no rigorous definition of the term "effective procedure." Nevertheless, no counterexample has yet been found, and the weight of evidence seems to favor affirmation of this claim.

Acceptance of Church's conjecture has an important and profound implication for the study of programming languages. Turing machines are wonderfully simple mechanisms, and it does not require many features in a language to simulate such a device. In the 1960s, for example, it was demonstrated that a Turing machine could be emulated in any language that possessed at least a conditional statement and a looping construct [Böhm 1966]. (This greatly misunderstood result was the major ammunition used to "prove" that the infamous goto statement was unnecessary.)

If we accept Church's conjecture, any language in which it is possible to simulate a Turing machine is sufficiently powerful to perform *any* realizable algorithm. (To solve a problem, find the Turing machine that produces the desired result, which by Church's conjecture must exist; then simulate the execution of the Turing machine in your favorite language.) Thus, arguments about the relative "power" of programming languages—if by power we mean "ability to solve problems"—are generally vacuous. The late Alan Perlis had a term for such an argument. He called it a "Turing Tarpit" because it is often so difficult to extricate oneself from it and so fundamentally pointless.

Note that Church's conjecture is, in a certain sense, almost the exact opposite of the Sapir-Whorf hypothesis. Church's conjecture states that in a fundamental way all programming languages are identical. Any idea that can be expressed in one language can, in theory, be expressed in any language. The Sapir-Whorf hypothesis claims that it is possible to have ideas that can be expressed in one language that cannot be expressed in another.

Many linguists reject the Sapir-Whorf hypothesis and instead adopt a sort of "Turing-equivalence" for natural languages. By this we mean that, with a sufficient amount of work, any idea can be expressed in any language. For example, while the language spoken by a native of a warm climate may not make it instinctive to examine a field of snow and categorize it by type or use, with time and training it certainly can be learned. Similarly, object-oriented techniques do not provide any new computational power that permits problems to be solved that cannot, *in theory*, be solved by other means. But object-oriented techniques *do* make it *easier* and more natural to address problems in a fashion that tends to favor the management of large software projects.

Thus, for both computer and natural languages the language will *direct* thoughts but cannot *proscribe* thoughts.

1.3 ▫ A New Paradigm

Object-oriented programming is frequently referred to as a new programming *paradigm*. Other programming paradigms include the imperative-programming paradigm (languages such as Pascal or C), the logic programming paradigm (Prolog), and the functional-programming paradigm (ML or Haskell).

It is interesting to examine the definition of the word "paradigm." The following is from the *American Heritage Dictionary of the English Language*.

> **par a digm** *n*. 1. A list of all the inflectional forms of a word taken as an illustrative example of the conjugation or declension to which it belongs. 2. Any example or model. [Late Latin *paradīgma*, from Greek *paradeigma*, model, from *paradeiknunai*, to compare, exhibit.]

At first blush, the conjugation or declension of Latin words would seem to have little to do with computer programming languages. To understand the connection, we must note that the word was brought into the modern vocabulary through an influential book, *The Structure of Scientific Revolutions*, by the historian of science Thomas Kuhn [Kuhn 1970]. Kuhn used the term in the second form, to describe a set of theories, standards, and methods that together represent a way of organizing knowledge—that is, a way of viewing the world. Kuhn's thesis was that revolutions in science occur when an older paradigm is reexamined, rejected, and replaced by another.

It is in this sense, as a model or example and as an organizational approach, that Robert Floyd used the term in his 1979 ACM Turing Award lecture [Floyd 1979], "The Paradigms of Programming." A programming paradigm is a way of conceptualizing what it means to perform computation and how tasks to be carried out on a computer should be structured and organized.

Although new to computation, the organizing technique that lies at the heart of object-oriented programming can be traced back at least as far as Carolus Linnaeus (1707–1778) (Figure 1.1). It was Linnaeus, you will recall, who categorized biological organisms using the idea of phylum, genus, species, and so on.

Paradoxically, the style of problem solving embodied in the object-oriented technique is frequently the method used to address problems in everyday life. Thus, computer novices are often able to grasp the basic ideas of object-oriented programming easily, whereas people who are more computer literate are often blocked by their own preconceptions. Alan Kay, for example, found that it was often easier to teach Smalltalk to children than to computer professionals [Kay 1977].

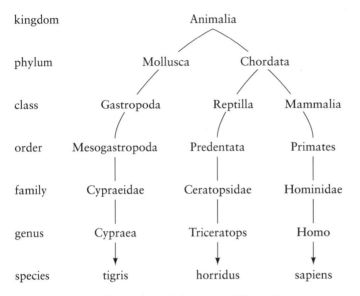

▫ Figure 1.1 —— The Linnaen Inheritance Hierarchy

In trying to understand exactly what is meant by the term *object-oriented programming*, it is useful to examine the idea from several perspectives. The next few sections outline two aspects of object-oriented programming; each illustrates a particular reason that this technique should be considered an important new tool.

1.4 ▫ A Way of Viewing the World

To illustrate some of the major ideas in object-oriented programming, let us consider first how we might go about handling a real-world situation and then ask how we could make the computer more closely model the techniques employed.

Suppose an individual named Chris wishes to send flowers to a friend named Robin, who lives in another city. Because of the distance, Chris cannot simply pick the flowers and take them to Robin in person. Nevertheless, it is a task that is easily solved. Chris simply walks to a nearby flower shop, run by a florist named Fred. Chris will tell Fred the kinds of flowers to send to Robin and the address to which they should be delivered. Chris can then be assured that the flowers will be delivered expediently and automatically.

1.4.1   Agents and communities

At the risk of belaboring a point, let us emphasize that the mechanism that was used to solve this problem was to find an appropriate *agent* (namely, Fred) and to pass to this agent a *message* containing a request. It is the *responsibility* of Fred to satisfy the request. There is some *method*—some algorithm or set of operations—used by Fred to do this. Chris does not need to know the particular method that Fred will use to satisfy the request; indeed, often the person making a request does not want to know the details. This information is usually *hidden* from inspection.

An investigation, however, might uncover the fact that Fred delivers a slightly different message to another florist in the city where Robin lives. That florist, in turn, perhaps has a subordinate who makes the flower arrangement. The florist then passes the flowers, along with yet another message, to a delivery person, and so on. Earlier, the florist in Robin's city had obtained the flowers from a flower wholesaler who, in turn, had interactions with the flower growers, each of whom had to manage a team of gardeners.

So, our first observation of object-oriented problem solving is that the solution to this problem required the help of many other individuals (Figure 1.2). Without their help, the problem could not be easily solved. We phrase this in a general fashion.

An object-oriented program is structured as a *community* of interacting agents called *objects*. Each object has a role to play. Each object provides a service or performs an action that is used by other members of the community.

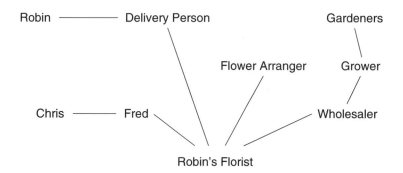

□ Figure 1.2 —— The community of agents in the flower delivery process

1.4.2   Messages and methods

The chain reaction that ultimately resulted in the solution to Chris's problem began with a request given to the florist, Fred. This request lead to other requests, which lead to still more requests, until the flowers ultimately reached Chris's friend, Robin. We see, therefore, that members of this community interact with each other by making requests. So, our next principle of object-oriented problem solving is the vehicle used to indicate an action to be performed.

> Action is initiated in object-oriented programming by the transmission of a *message* to an agent (an *object*) responsible for the action. The message encodes the request for an action and is accompanied by any additional information (arguments) needed to carry out the request. The *receiver* is the object to whom the message is sent. If the receiver accepts the message, it accepts the responsibility to carry out the indicated action. In response to a message, the receiver will perform some *method* to satisfy the request.

We have noted the important principle of *information hiding* in regard to message passing—that is, the client sending the request need not know the actual means by which the request will be honored. There is another principle, all too human, that we see is implicit in message passing. If there is a task to perform, the first thought of the client is to find somebody else he or she can ask to do the work. This second reaction often becomes atrophied in many programmers with extensive experience in conventional techniques. Frequently, a difficult hurdle to overcome is the idea in the programmer's mind that he or she must write everything and not use the services of others. An important part of object-oriented programming is the development of reusable components, and an important first step in the use of reusable components is a willingness to trust software written by others.

Messages Versus Procedure Calls

Information hiding is also an important aspect of programming in conventional languages. In what sense is a message different from, say, a procedure call? In both cases, there is a set of well-defined steps that will be initiated following the request. But there are two important distinctions.

The first is that in a message there is a designated *receiver* for that message; the receiver is some object to which the message is sent. In a procedure call, there is no designated receiver.

The second is that the *interpretation* of the message (that is, the method used to respond to the message) is determined by the receiver and can vary with different receivers. Chris could give a message to a friend named Elizabeth, for example, and she will understand it and a satisfactory outcome will be produced (that is, flowers will be delivered to their mutual friend Robin). However, the method Elizabeth uses to satisfy the request (in all likelihood, simply passing the request on to Fred) will be different from that used by Fred in response to the same request.

If Chris were to ask Kenneth, a dentist, to send flowers to Robin, Kenneth may not have a method for solving that problem. If he understands the request at all, he will probably issue an appropriate error diagnostic.

Let us move our discussion back to the level of computers and programs. There, the distinction between message passing and procedure calling is that in message passing there is a designated receiver, and the interpretation—the selection of a method to execute in response to the message—may vary with different receivers. Usually, the specific receiver for any given message will not be known until run time, so the determination of which method to invoke cannot be made until then. Thus, we say there is late *binding* between the message (function or procedure name) and the code fragment (method) used to respond to the message. This situation is in contrast to the very early (compile-time or link-time) binding of name to code fragment in conventional procedure calls.

1.4.3   Responsibilities

A fundamental concept in object-oriented programming is to describe behavior in terms of *responsibilities*. Chris's request for action indicates only the desired outcome (flowers sent to Robin). Fred is free to pursue any technique that achieves the desired objective and in doing so will not be hampered by interference from Chris.

By discussing a problem in terms of responsibilities we increase the level of abstraction. This permits greater *independence* between objects, a critical factor in solving complex problems. The entire collection of responsibilities associated with an object is often described by the term *protocol*.

A traditional program often operates by acting *on* data structures—for example, changing fields in an array or record. In contrast, an object-oriented program *requests* data structures (that is, objects) to perform a service. This difference between viewing software in traditional, structured terms and viewing it from an object-oriented perspective can be summarized by a twist on a well-known quote.

> Ask not what you can do *to* your data structures.
> Ask what your data structures can do *for* you.

1.4.4   Classes and instances

Although Chris has only dealt with Fred a few times, Chris has a rough idea of the transaction that will occur inside Fred's flower shop. Chris is able to make certain assumptions based on previous experience with other florists, and hence Chris can expect that Fred, being an instance of this category, will fit the general pattern. We can use the term Florist to represent the category (or *class*) of all florists. Let us incorporate these notions into our next principle of object-oriented programming.

> All objects are *instances* of a *class*. The method invoked by an object in response to a message is determined by the class of the receiver. All objects of a given class use the same method in response to similar messages.

1.4.5   Class hierarchies—inheritance

Chris has more information about Fred—not necessarily because Fred is a florist but because he is a shopkeeper. Chris knows, for example, that a transfer of money will be part of the transaction and that in return for payment Fred will offer a receipt. These actions are true of grocers, stationers, and other shopkeepers. Since the category Florist is a more specialized form of the category Shopkeeper, any knowledge Chris has of Shopkeepers is also true of Florists and, hence, of Fred.

One way to think about how Chris has organized knowledge of Fred is in terms of a hierarchy of categories (see Figure 1.3). Fred is a Florist, but Florist is a specialized form of Shopkeeper. Furthermore, a Shopkeeper is also a Human; so Chris knows, for example, that Fred is probably bipedal. A Human is a Mammal (therefore, they nurse their young and have hair), a Mammal is an Animal (therefore, it breathes

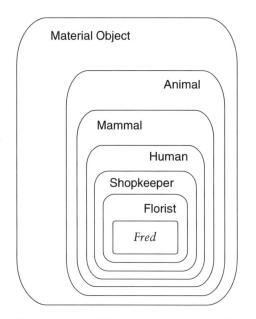

▣ Figure 1.3 ——The categories surrounding Fred

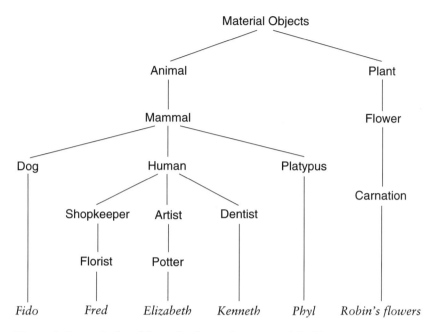

⊡ Figure 1.4 —— A class hierarchy for various material objects

oxygen), and an Animal is a Material Object (therefore, it has mass and weight). Thus, quite a lot of knowledge that Chris has that is applicable to Fred is not directly associated with him, or even with the category Florist.

The principle that knowledge of a more general category is also applicable to a more specific category is called *inheritance*. We say that the class Florist will inherit attributes of the class (or category) Shopkeeper.

There is an alternative graphical technique often used to illustrate this relationship, particularly when there are many individuals with differing lineages. This technique shows classes listed in a hierarchical treelike structure, with more abstract classes (such as Material Object or Animal) listed near the top of the tree and more specific classes, and finally individuals, listed near the bottom. Figure 1.4 shows this class hierarchy for Fred. This same hierarchy also includes Elizabeth; Chris's dog, Fido; Phyl the platypus, who lives at the zoo; and the flowers Chris is sending to Robin. Notice that the structure and interpretation of this type of diagram is similar to the biological hierarchy presented in Figure 1.1.

Any information that Chris has about Fred because Fred is an instance of class Human is also applicable to Elizabeth. Any information that Chris has about Fred because Fred is a Mammal is applicable to Fido as well. Any information about all members of Material Object is equally applicable to Fred and to his flowers. We capture this in the idea of inheritance.

> Classes can be organized into a hierarchical *inheritance* structure. A *child class* (or *subclass*) will inherit attributes from a *parent class* higher in the tree. An *abstract parent class* is a class (such as Mammal) for which there are no direct instances; it is used only to create subclasses.

1.4.6   Method binding and overriding

Phyl the platypus presents a problem for our simple organizing structure. Chris knows that mammals give birth to live children, and Phyl is certainly a Mammal, yet Phyl (or rather his mate Phyllis) lays eggs. To accommodate this, we need to find a technique to encode *exceptions* to a general rule.

We do this by decreeing that information contained in a subclass can *override* information inherited from a parent class. Most often, implementations of this approach take the form of a method in a subclass having the same name as a method in the parent class, combined with a rule for how the search for a method to match a specific message is conducted.

> The search for a method to invoke in response to a given message begins with the *class* of the receiver. If no appropriate method is found, the search is conducted in the *parent class* of this class. The search continues up the parent class chain until either a method is found or the parent class chain is exhausted. In the former case the method is executed; in the latter case, an error message is issued. If methods with the same name can be found higher in the class hierarchy, the method executed is said to *override* the inherited behavior.

Even if a compiler cannot determine which method will be invoked at run time, in many object-oriented languages, such as Java, it can determine whether there will be an appropriate method and issue an error message as a compile-time error diagnostic rather than as a run-time message.

The fact that both Elizabeth and Fred will react to Chris's messages but use different methods to respond is one form of *polymorphism*. As explained, that Chris does not, and need not, know exactly what method Fred will use to honor the request is an example of *information hiding*.

1.4.7   Summary of object-oriented concepts

Alan Kay, considered by some to be the father of object-oriented programming, identified the following characteristics as fundamental to OOP [Kay 1993]:

1. Everything is an *object*.

2. Computation is performed by objects communicating with each other, requesting that other objects perform actions. Objects communicate by sending and receiving *messages*. A message is a request for action bundled with whatever arguments may be necessary to complete the task.

3. Each object has its own *memory*, which consists of other objects.

4. Every object is an *instance* of a *class*. A class simply represents a grouping of similar objects, such as integers or lists.

5. The class is the repository for *behavior* associated with an object. That is, all objects that are instances of the same class can perform the same actions.

6. Classes are organized into a singly rooted tree structure, called the *inheritance hierarchy*. Memory and behavior associated with instances of a class are automatically available to any class associated with a descendant in this tree structure.

*1.5 ▫ Computation as Simulation

The view of programming represented by the example of sending flowers to a friend is very different from the conventional conception of a computer. The traditional model describing the behavior of a computer executing a program is a *process-state* or *pigeon-hole* model. In this view, the computer is a data manager, following some pattern of instructions, wandering through memory, pulling values out of various slots (memory addresses), transforming them in some manner, and pushing the results back into other slots (see Figure 1.5). By examining the values in the slots, one can determine the state of the machine or the results produced by a computation. Although this model may be a more or less accurate picture of what takes place inside a computer, it does little to help us understand how to solve problems using the computer, and it is certainly not the way most people (pigeon handlers and postal workers excepted) go about solving problems.

In contrast, in the object-oriented framework we never mention memory addresses, variables, assignments, or any of the conventional programming terms. Instead, we speak of objects, messages, and responsibility for some action. I quote Dan Ingalls's memorable phrase.

> Instead of a bit-grinding processor . . . plundering data structures, we have a universe of well-behaved objects that courteously ask each other to carry out their various desires [Ingalls 1981].

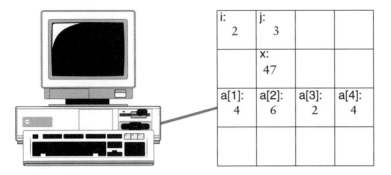

i: 2	j: 3		
	x: 47		
a[1]: 4	a[2]: 6	a[3]: 2	a[4]: 4

▫ Figure 1.5 ──── Visualization of imperative programming.

Another author has described object-oriented programming as "animistic": a process of creating a host of helpers that form a community and assist the programmer in the solution of a problem [Actor 1987].

This view of programming as creating a "universe" is in many ways similar to a style of computer simulation called "discrete event-driven simulation." In brief, in a discrete event-driven simulation the user creates computer models of the various elements of the simulation, describes how they will interact with one another, and sets them moving. This is almost identical to the average object-oriented program, in which the user describes what the various entities in the universe for the program are and how they will interact with one another, and then finally sets them in motion. Thus, in object-oriented programming, we have the view that *computation is simulation* [Kay 1977].

1.5.1   The power of metaphor

An easily overlooked benefit to the use of object-oriented techniques is the power of *metaphor*. When programmers think about problems in terms of behaviors and responsibilities of objects, they bring with them a wealth of intuition, ideas, and understanding from their everyday experiences. When envisioned as pigeon holes, mailboxes, or slots containing values, there is little in the programmer's background to provide insight into how problems should be structured.

Although anthropomorphic descriptions such as the quote by Ingalls may strike some people as odd, in fact they are a reflection of the great expositive power of metaphor. Journalists make use of metaphor every day, as in this description of object-oriented programming from *Newsweek* (Figure 1.6).

Unlike the usual programming method—writing software one line at a time—NeXT's "object-oriented" system offers larger building blocks that

□ Figure 1.6 —— Mr. Potato Head, an object-oriented toy (Hasbro, Inc.)

developers can quickly assemble the way a kid builds faces on Mr. Potato Head.

Possibly this feature, more than any other, is responsible for the frequent observation that it is sometimes easier to teach object-oriented programming concepts to computer novices than to computer professionals. Novice users quickly adapt the metaphors with which they are already comfortable from their everyday life, whereas seasoned computer professionals can be blinded by an adherence to more traditional ways of viewing computation.

1.5.2   Avoiding infinite regression

Of course, objects cannot always respond to a message by politely asking another object to perform some action. The result would be an infinite circle of requests, like two gentlemen politely waiting for the other to go first before entering a doorway, or like a bureaucracy of paper pushers, each passing on all papers to some other member of the organization. At some point, at least a few objects need to perform some work besides passing on requests to other agents. This work is accomplished differently in various object-oriented languages.

In blended object-oriented/imperative languages, such as C++, Object Pascal, and Objective-C, it is accomplished by methods written in the base (non-object-oriented) language. In more purely object-oriented languages, such as Smalltalk or Java, it is accomplished by "primitive" or "native" operations that are provided by the underlying system.

*1.6 ⊡ A Brief History

It is commonly thought that object-oriented programming is a relatively recent phenomenon in computer science. To the contrary, in fact, almost all the major concepts we now associate with object-oriented programs, such as objects, classes, and inheritance hierarchies, were developed in the 1960s as part of a language called Simula, designed by researchers at the Norwegian Computing Center. Simula, as the name suggests, was a language inspired by problems involving the simulation of real life systems. However, the importance of these constructs, even to the developers of Simula, was only slowly recognized [Nygaard 1981].

In the 1970s Alan Kay organized a research group at Xerox PARC (the Palo Alto Research Center). With great prescience, Kay predicated the coming revolution in personal computing that was to develop nearly a decade later (see, for example, his 1977 article in *Scientific American* [Kay 1977]). Kay was concerned with discovering a programming language that would be understandable to non-computer professionals, to ordinary people with no prior training in computer use.[1] He found in the notion of classes and computing as simulation a metaphor that could easily be understood by novice users, as he then demonstrated by a series of experiments conducted at PARC using children as programmers. The programming language developed by his group was named Smalltalk. This language evolved through several revisions during the decade. A widely read 1981 issue of *Byte* magazine did much to popularize the concepts developed by Kay and his team at Xerox.

Roughly contemporaneous with Kay's work was another project being conducted on the other side of the country. Bjarne Stroustrup, a researcher at Bell Laboratories who had learned Simula while completing his doctorate at Cambridge University in England, was developing an extension to the C language that would facilitate the creation of objects and classes [Stroustrup 1982]. This was to eventually evolve into the language C++ [Stroustrup 1994].

---

1. I have always found it ironic that Kay missed an important point. He thought that to *use* a computer one would be required to *program* a computer. Although he correctly predicted in 1977 the coming trend in hardware, few could have predicted at that time the rapid development of general purpose computer applications that was to accompany, perhaps even drive, the introduction of personal computers. Nowadays the vast majority of people who use personal computers have no idea how to program.

With the dissemination of information on these and other similar projects, an explosion of research in object-oriented programming techniques began. By the time of the first major conference on object-oriented programming in 1986, there were literally dozens of new programming languages vying for acceptance. These included Eiffel [Meyer 1988a], Objective-C [Cox 1986], Actor [Actor 1987], Object Pascal, and various Lisp dialects.

In the two decades since the 1986 OOPSLA conference, object-oriented programming has moved from being revolutionary to being mainstream and in the process has transformed a major portion of the field of computer science as a whole.

Summary ⊡

- Object-oriented programming is not simply a few new features added to programming languages. Rather, it is a new way of *thinking* about the process of decomposing problems and developing programming solutions.

- Object-oriented programming views a program as a collection of loosely connected agents, termed *objects*. Each object is responsible for specific tasks. It is by the interaction of objects that computation proceeds. In a certain sense, therefore, programming is nothing more or less than the simulation of a model universe.

- An object is an encapsulation of *state* (data values) and *behavior* (operations). Thus, an object is in many ways similar to a special purpose computer.

- The behavior of objects is dictated by the object *class*. Every object is an instance of some class. All instances of the same class will behave in a similar fashion (that is, invoke the same method) in response to a similar request.

- An object will exhibit its behavior by invoking a method (similar to executing a procedure) in response to a message. The interpretation of the message (that is, the specific method used) is decided by the object and may differ from one class of objects to another.

- Classes can be linked to each other by means of the notion of *inheritance*. Using inheritance, classes are organized into a hierarchical inheritance tree. Data and behavior associated with classes higher in the tree can also be accessed and used by classes lower in the tree. Such classes are said to inherit their behavior from the parent classes.

- Designing an object-oriented program is like organizing a community of individuals. Each member of the community is given certain responsibilities. The achievement of the goals for the community as a whole come about through the work of each member, and the interactions of members with each other.

- By reducing the interdependency among software components, object-oriented programming permits the development of reusable software systems. Such components can be created and tested as independent units, in isolation from other portions of a software application.

- Reusable software components permit the programmer to deal with problems on a higher level of abstraction. We can define and manipulate objects simply in terms of the messages they understand and a description of the tasks they perform, ignoring implementation details.

Further Reading ▫

I noted earlier that many consider Alan Kay to be the father of object-oriented programming. Like most simple assertions, this one is only somewhat supportable. Kay himself [Kay 1993] traces much of the influence on his development of Smalltalk to the earlier computer programming language Simula, developed in Scandinavia in the early 1960s [Dahl 1966; Kirkerud 1989]. A more accurate history would be that most of the principles of object-oriented programming were fully worked out by the developers of Simula but that these would have been largely ignored by the profession had they not been rediscovered by Kay in the creation of the Smalltalk programming language.

The term "software crisis" seems to have been coined by Doug McIlroy at a 1968 NATO conference on software engineering. It is curious that we have been in a state of crisis now for more than half the life of computer science as a discipline. Despite the end of the Cold War, the end of the software crisis seems to be no closer now than it was in 1968. See, for example, Gibb's article "Software's Chronic Crisis" in the September 1994 issue of *Scientific American* [Gibbs 1994].

To some extent, the software crisis may be largely illusory. For example, tasks considered exceedingly difficult five years ago seldom seem so daunting today. It is only the tasks that we wish to solve *today* that seem, in comparison, to be nearly impossible, which seems to indicate that the field of software development has, indeed, advanced steadily year by year.

The quote from the American linguist Edward Sapir is taken from "The Relation of Habitual Thought and Behavior to Language," reprinted in Benjamin Lee Whorf's book *Language, Thought and Reality* [Whorf 1956]. This book contains several interesting papers on the relationships between language and our habitual thinking processes. I urge any serious student of computer languages to read these essays; some of them have surprising relevance to artificial languages.

(An undergraduate once exclaimed to me, "I didn't know the Klingon was a linguist!")

Another interesting book along similar lines is *The Alphabet Effect* by Robert Logan [Logan 1986], which explains in terms of language why logic and science developed in the West, while for centuries China had superior technology. In a more contemporary investigation of the effect of natural language on computer science, J. Marshall Unger [Unger 1987] describes the influence of the Japanese language on the much-heralded Fifth Generation project.

The commonly held observation that Eskimo languages have many words for snow was debunked by Geoffrey Pullum in his book of essays on linguistics [Pullum 1991]. In his article "In Praise of Snow" in the January 1995 issue of *Atlantic Monthly*, Cullen Murphy pointed out that the vocabulary used to discuss snow among English speakers for whom a distinction between types of snow is important—namely, those who perform research on the topic—is every bit as large as, or larger than, that of the Eskimo.

Those who would argue in favor of the Sapir-Whorf hypothesis have a difficult problem to overcome—namely, the simple question "Can you give me an example?" Either they can, which (since it must be presented in the language of the speaker) serves to undercut their argument, or they cannot, which also weakens their argument. In any case, the point is irrelevant to our discussion. It is certainly true that groups of individuals with common interests tend to develop their own specialized vocabulary, and once developed, the vocabulary itself tends to direct their thoughts along paths that may not be natural to those outside the group. Such is the case with OOP. While object-oriented ideas can, with discipline, be used without an object-oriented language, the use of object-oriented terms helps direct the programmer's thought along lines that may not have been obvious without the OOP terminology.

My history is slightly imprecise with regard to Church's conjecture and Turing machines. Church actually conjectured about partial functions [Church 1936], which were later shown to be equivalent to computations performed with Turing machines [Turing 1936]. Kleene described the conjecture in the form we have here, also giving it the name by which it has become known. Rogers gives a good summary of the arguments for the equivalence of various computational models [Rogers 1967].

Information on the history of Smalltalk can be found in Kay's article from the History of Programming Languages conference [Kay 1993]. Bjarne Stroustrup has provided a history of C++ [Stroustrup 1994]. A more general history of OOP is presented in the *Handbook of Programming Languages* [Salus 1998].

Like most terms that have found their way into the popular jargon, *object-oriented* is used more often than it is defined. Thus, the question "What is object-oriented programming?" is surprisingly difficult to answer. Bjarne Stroustrup has quipped that many arguments appear to boil down to the following syllogism.

- X is good.
- Object-oriented is good.
- *Ergo,* X is object-oriented.

Roger King [Kim 1989] argued that his cat is object-oriented. After all, a cat exhibits characteristic behavior, responds to messages, is heir to a long tradition of inherited responses, and manages its own quite independent internal state.

Many authors have tried to provide a precise description of the properties a programming language must possess to be called *object-oriented*. See, for example, the analysis by Josephine Micallef [Micallef 1988] or Peter Wegner [Wegner 1986]. Wegner, for example, distinguishes *object-based* languages, which support only abstraction (such as Ada), from *object-oriented* languages, which must also support inheritance.

Other authors—notably Brad Cox [Cox 1990]—define the term much more broadly. To Cox, object-oriented programming represents the *objective* of programming by assembling solutions from collections of off-the-shelf subcomponents, rather than any particular *technology* we may use to achieve this objective. Rather than drawing lines that are divisive, we should embrace any and all means that show promise in leading to a new software Industrial Revolution. Cox's book on OOP [Cox 1986], although written early in the development of object-oriented programming and now somewhat dated, is nevertheless one of the most readable manifestos of the object-oriented movement.

Self-Study Questions □

1. What is the original meaning of the word *paradigm*?
2. How do objects interact with each other?
3. How are messages different from procedure calls?
4. What is the name applied to describe an algorithm that an object uses to respond to a request?
5. Why does the object-oriented approach naturally imply a high degree of information hiding?
6. What is a class? How are classes linked to behavior?
7. What is a class inheritance hierarchy? How is it linked to classes and behavior?
8. What does it mean for one method to override another method from a parent class?
9. What are the basic elements of the process-state model of computation?

10. How does the object-oriented model of computation differ from the process-state model?

11. In what way is an object-oriented program like a simulation?

Exercises ⊡

1. In an object-oriented inheritance hierarchy, each level is a more specialized form of the preceding level. Give an example of a hierarchy found in everyday life that has this property. Some types of hierarchy found in everyday life are not inheritance hierarchies. Give an example of a noninheritance hierarchy.

2. Look up the definition of *paradigm* in at least three dictionaries. Relate these definitions to computer programming languages.

3. Take a real world problem, such as the task of sending flowers in our example, and describe its solution in terms of agents (objects) and responsibilities.

4. If you are familiar with two or more distinct computer programming languages, give an example of a problem showing how one language would direct the programmer to one type of solution and a different language would encourage an alternative solution.

5. If you are familiar with two or more distinct natural languages, describe a situation that illustrates how one language directs the speaker in a certain direction and the other language encourages a different line of thought.

6. Argue either for or against the position that computing is basically simulation. (You may want to read Kay's 1977 *Scientific American* article.)

CHAPTER 2

Abstraction

If you open an atlas you will often first see a map of the world. This map will show only the most significant features. For example, it may show the various mountain ranges, the ocean currents, and other extremely large structures. But small features will almost certainly be omitted.

A subsequent map will cover a smaller geographical region and will typically possess more detail. For example, a map of a single continent (such as South America) may now include political boundaries and perhaps the major cities. A map over an even smaller region, such as a country, might include towns as well as cities and smaller geographical features, such as the names of individual mountains. A map of an individual large city might include the most important roads leading into and out of the city. Maps of smaller regions might even represent individual buildings.

Notice how, at each level, certain information has been included and certain information has been purposely omitted. There is simply no way to represent all the details when an artifact is viewed at a higher level of abstraction. And even if all the detail could be described (using tiny writing, for example), there is no way that people could assimilate or process such a large amount of information. Hence, details are simply left out.

Fundamentally, people use only a few simple tools to create, understand, or manage complex systems. One of the most important techniques is termed *abstraction.*

Consider the average person's understanding of an automobile. A layman's view of an automobile engine, for example, is a device that takes fuel as input and produces a rotation of the drive shaft as output. This rotation is too fast to connect to the wheels of the car directly, so a transmission is a mechanism used

Abstraction

Abstraction is the purposeful suppression, or hiding, of some details of a process or artifact, in order to bring out more clearly other aspects, details, or structures.

to reduce a rotation of several thousand revolutions per minute to a rotation of several revolutions per minute. This slower rotation can then be used to propel the car. This is not exactly correct, but it is sufficiently close for everyday purposes. We sometimes say that by means of abstraction we have constructed a *model* of the actual system.

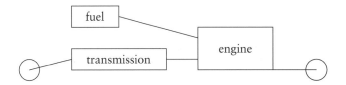

In forming an abstraction, or model, we purposely avoid the need to understand many details, concentrating instead of a few key features. We often describe this process with another term: *information hiding*.

Information Hiding

Information hiding is the purposeful omission of details in the development of an abstract representation.

2.1 ▣ Layers of Abstraction

In a typical program written in the object-oriented style there are many important levels of abstraction. The higher level abstractions are part of what makes an object-oriented program object-oriented.

At the highest level a program is viewed as a "community" of objects that must interact with each other in order to achieve their common goal.

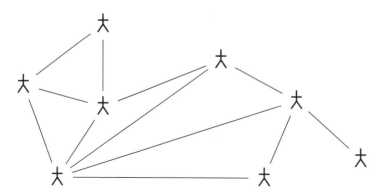

This notion of community finds expression in object-oriented development in two distinct forms. First, there is the community of programmers, who must interact with each other in the real world in order to produce their application. Second, there is the community of objects that they create, which must interact with each other in a virtual universe in order to further their common goals. Key ideas such as information hiding and abstraction are applicable to both levels.

Each object in this community provides a service that is used by other members of the organization. At this highest level of abstraction, the important features to emphasize are the lines of communication and cooperation and the way in which the members must interact with each other.

The next level of abstraction is not found in all object-oriented programs, nor is it supported in all object-oriented languages. However, many languages permit a group of objects working together to be combined into a unit. Examples of this idea include *packages* in Java, *name spaces* in C++, or *units* in Delphi. The unit allows certain names to be exposed to the world outside the unit, while other features remain hidden inside the unit.

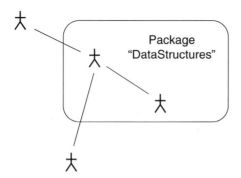

For readers familiar with concepts found in earlier languages, this notion of a unit is the heir to the idea of a *module* in languages such as C or Modula. Later in this chapter we will present a short history of programming language abstractions and note the debt that ideas of object-oriented programming owe to the earlier work on modules.

The next two levels of abstraction deal with the interactions between two individual objects. Often we speak of objects as proving a *service* to other objects. We build on this intuition by describing communication as an interaction between a *client* and a *server*.

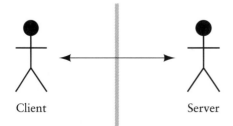

Client   Server

We are not using the term *server* in the technical sense of, say, a Web server. Rather, here the term *server* simply means an object that is providing a service. The two layers of abstraction refer to the two views of this relationship: the view from the client side and the view from the server side.

In a good object-oriented design we can describe and discuss the services that the server provides without reference to any actions that the client may perform in using those services. One can think of this as being like a billboard advertisement.

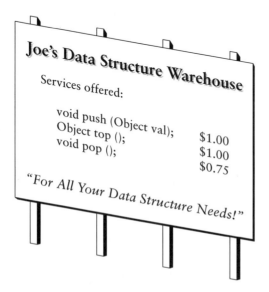

The billboard describes, for example, the services provided by a data structure, such as a Stack. Often this level of abstraction is represented by an interface, a classlike mechanism that defines behavior without describing an implementation.

```
interface Stack {
  public void push (Object val);
  public Object top () throws EmptyStackException;
  public void pop () throws EmptyStackException;
}
```

The next level of abstraction looks at the same boundary but from the server side. This level considers a concrete implementation of the abstract behavior. For example, there are any number of data structures that can be used to satisfy the requirements of a Stack. Concerns at this level deal with the way in which the services are being realized.

```
public class LinkedList implements Stack ... {
  public void pop () throws  EmptyStackException { ... }
      .
      .
      .
}
```

Finally, the last level of abstraction considers a single task in isolation—that is, a single method. Concerns at this level of abstraction deal with the precise sequence of operations used to perform just this one activity. For example, we might investigate the technique used to perform the removal of the most recent element placed into a stack.

```
public class LinkedList implements Stack ... {
      .
      .
      .
  public void pop () throws  EmptyStackException {
    if (isEmpty())
      throw new EmptyStackException();
    removeFirst(); // delete first element of list
  }
      .
      .
      .
}
```

Each level of abstraction is important at some point during software development. In fact, programmers are often called upon to quickly move back and forth between different levels of abstraction. We will see analysis of object-oriented programs performed at each of these levels of abstraction as we proceed through the book.

Finding the Right Level of Abstraction

In early stages of software development a critical problem is *finding the right level of abstraction*. A common error is to dwell on the lowest levels, worrying about the implementation details of various key components, rather than striving to ensure that the high-level organizational structure promotes a clean separation of concerns.

The programmer (or, in larger projects, the design team) must walk a fine line in trying to identify the right level of abstraction at any one point of time. One does not want to ignore or throw away too much detail about a problem, but also one must not keep so much detail that important issues become obscured.

2.2 □ Other Forms of Abstraction

Abstraction is used to help understand a complex system. In a certain sense, abstraction is the imposition of structure on a system. The structure we impose may reflect some real aspects of the system (a car really does have both an engine and a transmission), or it may simply be a mental abstraction we employ to aid in our understanding.

This idea of abstraction can be further subdivided into a variety of different forms (Figure 2.1). A common technique is to divide a layer into constituent parts. This is the approach we used when we described an automobile as being composed of the engine, the transmission, the body, and the wheels. The next level of understanding is then achieved by examining each of these parts in turn. This is nothing more than the application of the old maxim *divide and conquer*.

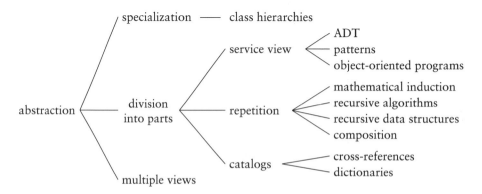

□ Figure 2.1 —— Some techniques for handling complexity, with examples

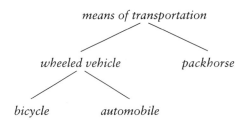

□ Figure 2.2 —— Layers of specialization

Other times we use different types of abstraction. Another form is the idea of layers of specialization (Figure 2.2). An understanding of an automobile is based, in part, on knowledge that it is a *wheeled vehicle*, which is in turn a *means of transportation*. There is other information we know about wheeled vehicles, and that knowledge is applicable to both an automobile and a bicycle. There is other knowledge we have about various different means of transportation, and that information is also applicable to packhorses as well as bicycles. Object-oriented languages make extensive use of this form of abstraction.

Yet another form of abstraction is to provide multiple views of the same artifact. Each of the views can emphasize certain detail and suppress others and thus bring out different features of the same object. A layman's view of a car, for example, is very different from a mechanic's.

Is-a and Has-a Abstraction

The idea of division into parts and division into specializations represents the two most important forms of abstraction used in object-oriented programming. These are commonly known as *is-a* and *has-a* abstractions.

Division into parts is *has-a* abstraction. The meaning of this term is easy to understand: A car "has-a" engine, it "has-a" transmission, and so on.

Specialization is *is-a* abstraction: A bicycle "is-a" wheeled vehicle, which in turn "is-a" means of transportation.

Both *is-a* and *has-a* abstractions will reappear in later chapters and be tied to specific programming language features.

2.2.1   Division into parts

The most common technique people use to help understand complex systems is to combine abstraction with a division into component parts. Our description of an automobile is an example of this. The next level of understanding is then achieved by taking each of the parts and performing the same sort of analysis at a finer level of detail. A slightly more precise description of an engine, for example, views it as a collection of cylinders, each of which converts an explosion of fuel into a vertical motion, and a crankshaft, which converts the up and down motion of the cylinder into a rotation.

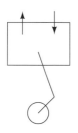

Another example might be organizing information about motion in a human body. At one level we are simply concerned with mechanics, and we consider the body as composed of bone (for rigidity), muscles (for movement), eyes and ears (for sensing), the nervous system (for transferring information), and skin (to bind it all together). At the next level of detail we might ask how the muscles work and consider issues such as cell structure and chemical actions. But chemical actions are governed by their molecular structure, and to understand molecules we break them into their individual atoms.

Any explanation must be phrased at the right level of abstraction. Trying to explain how a person can walk by understanding the atomic level details is almost certainly difficult, if not impossible.

2.2.2   Encapsulation and interchangeability

A key step in the creation of large systems is the division into components. Suppose instead of writing software we are part of a team working to create a new automobile. By separating the automobile into the parts *engine* and *transmission*, it is possible to assign people to work on the two aspects more or less independently of each other. We use the term *encapsulation* to mean that there is a strict division between the inner and the outer view. Those members of the team working on the engine need only an abstract (outside, as it were) view of the transmission, whereas those actually working on the transmission need the more detailed inside view.

An important benefit of encapsulation is that it permits us to consider the possibility of *interchangeability*. When we divide a system into parts, a desirable goal is that the interaction between the parts is kept to a minimum. For example, by encapsulating the behavior of the engine from that of a transmission we permit the ability to exchange one type of engine with another without incurring an undue impact on the other portions of the system.

For these ideas to be applicable to software systems, we need a way to discuss the task that a software component performs and separate this from the way the component fulfills this responsibility.

2.2.3   Interface and implementation

In software we use the terms *interface* and *implementation* to describe the distinction between the *what* aspects of a task and the *how* features, between the outside view and the inside view. An interface describes what a system is designed to do. This is the view that *users* of the abstraction must understand. The interface says nothing about how the assigned task is being performed. So to work, an interface is matched with an *implementation* that completes the abstraction. The designers of an engine will deal with the interface to the transmission, while the designers of the transmission must complete an implementation of this interface.

Similarly, a key step along the path to developing complex computer systems will be the division of a task into component parts. These parts can then be developed by different members of a team. Each component will have two faces: the interface that it shows to the outside world and an implementation that it uses to fulfill the requirements of the interface.

The division between interface and implementation not only makes it easier to understand a design at a high level (since the description of an interface is much simpler than the description of any specific implementation) but also makes it

Catalogs

When the number of components in a system becomes large, it is often useful to organize the items by means of a *catalog*. We use many different forms of catalog in everyday life. Examples include a telephone directory, a dictionary, or an Internet search engine. Similarly, there are a variety of different catalogs used in software. One example is a simple list of classes. Another catalog might be the list of methods defined by a class. A reference book that describes the classes found in the Java standard library is a very useful form of catalog. In each of these cases the idea is to provide the user a mechanism to quickly locate a single part (be it class, object, or method) from a larger collection of items.

possible to interchange the software components (as I can use any implementation that satisfies the specifications given by the interface).

2.2.4   The service view

The idea that an interface describes the service provided by a software component without describing the techniques used to implement the service is at the heart of a much more general approach to managing the understanding of complex software systems. It was this sort of abstraction that we emphasized in our flower sending story in Chapter 1. Ultimately in that story a whole community of people became involved in the process of sending flowers.

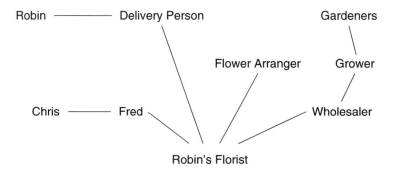

Each member of the community is providing a service that is used by other members of the group. No member could solve the problem on their own, and it is only by working together that the desired outcome is achieved.

2.2.5   Composition

Composition is another powerful technique used to create complex structures out of simple parts. The idea is to begin with a few primitive forms and add rules for combining forms to create new forms. The key insight in composition is to permit the combination mechanism to be used both on the new forms as well as the original primitive forms.

A good illustration of this technique is the concept of regular expressions. Regular expressions are a simple technique for describing sets of values, and they have been extensively studied by theoretical computer scientists. The description of a regular expression begins by identifying a basic alphabet—for example, the letters a, b, c, and d. Any single example of the alphabet is a regular expression. We next add a rule that says the composition of two regular expressions is a regular expression. By applying this rule repeatedly we see that any finite string of letters is a regular expression.

abaccaba

The next combining rule says that the alternation (represented by the vertical bar |) of two regular expressions is a regular expression. Normally we give this rule a lower precedence than composition, so the following pattern represents the set of three letter values that begin with ab and end with either an a, c, or d.

aba | abc | abd

Parentheses can be used for grouping, so the previous set can also be described as follows.

ab(a|c|d)

Finally, the * symbol (technically known as the kleene-star) is used to represent the concept "zero or more repetitions." By combining these rules we can describe quite complex sets. For example, the following describes the set of values that begin with a run of a's and b's followed by a single c or a two-character sequence dd, followed by the letter a.

(((a|b)*c)|dd)a

This idea of composition is also basic to type systems. We begin with the primitive types, such as int and boolean. The idea of a class then permits the user to create new types. These new types can include data fields constructed out of previous types, either primitive or user-defined. Since classes can build on previously defined classes, very complex structures can be constructed piece by piece.

```
class  Box { // a box is a new data type
   .
   .
   .
   private int value; // built out of the existing type int
}
```

Yet another application of the principle of composition is the way that many user interface libraries facilitate the layout of windows. A window is composed from a few simple data types, such as buttons, sliders, and drawing panels. Various different types of layout managers create simple structures. For example, a grid layout defines a rectangular grid of equal-sized components, a border layout manager permits the specification of up to five components in the north, south, east, west, and center of a screen. As with regular expressions, the key is that windows can be structured as part of other windows. Imagine, for example, that we want to define a window that has three sliders on the left, a drawing panel in the middle, a bank of 16 buttons organized four by four on the right, and a text output box running along the top. (We will develop just such an application

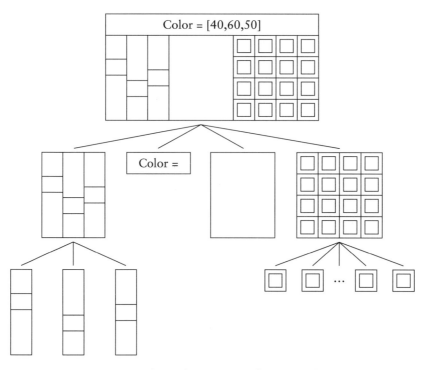

▣ Figure 2.3 —— Composition in the creation of user interfaces

in Chapter 22. A screen shot is shown in Figure 22.4.) We can do this by laying simple windows inside of more complex windows (Figure 2.3).

Many computer programs can themselves be considered a product of composition, where the method or procedure call is the mechanism of composition. We begin with the primitive statements in the language (assignments and the like). With these we can develop a library of useful functions. Using these functions as new primitives, we can then develop more complex functions. We continue, each layer being built on top of earlier layers, until eventually we have the desired application.

2.2.6   Layers of specialization

Yet another approach to dealing with complexity is to structure abstraction using layers of specialization. This is sometimes referred to as a *taxonomy*. For example, in biology we divide living things into animals and plants. Living things are then divided into vertebrates and invertebrates. Vertebrates eventually includes mammals, which can then be divided into cats, dogs, whales, and so on.

Nonstandard Behavior

Phyl and his friends remind us that there are almost never generalizations without their being exceptions. A platypus (such as phyl) is a mammal that lays eggs. Thus, while we might associate the tidbit of knowledge "gives birth to live young" with the category Mammal, we then need to amend this with the caveat "lays eggs" when we descend to the category Platypus.

Object-oriented languages will also need a mechanism to *override* information inherited from a more general category. We will explore this in more detail once we have developed the idea of class hierarchies.

The key difference between this and the earlier abstraction is that the more specialized layer of abstraction (for example, a cat) is indeed representative of the more general layer of abstraction (for example, an animal). This was not true when, in an earlier example, we descended from the characterization of a muscle to the description of different chemical interactions. These two different types of connections are sometimes described as *is-a* and *has-a* relationships.

However, in practice our reason for using either type of abstraction is the same. The principle of abstraction permits us to suppress some details so that we can more easily characterize a fewer number of features. For example, we can say that mammals are animals that have hair and nurse their young. By associating this fact at a high level of abstraction, we can then apply the information to all more specialized categories, such as cats and dogs.

The same technique is used in object-oriented languages. New interfaces can be formed from existing interfaces. A class can be formed using inheritance from an existing class. In doing so, all the properties (data fields and behavior) we associate with the original class become available to the new class.

In a case study later in this book we will examine the Java AWT (Abstract Windowing Toolkit) library. When a programmer creates a new application using the AWT, the main class is declared as a subclass of Frame, which in turn is linked to many other classes in the AWT library (Figure 2.4). A Frame is a special type of application window, but it is also a more specialized type of the general class Window. A Window can hold other graphical objects and is thus a type of Container. Each level of the hierarchy provides methods used by lower levels. Even the simplest application will likely use the following:

setTitle(String)	inherited from class Frame
setSize(int, int)	inherited from class Component
show()	inherited from class Window

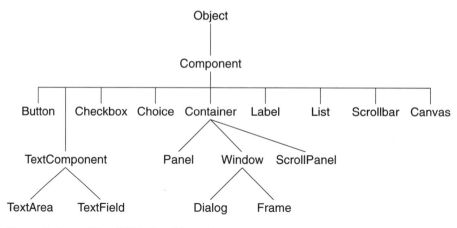

▫ Figure 2.4 —— The AWT class hierarchy

repaint()	inherited from class Component
paint()	inherited from Component, then overridden in the programmers new application class

2.2.7   Patterns

When faced with a new problem, most people will consider successful solutions to previous problems with similar characteristics. The previous problem can be used as a model, and the solution can be tried on the new problem, with any necessary changes to accommodate the different circumstances.

This insight lies behind the idea of a software *pattern*. A pattern is nothing more than an attempt to document a proven solution to a problem so that future problems can be more easily handled in a similar fashion. In the object-oriented world this idea has been used largely to describe patterns of interaction between the various members of an object community.

A simple example will illustrate this idea of a pattern. Imagine one is developing an application that will operate over a network. That means that part of the application will run on one computer, and part will run on another computer linked by a network connection. Creating the actual connection between the two computers and transmitting information along this connection are details that are perhaps not relevant to large portions of the application. One way to structure these relationships is to use a type of pattern termed a *proxy*. The proxy is an intermediary that hides the network connection. Objects can interact with the proxy and not be aware that any type of network connection is involved at all. When the proxy receives a request for data or action, it bundles the request as a package, transmits the package over the network, receives the response, unpackages the response, and hands it back to the client. In this fashion the client is completely unaware of the details of the network protocol.

Notice how the description of the pattern has captured certain salient points of the interaction (the need to hide the communication protocol from the client) while omitting many other aspects of the interaction (for example, the particular information being communicated between client and server). We will have more to say about patterns in Chapter 24.

*2.3 □ A Short History of Abstraction Mechanisms

Each of the abstraction mechanisms in this chapter was the end product of a long process of searching for ways to deal with complexity. Another way to appreciate the role of object-oriented programming is to quickly review the history of mechanisms that computer languages have used to manage complexity. When seen in this perspective, object-oriented techniques are not at all revolutionary but are rather a natural outcome of a progression from procedures, to modules, to abstract data types, and finally to objects.

2.3.1 Assembly language

The techniques used to control the first computers were hardly what we would today term a language. Memory locations were described by address (for example, location 372), not by name or purpose. Operations were similarly described by a numeric operation code. For example, an integer addition might be written as opcode 33, an integer subtraction as opcode 35. The following program might add the contents of location 372 to that of 376, then subtract from the result the value stored in location 377.

```
33    372    376
35    377    376
. . .   . . .   . . .
```

One of the earliest abstraction mechanisms was the creation of an assembler— a tool that could take a program written in a more human-friendly form and translate it into a representation suitable for execution by the machine. The assembler permitted the use of symbolic names. The previous instructions might now be written as follows.

ADDI   A,X
SUBI   B,X
. . .   . . .

This simple process was the first step in the long process of abstraction. Abstraction allowed the programmer to concentrate more effort on defining the task to be performed and less on the steps necessary to complete the task.

2.3.2 Procedures

Procedures and functions represent the next improvement in abstraction in programming languages. Procedures allowed tasks that were executed repeatedly, or executed with only slight variations, to be collected in one place and reused, rather than being duplicated several times. In addition, the procedure gave the first possibility for *information hiding*. One programmer could write a procedure, or a set of procedures, that was used by many others. Other programmers did not need to know the exact details of the implementation—they needed only the necessary interface. But procedures were not an answer to all problems. In particular, they were not an effective mechanism for information hiding, and they only partially solved the problem of multiple programmers using the same names.

To illustrate these problems, we can consider a programmer who must write a set of routines to implement a *simple stack*. Following good software engineering principles, our programmer first establishes the visible interface to her work— say, a set of four routines: init, push, pop, and top. She then selects some suitable implementation technique. There are many choices here, such as an array with a top-of-stack pointer, a linked list, and so on. Our intrepid programmer selects from among these choices, then proceeds to code the utilities, as shown in Figure 2.5.

It is easy to see that the data contained in the stack itself cannot be made local to any of the four routines, since they must be shared by all. But if the only choices are local variables or global variables (as they are in early programming languages, such as FORTRAN, or in C prior to the introduction of the static modifier), then the stack data must be maintained in global variables. However, if the variables are global, there is no way to limit the accessibility or visibility of these names. For example, if the stack is represented in an array named datastack, this fact must be made known to all the other programmers, since they may want to create variables using the same name and should be discouraged from doing so. This is true even though these data values are important only to the stack routines and should not have any use outside of these four procedures. Similarly, the names init, push, pop, and top are now reserved and cannot be used in other portions of the program for other purposes, even if those sections of code have nothing to do with the stack routines.

```
int datastack[100];
int datatop = 0;

void init()
{
  datatop = 0;
}

void push(int val)
{
  if (datatop < 100)
    datastack [datatop++] = val;
}

int top()
{
  if (datatop > 0)
    return datastack [datatop - 1];
  return 0;
}

int pop()
{
  if (datatop > 0)
    return datastack [--datatop];
  return 0;
}
```

▢ Figure 2.5 —— Failure of procedures in information hiding

2.3.3 Modules

The solution to the problem of global name space congestion was the introduction
of the idea of a module. In one sense, modules can be viewed simply as an
improved technique for creating and managing collections of names and their
associated values. Our stack example is typical in that there is some information
(the interface routines) that we want to be widely and publicly available, whereas
there are other data values (the stack data themselves) that we want restricted.
Stripped to its barest form, a *module* provides the ability to divide a name space
into two parts. The *public* part is accessible outside the module; the *private* part
is accessible only within the module. Types, data (variables), and procedures can

```
module StackModule;
  export push, pop, top; (* the public interface *)

  var
    (* since data values are not exported, they are hidden *)
    datastack : array [ 1 .. 100 ] of integer;
    datatop : integer;

  procedure push(val : integer) ...

  procedure top : integer ...

  procedure pop : integer ...

  begin        (* can perform initialization here *)
    datatop = 0;
  end;
end StackModule.
```

▫ Figure 2.6 —— A module for the stack abstraction

all be defined in either portion. A module encapsulation of the stack abstraction is shown in Figure 2.6.

David Parnas, who popularized the notion of modules, described the following two principles for their proper use.

1. One must provide the intended user with all the information needed to use the module correctly and *nothing more*.
2. One must provide the implementor with all the information needed to complete the module and *nothing more*.

The philosophy is much like the military doctrine of "need to know": If you do not need to know some information, you should not have access to it. This explicit and intentional concealment of information is what we have been calling *information hiding*.

Modules solve some, but not all, of the problems of software development. For example, they will permit our programmer to hide the implementation details of her stack, but what if the other users want to have two (or more) stacks?

As a more extreme example, suppose a programmer announces that he has developed a new type of numeric abstraction, called Complex. He has defined the arithmetic operations for complex numbers—addition, subtraction, multiplication, and so on—and has defined routines to convert numbers from conventional to complex. There is just one small problem: Only one complex number can be manipulated.

The complex number system would not be useful with this restriction, but this is just the situation in which we find ourselves with simple modules. Modules by themselves provide an effective method of information hiding, but they do not allow us to perform *instantiation*, which is the ability to make multiple copies of the data areas. To handle the problem of instantiation, computer scientists needed to develop a new concept.

2.3.4   Abstract data types

The development of the notion of an abstract data type was driven, in part, by two important goals. The first we have identified already. Programmers should be able to define their own new data abstractions that work much like the primitive system provided data types. This includes giving clients the ability to create multiple instances of the data type. But equally important, clients should be able to use these instances knowing only the operations that have been provided, without concern for how those operations were supported.

An *abstract data type* is defined by an abstract specification. The specification for our stack data type might list, for example, the trio of operations push, pop, and top. Matched with the ADT will be one or more different implementations. There might be several different implementation techniques for our stack—for example, one using an array and another using a linked list. As long as the programmer restricts himself to only the abstract specification, any valid implementation should work equally well.

The important advance in the idea of the ADT is to finally separate the notions of interface and implementation. Modules are frequently used as an implementation technique for abstract data types, although we emphasize that modules are an implementation technique and that the abstract data type is a more theoretical concept. The two are related but are not identical. To build an abstract data type, we must be able to do the following.

1. Export a type definition.
2. Make available a set of operations that can be used to manipulate instances of the type.
3. Protect the data associated with the type so that they can be operated on only by the provided routines.
4. Make multiple instances of the type.

As we have defined them, modules serve only as an information-hiding mechanism and thus directly address only list items 2 and 3, although the others can be accommodated via appropriate programming techniques. *Packages*, found in languages such as CLU and Ada, are an attempt to address more directly the issues involved in defining abstract data types.

In a certain sense, an object is simply an abstract data type. People have said, for example, that Smalltalk programmers write the most "structured" of all programs because they cannot write anything but definitions of abstract data types. It is true that an object definition is an abstract data type, but the notions of object-oriented programming build on the ideas of abstract data types and add to them important innovations in code sharing and reusability.

2.3.5   A service-centered view

Assembly language and procedures as abstraction mechanisms concentrated the programmer's view at the functional level: how a task should be accomplished. The movement toward modules and ADT is indicative of a shift from a function-centered conception of computation to a more data-centered view. Here it is the data values that are important—their structure, representation, and manipulation.

Object-oriented programming starts from this data-centered view of the world and takes it one step further. It is not that data abstractions, per se, are important to computation. Rather, an ADT is a useful abstraction because it can be defined in terms of the *service* it offers to the rest of a program. Other types of abstractions can be similarly defined, not in terms of their particular actions or their data values but in terms of the services they provide.

Assembly Language	*Function*
Functions and Procedures	Centered View
Modules	*Data*
Abstract Data Types	Centered View
Object-Oriented	*Service*
Programming	Centered View

Thus, object-oriented programming represents a third step in this sequence: from function-centered, to data-centered, and finally to service-centered view of how to structure a computer program.

2.3.6   Messages, inheritance, and polymorphism

In addition to this service-centered view of computing, object-oriented programming adds several important new ideas to the concept of the abstract data type. Foremost among these is *message passing*. Activity is initiated by a *request* to a specific object, not by the invoking of a function.

Implicit in message passing is the idea that the *interpretation* of a message can vary with different objects. That is, the behavior and response that the message elicits will depend on the object receiving it. Thus, push can mean one thing to a stack and a very different thing to a mechanical-arm controller. Since names for operations need not be unique, simple and direct forms can be used, leading to more readable and understandable code.

Finally, object-oriented programming adds the mechanisms of *inheritance* and *polymorphism*. Inheritance allows different data types to share the same code, leading to a reduction in code size and an increase in functionality. Polymorphism allows this shared code to be tailored to fit the specific circumstances of individual data types. The emphasis on the independence of individual components permits an incremental development process in which individual software units are designed, programmed, and tested before being combined into a large system. We will discuss all of these ideas in more detail in subsequent chapters.

Summary ▫

People deal with complex artifacts and situations every day. Thus, while many readers may not yet have created complex computer programs, they nevertheless will have experience in using the tools that computer scientists employ in managing complexity.

- The most basic tool is *abstraction*, the purposeful suppression of detail in order to emphasize a few basic features.
- *Information hiding* describes the part of abstraction in which we intentionally choose to ignore some features so that we can concentrate on others.
- Abstraction is often combined with a division into *components*. For example, we divided the automobile into the engine and the transmission. Components are carefully chosen so that they *encapsulate* certain key features and interact with other components through a simple and fixed *interface*.
- The division into components means we can divide a large task into smaller problems that can then be worked on more or less independently of each other. It is the responsibility of a developer of a component to provide an *implementation* that satisfies the requirements of the interface.
- A point of view that turns out to be very useful in developing complex software systems is the concept of a *service provider*. A software component is providing a service to other components with which it interacts. In real life we often characterize members of the communities in which we operate by the services they provide. (A delivery person is charged with transporting flowers from

a florist to a recipient.) Thus, this metaphor allows us to think about a large software system in the same way that we think about situations in our everyday lives.

- Another form of abstraction is a taxonomy—in object-oriented languages more often termed an *inheritance hierarchy*. Here the layers are more detailed representatives of a general category. An example of this type of system is a biological division into categories such as Living Thing-Animal-Mammal-Cat. Each level is a more specialized version of the previous. This division simplifies understanding, since knowledge of more general levels is applicable to many more specific categories. When applied to software this technique also simplifies the creation of new components, since if a new component can be related to an existing category, all the functionality of the older category can be used for free. (Thus, for example, by saying that a new component represents a Frame in the Java library, we immediately get features such as a menu bar as well as the ability to move and resize the window.)

- Finally, a particular tool that has become popular in recent years is the *pattern*. A pattern is simply a generalized description of a solution to a problem that has been observed to occur in many places and in many forms. The pattern described how the problem can be addressed and the reasons both for adopting the solution and for considering other alternatives. We will see several different types of patterns throughout this book.

Further Information ⊡

In the sidebar on page 33 we mention software catalogs. For the Java programmer, a very useful catalog is *The Java Developers Almanac*, by Patrick Chan [Chan 2000].

The concept of *patterns* actually grew out of work in architecture, specifically the work of Christopher Alexander [Alexander 1977]. The application of patterns to software is described by Gabriel [Gabriel 1996]. The best-known catalog of software Patterns is by Gamma et al. [Gamma 1995]. A more recent almanac that collects several hundred design patterns is [Rising 2000].

The criticism of procedures as an abstraction technique, because they fail to provide an adequate mechanism for information hiding, was first stated by William Wulf and Mary Shaw [Wulf 1973] in an analysis of many of the problems surrounding the use of global variables. These arguments were later expanded upon by David Hanson [Hanson 1981].

David Parnas originally described his principles in [Parnas 1972].

An interesting book that deals with the relationship between how people think and the way they form abstractions of the real word is Lakoff [Lakoff 1987].

Self-Study Questions ▫

1. What is abstraction?
2. Give an example of how abstraction is used in real life.
3. What is information hiding?
4. Give an example of how information hiding is used in real life.
5. What are the layers of abstraction found in an object-oriented program?
6. What do the terms *client* and *server* mean when applied to simple object-oriented programs?
7. What is the distinction between an interface and an implementation?
8. How does an emphasis on encapsulation and the identification of interfaces facilitate interchangeability?
9. What are the basic features of composition as a technique for creating complex systems out of simple parts?
10. How does a division based on layers of specialization differ from a division based on separation into parts?
11. What goal motivates the collection of software patterns?
12. What key idea was first realized by the development of procedures as a programming abstraction?
13. What are the basic features of a module?
14. How is an abstract data type different from a module?
15. In what ways is an object similar to an abstract data type? In what ways are they different?

Exercises ▫

1. Consider a relationship in real life, such as the interaction between a customer and a waiter in a resturant. Describe the interaction govering this relationship in terms of an interface for a customer object and a waiter object.
2. Take a relatively complex structure from real life, such as a building. Describe features of the building using the technique of division into parts, followed by a further refinement of each part into a more detailed description. Extend your description to at least three levels of detail.
3. Describe a collection of everyday objects using the technique of layers of specialization.

CHAPTER 3

Object-Oriented Design

A cursory explanation of object-oriented programming emphasizes the syntactic features of languages such as C++ or Delphi, as opposed to their older, non-object-oriented versions, C or Pascal. Thus, an explanation usually turns quickly to issues such as classes and inheritance, message passing, and virtual and static methods. But such a description will miss the most important point of object-oriented programming, which has nothing to do with syntax.

Working in an object-oriented language (that is, one that supports inheritance, message passing, and classes) is neither a necessary nor sufficient condition for doing object-oriented programming. As we emphasized in Chapters 1 and 2, the most important aspect of OOP is the creation of a universe of largely autonomous interacting agents. But how does one come up with such a system? The answer is a design technique driven by the determination and delegation of responsibilities. The technique described in this chapter is termed *responsibility-driven design*.[1]

---

1. The past few years have seen a poliferation of object-oriented design techniques. See the section on further reading at the end of this chapter for pointers to some of the alternatives. I have selected responsibility-driven design, developed by Rebecca Wirfs-Brock [Wirfs-Brock 1989b, Wirfs-Brock 1990] because it is one of the simplest, and it facilitates the transition from design to programming. Also in this chapter I introduce some of the notational techniques made popular by the Unified Modeling Language, or UML. However, space does not permit a complete introduction to UML, nor is it necessary for an understanding of subsequent material in the book.

3.1 ▫ Responsibility Implies Noninterference

As anyone who has raised children, or who can remember their own childhood, can attest, responsibility is a sword that cuts both ways. When you make an object (be it a child or a software system) responsible for specific actions, you expect a certain behavior, at least when the rules are observed. But just as important, responsibility implies a degree of independence or noninterference. If you tell a child that she is responsible for cleaning her room, you do not normally stand over her and watch while that task is being performed—that is not the nature of responsibility. Instead, you expect that, having issued a directive in the correct fashion, the desired outcome will be produced.

Similarly, in our flowers example, when Chris gave the request to the florist to deliver flowers to Robin, it was not necessary to stop to think about how the request would be serviced. The florist, having taken on the responsibility for this service, is free to operate without interference on the part of the customer, Chris.

The difference between conventional programming and object-oriented programming is in many ways the difference between actively supervising a child while she performs a task and delegating to the child responsibility for that performance. Conventional programming proceeds largely by doing something *to* something else—modifying a record or updating an array, for example. Thus, one portion of code in a software system is often intimately tied, by control and data connections, to many other sections of the system. Such dependencies can come about through the use of global variables, through use of pointer values, or simply through inappropriate use of and dependence on implementation details of other portions of code. A responsibility-driven design attempts to cut these links, or at least make them as unobtrusive as possible.

This notion might at first seem no more subtle than the concepts of information hiding and modularity, which are important to programming even in conventional languages. But responsibility-driven design elevates information hiding from a technique to an art. This principle of information hiding becomes vitally important when one moves from programming in the small to programming in the large.

One of the major benefits of object-oriented programming occurs when software subsystems are reused from one project to the next. For example, a simulation manager (such as the one we will develop in Chapter 7) might work for both a simulation of balls on a billiards table and a simulation of fish in a fish tank. This ability to reuse code implies that the software can have almost no domain-specific components; it must totally delegate responsibility for domain-specific behavior to application-specific portions of the system. The ability to create such reusable code is not one that is easily learned. It requires experience, careful examination of case studies (paradigms, in the original sense of the word), and use of a programming language in which such delegation is natural and easy to express. In subsequent chapters, we will see several such examples.

3.2 ▫ Programming in the Small and in the Large

The difference between the development of individual projects and of more sizable software systems is often described as programming in the small versus programming in the large.

Programming in the small characterizes projects with the following attributes.

- Code is developed by a single programmer or by a very small collection of programmers. A single individual can understand all aspects of a project from top to bottom, beginning to end.
- The major problem in the software development process is the design and development of algorithms for dealing with the problem at hand.

Programming in the large, on the other hand, characterizes software projects with features such as the following.

- The software system is developed by a large team, often consisting of people with many different skills. There may be graphic artists, design experts, as well as programmers. Individuals involved in the specification or design of the system may differ from those involved in the coding of individual components, who may differ as well from those involved in the integration of various components in the final product. No single individual can be responsible for the entire project or even understand all aspects of the project.
- The major problem in the software development process is the management of details and the communication of information between diverse portions of the project.

While the beginning student will usually be acquainted with programming in the small, aspects of many object-oriented languages are best understood as responses to the problems encountered while programming in the large. Thus, some appreciation of the difficulties involved in developing large systems is a helpful prerequisite to understanding OOP.

3.3 ▫ Why Begin with Behavior?

Why begin the design process with an analysis of behavior? The simple answer is that the behavior of a system is usually understood long before any other aspect.

Earlier software development methodologies (those popular before the advent of object-oriented techniques) concentrated on ideas such as characterizing the basic data structures or the overall structure of function calls, often within the creation of a formal specification of the desired application. But structural elements of the application can be identified only after a considerable amount of problem analysis. Similarly, a formal specification often ended up as a document understood by neither programmer nor client. But *behavior* is something that can be described almost from the moment an idea is conceived and (often unlike a formal specification) can be described in terms meaningful to both the programmers and the client.

Responsibility-Driven Design (RDD), developed by Rebecca Wirfs-Brock, is an object-oriented design technique that is driven by an emphasis on behavior at all levels of development. It is but one of many alternative object-oriented design techniques. We will illustrate the application of Responsibility-Driven Design with a case study.

3.4 ⊡ A Case Study in RDD

Imagine you are the chief software architect in a major computer firm. One day your boss walks into your office with an idea that, it is hoped, will be the next major success in your product line. Your assignment is to develop the *Interactive Intelligent Kitchen Helper* (Figure 3.1).

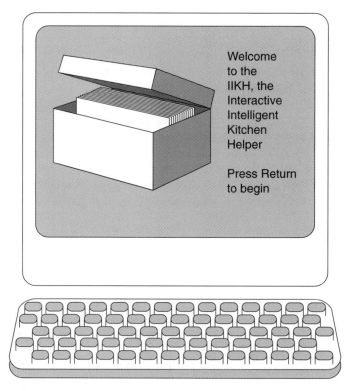

⊡ Figure 3.1 —— View of the Interactive Intelligent Kitchen Helper

The task given to your software team is stated in very few words (written on what appears to be the back of a slightly used dinner napkin, in handwriting that appears to be your boss's).

3.4.1 The Interactive Intelligent Kitchen Helper

Briefly, the Interactive Intelligent Kitchen Helper (IIKH) is a PC-based application that will replace the index-card system of recipes found in the average kitchen. But more than simply maintaining a database of recipes, the kitchen helper assists in the planning of meals for an extended period—say, a week. The user of the IIKH can sit down at a terminal, browse the database of recipes, and interactively create a series of menus. The IIKH will automatically scale the recipes to any number of servings and will print out menus for the entire week, for a particular day, or for a particular meal. It will also print an integrated grocery list of all the items needed for the recipes for the entire period.

As is usually true with the initial descriptions of most software systems, the specification for the IIKH is highly ambiguous on a number of important points. It is also true that, in all likelihood, the eventual design and development of the software system to support the IIKH will require the efforts of several programmers working together. Thus, the initial goal of the design team must be to clarify the ambiguities in the description and to outline how the project can be divided into components to be assigned for development to individual team members.

The fundamental cornerstone of object-oriented programming is to characterize software in terms of *behavior*—that is, actions to be performed. We will see this repeated on many levels in the development of the IIKH. Initially, the team will try to characterize, at a very high level of abstraction, the behavior of the entire application. This then leads to a description of the behavior of various software subsystems. Only when all behavior has been identified and described will the software design team proceed to the coding step. In the next several sections we will trace the tasks the software design team will perform in producing this application.

3.4.2 Working through scenarios

The first task is to refine the specification. As we have already noted, initial specifications are almost always ambiguous and unclear on anything except the most general points. There are several goals for this step. One objective is to get a better handle on the "look and feel" of the eventual product. This information can then be carried back to the client (in this case, your boss) to see if it is in agreement with the original conception. It is likely, perhaps inevitable, that the specifications for the final application will change during the creation of the software system,

Simple Browsing

Alice Smith sits down at her computer and starts the IIKH. When the program begins, it displays a graphical image of a recipe box and identifies itself as the IIKH, product of IIKH incorporated. Alice presses the return button to begin.

In response to the key press, Alice is given a choice of a number of options. She elects to browse the recipe index, looking for a recipe for salmon that she wishes to prepare for dinner the next day. She enters the keyword "salmon" and is shown in response a list of various recipes. She remembers seeing an interesting recipe that used dill weed as a seasoning. She refines the search, entering the words "salmon" and "dill weed." This narrows the search to two recipes.

She selects the first. This brings up a new window in which an attractive picture of the finished dish is displayed, along with the list of ingredients, preparation steps, and expected preparation time. After examining the recipe, Alice determines it is not the recipe she wanted. She returns to the search result page and selects the second alternative.

Examining this dish, Alice decides this is the one she had in mind. She requests a printout of the recipe, and the output is spooled to her printer. Alice selects "quit" from a program menu, and the application quits.

▫ **Figure 3.2** —— An example scenario

and it is important that the design be developed to easily accommodate change and that potential changes be noted as early as possible. Equally important, at this point very high-level decisions can be made concerning the structure of the eventual software system. In particular, the activities to be performed can be mapped onto components.

In order to uncover the fundamental behavior of the system, the design team first creates a number of *scenarios*. That is, the team acts out the running of the application just as if it already possessed a working system. An example scenario is shown in Figure 3.2.

3.4.3   Identification of components

The engineering of a complex physical system, such as a building or an automobile engine, is simplified by dividing the design into smaller units. So, too, the engineering of software is simplified by the identification and development of software components. A *component* is simply an abstract entity that can perform tasks— that is, fulfill some responsibilities. At this point, it is not necessary to know exactly the eventual representation for a component or how a component will perform a task. A component may ultimately be turned into a function, a structure or class, or a collection of other components. At this level of development there are just two important characteristics.

- A component must have a small, well-defined set of responsibilities.
- A component should interact with other components to the minimal extent possible.

We will shortly discuss the reasoning behind the second characteristic. For the moment we are simply concerned with the identification of component responsibilities.

3.5 ◻ CRC Cards—Recording Responsibility

As the design team walks through the various scenarios they have created, they identify the components that will be performing certain tasks. Every activity that must take place is identified and assigned to some component as a responsibility.

Component Name	Collaborators
Description of the responsibilities assigned to this component	*List of other components*

As part of this process, it is often useful to represent components using small index cards. Written on the face of the card is the name of the software component, the responsibilities of the component, and the names of other components with which the component must interact. Such cards are sometimes known as CRC (Component, Responsibility, Collaborator) cards and are associated with each software component. As responsibilities for the component are discovered, they are recorded on the face of the CRC card.

3.5.1 Give components a physical representation

While working through scenarios, it is useful to assign CRC cards to different members of the design team. The member holding the card representing a component records the responsibilities of the associated software component and acts as the "surrogate" for the software during the scenario simulation. He or she describes the activities of the software system, passing "control" to another member when the software system requires the services of another component.

An advantage of CRC cards is that they are widely available, inexpensive, and erasable. This encourages experimentation, since alternative designs can be tried, explored, or abandoned with little investment. The physical separation of the cards encourages an intuitive understanding of the importance of the logical separation of the various components, helping to emphasize the cohesion and coupling (which we will describe shortly). The constraints of an index card are also a good measure of approximate complexity. A component that is expected to perform more tasks than can fit easily in this space is probably too complex, and the team should find a simpler solution, perhaps by moving some responsibilities elsewhere to divide a task between two or more new components.

3.5.2   The what/who cycle

As we noted at the beginning of this discussion, the identification of components takes place during the process of imagining the execution of a working system. Often this proceeds as a cycle of what/who questions. First, the design team identifies *what* activity needs to be performed next. This is immediately followed by answering the question of *who* performs the action. In this manner, designing a software system is much like organizing a collection of people, such as a club. Any activity that is to be performed must be assigned as a responsibility to some component.

A popular bumper sticker states that phenomena can and will spontaneously occur. (The bumper sticker uses a slightly shorter phrase.) We know, however, that in real life this is seldom true. If any action is to take place, there must be an agent assigned to perform it. Just as in the running of a club any action to be performed must be assigned to some individual, in organizing an object-oriented program all actions must be the responsibility of some component. The secret to good object-oriented design is to first establish an agent for each action.

3.5.3   Documentation

At this point the development of documentation should begin. Two documents should be essential parts of any software system: the user manual and the system design documentation. Work on both of these can commence even before the first line of code has been written.

The user manual describes the interaction with the system from the user's point of view; it is an excellent means of verifying that the development team's conception of the application matches the client's. Since the decisions made in creating the scenarios will closely match the decisions the user will be required to make in the eventual application, the development of the user manual naturally dovetails with the process of walking through scenarios.

Before any actual code has been written, the mindset of the software team is most similar to that of the eventual users. Thus, it is at this point that the developers can most easily anticipate the sort of questions to which a novice user will need answers. A user manual is also an excellent tool to verify that the programming team is looking at the problem in the same way that the client intended. A client seldom presents the programming team with a complete and formal specification, and thus some reassurance and two-way communication early in the process, before actual programming has begun, can prevent major misunderstandings.

The second essential document is the design documentation. The design documentation records the major decisions made during software design and should thus be produced when these decisions are fresh in the minds of the creators and not after the fact when many of the relevant details will have been forgotten. It is often far easier to write a general global description of the software system early in the development. Too soon, the focus will move to the level of individual components or modules. While it is also important to document the module level, too much concern with the details of each module will make it difficult for subsequent software maintainers to form an initial picture of the larger structure.

CRC cards are one aspect of the design documentation, but many other important decisions are not reflected in them. Arguments for and against any major design alternatives should be recorded, as well as factors that influenced the final decisions. A log or diary of the project schedule should be maintained. Both the user manual and the design documents are refined and evolve over time in exactly the same way the software is refined and evolves.

3.6 □ Components and Behavior

To return to the IIKH, the team decides that when the system begins, the user will be presented with an attractive, informative window (see Figure 3.1). The responsibility for displaying this window is assigned to a component called the Greeter. In some as yet unspecified manner (perhaps by pull-down menus, button or key presses, or use of a pressure-sensitive screen), the user can select one of several actions. Initially, the team identifies just five actions.

1. Casually browse the database of existing recipes but without reference to any particular meal plan.
2. Add a new recipe to the database.
3. Edit or annotate an existing recipe.
4. Review an existing plan for several meals.
5. Create a new plan of meals.

```
┌─────────────────────────────────────────────────────────────────┐
│                                                                   │
│   Greeter                            Collaborators                │
│                                                                   │
│                                      Database Manager             │
│   Display informative initial message   Plan Manager             │
│   Offer user choice of options                                    │
│   Pass control to either                                          │
│         Recipe Database Manager                                   │
│         Plan Manager for processing                               │
│                                                                   │
│                                                                   │
│                                                                   │
└─────────────────────────────────────────────────────────────────┘
```

▣ Figure 3.3 —— CRC card for the Greeter

These activities seem to divide themselves naturally into two groups. The first three are associated with the recipe database; the latter two are associated with menu plans. As a result, the team next decides to create components corresponding to these two responsibilities. Continuing with the scenario, the team elects to ignore the meal plan management for the moment and move on to refine the activities of the Recipe Database component. Figure 3.3 shows the initial CRC card representation of the Greeter.

Broadly speaking, the responsibility of the recipe database component is simply to maintain a collection of recipes. We have already identified three elements of this task: The recipe component database must facilitate browsing the library of existing recipes, editing the recipes, and including new recipes in the database.

3.6.1   Postponing decisions

There are a number of decisions that must eventually be made concerning how best to let the user browse the database. For example, should the user first be presented with a list of categories, such as "soups," "salads," "main meals," and "desserts"? Alternatively, should the user be able to describe keywords to narrow a search, perhaps by providing a list of ingredients, and then see all the recipes that contain those items ("almonds, strawberries, cheese") or a list of previously inserted keywords ("Bob's favorite cake")? Should scroll bars be used or simulated thumbholes in a virtual book? These are fun to think about, but the important point is that such decisions do not need to be made at this point (see the next section). Since they affect only a single component and do not affect the functioning of any other system, all that is necessary to continue the scenario is to assert that by some means the user can select a specific recipe.

3.6.2   Preparing for change

It has been said that all that is constant in life is the inevitability of uncertainty and change. The same is true of software. No matter how carefully one tries to develop the initial specification and design of a software system, it is almost certain that, sometime during the life of the system, changes in the user's needs or requirements will force changes to be made to the software. Programmers and software designers need to anticipate this and plan accordingly.

- The primary objective is that changes should affect as few components as possible. Even major changes in the appearance or functioning of an application should be possible with alterations to only one or two sections of code.
- Try to predict the most likely sources of change and isolate the effects of such changes to as few software components as possible. The most likely sources of change are interfaces, communication formats, and output formats.
- Try to isolate and reduce the dependency of software on hardware. For example, the interface for recipe browsing in our application may depend in part on the hardware on which the system is running. Future releases may be ported to different platforms. A good design will anticipate this change.
- Reducing coupling between software components will reduce the dependence of one on another and increase the likelihood that one can be changed with minimal effect on the other.
- In the design documentation, maintain careful records of the design process and the discussions surrounding all major decisions. It is almost certain that the individuals responsible for maintaining the software and designing future releases will have at least some members different from the team producing the initial release. The design documentation will allow future teams to know the important factors behind a decision and help them avoid spending time discussing issues that have already been resolved.

3.6.3   Continuing the scenario

Each recipe will be identified with a specific recipe component. Once a recipe is selected, control is passed to the associated recipe object. A recipe must contain certain information. Basically, it consists of a list of ingredients and the steps needed to transform the ingredients into the final product. In our scenario, the recipe component must also perform other activities. For example, it will display the recipe interactively on the terminal screen. The user may be given the ability to annotate or change either the list of ingredients or the instruction portion. Alternatively, the user may request a printed copy of the recipe. All of these actions are the responsibility of the Recipe component. (For the moment, we will continue to describe the Recipe in singular form. During design we can think of this as a prototypical recipe that stands in place of a multitude of actual recipes. We will later return to a discussion of singular versus multiple components.)

Having outlined the actions that must take place to permit the user to browse the database, we return to the recipe database manager and pretend the user has indicated a desire to add a new recipe. The database manager somehow decides in which category to place the new recipe (again, the details of how this is done are unimportant for our development at this point), requests the name of the new recipe, and then creates a new recipe component, permitting the user to edit this new blank entry. Thus, the responsibilities of performing this new task are a subset of those we already identified in permitting users to edit existing recipes.

Having explored the browsing and creation of new recipes, we return to the Greeter and investigate the development of daily menu plans, which is the Plan Manager's task. In some way (again, the details are unimportant here) the user can save existing plans. Thus, the Plan Manager can either be started by retrieving an already developed plan or by creating a new plan. In the latter case, the user is prompted for a list of dates for the plan. Each date is associated with a separate Date component. The user can select a specific date for further investigation, in which case control is passed to the corresponding Date component. Another activity of the Plan Manager is printing out the recipes for the planning period. Finally, the user can instruct the Plan Manager to produce a grocery list for the period.

The Date component maintains a collection of meals as well as any other annotations provided by the user (birthday celebrations, anniversaries, reminders, and so on). It prints information on the display concerning the specified date. By some means (again unspecified), the user can indicate a desire to print all the information concerning a specific date or choose to explore in more detail a specific meal. In the latter case, control is passed to a Meal component.

The Meal component maintains a collection of augmented recipes, where the augmentation refers to the user's desire to double, triple, or otherwise increase a recipe. The Meal component displays information about the meal. The user can add or remove recipes from the meal or can instruct that information about the meal be printed. In order to discover new recipes, the user must be permitted at this point to browse the recipe database. Thus, the Meal component must interact with the recipe database component. The design team will continue in this fashion, investigating every possible scenario. The major category of scenarios we have not developed here is exceptional cases. For example, what happens if a user selects a number of keywords for a recipe and no matching recipe is found? How can the user cancel an activity, such as entering a new recipe, if he or she decides not to continue? Each possibility must be explored, and the responsibilities for handling the situation must be assigned to one or more components.

Having walked through the various scenarios, the software design team eventually decides that all activities can be adequately handled by six components (Figure 3.4). The Greeter needs to communicate only with the Plan Manager and the Recipe Database components. The Plan Manager needs to communicate only with

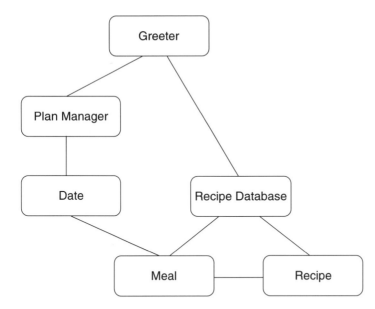

Figure 3.4 —— Communication between the six components in the IIKH

the Date component and the Date agent only with the Meal component. The Meal component communicates with the Recipe Manager and, through this agent, with individual recipes.

3.6.4   Interaction diagrams

While the process in Figure 3.4 may illustrate the static relationships between components, it is not very good for describing their dynamic interactions during the execution of a scenario. A better tool for this purpose is an *interaction diagram*. Figure 3.5 shows the beginning of an interaction diagram for the interactive kitchen helper. In the diagram, time moves forward from the top to the bottom. Each component is represented by a labeled vertical line. A component sending a message to another component is represented by a horizontal arrow from one line to another. Similarly, a component returning control and perhaps a result value back to the caller is represented by an arrow. (Some authors use two different arrow forms, such as a solid line to represent message passing and a dashed line to represent returning control.) The commentary on the right side of the figure explains more fully the interaction taking place.

   With a time axis, the interaction diagram is able to describe better the sequencing of events during a scenario. For this reason, interaction diagrams can be a useful documentation tool for complex software systems.

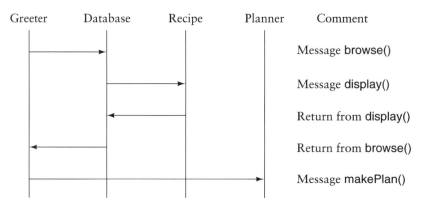

Greeter   Database   Recipe   Planner   Comment

Message **browse()**

Message **display()**

Return from **display()**

Return from **browse()**

Message **makePlan()**

▢ Figure 3.5 —— An example interaction diagram

3.7 ▢ Software Components

In this section we will explore a software component in more detail. As is true of all but the most trivial ideas, there are many aspects to this seemingly simple concept.

3.7.1   Behavior and state

We have already seen how components are characterized by their behavior—that is, by what they can do. But components may also hold certain information. Let us take as our prototypical component a Recipe structure from the IIKH. One way to view such a component is as a pair consisting of *behavior* and *state*.

- The *behavior* of a component is the set of actions it can perform. The complete description of all the behavior for a component is sometimes called the *protocol*. For the Recipe component this includes activities such as editing the preparation instructions, displaying the recipe on a terminal screen, or printing a copy of the recipe.

- The *state* of a component represents all the information held within it at a given point of time. For our Recipe component the state includes the ingredients and preparation instructions. Notice that the state is not static and can change over time. For example, by editing a recipe (a behavior) the user can make changes to the preparation instructions (part of the state).

It is not necessary that all components maintain state information. For example, it is possible that the Greeter component will not have any state since it does not need to remember any information during the course of execution. However, most components will consist of a combination of behavior and state.

3.7.2 Instances and classes

The separation of state and behavior permits us to clarify a point we avoided in our earlier discussion. Note that in the real application there will probably be many different recipes. However, all of these recipes will *perform* in the same manner. That is, the behavior of each recipe is the same; it is only the state— the individual lists of ingredients and instructions for preparation—that differs between individual recipes. In the early stages of development our interest is in characterizing the behavior common to all recipes; the details particular to any one recipe are unimportant.

The term *class* is used to describe a set of objects with similar behavior. We will see in later chapters that a class is also used as a syntactic mechanism in almost all object-oriented languages. An individual representative of a class is known as an *instance*. Note that behavior is associated with a class, not with an individual. That is, all instances of a class will respond to the same instructions and perform in a similar manner. On the other hand, state is a property of an individual. We see this in the various instances of the class Recipe. They can all perform the same actions (editing, displaying, printing) but use different data values.

3.7.3 Coupling and cohesion

Two important concepts in the design of software components are coupling and cohesion. Cohesion is the degree to which the responsibilities of a single component form a meaningful unit. High cohesion is achieved by associating in a single component tasks that are related in some manner. Probably the most frequent way in which tasks are related is through the necessity to access a common data value. This is the overriding theme that joins, for example, the various responsibilities of the Recipe component.

Coupling, on the other hand, describes the relationship between software components. In general, it is desirable to reduce the amount of coupling as much as possible, since connections between software components inhibit ease of development, modification, or reuse.

In particular, coupling is increased when one software component must access data values—the state—held by another component. Such situations should almost always be avoided in favor of moving a task into the list of responsibilities of the component that holds the necessary data. For example, one might conceivably first assign responsibility for editing a recipe to the Recipe Database component, since it is while performing tasks associated with this component that the need to edit a recipe first occurs. But if we did so, the Recipe Database agent would need the ability to directly manipulate the state (the internal data values representing the list of ingredients and the preparation instructions) of an individual recipe. It is better to avoid this tight connection by moving the responsibility for editing to the recipe itself.

3.7.4   Interface and implementation—Parnas's principles

The emphasis on characterizing a software component by its behavior has one extremely important consequence. It is possible for one programmer to know how to *use* a component developed by another programmer without needing to know how the component is *implemented*. For example, suppose each of the six components in the IIKH is assigned to a different programmer. The programmer developing the Meal component needs to allow the IIKH user to browse the database of recipes and select a single recipe for inclusion in the meal. To do this, the Meal component can simply invoke the browse behavior associated with the Recipe Database component, which is defined to return an individual Recipe. This description is valid regardless of the particular implementation used by the Recipe Database component to perform the actual browsing action.

The purposeful omission of implementation details behind a simple interface is known as *information hiding*. We say the component *encapsulates* the behavior, showing only how the component can be used but not the detailed actions it performs. This naturally leads to two different views of a software system. The interface view is the face seen by other programmers. It describes *what* a software component can perform. The implementation view is the face seen by the programmer working on a particular component. It describes *how* a component goes about completing a task.

The separation of interface and implementation is perhaps *the* most important concept in software engineering. Yet it is difficult for students to understand or to motivate. Information hiding is largely meaningful only in the context of multiperson programming projects. In such efforts, the limiting factor is often not the amount of coding involved but the amount of communication required between the various programmers and between their respective software systems. As we will describe shortly, software components are often developed in parallel by different programmers and in isolation from each other.

There is also an increasing emphasis on the reuse of general-purpose software components in multiple projects. For this to be successful, there must be minimal and well-understood interconnections between the various portions of the system. As we noted in the previous chapter, these ideas were captured by computer scientist David Parnas in a pair of rules known as *Parnas's principles*.

- The developer of a software component must provide the intended user with all the information needed to make effective use of the services provided by the component and should provide *no* other information.

- The developer of a software component must be provided with all the information necessary to carry out the given responsibilities assigned to the component and should be provided with *no* other information.

A consequence of the separation of interface from implementation is that a programmer can experiment with several different implementations of the same structure without affecting other software components.

3.8 ▫ Formalize the Interface

We continue with the description of the IIKH development. In the next several steps the descriptions of the components will be refined. The first step in this process is to formalize the patterns and channels of communication.

A decision should be made as to the general structure that will be used to implement each component. A component with only one behavior and no internal state may be made into a function—for example, a component that simply takes a string of text and translates all capital letters to lowercase. Components with many tasks are probably more easily implemented as classes. Names are given to each of the responsibilities identified on the CRC card for each component, and these will eventually be mapped onto method names. Along with the names, the types of any arguments to be passed to the function are identified. Next, the information maintained within the component itself should be described. All information must be accounted for. If a component requires some data to perform a specific task, the source of the data, either through argument or global value or maintained internally by the component, must be clearly identified.

3.8.1 Coming up with names

Careful thought should be given to the names associated with various activities. Shakespeare said that a name change does not alter the object being described ("a rose by any other name . . . "), but certainly not all names will conjure up the same mental images in the listener. As government bureaucrats have long known, obscure and idiomatic names can make even the simplest operation sound intimidating. The selection of useful names is extremely important, since names create the vocabulary with which the eventual design will be formulated. Names should be internally consistent, meaningful, preferably short, and evocative in the context of the problem. Often a considerable amount of time is spent finding just the right set of terms to describe the tasks performed and the objects manipulated. Far from being a barren and useless exercise, proper naming early in the design process greatly simplifies and facilitates later steps.

The following general guidelines have been suggested.

- Use pronounceable names. As a rule of thumb, if you cannot read a name out loud, it is not a good one.
- Use capitalization (or underscores) to mark the beginning of a new word within a name, such as "CardReader" or "Card_reader," rather than the less readable "cardreader."
- Examine abbreviations carefully. An abbreviation that is clear to one person may be confusing to the next. Is a "TermProcess" a terminal process, something that terminates processes, or a process associated with a terminal?
- Avoid names with several interpretations. Does the empty function tell whether something is empty, or does it empty the values from the object?
- Avoid digits within a name. They are easy to misread as letters (0 as O, 1 as l, 2 as Z, 5 as S).
- Name functions and variables that yield Boolean values so they describe clearly the interpretation of a true or false value. For example, "PrinterIsReady" clearly indicates that a true value means the printer is working, whereas "PrinterStatus" is much less precise.
- Take extra care in the selection of names for operations that are costly and infrequently used. By doing so, errors caused by using the wrong function can be avoided.

Once names have been developed for each activity, the CRC cards for each component are redrawn, with the name and formal arguments of the function used to elicit each behavior identified. An example of a CRC card for the Date component is shown in Figure 3.6. What is not yet specified is how each component will perform the associated tasks.

Date	Collaborators
	Plan Manager
Maintain information about specific date	Meal
Date (year, month, date)—create new date	
DisplayAndEdit()—display date information	
in window allowing user to edit entries	
BuildGroceryList(List &)—add items from	
all meals to grocery list	

▢ Figure 3.6 —— Revised CRC card for the Date component

Once more, scenarios or role playing should be carried out at a more detailed level to ensure that all activities are accounted for and that all necessary information is maintained and made available to the responsible components.

3.9 ▫ Designing the Representation

At this point, if not before, the design team can be divided into groups, each responsible for one or more software components. The task now is to transform the description of a component into a software system implementation. The major portion of this process is designing the data structures that will be used by each subsystem to maintain the state information required to fulfill the assigned responsibilities.

It is here that the classic data structures of computer science come into play. The selection of data structures is an important task, central to the software design process. Once they have been chosen, the code used by a component in the fulfillment of a responsibility is often almost self-evident. But data structures must be carefully matched to the task at hand. A wrong choice can result in complex and inefficient programs, while an intelligent choice can result in just the opposite.

It is also at this point that descriptions of behavior must be transformed into algorithms. These descriptions should then be matched against the expectations of each component listed as a collaborator, to ensure that expectations are fulfilled and necessary data items are available to carry out each process.

3.10 ▫ Implementing Components

Once the design of each software subsystem is laid out, the next step is to implement each component's desired behavior. If the previous steps were correctly addressed, each responsibility or behavior will be characterized by a short description. The task at this step is to implement the desired activities in a computer language. In a later section we will describe some of the more common heuristics used in this process.

If they were not determined earlier (say, as part of the specification of the system), then decisions can now be made on issues that are entirely self-contained within a single component. A decision we saw in our example problem was how best to let the user browse the database of recipes.

As multiperson programming projects become the norm, it becomes increasingly rare that any one programmer will work on all aspects of a system. More often, the skills a programmer will need to master are understanding how one section of code fits into a larger framework and how to work well with other members of a team.

Often in the implementation of one component it will become clear that certain information or actions might be assigned to yet another component that will act "behind the scene," with little or no visibility to users of the software abstraction. Such components are sometimes known as *facilitators*. We will see examples of facilitators in some of the later case studies.

An important part of analysis and coding at this point is characterizing and documenting the necessary preconditions a software component requires to complete a task, and verifying that the software component will perform correctly when presented with legal input values.

3.11 ▫ Integration of Components

Once software subsystems have been individually designed and tested, they can be integrated into the final product. This is often not a single step but part of a larger process. Starting from a simple base, elements are slowly added to the system and tested using *stubs*—simple dummy routines with no behavior or with very limited behavior—for the as yet unimplemented parts.

For example, in the development of the IIKH, it would be reasonable to start integration with the Greeter component. To test the Greeter in isolation, stubs are written for the Recipe Database manager and the daily Meal Plan manager. These stubs need not do any more than print an informative message and return. With these, the component development team can test various aspects of the Greeter system (for example, that button presses elicit the correct response). Testing of an individual component is often referred to as *unit testing*.

Next, one or the other of the stubs can be replaced by more complete code. For example, the team might decide to replace the stub for the Recipe Database component with the actual system, maintaining the stub for the other portion. Further testing can be performed until it appears that the system is working as desired. (This is sometimes referred to as *integration testing*.)

The application is finally complete when all stubs have been replaced with working components. The ability to test components in isolation is greatly facilitated by the conscious design goal of reducing connections between components, since this reduces the need for extensive stubbing.

During integration it is not uncommon for an error to be manifested in one software system and yet to be caused by a coding mistake in another system. Thus, testing during integration can involve the discovery of errors, which then results in changes to some of the components. Following these changes the components should be once again tested in isolation before an attempt to reintegrate the software, once more, into the larger system. Reexecuting previously developed test cases following a change to a software component is sometimes referred to as *regression testing*.

3.12 ⊡ Maintenance and Evolution

It is tempting to think that once a working version of an application has been delivered the task of the software development team is finished. Unfortunately, that is almost never true. The term *software maintenance* describes activities subsequent to the delivery of the initial working version of a software system. A wide variety of activities fall into this category.

- Errors, or *bugs*, can be discovered in the delivered product. These must be corrected, either in updates or corrections to existing releases or in subsequent releases.
- Requirements may change, perhaps as a result of government regulations or standardization among similar products.
- Hardware may change. For example, the system may be moved to different platforms, or input devices, such as a pen-based system or a pressure-sensitive touch screen, may become available. Output technology may change—for example, from a text-based system to a graphical window-based arrangement.
- User expectations may change. Users may expect greater functionality, lower cost, and easier use. This can occur as a result of competition with similar products.
- Better documentation may be requested by users.

A good design recognizes the inevitability of changes and plans an accommodation for them from the very beginning.

Summary ⊡

In this chapter we have presented a very abbreviated introduction to the basic ideas of object-oriented modeling and design. References in the following section can be consulted for more detailed discussion of this topic.

Object-oriented design differs from conventional software design in that the driving force is the assignment of responsibilities to different software components. No action will take place without an agent to perform the action, and hence every action must be assigned to some member of the object community. Conversely, the behavior of the members of the community taken together must be sufficient to achieve the desired goal.

The emphasis on *behavior* is a hallmark of object-oriented programming. Behavior can be identified in even the most rudimentary descriptions of a system, long before any other aspect can be clearly discerned. By constantly being driven by behavior, responsibility-driven design moves smoothly from problem description to software architecture to code development to finished application.

Further Reading ⊡

Responsibility-driven design was developed and first described by Rebecca Wirfs-Brock [Wirfs-Brock 1989b, Wirfs-Brock 1990]. There are many other object-oriented design techniques, such as that of Jacobson [Jacobson 1994] or Rumbaugh [Rumbaugh 1991], but I like responsibility-driven design because it is among the simplest to explain and is therefore a good introduction to object-oriented design and modeling.

Much of the most recent work in the field of object-oriented design has centered on UML, the *Unified Modeling Language*. I are not going to discuss UML in detail in this book, although I do use some of their notation in describing class diagrams. A good introduction to UML is [Booch 1999]. A slightly simpler explanation is found in [Alhir 1998].

Other good books on object-oriented design include [Rumbaugh 1991] and [Henderson-Sellers 1992].

CRC cards were developed by Beck [Beck 1989]. A more in-depth book-length treatment of the idea is [Bellin 1997].

Parnas's principles were first presented in [Parnas 1972].

The guidelines on names presented in Section 3.8.1 are from [Keller 1990].

Self-Study Questions ⊡

1. What are the key features of responsibility-driven design?
2. What are some key differences between programming in the small and programming in the large?
3. Why can a design technique based on behavior be applied more easily to poorly defined problems than can, say, a design approach based on data structures?
4. What is a scenario?
5. What are the basic elements of a component?
6. What is a CRC card? What do the letters stand for?
7. What is the what/who cycle?
8. Why should a user manual be developed before coding begins?
9. What are the major sources of change that can be expected during the lifetime of most long-lived software applications?
10. What information is conveyed by an interaction diagram?
11. What are Parnas's principles?
12. Why is the selection of good names an important aspect of a successful software design effort? What are some guidelines for choosing names?

13. What is integration testing?
14. What is software maintenance?

Exercises ⊡

1. Describe the responsibilities of an organization that includes at least six types of members. Examples of such organizations are a school (students, teachers, principal, janitor), a business (secretary, president, worker), and a club (president, vice president, member). For each member type, describe the responsibilities and the collaborators.

2. Create a scenario for the organization you described in Exercise 1 using an interaction diagram.

3. For a common game such as Solitaire or Twenty-one, describe a software system that will interact with the user as an opposing player. Example components include the deck and the discard pile.

4. Describe the software system to control an ATM (automated teller machine). Give interaction diagrams for various scenarios that describe the most common uses of the machine.

CHAPTER 4

Classes and Methods

Although they may use different terms, all object-oriented languages have the features introduced in Chapter 1 in common: *classes*, *instances*, *message passing*, *methods*, and *inheritance*. As noted already, the use of different terms for similar concepts is rampant in object-oriented programming languages. We will use a consistent and, we hope, clear terminology for all languages, and we will note in language-specific sections the various synonyms for our terms. Readers can refer to the glossary at the end of the book for explanations of unfamiliar terms.

This chapter will describe the definition or creation of classes, and Chapter 5 will outline their dynamic use. Here we will illustrate the mechanics of declaring a class and defining methods associated with instances of the class. In Chapter 5 we will examine how instances of classes are created and how messages are passed to those instances. For the most part we will defer an explanation of the mechanics of inheritance until Chapter 8.

4.1 ▫ Encapsulation

In Chapter 1, we noted that object-oriented programming, and objects in particular, can be viewed from many perspectives. In Chapter 2 we described the many levels of abstraction from which one could examine a program. In this chapter, we wish to view objects as examples of *abstract data types*.

Programming that uses data abstractions is a methodological approach to problem solving where information is consciously hidden in a small part of a program. In particular, the programmer develops a series of abstract data types, each of which can be viewed as having two faces. This is similar to the dichotomy in Parnas's principles, discussed in Chapter 3. From the outside, a client (user) of

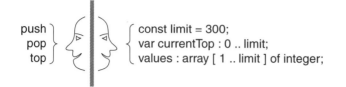

push ⎫
pop ⎬   const limit = 300;
top ⎭   var currentTop : 0 .. limit;
         values : array [1 .. limit] of integer;

▢ Figure 4.1 ——The interface and implementation faces of a stack

an abstract data type sees only a collection of operations that defines the behavior of the abstraction. On the other side of the interface, the programmer defining the abstraction sees the data variables that are used to maintain the internal state of the object.

For example, in an abstraction of a stack data type, the user would see only the description of the legal operations—say, push, pop, and top. The implementor, on the other hand, needs to know the actual concrete data structures used to implement the abstraction (Figure 4.1). The concrete details are encapsulated within a more abstract framework.

We have been using the term *instance* to mean a representative, or example, of a class. We will accordingly use the term *instance variable* to mean an internal variable maintained by an instance. Other terms we will occasionally use are *data field*, or *data members*. Each instance has its own collection of instance variables. These values should not be changed directly by clients but only by methods associated with the class.

A simple view of an object is, then, a combination of *state* and *behavior*. The state is described by the instance variables, whereas the behavior is characterized by the methods. From the outside, clients can see only the behavior of objects. From the inside, the methods provide the appropriate behavior through modifications of the state as well as by interacting with other objects.

4.2 ▢ Class Definitions

Throughout this chapter and the next we will use as an example the development of a playing card abstraction like one in a card game application. We will develop this abstraction through a sequence of refinements, each refinement incorporating a small number of new features.

We start by imagining that a playing card can be abstracted as a container for two data values: the card rank and card suit. We can use a number between 1 and 13 to represent the rank (1 is ace; 11, 12, and 13 are jack, queen, and king). To represent the suit we can use an enumerated data type if our language provides such facilities. In languages that do not have enumerated data types we can use symbolic constants and integer values from 1 to 4. (The advantage of the enumerated data type is that type errors are avoided, since we can guarantee the suit is one of the four specified values. If we use integers for this purpose, then nothing prevents a programmer from assigning an invalid integer number—for example, 42—to the suit variable.)

4.2.1 C++, Java, and C#

We begin by looking at class definitions in three very similar languages: C++, Java, and C#. The syntax used by these three languages in shown in Figure 4.2. There are some superficial differences: For example a class definition is terminated by a semicolon in C++ but not in the other two. Visibility modifiers (that is, public) mark an entire block of declarations in C++ and are placed on each declaration independently in the other two languages. In C++ and C# a programmer can define an enumerated data type for representing the playing card suits. By placing the definition inside the class, in C++ the programmer makes clear the link between the two data types. (This is not possible in C#.) Outside of the class definition the symbolic constants that represent the suits must be prefixed by the class name, as in C++.

```
if (aCard.suit() == PlayingCard::Diamond) ...
```

or by the type name as in C#:

```
if (aCard.suit() == Suits.Diamond) ...
```

Here aCard is the name of an instance of PlayingCard, and we are invoking the method named suit in order to test the suit of the card. The data fields suitValue and rankValue represent the instance data for this abstraction. Each instance of the class PlayingCard will have its own separate field, maintaining its own suit and rank value. Notice that the value of the suit is obtained by invoking a method named suit, which simply returns the data field named suitValue.

The first letter of the class name has here been capitalized. This is a convention many languages follow, although not universally (in particular, many C++ programmers prefer to use names that are in all lowercase letters). Normally instance variables are given names that are not capitalized to make it easier to distinguish between the two categories. Some languages, such as Delphi Pascal, have other conventions.

Enumerated data types are not provided by the language Java, and so the programmer typically resorts to defining a series of symbolic constants. A symbolic constant is characterized by the two modifiers final and static. In Java the modifier final means that the assignment of the name cannot subsequently be changed. The modifier static means that there exists only one instance of a variable, regardless

C++

```
class PlayingCard {
public:
    enum Suits {Spade, Diamond, Club, Heart};

    Suits suit () { return suitValue; }
    int   rank () { return rankValue; }

private:
    Suits suitValue;
    int   rankValue;
};
```

Java

```
class PlayingCard {
    public  int suit () { return suitValue; }
    public  int rank () { return rankValue; }

    private int suitValue;
    private int rankValue;

    public static final int Spade = 1;
    public static final int Diamond = 2;
    public static final int Club = 3;
    public static final int Heart = 4;
}
```

C#

```
class PlayingCard {
enum Suits {Spade, Diamond, Club, Heart};
    public Suits suit () { return suitValue; }
    public int   rank () { return rankValue; }

    private Suits suitValue;
    private int   rankValue;
}
```

□ Figure 4.2 —— A simple class definition in C++, Java, and C#

of how many instances of the class are created. Taken together, the two define a unique variable that cannot change—that is, a constant.

Note the essential difference between the data fields suitValue and rankValue and the constants Heart, Spade, Diamond, and Club in the Java definition. Because the latter are declared as static, they exist outside of any one instance of the class and are shared by all instances. The suit and rank fields, on the other hand, are not static, and hence each instance of the class will have its own copy of these values.

Visibility Modifiers

Note the use of the terms public and private in several places in these examples. These are *visibility* modifiers. All three languages, as well as a number of other object-oriented programming languages, provide a way of describing features that are known and can be used *outside* the class definition and distinguishing those from features that can only be used *within* a class definition. The latter are indicated by the keyword private.

4.2.2   Apple Object Pascal and Delphi Pascal

The next two languages we examine are also very similar. Both Apple's Object Pascal language and Borland's Delphi Pascal (called Kylix on Linux platforms) were based on an earlier language named simply Pascal. Thus, many features derived from the original language are the same. However, the two vendors have extended the language in slightly different ways (Figure 4.3).

Both languages permit the creation of enumerated data types, similar to C++. The Apple version of the language uses the keyword object to declare a new class (and hence classes are sometimes termed *object types* in that language). The Delphi language uses the keyword class and further requires that every class inherit from some existing class. We have here used the class TObject for this purpose. It is conventional in Delphi that all classes must have names that begin with the letter T. Delphi uses visibility modifiers; the Apple language does not. Finally, the Delphi language requires the creation of a constructor, a topic we will return to shortly.

4.2.3   Smalltalk

Smalltalk does not actually have a textual representation of a class. Instead, classes are described using an interactive interface called the browser. A screen shot of the browser is shown in Figure 4.4. Using the browser, the programmer can define a new class using a message sent to the parent class Object. As in Delphi Pascal, all classes in Smalltalk must name a specific parent class from which they will inherit.

Object Pascal

```
type
    Suits = (Heart, Club, Diamond, Spade);

    PlayingCard = object
        suit : Suits;
        rand : integer;
    end;
```

Delphi Pascal

```
type
    Suits = (Heart, Club, Diamond, Spade);

    TPlayingCard = class (TObject)
        public
            constructor Create (r : integer; s : Suits);

            function suit : Suits;
            function rank : int;

        private
            suitValue : Suits;
            rankValue : integer;
    end;
```

▫ Figure 4.3 —— Class definitions in Object Pascal and Delphi Pascal

System Browser			
Graphics	Array	insertion	add:
Collections	Bag	removal	addAll:
Numerics	Set	testing	——
System	Dictionary	printing	

Object subclass: #PlayingCard
    instanceVariableNames: 'suit rank'
    classVariableNames: ' '
    category: 'Playing Card Application'			

▫ Figure 4.4 —— A view of the Smalltalk browser

CLOS

```
(defclass PlayingCard ( ) (rank suit) )
```

Eiffel

```
class PlayingCard
feature
    Spade, Diamond, Heart, Club : Integer is Unique;

    suit : integer;
    rank : integer;
end
```

Objective-C

```
enum suits {Heart, Club, Diamond, Spade};

@ interface PlayingCard : Object
{
    suits suit;
    int rank;
}
@end
```

Python

```
class PlayingCard:
    "A playing card class"
    def __init__ (self, s, r):
        self.suit = s
        self.rank = r
```

⊡ Figure 4.5 —— Class definitions in other object-oriented languages

Figure 4.4 illustrates the creation of the class PlayingCard with two instance data fields.

4.2.4 Other languages

Throughout the book, we refer to a number of languages, particularly when they include features that are unique or not widely found in alternative languages. Some of these include Objective-C, CLOS, Eiffel, Dylan, and Python. Class definitions for some of these are shown in Figure 4.5. Python is interesting in that indentation levels, rather than beginning and ending tokens, are used to indicate class, function, and statement nesting.

4.3 ▫ Methods

In the next revision of our playing card abstraction we make the following changes.

- We add a method that will return the face color of the card, either red or black.
- We add a data field to maintain whether the card is faceup or facedown and methods both to test the state of this value and to flip the card.

A typical class that illustrates these changes is the C# definition shown in Figure 4.6. Some features to note are that we have added a second enumerated data type to represent the colors, and the data fields (including the third data field representing the faceup state of the card) are declared private. By declaring the

```
class PlayingCard {
  // constructor, initialize new playing card
  public PlayingCard (Suits is, int ir)
    { suit = is; rank = ir; faceUp = true; }

  // operations on a playing card
  public boolean isFaceUp   ()            { return faceUp; }
  public int      rank       ()            { return rankValue; }
  public Suits    suit       ()            { return suitValue; }
  public void     setFaceUp (boolean up) { faceUp = up; }
  public void     flip       ()            { setFaceUp( !faceUp);}
  public Color    color      ()            {
    if ((suit() == Suits.Diamond) || (suit() == Suits.Heart))
      return Color.Red;
    return Color.Black;
  }
  // private data values
  private Suits suitValue;
  private int rankValue;
  private boolean faceUp;
}
```

▫ Figure 4.6 —— The revised PlayingCard class in C#

data fields private it means that access outside the class definition is not permitted. This guarantees that the only way the data fields will be modified is by methods associated with the class. Most object-oriented style guidelines will instruct that data fields should never be declared public and should always be private or protected, the latter a third level of protection we will discuss after we introduce inheritance in Chapter 8.

The constructor is a special method that has the same name as the class and is used to initialize the data fields in an object. As we noted earlier, we will discuss constructors in more detail in the next chapter.

Where access to data fields must be provided, good object-oriented style says that access should be mediated by methods defined in the class. A method that does nothing more than return the value of a data field is termed an *accessor* or, sometimes, a *getter*. An example is the method isFaceUp, which returns the value of the data field faceUp. Another example is the method rank, which return the value of the rankValue data field.

Why is it better to use a method for this simple action rather than permitting access to the data field directly? One reason is that the method makes the data field *read-only*. A function can only be called, whereas a data field can be both read and written. By the combination of a private data field and a public accessor we ensure the rank of the playing card cannot change once it has been created.

The naming conventions for the methods shown here are typical. It is good practice to name a method that returns a boolean value with a term that begins with is and indicates the meaning when a true value is returned. Following this convention makes it easy to understand the use of the method in a conditional statement, such as the following.

```
if (aCard.isFaceUp()) ...
```

Here aCard is once again an instance of class PlayingCard. Many style guidelines suggest that all other accessor methods should begin with the word get to most clearly indicate that the most important purpose of the method is to simply get the value of a data field. Again this convention makes it easy to understand statements that use this method.

```
int cardRank = aCard.getRank();
```

However, this convention is not universally advocated. In particular, we will continue to use the simpler names rank and suit for our methods.

Methods whose major purpose is simply to set a value are termed *mutator methods* or *setters*. As the name suggests, a setter most generally is named beginning with the word set. An example setter is the method setFaceUp, which sets the value for the faceUp accessor.

```
class PlayingCard {
    .
    .
    .

    void setFaceUp (boolean up) { faceUp = up; }
    .
    .
    .
}
```

The method flip is neither a getter nor a setter, since it neither gets nor sets a data field. It is simply a method. The method color is not technically a getter, since it is not getting a data field held by the class. Nevertheless, because it is returning an attribute of the object, some style guidelines would suggest that a better name would be getColor.

Visibility modifiers are not found in the language Smalltalk. By default all data fields are private—that is, accessible only within the class definition itself. To allow access to a data field, an accessor method must be provided.

```
rank
    " return the face value of a card  "
    ↑ rank
```

The convention of using get names is not widely followed in Smalltalk. Instead, it is conventional for accessor methods to have the same name as the data field they are returning. No confusion arises in the Smalltalk system, but we reserve comment on confusion that can arise in the programmer's mind.

4.3.1 Order of methods in a class declaration

For the most part, programming languages do not specify the order that methods are declared within a class definition. However, the order can have a significant impact on readability, an issue that is often of critical importance to programmers. Many style guidelines offer conflicting advice on this issue. The following are some of the most significant considerations:

- Important features should be listed earlier in the class definition, less important features listed later.
- Constructors are one of the most important aspects of an object definition and hence should appear very near the top of a class definition.
- The declaration of methods should be grouped to facilitate finding the body associated with a given message selector. Ways of doing this include listing methods in alphabetical order or grouping methods by their purpose.
- Private data fields are important only to the class developer. They should be listed near the end of a class definition.

C++

```
class PlayingCard {
public:
        .
        .
        .
        const int rank; // since immutable, can allow
        const Suits suit; // public access to data field
};
```

Java

```
class PlayingCard {
        .
        .
        .
        public final int rank;
        public final int suit;
}
```

▫ Figure 4.7 —— Syntax for defining immutable data values

4.3.2   Constant or immutable data fields

As an alternative to accessor methods, some programming languages provide a way to specify that a data field is constant, or *immutable*. This means that once set, the value of the data field cannot subsequently be changed. With this restriction there is less need to hide access to a data value behind a method.

Two different ways of describing constant data fields are shown in Figure 4.7. Such a field is declared as final in Java. The modifier const is used in C++ for much the same purpose.

4.3.3   Separating definition and implementation

Some languages, such as Java and C#, place the body of a method directly in the class definition, as shown in Figure 4.6. Other languages, such as C++ and Object Pascal, separate these two aspects. In C++ the programmer has a choice. Small methods can be defined in the class, while larger methods are defined outside. A C++ class definition for our playing card abstraction might look something like the following.

```
class PlayingCard {
public:
    // enumerated types
```

```
enum Suits {Spade, Diamond, Club, Heart};
enum Colors {Red, Black};

// constructor, initialize new playing card
PlayingCard (Suits is, int ir)
  { suit = is; rank = ir; faceUp = true; }

// operations on a playing card
boolean isFaceUp  ()            { return faceUp; }
void    setFaceUp (bool up)  { faceUp = up; }
void    flip       ()            { setFaceUp( ! faceUp); }
int     rank       ()            { return rankValue; }
Suits   suit       ()            { return suitValue; }
Colors  color      () ;
private:      // private data values
  Suits suitValue;
  int rankValue;
  boolean faceUp;
};
```

Notice the body of the method color has been omitted, since it is longer than the other methods defined in this class. A subsequent method definition (sometimes termed a *function member*) provides the body of the function.

```
PlayingCard::Colors PlayingCard::color ( )
{
  // return the face color of a playing card
  if ((suit == Diamond) || (suit == Heart))
    return Red;
  return Black;
}
```

The method heading is very similar to a normal C-style function definition, except the name has been expanded into a *fully qualified* name. The qualified name provides both the class name and the method name for the method being defined. This is analogous to identifying a person by both their given and family names (for example, "Chris Smith").

C++ programmers have the choice between defining methods in-line as part of the class definition or defining them in a separate section of the program. Typically only methods that are one or two statements long are placed in-line, and anything more complex than one or two lines is defined outside the class.

There are two reasons for placing a method body outside the class definition. Method bodies that are longer than one statement can obscure other features of the class definition, and thus removing long method bodies can improve readability. (Readability, however, is in the eye of the beholder. Not all programmers think that this separation improves readability, since the programmer must now look in two different places to find a method body.) A second reason involves semantics. When method bodies are declared within a class definition, a C++ compiler is permitted (although not obligated) to expand invocations of the method directly in-line without creating a function call. An in-line definition can be executed much faster than the combination of function call and method body.

Often the class definition and the larger method bodies in a C++ program will not even be found in the same file. The class heading will be given in an *interface file* (by convention a file with the extension .h on Unix systems or .hpp on Windows systems), whereas the function bodies will be found in an implementation file (by convention a file with the extension .cpp or .C).

Objective-C also separates a class definition from a class implementation. The definition includes a description of methods for the class. These are indicated by a + or − sign, followed by the return type in parentheses followed by a description of the method.

```
@ interface PlayingCard : Object
{
    int suit;
    int rank;
    int faceUp;
}

+ suit: (int) s rank: (int) i
- (int) color;
- (int) rank;
- (int) suit;
- (int) isFaceUp;
- (void) flip;
@ end
```

The implementation section then provides the body of the methods.

```
@ implementation PlayingCard

- (int) color
{
    if ((suit == Diamond) || (suit == Heart))
        return red;
    return black;
}
```

```
- (int) rank
{
  return rank;
}
... ./* other method bodies */
@ end
```

Object Pascal and Delphi similarly separate the class definition from the method function bodies, but the two parts remain in the same file. The class definitions are described in a section labeled with the name interface, and the implementations are found in a section labeled, clearly enough, implementation. The following is a Delphi example.

```
interface

type
  Suits = (Heart, Club, Diamond, Spade);
  Colors = (Red, Black);

  TPlayingCard = class (TObject)
    public
      constructor Create (r : integer; s : Suits);
      function color : Colors;
      function isFaceUp : boolean;
      procedure flip;
      function rank : integer;
      function suit : Suits;
    private
      suit : Suits;
      rank : integer;
      faceUp : boolean;
  end;
implementation
  function TPlayingCard.color : Colors;
  begin
    case suit of
      Diamond: color := Red;
      Heart: color := Red;
      Spade: color := Black;
      Club: color := Black;
  end

  ... (* other methods similarly defined *)
end.
```

Note that fully qualified names in Pascal are formed using a period between the class name and the method name instead of the double colon used by C++.

In CLOS, accessor functions can be automatically created when a class is defined, using the :accessor keyword followed by the name of the accessor function.

```
(defclass PlayingCard ()
  ((rank :accessor getRank) (suit :accessor getSuit) ))
```

Other methods are defined using the function defmethod. Unlike Java or C++, the receiver for the method is named as an explicit parameter.

```
(defmethod color ((card PlayingCard))
  (cond
    ((eq (getSuit card) 'Diamond) 'Red)
    ((eq (getSuit card) 'Heart) 'Red)
    (t 'Black)))
```

The receiver must also be named as an explicit parameter in Python.

```
class PlayingCard:
  "A playing card class"
  def __init__ (self, s, r):
    self.suit = s
    self.rank = r
  def rank (self)
    return self.rank
  def color (self)
    if self.suit == 1 or self.suit == 2
      return 1
    return 0
```

*4.4 □ Variations on Class Themes

While the concept of a class is fundamental to object-oriented programming, some languages go further in providing variations on this basic idea. In the following sections we describe some of the more notable among these variations.

4.4.1 Methods without classes in Oberon

The language Oberon does not have classes in the sense of other object-oriented languages but only the more traditional concept of data records. Nevertheless, it does support message passing, including many of the dynamic method-binding features found in object-oriented languages.

A method in Oberon is not defined inside a record but is instead declared using a special syntax where the receiver is described in an argument list separately from the other arguments. Often the receiver is required to be a pointer type rather than the data record type.

```
TYPE
   PlayingCard = POINTER TO PlayingCardDesc;

   PlayingCardDesc = RECORD
      suit : INTEGER;
      rank : INTEGER;
      faceUp: BOOLEAN;
   END

PROCEDURE (aCard: PlayingCard) setFaceUp (b : BOOLEAN);
BEGIN
   aCard.faceUp = b;
END
```

The record PlayingCardDesc contains the data fields, which can be modified by the procedure setFaceUp, which must take a pointer to a playing card as a receiver.

4.4.2 Interfaces

Some object-oriented languages, such as Java, support a concept called an *interface*. An interface defines the protocol for certain behavior but does not provide an implementation. The following is an example interface describing objects that can read from and write to an input/output stream.

```
public interface Storing {
   void writeOut (Stream s);
   void readFrom (Stream s);
};
```

Like a class, an interface defines a new type. This means that variables can be declared simply by the interface name.

```
Storing storableValue;
```

A class can indicate that it implements the protocol defined by an interface. Instances of the class can be assigned to variables declared as the interface type.

```
public class BitImage implements Storing {
   void writeOut (Stream s) {
      // ...
   }
   void readFrom (Stream s) {
```

```
    // ...
  }
};
```

```
    storableValue = new BitImage();
```

The use of interfaces is very similar to the concept of inheritance, and thus we will return to a more detailed consideration of interfaces in Chapter 8.

4.4.3 Properties

Delphi, Visual Basic, C#, and other programming languages (both object-oriented and not) incorporate an idea called a property. A property is manipulated syntactically in the fashion of a data field but operates internally like a method. That is, a property can be read as an expression or assigned to as a value.

```
writeln ('rank is ', aCard.rank); (* rank is property of card *)
aCard.rank = 5; (* changing the rank property *)
```

However, in both cases the value assigned or set will be mediated by a function rather than a simple data value. In Delphi a property is declared using the keyword property and the modifiers read and write. The values following the read and write keyword can be either a data field or a method name. The read attribute will be invoked when a property is used in the fashion of an expression, and the write attribute when the property is the target of an assignment. Having a read attribute and no write makes a property read only. We could recast our rank and suit values as properties as follows.

```
type
  TPlayingcard = class (TObject)
    public
      .
      .
      .
      property rank : Integer read rankValue;
      property suit : Suits read suitValue write suitValue;
    private
      rankValue : Integer;
      suitValue : Suits;
  end;
```

Here we have made rank read only but allowed suit to be both read and written. It is also possible to make a property write-only, although this is not very common.

In C# a property is defined by writing a method without an argument list, and including either a get or a set section.

```
public class PlayingCard {
  public int rank {
    get
    {
      return rankValue;
    }
    set
    {
      rankValue = value;
    }
  }
  .
  .
  .

  private int rankValue;
}
```

A get section must return a value. A set section can use the pseudo-variable value to set the property. If no set section is provided, the property is read-only. If no get section is given, the property is write only. Properties are commonly used in C# programs for functions that take no arguments and return a value.

4.4.4 Forward definitions

A program can sometimes require that two or more classes each have references to the other. This situation is termed *mutual recursion*. We might need to represent the horse and buggy trade—for example, where every horse is associated with their own buggy and every buggy with one horse. Some languages will have little trouble with this. Java, for example, scans an entire file before it starts to generate code, and so classes that are referenced later in a file can be used earlier in a file with no conflict.

Other languages, such as C++, deal with classes and methods one by one as they are encountered. A name must have at least a partial definition before it can be used. In C++ this often results in the need for a *forward definition*. A definition that serves no other purpose than to place a name in circulation, leaving the completion of the definition until later. Our horse and buggy example might require something like the following.

```
class Horse; // forward definition

class Buggy {
  .
  .
  .
  Horse * myHorse;
};
```

```
class Horse {
    .
    .
    .
    Buggy * myBuggy;
};
```

The first line simply indicates that Horse is the name of a class and that the definition will be forthcoming shortly. Knowing only this little bit of information, however, is sufficient for the C++ compiler to permit the creation of a pointer to the unknown class.

Of course, nothing can be done with this object until the class definition has been read. Solving this problem requires a careful ordering of the class definitions and the implementations of their associated methods: first one class definition, then the second class definition, then methods from the first class, and finally methods from the second.

4.4.5 Inner or nested classes

Both Java and C++ allow the programmer to write one class definition inside of another. Such a definition is termed an *inner class* in Java and a *nested class* in C++. Despite the similar appearances, there is a major semantic difference between the two concepts. An inner class in Java is linked to a specific instance of the surrounding class (the instance in which it was created) and is permitted access to data fields and methods in this object. A nested class in C++ is simply a naming device. It restricts the visibility of features associated with the inner class, but otherwise the two are not related.

To illustrate the use of nested classes, let us imagine that a programmer wants to write a doubly linked list abstraction in Java. The programmer might decide to place the Link class inside the List abstraction.

```
// Java List class
class List {
  private Link firstElement = null;
  public void push_front(Object val)
    {
      if (firstElement == null)
        firstElement = new Link(val, null, null);
      else
        firstElement.addBefore (val);
    }

    ... // other methods omitted

    private class Link { // inner class definition
```

```
public Object value;
public Link forwardLink;
public Link backwardLink;

public Link (Object v, Link f, Link b)
    { value = v; forwardLink = f; backwardLink = b; }
public void addBefore (Object val)
{
  Link newLink = new Link(val, this, backwardLink);
  if (backwardLink == null)
    firstElement = newLink;
  else {
    backwardLink.forwardLink = newLink;
    backwardLink = newLink;
  }
}
}
... // other methods omitted
  }
}
```

Note that the method addBefore references the data field firstElement in order to handle the special case where an element is being inserted into the front of a list. A direct translation of this code into C++ will produce the following.

```
// C++ List class
class List {
private:
  class Link;  // forward definition
  Link * firstElement;

  class Link { // nested class definition
  public:
    int value;
    Link * forwardLink;
    Link * backwardLink;

    Link (int v, Link * f, Link * b)
      { value = v; forwardLink = f; backwardLink = b; }

    void addBefore (int val)
    {
      Link * newLink = new Link(val, this, backwardLink);
      if (backwardLink == 0)
```

```
        firstElement = newLink; // ERROR!
      else {
        backwardLink->forwardLink = newLink;
        backwardLink = newLink;
      }
    }

    ... // other methods omitted
    };

public:
  void push_front(int val)
  {
    if (firstElement == 0)
      firstElement = new Link(val, 0, 0);
    else
      firstElement->addBefore (val);
  }
  ... // other methods omitted
};
```

It has been necessary to introduce a forward reference for the Link class so the pointer firstElement could be declared before the class was defined. Also C++ uses the value zero for a null element rather than the pseudo-constant null. Finally, links are pointers, rather than values, and so the pointer access operator is necessary. But the feature to note occurs on the line marked as an error. The class Link is not permitted to access the variable firstElement because the scope for the class is not actually nested in the scope for the surrounding class. In order to access the List object, it would have to be explicitly available through a variable. In this case, the most reasonable solution would probably be to have the List method pass itself as argument, using the pseudo-variable this, to the inner Link method addBefore. (An alternative solution, having each Link maintain a reference to its creating List, is probably too memory intensive.)

```
class List {
  Link * firstElement;

  class Link {
    void addBefore (int val, List * theList)
    {
      .
      .
      .
      if (backwardLink == 0)
```

```
          theList->firstElement = newLink;

            .
            .
            .
    }
  };
public:
  void push_front(int val)
  {

        .
        .
        .
        // pass self as argument
      firstElement->addBefore (val, this);
  }
  ... // other methods omitted
};
```

When nested class methods are defined outside the class body, the name may require multiple levels of qualification. The following, for example, would be how the method addBefore would be written in this fashion.

```
void List::Link::addBefore (int val, List * theList)
{
  Link * newLink = new Link(val, this, backwardLink);
  if (backwardLink == 0)
    theList->firstElement = newLink;
  else {
    backwardLink->forwardLink = newLink;
    backwardLink = newLink;
  }
}
```

The name of the function indicates that this is the method addBefore that is part of the class Link, which is in turn defined as part of the class List.

4.4.6   Class data fields

In many problems it is useful to have a common data field that is shared by all instances of a class. However, the manipulation of such an object creates a curious paradox for the object-oriented language designer. To understand this problem, consider that the reason for the invention of the concept of a class was to reduce the amount of work necessary to create similar objects; every instance of a class has exactly the same behavior as every other instance. Now imagine that we have somehow defined a common data area shared by all instances of a class, and think about the task of initializing this common area. There seem to be two choices, neither satisfactory. Either everybody performs the initialization task (and the field is initialized and reinitialized over and over again), or nobody does (leaving the data area uninitialized).

Resolving this paradox requires moving outside of the simple class/method/instance paradigm. Another mechanism, not the objects themselves, must take responsibility for the initialization of shared data. If objects are automatically initialized to a special value (such as zero) by the memory manager, then every instance can test for this special value and perform initialization if they are the first. However, there are other (and better) techniques.

In both C++ and Java, shared data fields are created using the static modifier. We have seen this already in the creation of symbolic constants in Java. In Java the intialization of a static data field is accomplished by a *static block*, which is executed when the class is loaded. For example, suppose we wanted to keep track of how many instances of a class have been created.

```
class CountingClass {

  CountingClass () {
    count = count + 1; // increment count
      .
      .
      .
  }
      .
      .
      .
  private static int count; // shared by all

  static {  // static block
    count = 0;
  }
}
```

In C++ there are two different mechanisms. Data fields that are static (or const) and represented by primitive data types can be initialized in the class body, as we have seen already. Alternatively, a global initialization can be defined that is separate from the class:

```
class CountingClass {
public:
  CountingClass () { count++; ... }

private:
  static int count;
};
```

```
// global initialization is separate from class
int CountingClass::count = 0;
```

In C# static data fields can be initialized by a static constructor, a constructor method that is declared static. This constructor is not permitted to have any arguments.

In Python class data fields are simply named at the level of methods, whereas instance variables are named inside of methods (typically inside the constructor method).

```
class CountingClass:
  count = 0
  def __init__ (self)
    self.otherField = 3
```

4.4.7   Classes as objects

In a number of languages (Smalltalk, Java, many others) a class is itself an object. Of course, one must then ask what class represents the category to which this object belongs—that is, what class is the class? In most cases there is a special class, typically named Class, that is the class for classes.

Since objects are classes, they have behavior. What can you do with a class? Frequently, the creation of an instance of the class is simply a message given to a class object. This occurs in the following example from Smalltalk.

```
aCard <- PlayingCard new.  "message new given to object PlayingCard"
```

Other common behaviors include returning the name of the class, the size of instances of the class, or a list of messages that instances of the class will recognize. The following bit of Java code illustrates one use.[1]

```
    Object obj = new PlayingCard();
    Class c = obj.getClass();
    System.out.println("class is " + c.getName());
PlayingCard
```

We will return to an exploration of classes as objects when we investigate the concept of *reflection* in Chapter 25.

---

1. In noninteractive languages it is sometimes difficult to show the relationship between program statements and their output. Throughout the rest of the book we will use the convention illustrated by this example, indenting a sequence of statement and then showing the resulting output without indentation. The reader will hopefully be able to distinguish the executable statements from the nonexecutable output.

Summary ⊡

In this chapter we have started our exploration of the concept of *class* in object-oriented languages. We have described the syntax for class and method definitions in various languages, including Java, C++, C#, Object Pascal, Objective-C, and Eiffel. Throughout the text we will occasional refer to other example languages as well.

Some of the features of classes that we have seen in this chapter include the following.

- Visibility modifiers. The keywords public and private that are used to control the visibility, and hence the manipulation, of class features.
- Getter and Setter functions. Sometimes termed accessors and mutators, these are methods that provide access to data fields. By using methods rather than providing direct access, programmers have greater control over the way data is modified and where it can be used.
- Constant, or immutable, data fields. These data fields are guaranteed to not change during the course of execution.
- Interfaces. These classlike entities describe behavior but do not provide an implementation.
- Nested classes. These class definitions appear inside other class definitions.
- Class data fields. The particular paradox arises over the initialization data fields that are shared in common among all instances of a class.

Further Reading ⊡

The Apple Object Pascal language was originally defined by Larry Tesler of Apple Computer [Tesler 1985]. The Borland language was originally known as Turbo Pascal [Turbo 1988]. More recent descriptions of the Delphi version of this language can be found in [Lischner 2000, Kerman 2002].

The classic definition of the language Smalltalk is [Goldberg 1983]. More recent treatments of the language include [LaLonde 1990b, Smith 1995]. A popular public-domain version of Smalltalk is Squeak [Guzdial 2001].

The Java language is described in [Arnold 2000]. A good tutorial on Java can be found in [Campione 1998]. In Java and C++ the concept of *interfaces* is closely related to the concept of a class. We will discuss interfaces when we examine inheritance in Chapter 8. A good style guidebook for Java programmers is [Vermeulen 2000].

Since C# is a relatively recent language there are still only a few published references. Two recent sources are [Gunnerson 2000, Albahari 2001]. Since C#

is a relatively recent language there are still only a few published references. Two recent sources are [Gunnerson 2000; Albahari 2001].

Objective-C was created as an extension to C at about the same time that C++ was developed. A good introduction to Objective-C is the book written by its creator, Brad Cox [Cox 1986]. Python is described in [Beazley 2000].

An interesting question is whether classes are necessary for object-oriented programming. It turns out that you can achieve much of the desirable characteristics of object-oriented languages without using classes by means of an idea termed *delegation* [Lieberman 1986]. However, in the period between when delegation languages were first proposed and the present there has not been a groundswell of support for this idea, so most people seem to prefer classes.

Self-Study Questions ▣

1. What is the difference between a class declaration and an object declaration (the latter also known as an instantiation)?
2. What is an instance variable?
3. What are the two most basic aspects of a class?
4. What is the meaning of the modifiers final and static in Java? How do these two features combine to form a symbolic constant?
5. What does the term public mean? What does the term private mean?
6. What is a constructor?
7. What is an accessor method? What is the advantage of using accessor methods instead of providing direct access to a data field?
8. What is a mutator, or setter, method?
9. What are some guidelines for selecting the order of features in a class definition?
10. What is an immutable data field?
11. What is a fully qualified name?
12. How is an interface different from a class? How is it similar?
13. What is an inner or nested class?
14. Explain the paradox arising from the initialization of common data fields or class data fields.

Exercises ▣

1. Suppose you were required to program in a non-object-oriented language such as Pascal or C. How would you simulate the notion of classes and methods?

2. In Smalltalk and Objective-C, methods that take multiple arguments are described using a keyword to separate each argument; in C++ the argument list follows a single method name. Describe some of the advantages and disadvantages of each approach. In particular, explain the effect on readability and understandability.

3. A digital counter is a bounded counter that turns over when its integer value reaches a certain maximum. Examples include the numbers in a digital clock and the odometer in a car. Define a class description for a bounded counter. Provide the ability to set maximum and minimum values, to increment the counter, and to return the current counter value.

4. Write a class description for complex numbers. Write methods for addition, subtraction, and multiplication of complex numbers.

5. Write a class description for a fraction, a rational number composed of two integer values. Write methods for addition, subtraction, multiplication, and division of fractions. How do you handle the reduction of fractions to lowest-common-denominator form?

6. Consider the following two combinations of class and function in C++. Explain the difference in using the function addi as the user would see it.

```
class example1 {
public:
   int i;
};

int addi(example1 & x, int j)
{
   x.i = x.i + j;
   return x.i;
}

class example2 {
public:
   int i;
   int addi(int j)
      { i = i + j; return i; }
};
```

7. In both the C++ and Objective-C versions of the playing card abstraction, the modular division instruction is used to determine the color of a card based on the suit value. Is this a good practice? Discuss a few of the advantages and disadvantages. Rewrite the methods to remove the dependency on the particular values associated with the suits.

8. Do you think it is better to have the access modifiers private and public associated with every individual object, as in Java, or used to create separate areas in the declaration, as in C++, Objective-C, and Delphi Pascal? Give reasons to support your view.

9. Contrast the encapsulation provided by the class mechanism with the encapsulation provided by the module facility. How are they different? How are they the same?

CHAPTER 5

Messages, Instances, and Initialization

In Chapter 4 we briefly outlined some of the compile-time features of object-oriented programming languages. That is, we described how to create new types, new classes, and new methods. In this chapter, we continue our exploration of the mechanics of object-oriented programming by examining the *dynamic* features. These include how values are instantiated (or created), how they are initialized, and how they communicate with each other by means of message passing.

In the first section, we explore the mechanics of message passing. Then we investigate creation and initialization. By *creation* we mean the allocation of memory space for a new object and the binding of that space to a name. By *initialization* we mean not only the setting of initial values in the data area for the object, similar to the initialization of fields in a record, but also the more general process of establishing the initial conditions necessary for the manipulation of an object. The degree to which this latter task can be hidden from clients who use an object in most object-oriented languages is an important aspect of *encapsulation*, which we identified as one of the principle advantages of object-oriented techniques over other programming styles.

5.1 ⊡ Message-Passing Syntax

We are using the term *message passing* (sometimes also called *method lookup*) to mean the dynamic process of asking an object to perform a specific action. In Chapter 1 we informally described message passing and noted how a message differs from an ordinary procedure call.

- A *message* is always given *to* some object, called the *receiver*.
- The action performed in response to the message is not fixed but may differ, depending on the class of the receiver. That is, different objects may accept the same message and yet perform different actions.

There are three identifiable parts to any message-passing expression. These are the *receiver* (the object to which the message is being sent), the *message selector* (the text that indicates the particular message being sent), and the *arguments* used in responding to the message.

aGame · displayCard (aCard, 42, 27)
  receiver   *selector*   *arguments*

As Figure 5.1 indicates, the most common syntax for message passing uses a period to separate the receiver from the message selector. Minor variations include features such as whether an empty pair of parentheses is required when a method has no arguments (they can be omitted in Pascal and some other languages).

Smalltalk and Objective-C use a slightly different syntax. In these languages a space is used as a separator. Unary messages (messages that take no argument) are simply written following the receiver. Messages that take arguments are written using *keyword notation*. The message selector is split into parts, one part before each argument. A colon follows each part of the key.

```
aGame display: aCard atLocation: 45 and: 56.
```

In Smalltalk even binary operations, such as addition, are interpreted as a message sent to the left value with the right value as argument.

```
z <- x + y.   " message to x to add y to itself and return sum "
```

It is possible to define binary operators in C++ to have similar meanings. In Objective-C a Smalltalk-like message is enclosed in a pair of brackets, termed a *message passing expression*. The brackets only surround the message itself. They do not, for example, surround an assignment that places the result of a message into a variable.

```
int cardrank = [ aCard getRank ];
```

The syntax used in CLOS follows the traditional Lisp syntax. All expressions in Lisp are written as parentheses-bounded lists. The operation is the first element of the list, followed by the arguments. The receiver is simply the first argument.

C++, C#, Java, Python, Ruby

```
aCard.flip ();
aCard.setFaceUp(true);
aGame.displayCard(aCard, 45, 56);
```

Pascal, Delphi, Eiffel, Oberon

```
aCard.flip;
aCard.setFaceUp(true);
aGame.displayCard(aCard, 45, 56);
```

Smalltalk

```
aCard flip.
aCard setFaceUp: true.
aGame display: aCard atLocation: 45 and: 56.
```

Objective-C

```
[ aCard flip ].
[ aCard setFaceUp: true ].
[ aGame display: aCard atLocation: 45 and: 56 ]
```

CLOS

```
(flip aCard)
(setFaceUp aCard true)
(displayCard aGame 45 56)
```

☐ Figure 5.1 —— Message passing syntax in various languages

5.2 ☐ Statically and Dynamically Typed Languages

Languages can be divided into two groups, depending on whether they are statically or dynamically typed. Fundamentally, a statically typed language associates types with variables (usually the binding is established by means of declaration statements), whereas a dynamically typed language treats variables simply as names and associates types with values. Java, C++, C#, and Pascal are statically typed languages, whereas Smalltalk, CLOS, and Python are dynamically typed.

Objective-C holds a curious middle ground between the two camps. In Objective-C a variable can be declared with a fixed type, and if so, the variable is statically typed. On the other hand, a variable can also be declared using the object type id. A variable declared in this fashion can hold any object value and hence is dynamically typed.

```
PlayingCard aCard;  /* a statically typed variable */
id anotherCard; /* a dynamically typed variable */
```

The difference between statically typed languages and dynamically typed languages is important in regard to message passing because a statically typed language will use the type of the receiver to check, at compile time, that a receiver will understand the message it is being presented. A dynamically typed language, on the other hand, has no way to verify this information at compile time. Thus, in a dynamically typed language a message can generate a run-time error if the receiver does not understand the message selector. Such a run-time error can never occur in a statically typed language.

5.3 ▫ Accessing the Receiver from within a Method

As we indicated at the beginning of this chapter, a message is always passed to a receiver. In most object-oriented languages, however, the receiver does not appear in the argument list for the method. Instead, the receiver is only implicitly involved in the method definition. In those rare situations when it is necessary to access the receiver value from within a method body, a *pseudo-variable* is used. A pseudo-variable is like an ordinary variable, only it need not be declared and cannot be modified. (The term *pseudo constant* might therefore seem more appropriate, but this term does not seem to be used in any language definitions.)

The pseudo-variable that designates the receiver is named this in Java and C++, Current in Eiffel, and self in Smalltalk, Objective-C, Object Pascal, and many other languages. The pseudo-variable can be used as if it refers to an instance of the class. For example, the method color could be written in Pascal as follows.

```
function PlayingCard.color : colors;
begin
  if (self.suit = Heart) or (self.suit = Diamond) then
    color := Red
  else
    color := Black;
end
```

In most languages the majority of uses of the receiver pseudo-variable can be omitted. If a data field is accessed or a method is invoked without reference to a receiver, it is implicitly assumed that the receiver pseudo-variable is the intended basis for the message. We saw this earlier in the method flip, which acted by invoking the method setFaceUp.

```
class PlayingCard {
    .
    .
    .
    public void flip () { setFaceUp( ! faceUp ); }
    .
    .
    .
}
```

The method could be rewritten to make the receivers explicit, as follows.

```
class PlayingCard {
    .
    .
    .
    public void flip () { this.setFaceUp( ! this.faceUp); }
    .
    .
    .
}
```

One place where the use of the variable often cannot be avoided is when a method wishes to pass itself as an argument to another function, as in the following bit of Java.

```
class QuitButton extends Button implements ActionListener {
    public QuitButton () {
        .
        .
        .
        // install ourselves as a listener for button events
        addActionListener(this);
    }
    .
    .
    .
};
```

Some style guidelines for Java suggest the use of this when arguments in a constructor are used to initialize a data member. The same name can then be used for the argument and the data member, with the explicit this being used to distinguish the two names.

```
class PlayingCard {
    public PlayingCard (int suit, int rank) {
        this.rank = rank; // this.rank is the data member
        this.suit = suit;  // rank is the argument value
```

```
   this.faceUp = true;
 }
     .
     .
     .
 private int suit;
 private int rank;
 private boolean faceUp;
}
```

A few object-oriented languages, such as Python, CLOS, or Oberon, buck the trend and require that the receiver be declared explicitly in a method body. In Python, for example, a message might appear to have two arguments, as follows,

```
aCard.moveTo(27, 3)
```

but the corresponding method would declare three parameter values.

```
class PlayingCard:
  def moveTo (self, x, y):
     .
     .
     .
```

While the first argument could in principle be named anything, it is common to name it self or this to indicate the association with the receiver pseudo-variables in other languages. Examples in the previous chapter illustrated the syntax used by CLOS and Oberon, which also must name the receiver as an argument.

5.4 ▫ Object Creation

In most conventional programming languages, variables are created by means of a declaration statement, as in the following Pascal example.

```
var
  sum : integer;
begin
  sum := 0.0;
     .
     .
     .
end;
```

Some programming languages allow the user to combine declaration with initialization, as in the following Java example.

```
int sum = 0.0; // declare and initialize variable with zero
     .
     .
     .
```

A variable declared within the bounds of a function or procedure generally exists only as long as the procedure is executing. The same is true for some object-oriented languages. The following declaration statement, for example, can be used to create a variable in C++.

```
PlayingCard aCard(Diamond, 4);   // create 4 of diamonds
```

Most object-oriented languages, however, separate the process of variable naming from the process of object creation. The declaration of a variable only creates the name by which the variable will be known. To create an object value the programmer must perform a separate operation. Often this operation is denoted by the operator new, as in this Smalltalk example.

```
| aCard |   " name a new variable named aCard "

aCard <- PlayingCard new.   " allocate memory space to variable "
```

The syntax used in object creation for various different languages is shown in Figure 5.2. Python does not use the new operator explicitly. Instead, in Python, creation occurs when a class name is used in the fashion of a function.

5.4.1 Creation of arrays of objects

The creation of an array of objects presents two levels of complication. There is the allocation and creation of the array itself and then the allocation and creation of the objects that the array will hold.

In C++ these features are combined, and an array will consist of objects that are each initialized using the default (that is, no-argument) constructor (see Section 5.6).

```
// create an array of 52 cards, all the same
PlayingCard cardArray [52];
```

In Java, on the other hand, a superficially similar statement has a very different effect. The new operator used to create an array creates only the array. The values held by the array must be created separately, typically in a loop.

```
PlayingCard cardArray[ ] = new PlayingCard[13];
for (int i = 0; i < 13; i++)
   cardArray[i] = new PlayingCard(Spade, i+1);
```

A frequent source of error for C or C++ programmers moving to Java is to forget that in Java the allocation of an array occurs separately from the allocation of the elements the array will contain.

C++

```
PlayingCard * aCard = new PlayingCard(Diamond, 3);
```

Java, C#

```
PlayingCard aCard = new PlayingCard(Diamond, 3);
```

Object Pascal

```
var
    aCard : ^ PlayingCard;
begin
    new (aCard);
    .
    .
    .
end
```

Objective-C

```
aCard = [ PlayingCard new ];
```

Python

```
aCard = PlayingCard(2, 3)
```

Ruby

```
aCard = PlayingCard.new
```

Smalltalk

```
aCard <- PlayingCard new.
```

▫ Figure 5.2 —— Syntax used for object creation

5.5 ▫ Pointers and Memory Allocation

All object-oriented languages use pointers in their underlying representation. Not all languages expose this representation to the programmer. It is sometimes said that "Java has no pointers" as a point of contrast to C++. A more accurate statement would be that Java has no pointers that the programmer can see, since all object references are in fact pointers in the internal representation.

The issue is important for three reasons. Pointers normally reference memory that is *heap allocated* and thus does not obey the normal rules associated with variables in conventional imperative languages. In an imperative language, a value created inside a procedure will exist as long as the procedure is active and will disappear when the procedure returns. A heap allocated value, on the other hand, will continue to exist as long as there are references to it, which often will be much longer than the lifetime of the procedure in which it is created.

The second reason is that heap-based memory must be recovered in one fashion or another—a topic we address in the next section.

A third reason is that some languages, notably C++, distinguish between conventional values and pointer values. In C++ a variable that is declared in the normal fashion, a so-called *automatic* variable, has a lifetime tied to the function in which it is created. When the procedure exits, the memory for the variable is recovered.

```
void exampleProcedure
{
  PlayingCard ace(Diamond, 1);
  .
  .
  .
  // memory is recovered for ace
  // at end of execution of the procedure
}
```

Values that are assigned to pointers (or as *references*, which are another form of pointers) are not tied to procedure entry. Such values differ from automatic variables in a number of important respects. As we will note in the next section, memory for such values must be explicitly recovered by the programmer. When we introduce inheritance in Chapter 8, we will see that such values also differ in the way they use that feature.

5.5.1 Memory recovery

Memory created using the new operator is known as *heap-based* memory or, simply, *heap* memory. Unlike ordinary variables, heap-based memory is not tied to procedure entry and exit. Nevertheless, memory is always a finite commodity, and hence some mechanism must be provided to recover memory values. Memory that has been allocated to object values is then recycled and used to satisfy subsequent memory requests.

There are two general approaches to the task of memory recovery. Some languages (such as C++ and Delphi Pascal) insist the programmer indicate when an object value is no longer being used by a program and hence can be recovered and recycled. The keywords used for this purpose vary from one language to another. In Object Pascal the keyword is free, as in the following example.

```
free aCard;
```

Objective-C uses the same keyword but written as a message with the receiver first.

```
[ aCard free ];
```

In C++ the keyword is delete:

```
delete aCard;
```

When an array is deleted, a pair of square braces must be placed after the keyword.

```
delete [ ] cardArray;
```

The alternative to having the programmer explicitly manage memory is an idea termed *garbage collection*. A language that uses garbage collection (such as Java, C#, Smalltalk, or CLOS) monitors the manipulation of object values and will automatically recover memory from objects that are no longer being used. Generally garbage collection systems wait until memory is nearly exhausted, then will suspend execution of the running program while they recover the unused space before finally resuming execution. Garbage collection uses a certain amount of execution time, which may make it more costly than the alternative of insisting that programmers free their own memory. But garbage collection prevents a number of common programming errors.

- It is not possible for a program to run out of memory because the programmer forgot to free up unused memory. (Programs can still run out of memory if the total memory required at any one time exceeds the available memory, of course.)

- It is not possible for a programmer to try to use memory after it has been freed. Freed memory can be reused, and hence the contents of the memory values may be overwritten. Using a value after it has been freed can therefore cause unpredictable results.

```
PlayingCard * aCard = new PlayingCard(Spade, 1);
    .
    .
    .
delete aCard;
    .
    .
    .
cout << aCard.rank(); // attempt to use after deletion
```

- It is not possible for a programmer to try and free the same memory value more than once. Doing this can also cause unpredictable results.

```
Playingcard * aCard = new PlayingCard(Space, 1);
    .
    .
    .
delete aCard;
    .
    .
    .
delete aCard; // deleting an already deleted value
```

When a garbage collection system is not available, it is often necessary to ensure that every dynamically allocated memory object has a designated *owner* in order to avoid these problems. The owner of the memory is responsible for ensuring that the memory location is used properly and is freed when it is no longer required. In large programs, as in real life, disputes over the ownership of shared resources can be a source of difficulty.

When a single object cannot be designated as the owner of a shared resource, another common technique is to use *reference counts*. A reference count is a count of the number of pointers that reference the shared object. Care is needed to ensure that the count is accurate. Whenever a new pointer is added the count is incremented, and whenever a pointer is removed the count is decremented. When the count reaches zero, it indicates that no pointers refer to the object, and its memory can be recovered.

As with the arguments for and against dynamic typing, the arguments for and against garbage collection tend to pit efficiency against flexibility. Automatic garbage collection can be expensive, since it necessitates a run-time system to manage memory. On the other hand, the cost of memory errors can be equally expensive.

5.6 ◻ Constructors

As we indicated in Chapter 4, a constructor is a method that is used to initialize a newly created object. Linking creation and initialization together has many beneficial consequences. Most importantly, it guarantees that an object can never be used before it has been properly initialized. When creation and initialization are separated (as they must be in languages that do not have constructors), a programmer can easily forget to call an initialization routine after creating a new value, often with unfortunate consequences. A less common problem, although often just as unfortunate, is to invoke an initialization procedure twice on the same value. This problem, too, is avoided by the use of constructors.

In Java and C++ a constructor can be identified by the fact that it has the same name as the class in which it appears. Another small difference is that constructors do not declare a return type.

```
class PlayingCard {  // a Java constructor
  public PlayingCard (int s, int r) {
    suit = s;
    rank = r;
    faceUp = true;
  }
  .
  .
  .
}
```

When memory is allocated using the new operator, any arguments required by the constructor appear following the class name.

```
aCard = new PlayingCard(PlayingCard.Diamond, 3);
```

Data fields in Java (as well as in C#) that are initialized with a simple value, independent of any constructor argument, can be assigned a value at the point they are declared, even if they are subsequently reassigned.

```
class Complex {  // complex numbers
  public Complex (double rv) { realPart = rv; }

  public double realPart = 0.0;   // initialize data areas
  public double imagPart = 0.0;  // to zero
}
```

A similar syntax can be used in C++ if the data members are declared to be static and/or const.

In C++, C#, and Java there can be more than one function definition that uses the same name, as long as the number, type, and order of arguments are sufficient to distinguish which function is intended in any invocation. This facility is frequently used with constructors, allowing the creation of one constructor to be used when no arguments are provided and another to be used with arguments.

```
class PlayingCard {
public:
  PlayingCard ( )   // default constructor,
      // used when no arguments are given
    { suit = Diamond; rank = 1; faceUp = true; }

  PlayingCard (Suit is) // constructor with one argument
    { suit = is; rank = 1; faceUp = true; }

  PlayingCard (Suit is, int ir) // constructor with two arguments
    { suit = is; rank = ir; faceUp = true; }
};
```

The combination of number, type, and order of arguments is termed a function *type signature*. We say that the meaning of an overloaded constructor (or any other overloaded function, for that matter) is resolved by examining the type signature of the invocation.

```
PlayingCard cardOne; // invokes default
PlayingCard * cardTwo = new PlayingCard;
PlayingCard cardThree(PlayingCard.Heart);
PlayingCard * cardFour = new PlayingCard(PlayingCard.Spade, 6);
```

In C++ one must be careful to omit the parentheses from an invocation of the default constructor. Using parentheses in this situation is legal, but it has an entirely different meaning.

```
PlayingCard cardFive; // creates a new card
PlayingCard cardSix(); // forward definition for function
                       // named cardSix that returns a PlayingCard
```

On the other hand, when using the new operator and no arguments, parentheses are omitted in C++ but not in Java or C#.

```
PlayingCard cardSeven = new PlayingCard(); // Java
PlayingCard * cardEight = new PlayingCard; // C++
```

Constructors in C++ can also use a slightly different syntax to specify the initial value for data members. A colon, followed by a named value in parentheses, is termed an *initializer*. Our constructor written using initializer syntax would look as follows.

```
Class PlayingCard {
public:
  PlayingCard (Suits is, int ir)
    : suit(is), rank(ir), faceUp(true) { }
  .
  .
  .
};
```

For simple values such as integers there is no difference between the use of an initializer and the use of an assignment statement within the body of the constructor. We will subsequently encounter different forms of initialization that can only be performed in C++ by means of an initializer.

Constructors in Objective-C need not have the same name as the class, and are signified by the use of a plus sign, rather than a minus sign, in the first column of their definition. Such a function is termed a *factory method*. The factory method uses the new operator to perform the actual memory allocation, then performs whatever actions are necessary to initialize the object.

```
@ implementation PlayingCard

+  suit: (int) s rank: (int) r {
   self = [ Card new ];
   suit = s;
   rank = r;
   return self;
}


@end
```

Factory methods are invoked using the class as the receiver, rather than an instance object.

```
PlayingCard aCard = [ PlayingCard suit: Diamond rank: 3 ];
```

Constructors in Python all have the unusual name __init__. When an object is created, the init function is implicitly invoked, passing as an argument the newly created object and any other arguments used in the creation expression.

```
aCard = PlayingCard(2, 3)
   # invokes PlayingCard.__init__(aCard, 2 3)
```

In Apple Object Pascal there are no constructors. New objects are created using the operator new, and often programmers define their own initialization routines that should be invoked using the newly created object as receiver. The Delphi version of Object Pascal is much closer to C++. In Delphi programmers can define a constructor, although unlike C++, this function need not have the same name as the class. It is typical (although not required) to use the name Create as a constructor name.

```
interface
  type
    TPlayingCard = class (TObject)
      constructor Create (is : Suits, ir : integer);
        .
        .
        .
    end;
implementation
  constructor TPlayingCard.Create (is : Suits, ir : integer);
  begin
    suit = is;
    rank = ir;
    faceUp = true;
  end;
```

New objects are then created using the constructor method with the class as receiver.

```
aCard := TPlayingCard.Create (Spade, 4);
```

*5.6.1   The orthodox canonical class form

Several authors of style guides for C++ have suggested that almost all classes should define four important functions. This has come to be termed the *orthodox canonical class* form. The four important functions are:

- A default constructor. This is used internally to initialize objects and data members when no other value is available.
- A copy constructor. This is used, among other places, in the implementation of call-by-value parameters.
- An assignment operator. This is used to assign one value to another.
- A destructor. This is invoked when an object is deleted. (We will shortly give an example to illustrate the use of destructors.)

We have already seen a default constructor. This is simply a constructor that takes no arguments. A copy constructor takes a reference to an instance of the class as an argument and initializes itself as a copy of the argument.

```
class PlayingCard {
public:
      .
      .
      .

   PlayingCard (PlayingCard & aCard)
   {
         // initialize ourself as copy of argument
      rank = aCard.getRank();
      suit = aCard.getSuit();
      faceUp = aCard.isFaceUp();
   }
      .
      .
      .
};
```

The system will implicitly create default versions of each of these if the user does not provide an alternative. However, in many situations (particulary those involving the management of dynamically allocated memory) the default versions are not what the programmer might wish. Even if empty bodies are supplied for these functions, writing the class body will at least suggest that the program designer has *thought* about the issues involved in each of these. Furthermore, appropriate use of visibility modifiers gives the programmer great power in allowing or disallowing different operations used with the class.

5.6.2 Constant values

In Chapter 4 we pointed out that some languages, such as C++ and Java, permit the creation of data fields that can be assigned once and thereafter are not allowed to change. Having introduced constructors, we can now complete that discussion by showing how such values can be initialized.

In Java an immutable data field is simply declared as final and can be initialized directly.

```
class ListofImportantPeople {
public:
  final int max = 100; // maximum number of people
  .
  .
  .
}
```

Alternatively, a final value can be assigned in the constructor. If there is more than one constructor, each constructor must initialize the data field.

```
class PlayingCard {
  public PlayingCard ( )
    { suit = Diamond; rank = 1; faceUp = true; }
  public PlayingCard ( int is, int ir)
    { suit = is; rank = ir; faceUp = true; }
  .
  .
  .

  public final int suit;   // suit and rank are
  public final int rank;   // immutable
  private boolean faceUp; // faceUp is not
}
```

Immutable values in C++ are designated using the keyword const. They can only be given a value using an initializer clause in a constructor.

```
class PlayingCard {
public:
  PlayingCard () : suit(Diamond), rank(1) { faceUp = true; }
  PlayingCard (Suits is, int ir) : suit(is), rank(ir)
    { faceUp = true; }
  .
  .
  .
```

```
   const Suits suit;
   const int rank;
private:
   boolean faceUp;
};
```

There is one subtle but nevertheless important difference between const and final values. The const modifier in C++ says that the associated value is truly constant and is not allowed to change. The final modifier in Java only asserts that the associated variable will not be assigned a new value. Nothing prevents the value itself from changing its own internal state—for example, in response to messages. To illustrate this, consider the following definition for a data type named Box.

```
class Box {
   public void setValue (int v);
   public int getValue () { return v; }
   private int v = 0;
}
```

Declaring a variable using the final modifier simply means it will not be reassigned; it does not mean it will not change.

```
final aBox = new Box(); // can be assigned only once
aBox.setValue(8); // but can change
aBox.setValue(12); // as often as you like
```

A variable declared using the const modifier in C++, on the other hand, is not allowed to change in any way, not even in its internal state. (Individual fields can be named as mutable, in which case they are allowed to change even within a const object. However, use of this facility is rare.)

5.7 ▫ Destructors and Finalizers

A constructor allows the programmer to perform certain actions when an object value is created (when it is being born, so to speak). Occasionally it is useful to also be able to specify actions that should be performed at the other end of a values lifetime, when the variable is about to die and have its memory recovered.

This can be performed in C++ using a method termed a *destructor*. The destructor is invoked automatically whenever memory space for an object is released. For automatic variables, space is released when the function containing the declaration for the variable is exited. For dynamically allocated variables, space is released with the operator delete. The destructor function is written as the name of the class preceded by a tilde (˜). It does not take any arguments and is never directly invoked by the user.

A simple but clever function will illustrate the use of constructors and destructors. The class Trace defines a simple class that can be used to trace the flow of execution. The constructor class takes as argument a descriptive string and prints a message when space for the associated variable is allocated (which is when the procedure containing the declaration is entered). A second message is printed by the destructor when space for the variable is released, which occurs when the procedure is exited.

```
class Trace {
public:
  // constructor and destructor
  Trace  (string);
  ~Trace  ();
private:
  string text;
};


Trace::Trace (string t) : text(t)
{   cout << "entering " << text << endl; }

Trace::~Trace ()
{   cout << "exiting " << text << endl; }
```

To trace the flow of execution, the programmer simply creates a declaration for a dummy variable of type Trace in each procedure to be traced. Consider the following pair of routines.

```
void procedureA ()
{
  Trace dummy ("procedure A");
  procedureB (7);
}

void procedureB (int x)
{
  Trace dummy ("procedure B");
  if (x < 5) {
    Trace aaa("true case in Procedure B");
    .
    .
    .
  }
  else {
```

```
      Trace bbb("false case in Procedure B");
         .
         .
         .
      }
   }
```

By their output, the values of type Trace will trace out the flow of execution. A
typical output as follows.

```
entering procedure A
entering procedure B
entering false case in Procedure B
   .
   .
   .
exiting false case in Procedure B
exiting procedure B
exiting procedure A
```

Delphi Pascal also supports a form of destructor. A destructor function (usually
called Destroy) is declared by the keyword destructor. When a dynamically allocated
object is freed, the memory management system will call the destructor function.

```
type
   TPlayingCard = class (TObject)
      .
      .
      destructor Destroy;
   end;

destructor PlayingCard.Destroy;
begin
   (* whatever housekeeping is necessary *)
      .
      .
end;
```

Java and Eiffel have similar facilities, although since both languages use
garbage collection, their utilization is different. A method named finalize in Java
will be invoked just before the point where a variable is recovered by the garbage
collection system. Since this can occur at any time, or it may never occur, the use
of this facility is much less common than the use of destructors in C++.

```
class FinalizeExample {
   public void finalize () {
```

```
        System.out.println("finally doing finalization");
        System.exit(0);
    }
}
    .
    .
    .
    // first create an instance
    Object x = new FinalizeExample();
    // redefining x releases memory
    x = new Integer(3);
    // now do lots of memory allocations
    // at some indeterminent point garbage collection
    // will occur and final method will be called
    for (int i = 0; i < 1000; i++) {
        System.out.println("i is " + i);
        for (int j = 0; j < 1000; j++)
            x = new Integer(j);
    }
```

In Eiffel the same effect is achieved by inheriting from the class Memory and overriding the method dispose. (We will discuss inheritance and overriding later in Chapter 8.)

*5.8 ▫ Metaclasses in Smalltalk

The discussion of object creation provides an excuse to introduce a curious concept found in Smalltalk and a few similar languages, termed *metaclasses*. To understand metaclasses, note first that methods are associated not with objects but with classes. That is, if we create a playing card, the methods associated with the card are found not in the object itself but in the class PlayingCard.

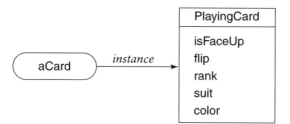

But in Smalltalk classes *are* objects. We explored this briefly in the previous chapter. Thus classes themselves respond to certain messages, such as the object creation message new.

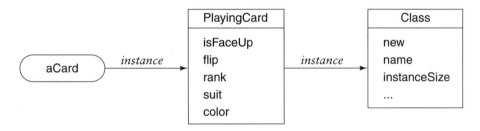

Given this situation, let us now imagine that we want to create a method that can be used in the fashion of a constructor. That is, we want a method—let us call it rank:suit:—that can be given to a specific class object—say, PlayingCard—and when executed it will both create a new instance and ensure it is properly initialized. Where in the picture just given can this method be placed? It cannot be part of the methods held by PlayingCard, since those are methods that are to be executed by *instances* of the class, and at the time of creation we do not yet have an instance. Nor can it be part of the methods held by Class, since those represent behavior common to all classes, and our initialization is something we want to do only for this one class.

The solution is to create a new "hidden" class, termed a metaclass. The object named PlayingCard is not actually an instance of Class but is in reality an instance of MetaPlayingCard, which is formed from inheritance from Class.[1] Initialization specific behavior can then be placed in this new class.

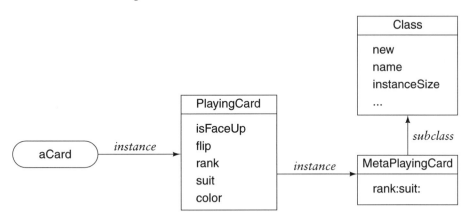

The behavior placed in the class MetaPlayingCard is understood by the object PlayingCard and by no other object. This object is the only instance of the class.

---

1. We are being slightly premature in presenting the discussion here, since inheritance will not be discussed in detail until Chapter 8. But the intuitive description of inheritance given in Chapter 1 is sufficient to understand the concept of metaclasses.

Smalltalk browsers generally hide the existence of metaobjects from programmers, calling such methods by the term *class methods* and acting as if they were associated with the same class as other methods. But behind the browser, class methods are simply ordinary methods associated with metaclasses.

Summary ▣

In this chapter we have examined the syntax and techniques used on object creation and initialization for each of the different languages we are considering.

- We have examined the syntax used for message passing.
- We introduced the two major categories of programming languages, statically and dynamically typed languages. In a statically typed language, types are associated with variables, whereas in a dynamically typed language a variable is simply a name, and types are associated with values.
- In many languages the receiver of a message can be accessed from within the body of the method used to respond to the message. The receiver is represented by a pseudo-variable. This variable can be named this, self, or current (depending on the language being used).
- Automatic memory allocates the lifetime of an object with the procedure in that it is declared. Heap-based memory is explicitly allocated (in most languages using an operator named new) and is either explicitly deallocated or recovered by a garbage collection system.
- A constructor ties together the two tasks of memory allocation and initialization. This ensures that all objects that are allocated are properly initialized.
- A destructor is executed when a value is deleted.
- Finally, we have examined how metaclasses in Smalltalk address the problem of creation and initialization in that language.

Further Reading ▣

The works cited at the end of the previous chapter should be consulted for more detailed information on any of the languages we are considering in this book.

Cohen [Cohen 1981] provides a good overview of garbage collection techniques. An interesting comparison between garbage collection and automatic memory allocation is given by Appel [Appel 1987]. Techniques for Reference counting in C++ are described in [Budd 1999].

Metaclasses in Smalltalk will be examined in detail in Chapter 25.

Self-Study Questions ▫

1. In what ways is a message passing operation different from a procedure call?
2. What are the three parts of a message passing expression?
3. How does Smalltalk-style keyword notation differ from Java or C++ style notation?
4. What is the difference between a statically typed language and a dynamically typed language?
5. Why are run-time errors of the form "receiver does not understand message" not common in statically typed languages? Why are they more common in dynamically typed languages?
6. What does the pseudo-variable this (or self in Smalltalk) refer to?
7. What is the difference between stack allocated and heap allocated memory?
8. What are the two general approaches to recovery of heap allocated memory?
9. What common programming errors does the use of a garbage collection system eliminate?
10. What two tasks are brought together by a constructor?
11. When is a destructor method executed?
12. What is a metaclass? What problem is solved through the use of metaclasses?

Exercises ▫

1. Write a method copy for the class Card of Chapter 4. This method should return a new instance of the class Card with the suit and rank fields initialized to be the same as the receiver.
2. In a language that does not provide direct support for immutable instance variables, how might you design a software tool that would help to detect violations of access? (Hint: The programmer can provide directives in the form of comments that tell the tool which variables should be considered immutable.)
3. We have seen two styles for invoking methods. The approach used in C++ is similar to a conventional function call. The Smalltalk and Objective-C approaches separate arguments with keyword identifiers. Which do you think is more readable? Which is more descriptive? Which is more error-prone? Present short arguments to support your opinions.
4. How might you design a tool to detect the different types of memory allocation and free problems described in Section 5.5.1?

5. Andrew Appel [Appel 1987] argues that under certain circumstances heap-based memory allocation can be more efficient than stack-based memory allocation. Read this article and summarize the points of Appel's argument. Are the situations in which this is true likely to be encountered in practice?

6. Write a short (two- or three-paragraph) essay arguing for or against automatic memory-management (garbage-collection) systems.

CHAPTER 6

A Case Study: The Eight-Queens Puzzle

This chapter presents the first of several case studies (or paradigms, in the original sense of the word) of programs written in an object-oriented style. The programs in this chapter will be rather small so we can present versions in several different languages. Later case studies will be presented in only one language.

After first describing the problem, we will discuss how an object-oriented solution would differ from another type of solution. The chapter then concludes with a solution written in each language.

6.1 □ The Eight-Queens Puzzle

In the game of chess, the queen can attack any piece that lies on the same row, on the same column, or along a diagonal. The *eight-queens* is a classic logic puzzle. The task is to place eight queens on a chessboard in such a fashion that no queen can attack any other queen. A solution is shown in Figure 6.1, but this solution is not unique. The eight-queens puzzle is often used to illustrate problem-solving or backtracking techniques.

How would an object-oriented solution to the eight-queens puzzle differ from a solution written in a conventional imperative programming language? In a conventional solution, some sort of data structure would be used to maintain the positions of the pieces. A program would then solve the puzzle by systematically manipulating the values in these data structures, testing each new position to see whether it satisfied the property that no queen can attack any other.

We can provide an amusing but nevertheless illustrative metaphor for the difference between a conventional and an object-oriented solution. A conventional program is like a human being sitting above the board and moving the chess

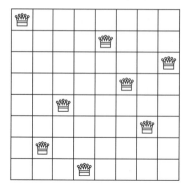

▢ Figure 6.1 ——— One solution to the eight-queens puzzle

pieces, which have no animate life of their own. In an object-oriented solution, on the other hand, we will empower the *pieces* to solve the problem themselves. That is, instead of a single monolithic entity controlling the outcome, we will distribute responsibility for finding the solution among many interacting agents. It is as if the chess pieces themselves are animate beings who interact with each other and take charge of finding their own solution.

Thus, the essence of our object-oriented solution will be to create objects that represent each of the queens and to provide them with the abilities to discover the solution. With the computing-as-simulation view of Chapter 1, we are creating a model universe, defining behavior for the objects in this universe, and then setting the universe in motion. When the activity of the universe stabilizes, the solution has been found.

6.1.1 Creating objects that find their own solution

How might we define the behavior of a queen object so that a group of queens working together can find a solution on their own? The first observation is that, in any solution, no two queens can occupy the same column, and consequently no column can be empty. At the start we can therefore assign a specific column to each queen and reduce the problem to the simpler task of finding an appropriate row.

To find a solution it is clear that the queens will need to communicate with each other. Realizing this, we can make a second important observation that will greatly simplify our programming task—namely, each queen needs to know only about the queens to her immediate left. Thus, the data values maintained for each queen will consist of three values: a column value, which is *immutable*; a row value,

---

Queen

initialize—initialize row, then find first acceptable
   solution for self and neighbor
advance—advance row and find next acceptable
   solution
canAttack—see whether a position can be attacked
   by self or neighbors

Queen—data values

row—current row number (changes)
column—column number (fixed)
neighbor—neighbor to left (fixed)

 Figure 6.2 —— Front and back sides of the queen CRC card

which is altered in pursuit of a solution; and the neighboring queen to the immediate left.

    Let us define an *acceptable solution for column n* to be a configuration of columns 1 through *n* in which no queen can attack any other queen in those columns. Each queen will be charged with finding acceptable solutions between herself and her neighbors on her left. We will find a solution to the entire puzzle by asking the rightmost queen to find an acceptable solution. A CRC-card description of the class Queen, including the data managed by each instance (recall that this information is described on the back side of the card), is shown in Figure 6.2.

6.2  Using Generators

As with many similar problems, the solution to the eight-queens puzzle involves two interacting steps: *generating* possible partial solutions and *filtering out* solutions that fail to satisfy some later goal. This style of problem solving is sometimes known as the *generate and test* paradigm.

Let us consider the filter step first, since it is easier. For the system to test a potential solution, it is sufficient for a queen to take a coordinate (row-column) pair and produce a Boolean value that indicates whether that queen or any queen to her left can attack the given location. A pseudo-code algorithm that checks to see whether a queen can attack a specific position is given here. The procedure canAttack uses the fact that for a diagonal motion, the differences in rows must be equal to the differences in columns.

```
function queen.canAttack(testRow , testColumn) -> boolean
  /* test for same row */
  if row = testRow then
    return true

  /* test diagonals */
  columnDifference := testColumn - column
  if (row + columnDifference = testRow) or
    (row - columnDifference = testRow)
      then return true

  /* we can't attack, see if neighbor can */
  return neighbor.canAttack(testRow, testColumn)
end
```

6.2.1   Initialization

We will divide the task of finding a solution into parts. The method initialize establishes the initial conditions necessary for a queen object, which in this case simply means setting the data values. This is usually followed immediately by a call on findSolution to discover a solution for the given column. Because such a solution will often not be satisfactory to subsequent queens, the message advance is used to advance to the next solution.

A queen in column n is initialized by being given a column number and the neighboring queen (the queen in column $n - 1$). At this level of analysis, we will leave unspecified the actions of the leftmost queen, who has no neighbor. We will explore various alternative actions in the example problems we subsequently present. We will assume the neighbor queens (if any) have already been initialized, which includes their having found a mutually satisfactory solution. The queen in the current column simply places herself in row 1. A pseudo-code description of the algorithm is as follows.

```
function queen.initialize(col, neigh) -> boolean

    /* initialize our column and neighbor values */
```

```
   column := col
   neighbor := neigh

      /* start in row 1 */
   row := 1
   return findSolution;
end
```

6.2.2   Finding a solution

To find a solution, a queen simply asks its neighbors if they can attack. If so, then the queen advances herself, if possible (returning failure if she cannot). When the neighbors indicate they cannot attack, a solution has been found.

```
function queen.findSolution -> boolean

      /* test positions */
   while neighbor.canAttack (row, column) do
     if not self.advance then
        return false

      /* found a solution */
   return true
end
```

As we noted in Chapter 5, the pseudo-variable self denotes the receiver for the current message. In this case we want the queen who is being asked to find a solution to pass the message advance to herself.

6.2.3   Advancing to the next position

The procedure advance divides into two cases. If we are not at the end, the queen simply advances the row value by 1. Otherwise, she has tried all positions and not found a solution, so nothing remains but to ask her neighbor for a new solution and start again from row 1.

```
function queen.advance -> boolean

      /* try next row */
   if row < 8 then begin
     row := row + 1
     return self.findSolution
   end
```

```
    /* cannot go further */
    /* move neighbor to next solution */
  if not neighbor.advance then
    return false

    /* start again in row 1 */
  row := 1
  return self.findSolution
end
```

The one remaining task is to print out the solution. This is most easily accomplished by a simple method, print, that is rippled down the neighbors.

```
procedure print
  neighbor.print
  write row, column
end
```

6.3 ▫ The Eight-Queens Puzzle in Several Languages

In this section we present solutions to the eight-queens puzzle in several of the programming languages we are considering. Examine each variation, and compare how the basic features provided by the language make subtle changes to the final solution. In particular, examine the solutions written in Smalltalk and Objective-C, which use a special class for a sentinel value, and contrast this with the solutions given in Object Pascal, C++, or Java, all of which use a null pointer for the leftmost queen and thus must constantly test the value of pointer variables.

6.3.1   The eight-queens puzzle in Object Pascal

The class definition for the eight-queens puzzle in Apple Object Pascal is shown below. A subtle but important point is that this definition is recursive; objects of type Queen maintain a data field that is itself of type Queen. This is sufficient to indicate that declaration and storage allocation are not necessarily linked; if they were, an infinite amount of storage would be required to hold any Queen value. We will contrast this with the situation in C++ when we discuss that language.

```
type
  Queen = object
    (* data fields *)
    row :    integer;
```

```
  column :  integer;
  neighbor :  Queen;

    (* initialization *)
  procedure initialize (col : integer; ngh : Queen);

    (* operations *)
  function   canAttack
        (testRow, testColumn : integer) : boolean;
  function   findSolution : boolean;
  function   advance : boolean;
  procedure  print;
end;
```

The class definition for the Delphi language differs only slightly, as shown below. The Borland language allows the class declaration to be broken into public and private sections, and it includes a constructor function, which we will use in place of the initialize routine.

```
TQueen = class (TObject)
public
    constructor Create (initialColumn : integer; nbr : TQueen);
    function findSolution : boolean;
    function advance : boolean;
    procedure print;

private
    function canAttack (testRow, testColumn : integer) : boolean;
    row : integer;
    column : integer;
    neighbor : TQueen;
end;
```

The pseudo-code presented in the earlier sections is reasonably close to the Pascal solution, with two major differences. The first is the lack of a return statement in Pascal, and the second is the necessity to first test whether a queen has a neighbor before passing a message to that neighbor. The functions findSolution and advance, shown following, illustrate these differences. (Note that Delphi Pascal differs from standard Pascal in permitting short-circuit interpretation of the and and or directives, in the fashion of C++. Thus, the code for the Delphi language could, in a single expression, combine the test for neighbor being non-null and the passing of a message to the neighbor.)

```
function Queen.findSolution : boolean;
var
  done : boolean;
begin
  done := false;
  findsolution := true;

    (* test positions *)
  if neighbor <> nil then
    while not done and neighbor.canAttack(row, column) do
      if not self.advance then begin
        findSolution := false;
        done := true;
      end;
end;


function Queen.advance : boolean;
begin
  advance := false;
    (* try next row *)
  if row < 8 then begin
    row := row + 1;
    advance := self.findSolution;
  end
  else begin
      (* cannot go further *)
      (* move neighbor to next solution *)
    if neighbor <> nil then
      if not neighbor.advance then
        advance := false
      else begin
        row := 1;
        advance := self.findSolution;
      end;
  end;
end;
```

The main program allocates space for each of the eight queens and initializes the queens with their column number and neighbor value. Since during initialization the first solution will be discovered, it is only necessary for the queens to print their solution. The code to do this in Apple Object Pascal is shown next.

In this case neighbor and i are temporary variables used during initialization, and lastQueen is the most recently created queen.

```
begin
  neighbor := nil;
  for i := 1 to 8 do begin
      (* create and initialize new queen *)
    new (lastQueen);
    lastQueen.initial (i, neighbor);
    if not lastQueen.findSolution then
      writeln('no solution');
      (* newest queen is next queen neighbor *)
    neighbor := lastQueen;
  end;

    (* print the solution *)
  lastQueen.print;

  end;
end.
```

By providing explicit constructors that combine new object creation and initialization, the Delphi language allows us to eliminate one of the temporary variables. The main program for the Delphi language is as follows.

```
begin
  lastQueen := nil;
  for i := 1 to 8 do begin
      // create and initialize new queen
    lastQueen := Queen.create(i, lastQueen);
    lastQueen.findSolution;
    end;

    // print the solution
  lastQueen.print;
end;
```

6.3.2   The eight-queens puzzle in C++

The most important difference between the pseudo-code description of the algorithm presented earlier and the eight-queens puzzle as actually coded in C++ is the explicit use of pointer values. The following is the class description for the class Queen. Each instance maintains, as part of its data area, a pointer to another queen value. Note that unlike the Object Pascal solution, in C++ this value must be declared explicitly as a pointer rather than an object value.

```
class Queen {
public:
    // constructor
  Queen (int, Queen *);

    // find and print solutions
  bool findSolution();
  bool advance();
  void print();

private:
    // data fields
  int row;
  const int column;
  const Queen * neighbor;

    // internal method
  bool canAttack (int, int);
};
```

As in the Delphi Pascal solution, we have subsumed the behavior of the method initialize in the constructor. We will describe this shortly.

There are three data fields. The integer data field column has been marked as const. This identifies the field as an immutable value, which cannot change during execution. The third data field is a pointer value, which either contains a null value (that is, points at nothing) or points to another queen.

Since initialization is performed by the constructor, the main program can simply create the eight queen objects and then print their solution. The variable lastQueen will point to the most recent queen created. This value is initially a null pointer—it points to nothing. A loop then creates the eight values, initializing each with a column value and the previous queen value. When the loop completes, the leftmost queen holds a null value for its neighbor field while every other queen points to its neighbor, and the value lastQueen points to the rightmost queen.

```
void main() {
  Queen * lastQueen = 0;

  for (int i = 1; i <= 8; i++) {
    lastQueen = new Queen(i, lastQueen);
    if (! lastQueen->findSolution())
```

```
        cout << "no solution\n";
    }

    lastQueen->print();
}
```

We will describe only those methods that illustrate important points. The complete solution can be examined in Appendix A.

The constructor method must use the initialization clauses on the heading to initialize the constant value column, since it is not permitted to use an assignment operator to initialize instance fields that have been declared const. An initialization clause is also used to assign the value neighbor, although we have not declared this field as constant.

```
Queen::Queen(int col, Queen * ngh) : column(col), neighbor(ngh)
{
    row = 1;
}
```

Because the value of the neighbor variable can be either a queen or a null value, a test must be performed before any messages are sent to the neighbor. This is illustrated in the method findSolution. The use of short-circuit evaluation in the logical connectives and the ability to return from within a procedure simplify the code in comparison to the Object Pascal version, which is otherwise very similar.

```
bool Queen::findSolution()
{
    while (neighbor && neighbor->canAttack(row, column))
        if (! advance())
            return false;
    return true;
}
```

The advance method must similarly test to make certain there is a neighbor before trying to advance the neighbor to a new solution. When passing a message to oneself, as in the recursive message findSolution, it is not necessary to specify a receiver.

```
bool Queen::advance()
{
    if (row < 8) {
        row++;
        return findSolution();
    }
```

```
      if (neighbor && ! neighbor->advance())
        return false;

      row = 1;
      return findSolution();
    }
```

6.3.3   The eight-queens puzzle in Java

The solution in Java is in many respects similar to the C++ solution. However, in Java the bodies of the methods are written directly in place, and public or private designations are placed on the class definitions themselves. The following is the class description for the class Queen, with some of the methods omitted.

```
class Queen {
    // data fields
  private int row;
  private int column;
  private Queen neighbor;

    // constructor
  Queen (int c, Queen n) {
      // initialize data fields
    row = 1;
    column = c;
    neighbor = n;
    }

  public boolean findSolution() {
    while (neighbor != null &&
        neighbor.canAttack(row, column))
      if (! advance())
        return false;
    return true;
    }

  public boolean advance() { ...  }

  private boolean canAttack(int testRow, int testColumn) { ...  }

  public void paint (Graphics g) { ...  }
  }
```

Unlike in C++, in Java the link to the next queen is simply declared as an object of type Queen and not as a pointer to a queen. Before a message is sent to the neighbor instance variable, an explicit test is performed to see if the value is null.

Since Java provides a rich set of graphics primitives, this solution will differ from the others in actually drawing the final solution as a board. The method paint will draw an image of the queen, then print the neighbor images.

```java
class Queen {
    .
    .
    .
    public void paint (Graphics g) {
        // x, y is upper left corner
        // 10 and 40 give slight margins to sides
        int x = (row - 1) * 50 + 10;
        int y = (column - 1) * 50 + 40;
        g.drawLine(x+5, y+45, x+45, y+45);
        g.drawLine(x+5, y+45, x+5, y+5);
        g.drawLine(x+45, y+45, x+45, y+5);
        g.drawLine(x+5, y+35, x+45, y+35);
        g.drawLine(x+5, y+5, x+15, y+20);
        g.drawLine(x+15, y+20, x+25, y+5);
        g.drawLine(x+25, y+5, x+35, y+20);
        g.drawLine(x+35, y+20, x+45, y+5);
        g.drawOval(x+20, y+20, 10, 10);
        // then draw neighbor
        if (neighbor != null)
            neighbor.paint(g);
    }
}
```

The graphics routines draw a small crown, which looks like this.

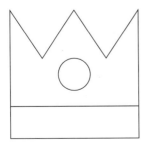

Java does not have global variables or functions that are not member functions. As we will describe in more detail in Chapter 22, a program is created by the defining of a subclass of the system class JFrame and then the overriding of certain methods. Notably, the constructor is used to provide initialization for the application, and the method paint is used to redraw the screen. Mouse events and window events are handled by creating *listener objects* that will execute when their associated event occurs. We will describe listeners in much greater detail in later sections. We name the application class QueenSolver and define it as follows.

```java
public class QueenSolver extends JFrame {

  public static void main(String [ ] args) {
    QueenSolver world = new QueenSolver();
    world.show();
  }

  private Queen lastQueen = null;

  public QueenSolver() {
    setTitle("8 queens");
    setSize(600, 500);
    for (int i = 1; i <= 8; i++) {
      lastQueen = new Queen(i, lastQueen);
      lastQueen.findSolution();
    }
    addMouseListener(new MouseKeeper());
    addWindowListener(new CloseQuit());
  }

  public void paint(Graphics g) {
    super.paint(g);
    // draw board
    for (int i = 0; i <= 8; i++) {
      g.drawLine(50 * i + 10, 40, 50*i + 10, 440);
      g.drawLine(10, 50 * i + 40, 410, 50*i + 40);
    }
    g.drawString("Click Mouse for Next Solution", 20, 470);
    // draw queens
    lastQueen.paint(g);
  }

  private class CloseQuit extends WindowAdapter {
    public void windowClosing (WindowEvent e) {
```

```
      System.exit(0);
    }
  }

  private class MouseKeeper extends MouseAdapter {
    public void mousePressed (MouseEvent e) {
      lastQueen.advance();
      repaint();
    }
  }
}
```

Note that the application class must be declared as public because it must be accessible to the main program.

6.3.4   The eight-queens puzzle in Objective-C

The interface description for our class Queen is as follows.

```
@interface Queen : Object
{   /* data fields */
  int row;
  int column;
  id neighbor;
}

  /* methods */
- (void) initialize: (int) c neighbor: ngh;
- (int)  advance;
- (void) print;
- (int)  canAttack: (int) testRow column: (int) testColumn;
- (int)  findSolution;

@end
```

Each queen will maintain three data fields: a row value, a column, and the neighbor queen. The last is declared with the data type id. This declaration indicates that the value being held by the variable is an object type, although not necessarily a queen.

In fact, we can use this typeless nature of variables in Objective-C to our advantage. We will employ a technique that is not possible, or at least not as easy, in a more strongly typed language such as C++ or Object Pascal. Recall that the leftmost queen does not have any neighbor. In the C++ solution, this was indicated by the null, or empty, value in the neighbor pointer variable in the leftmost queen.

In the current solution, we will instead create a new type of class, a *sentinel value*. The leftmost queen will point to this sentinel value, thereby ensuring that every queen has a valid neighbor.

Sentinel values are frequently used as endmarkers and are found in algorithms that manipulate linked lists, such as our linked list of queen values. The difference between an object-oriented sentinel and a more conventional value is that an object-oriented sentinel value can be *active*—it can have *behavior*—which means it can respond to requests.

What behaviors should our sentinel value exhibit? Recall that the neighbor links in our algorithm were used for two purposes. The first was to ensure that a given position could not be attacked. Our sentinel value should always respond negatively to such requests, since it cannot attack any position. The second use of the neighbor links was in a recursive call to print the solution. In this case our sentinel value should simply return, since it does not have any information concerning the solution.

Putting these together yields the following implementation for our sentinel queen.

```
@implementation SentinelQueen : Object
- (int) advance
{
  /* do nothing */
  return 0;
}


- (int) findSolution
{
  /* do nothing */
  return 1;
}


- (void) print
{
  /* do nothing */
}


- (int) canAttack: (int) testRow column: (int) testColumn;
{
  /* cannot attack */
  return 0;
}
@end
```

In the full solution there is an implementation section for SentinelQueen but no interface section. This omission is legal, although the compiler will provide a warning, since it is somewhat unusual.

The use of the sentinel allows the methods in class Queen to simply pass messages to their neighbor without first determining whether she is the leftmost queen. The method for canAttack, for example, illustrates this use.

```
- (int) canAttack: (int) testRow column: (int) testColumn
{  int columnDifference;

   /* can attack same row */
   if (row == testRow)
     return 1;

   columnDifference = testColumn - column;
   if ((row + columnDifference == testRow) ||
     (row - columnDifference == testRow))
       return 1;

   return [ neighbor canAttack:testRow column: testColumn ];
}
```

Within a method, a message sent to the receiver is denoted by a message sent to the pseudo-variable self.

```
- (void) initialize: (int) c neighbor: ngh
{
   /* set the constant fields */
   column = c;
   neighbor = ngh;
   row = 1;
}

- (int) findSolution
{
   /* loop until we find a solution */
   while ([neighbor canAttack: row and: column ])
     if (! [self advance])
       return 0; /* return false */
   return 1; /* return true */
}
```

Other methods are similar and are not described here.

6.3.5   The eight-queens puzzle in Smalltalk

The solution to the eight-queens puzzle in Smalltalk is in most respects very similar to the solution given in Objective-C. Like Objective-C, Smalltalk handles the fact that the leftmost queen does not have a neighbor by defining a special *sentinel* class. The sole purpose of this class is to provide a target for the messages sent by the leftmost queen.

The sentinel value is the sole instance of the class SentinelQueen, a subclass of class Object, which implements the following three methods.

```
{advance}

    " sentinels do not attack "
    ↑ false


{canAttack:} row {column:} column
    " sentinels cannot attack "
    ↑ false


{result}
    " return empty list as result "
    ↑ List new
```

One difference between the Objective-C and Smalltalk versions is that the Smalltalk code returns the result as a list of values rather than printing it on the output. The techniques for printing output are rather tricky in Smalltalk and vary from implementation to implementation. By returning a list we can isolate these differences in the calling method.

The class Queen is a subclass of class Object. Instances of class Queen maintain three instance variables: a row value, a column value, and a neighbor. Initialization is performed by the method setColumn:neighbor.

```
{setColumn:} aNumber {neighbor:} aQueen
    " initialize the data fields "
  column := aNumber.
  neighbor := aQueen.
  row := 1.
```

The canAttack method differs from the Objective-C counterpart only in syntax.

```
{canAttack:} testRow {column:} testColumn | columnDifference |
  columnDifference := testColumn - column.
  (((row = testRow) or:
    [ row + columnDifference = testRow]) or:
```

```
    [ row - columnDifference = testRow])
      ifTrue: [ ↑ true ].
↑ neighbor canAttack: testRow column: testColumn
```

Rather than testing for the negation of a condition, Smalltalk provides an explicit ifFalse statement, which is used in the method advance.

```
{advance}
    " first try next row "
  (row < 8)
    ifTrue: [ row := row + 1. ↑ self findSolution ].
    " cannot go further, move neighbor "
  (neighbor advance) ifFalse: [ ↑ false ].
    " begin again in row 1 "
  row := 1.
↑ self findSolution
```

The while loop in Smalltalk must use a block as the condition test, as in the following.

```
{findSolution}
  [ neighbor canAttack: row column: column ]
    whileTrue: [ self advance ifFalse: [ ↑ false ] ].
↑ true
```

A recursive method is used to obtain the list of answer positions. Recall that an empty list is created by the sentinel value in response to the message result.

```
{result}
↑ neighbor result; addLast: row
```

A solution can be found by invocation of the following method, which is not part of class Queen but is instead attached to some other class, such as Object.

```
{solvePuzzle} | lastQueen |
  lastQueen := SentinelQueen new.
  1 to: 8 do: [:i | lastQueen := (Queen new)
    setColumn: i neighbor: lastQueen.
    lastQueen findSolution ].
↑ lastQueen result
```

6.3.6 The eight-queens puzzle in Ruby

Ruby is a recent scripting language, similar in spirit to Python or Perl. There are only functions in Ruby—every method returns a value, which is simply the value of the last statement in the body of the method. A feel for the syntax for Ruby can be found by the definition of the sentinel queen, which can be written as follows.

```ruby
class NullQueen

  def canAttack(row, column)
    false
  end

  def first?
    true
  end

  def next?
    false
  end

  def getState
    Array.new
  end

end
```

The class Queen handles all but the last case. In Ruby, instance variables must begin with an at-sign (@). Thus, the initialization method is written as follows.

```ruby
class Queen

  def initialColumn(column, neighbor)
    @column = column
    @neighbor = neighbor
    nil
  end
  .
  .
  .
end
```

Conditional statements are written in a curious form where the expression is given first, followed by the if keyword. This is illustrated by the method canAttack.

```ruby
def canAttack(row, column)
  return true if row == @row

  cd = (column - @column).abs
```

```
    rd = (row - @row).abs
    return true if cd == rd

    @neighbor.canAttack(row, column)
end
```

The remainder of the Ruby solution can be found in Appendix A.

Summary ⊡

In this first case study we have examined a classic puzzle, how to place eight queens on a chessboard in such a way that no queen can attack any of the others. While the problem is moderately intriguing, our interest is not so much in the problem itself but in the way the solution to the problem has been structured. We have addressed the problem by making the queens into independent agents, who then work among themselves to discover a solution.

Further Reading ⊡

A solution to the eight-queens puzzle constructed without the use of a sentinel value was described in my earlier book on Smalltalk [Budd 1987].

The eight-queens puzzle is found in many computing texts. See [Griswold 1983, Budd 1987, Berztiss 1990] for some representative examples.

For further information on the general technique termed *generate* and *test*, see [Hanson 1981] or [Berztiss 1990].

The solution in Ruby was written by Mike Stok. Further information on Ruby can be found in [Thomas 2001].

Self-Study Questions ⊡

1. What is the eight-queens puzzle?
2. In what way is the object-oriented solution presented here different from a conventional solution?
3. What is the generate and test approach to finding a solution in a space of various alternative possibilities?
4. What is a sentinel? (The term is introduced in the solution presented in Objective-C.)

Exercises ⊡

1. Modify any one of the programs to produce all possible solutions rather than just one. How many possible solutions are there for the eight-queens puzzle? How many of these are rotations of other solutions? How might you filter out rotations?

2. Can you explain why the sentinel class in the Objective-C and Smalltalk versions of the eight-queens puzzle do not need to provide an implementation for the method findSolution, despite the fact that this message is passed to the neighbor value in the method advance?

3. Suppose we generalize the eight-queens problem to the N-queens problem, where the task is to place N queens on an N by N chessboard. How must the programs be changed?

    It is clear that there are values for N for which no solution exists (consider N = 2 or N = 3, for example). What happens when your program is executed for these values? How might you produce more meaningful output?

4. Using whatever graphics facilities your system has, alter one of the programs to display dynamically the positions of each queen on a chessboard as the program advances. What portions of the program need to know about the display?

CHAPTER 7

A Case Study:
A Billiards Game

In our second case study, we will develop a simple simulation of a billiard table.[1] The program is written in Delphi Pascal.[2] As with the eight-queens program, the design of this program will stress the creation of autonomous interacting agents working together to produce the desired outcome.

7.1 □ The Elements of Billiards

The billiard table as the user sees it consists of a window containing a rectangle with holes (pockets) in the corners, 15 colored balls, and 1 white cue ball. By clicking the mouse the user simulates striking the cue ball, imparting a certain amount of energy to it. The direction of motion for the cue ball will be opposite to that of the mouse position in relation to the cue. Once a ball has energy it will start to move, reflecting off of walls, falling into holes, and potentially striking other balls. When a ball strikes another ball, some of the energy of the first is

---

1. The game implemented by the program described in this chapter does not correspond to any actual game. It is not pool or billiards but simply balls moving around a table consisting of walls and holes.

2. Discussion of Delphi Pascal is complicated by the fact that graphical user interface elements of Delphi programs are constructed visually, using the integrated development environment. This style of design will be familiar to users of Visual Basic. However, the user interface aspects are not relevant to our purposes, which is the investigation of Delphi as an object-oriented programming language. The references at the end of the chapter provide pointers to further information regarding these other aspects of Delphi.

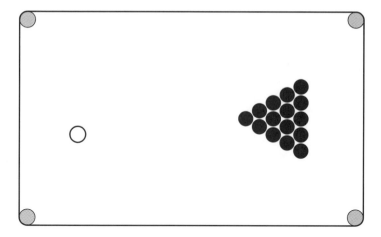

▢ Figure 7.1 ——— Billiard table

given to the second, while the direction of movement of the two balls is changed by the collision.

7.2 ▢ Graphical Objects

The heart of the simulation are three linked lists of *graphical objects*, which comprise the walls, holes, and balls. Each graphical object will include a link field and a field indicating the region of the screen occupied by the object.[3]

A simplifying assumption we have made is that all graphical objects occupy rectangular regions. This is, of course, quite untrue for a round object such as a ball. A more realistic alternative would have been to write a procedure that determined whether two balls have intersected based on the geometry of the ball rather than on the intersection of their regions. Once again, the complexity of the procedure would only have detracted from the issues we wish to address in our case study.

---

3. There are clear conflicts in ordering in the presentation of this case study. On the one hand, it is important for the reader to see examples of object-oriented principles as soon as possible; thus, placing this particular case study early in the book is desirable. On the other hand, this program, like almost all object-oriented programs, would benefit from more advanced techniques, which we will not discuss until later. In particular, the graphical objects might be better described by an inheritance hierarchy, such as we will discuss in Chapter 8. Similarly, it is generally considered poor programming practice for the objects being maintained on a linked list to hold the link fields as part of their data area; a better design would be to separate the container from the elements in the list. Solving this problem is nontrivial and introduces complications not particularly relevant to the points addressed here. We will discuss container classes in Chapter 19.

The primary objective in this case study is the way in which responsibility for behavior has been vested in the objects themselves. Every graphical object knows not only how to draw itself but how to move and how to interact with the other objects in the simulation.

7.2.1 The wall graphical object

The first of our three graphical objects is a wall. It is defined by the following class description.

```
TWall = class(TObject)
public
  constructor create
    (ix, iy, iw, ih : Integer; cf : Real; ilink : TWall);
  procedure draw (canvas : TCanvas);
  function hasIntersected(aBall : Tball) : Boolean;
  procedure hitBy (aBall : TBall);
private
  x, y : Integer;
  height, width : Integer;
  convertFactor : Real;
  link : TWall;
end;
```

The x and y fields represent the upper-left corner of the wall, while the height and width fields maintain the size. The link field maintains a linked list of wall objects. The constructor simply defines the region of the wall and sets the convert factor.

```
constructor TWall.create
  (ix, iy, iw, ih : Integer; cf : Real; ilink : Twall);
begin
  x := ix;
  y := iy;
  height := ih;
  width := iw;
  convertFactor := cf;
  link := ilink;
end;
```

A wall can be drawn simply by printing a solid rectangle. A graphics library routine performs this task.

```
procedure TWall.draw(canvas: TCanvas);
begin
        with canvas do begin
                Brush.Style := bsSolid;
                Brush.Color := clBlack;
                fillRect(Rect(x, y, x + width, y + height));
        end;
end;
```

The most interesting behavior of a wall occurs when it has been struck by a ball. The direction of the ball is modified by use of the convert factor for the wall. (Convert factors are either zero or pi, depending on whether the wall is horizontal or vertical.) The ball subsequently moves off in a new direction.

```
procedure TWall.hitBy (aBall : TBall);
begin
    { bounce the ball off the wall }
  aBall.direction := convertFactor - aBall.direction;
end;
```

7.2.2   The hole graphical object

A hole is defined by the following class description.

```
THole = class(TObject)
public
  constructor create (ix, iy : Integer; ilink : THole);
  procedure draw (canvas : TCanvas);
  function hasIntersected(aBall : TBall) : Boolean;
  procedure hitBy (aBall : TBall);
private
  x, y : Integer;
  link : THole;
end;
```

As with walls, the initialization and drawing of holes is largely a matter of invoking the correct library routines.

```
constructor THole.create(ix, iy : Integer; ilink : THole);
begin
  x := ix;
  y := iy;
  link := ilink;
end;
```

```
procedure THole.draw(canvas : TCanvas);
begin
       with canvas do begin
               Brush.Style := bsSolid;
               Brush.Color := clBlack;
               Ellipse(x-5, y-5, x+5, y+5);
       end;
end;
```

Of more interest is what happens when a hole is struck by a ball. There are two cases. If the ball happens to be the cue ball (which is identified with a global variable, CueBall), it is placed back into play at a fixed location. Otherwise, all the energy is drained from the ball, and it is moved off the table to a special display area.

```
procedure THole.hitBy (aBall : TBall);
begin
    { drain enery from ball }
  aBall.energy := 0.0;

    { move ball }
  if aBall = CueBall then
    aBall.setCenter(50, 100)
  else begin
    saveRack := saveRack + 1;
    aBall.setCenter (10 + saveRack * 15, 250);
  end;
end;
```

7.2.3   The ball graphical object

Our final graphical object is the ball, defined by the following class description:

```
TBall = class(TObject)
public
  constructor create (ix, iy : Integer; iLink : TBall);
  procedure draw (canvas : TCanvas);
  function hasIntersected(aBall : Tball) : Boolean;
  procedure hitBy (aBall : TBall);
  procedure update;
  procedure setCenter (nx, ny : Integer);
  procedure setDirection (nd : Real);
private
```

```
        x, y : Integer;
        direction : Real;
        energy : Real;
        link : TBall;
    end;
```

In addition to the link and rectangle regions common to the other objects, a ball maintains two new data fields: a direction, measured in radians, and an energy, which is an arbitrary real value. Like a hole, a ball is initialized by arguments that specify the center of the ball. Initially a ball has no energy and a direction of zero.

```
constructor TBall.create(ix, iy : Integer; iLink : TBall);
begin
        setCenter(ix, iy);
        setDirection(0.0);
        energy := 0.0;
        link := iLink;
end;

procedure TBall.setCenter(nx, ny : Integer);
begin
        x := nx;
        y := ny;
end;

procedure TBall.setDirection(nd : Real);
begin
        direction := nd;
end;
```

A ball is drawn either as a frame or as a solid circle, depending on whether or not it represents the cue ball.

```
procedure TBall.draw(canvas : TCanvas);
begin
        with canvas do begin
                Brush.Style := bsSolid;
                if (self = cueBall) then
                        Brush.Color := clWhite
                else
                        Brush.Color := clBlack;
                Ellipse(x-5, y-5, x+5, y+5);
        end;
end;
```

The method update is used to update the position of the ball. If the ball has a nontrivial amount of energy, it moves slightly and then checks to see if it has hit another object. A global variable named ballMoved is set to true if any ball on the table has moved. If the ball has hit another object, it notifies the second object that it has been struck. This notification process is divided into three steps, corresponding to hitting holes, walls, and other balls. Inheritance, which we will study in Chapter 8, will provide a means by which these three tests can be combined into a single loop.

```
procedure TBall.update;
var
   hptr : THole;
   wptr : TWall;
   bptr : TBall;
   dx, dy : integer;
begin
   if energy > 0.5 then begin
     ballMoved := true;
       { decrease energy }
     energy := energy - 0.05;
       { move ball }
     dx := trunc(5.0 * cos(direction));
     dy := trunc(5.0 * sin(direction));
               x := x + dx;
               y := y + dy;

       { see if we hit a hole }
     hptr := listOfHoles;
     while (hptr <> nil) do
       if hptr.hasIntersected(self) then begin
         hptr.hitBy(self);
         hptr := nil;
       end
       else
         hptr := hptr.link;

       { see if we hit a wall }
     wptr := listOfWalls;
     while (wptr <> nil) do
       if wptr.hasIntersected(self) then begin
         wptr.hitBy(self);
         wptr := nil;
       end
```

```
      else
        wptr := wptr.link;

      { see if we hit a ball }
    bptr := listOfBalls;
    while (bptr <> nil) do
      if (bptr <> self) and bptr.hasIntersected(self) then begin
        bptr.hitBy(self);
        bptr := nil;
      end
      else
        bptr := bptr.link;
  end;
end;
```

When one ball strikes another ball, the energy of the first one is split, and half is given to the second one. The angles of both are also changed. (The physics is not exactly correct, but the results look reasonably realistic.)

```
procedure TBall.hitBy (aBall : TBall);
var
  da : real;
begin
    { cut the energy of the hitting ball in half }
  aBall.energy := aBall.energy / 2.0;

    { and add it to our own }
  energy := energy + aBall.energy;

    { set our new direction }
  direction := hitAngle(self.x - aBall.x, self.y - aBall.y);

    { and set the hitting balls direction }
  da := aBall.direction - direction;
  aBall.direction := aBall.direction + da;

    { continue our update }
  update;
end;

function hitAngle (dx, dy : real) : real;
  const
    PI = 3.14159;
```

```
    var
       na : real;
    begin
      if (abs(dx) < 0.05) then
        na := PI / 2
      else
        na := arctan (abs(dy / dx));
      if (dx < 0) then
        na := PI - na;
      if (dy < 0) then
        na := - na;
      hitAngle := na;
    end;
```

7.3 ▫ The Main Program

The previous section described the static characteristics of the program. The dynamic characteristics are set in motion when a mouse press occurs, at which time the following function is invoked.

```
procedure TfrmGraphics.DoClick (Sender: TObject;
    Button: TMouseButton; Shift: TShiftState; X, Y: Integer);
var
    bptr : TBall;
begin
    cueBall.energy := 20.0;
    cueBall.setDirection(hitAngle(cueBall.x - x, cueBall.y - y));
      { then loop as long as called for }
    ballMoved := true;
    while ballMoved do begin
      ballMoved := false;
      bptr := listOfBalls;
      while bptr <> nil do begin
        bptr.update;
        bptr := bptr.link;
      end;
    end;
end;
```

The remainder of the program is relatively straightforward and will not be presented here. The complete source is given in Appendix B. The majority of the code is concerned with the initialization of the new objects and with the event loop that waits for the user to perform an action. The programmer uses the Delphi development environment to match events, such as mouse presses, with procedures, such as DoClick.

To stress the point we made at the beginning of this chapter, the most important feature of this case study is the way control has been decentralized and the objects themselves have been given the power to control and direct the flow of execution. When a mouse press occurs, all that happens is that the cue ball is provided with a certain amount of energy. Thereafter, the interaction of the balls drives the simulation.

7.4 ▢ Using Inheritance

In Chapter 1 we informally introduced inheritance, and in Chapter 8 we discuss how inheritance works in each of the languages we are considering. In this section we describe how inheritance can be used to simplify the billiards simulation, foreshadowing the discussion we will present in the next chapter. The reader may wish to return to this section after reading the general treatment of inheritance in Chapter 8.

We have, in fact, been using inheritance throughout our development of the classes for our application. All of our classes inherit from the system class TObject, but since we did not use any behavior from this class, the issue was not very important. Now we will create parent classes that do embody useful behavior.

The first step in using inheritance in our billiards simulation is to define a general class for "graphical objects." This class includes all three items: balls, walls, and holes. The parent class is defined as follows.

```
type
 TBall = class; (* forward declaration *)

 TGraphicalObject = (TObject)
 public
     constructor Create(ix, iy : Integer; il : TGraphicalObject);
     procedure draw (canvas : TCanvas); virtual; abstract;
     function hasIntersected (aBall : TBall): Boolean; virtual; abstract;
     procedure hitBy (aBall : TBall); virtual; abstract;
     procedure update; virtual;
 private
     x, y : Integer;
     link : TGraphicalObject;
 end;
```

Note the forward declaration for the class TBall. This allows the class TGraph-icalObject to declare arguments of type TBall, even though the class definition has not yet been seen.

Every graphical object has a location and a link. The constructor sets these values. The methods draw, hasIntersected, and hitBy are declared as virtual and abstract. This means they are not defined in the parent class but must be redefined in the child classes. The method update is declared as virtual but not abstract. In the parent class it is defined to do nothing. This behavior will be overridden by class TBall but not by the other two.

The classes Ball, Wall, and Hole are then declared as subclasses of the general class GraphicalObject and need not repeat the declarations for data areas or functions unless they are being overridden.

```
THole = class(TGraphicalObject)
public
  constructor create
    (ix, iy : Integer; ilink : TGraphicalObject); overload;
  procedure draw (canvas : TCanvas);  override;
  function hasIntersected(aBall : TBall) : Boolean;  override;
  procedure hitBy (aBall : TBall); override;
end;
```

Compare this declaration to the one given earlier and note how we have now eliminated the declaration for the data fields, since they have been moved to the parent class.

Constructors for the child classes must explicitly invoke the constructors for their parent classes, as in the following constructor for class TBall.

```
constructor TBall.Create (ix, iy : Integer; iLink : TGraphicalObject);
begin
  inherited Create(ix, iy, iLink);
  setDirection(0.0);
  energy := 0.0;
end;
```

By making CueBall a subclass of Ball, we can eliminate the conditional statement in the routine that draws the ball's image.

```
TCueBall = class(TBall)
public
        procedure draw (canvas : TCanvas); override;
end;


procedure TBall.draw(canvas : TCanvas);
```

```
begin
        with canvas do begin
                Brush.Style := bsSolid;
                Brush.Color := clBlack;
                Ellipse(x-5, y-5, x+5, y+5);
        end;
end;

procedure TCueBall.draw (canvas : TCanvas);
begin
        with canvas do begin
                Brush.Style := bsSolid;
                Brush.Color := clWhite;
                Ellipse(x-5, y-5, x+5, y+5);
        end;
end;
```

The greatest simplification comes from the fact that it is now possible to keep all graphical objects on a single linked list. Thus, the routine that draws the entire screen, for example, can be written as follows.

```
procedure TfrmGraphics.DrawExample(Sender: TObject);
var
  gptr : TGraphicalObject;
begin
  with imgGraph.Canvas do begin
    Brush.Color := clWhite;
    Brush.Style := bsSolid;
    FillRect(Rect(0, 0, 700, 700));
  end;
  gptr := listOfObjects;
  while (gptr <> nil) do begin
    gptr.draw(imgGraph.Canvas);
    gptr := gptr.link;
  end;
end;
```

The most important point in this code concerns the invocation of the function draw within the loop. Despite the fact that there is only one function call written here, sometimes the function invoked will be from class TBall; at other times it will be from class TWall or class THole. The fact that one function call might result in many different function bodies being invoked is a form of *polymorphism*. We will discuss this important topic in more detail in Chapter 14.

The routine that tests to see if a moving ball has hit anything in the function Ball.update is similarly simplified. This can be seen in the complete source listing provided in Appendix B.

Summary ▣

In our second case study we examined a graphical program that simulates the behavior of a pool table. Once more our motivation for presenting the case study was not so much the problem being addressed as it was the manner in which the problem was being solved. The balls, holes, and walls in the game are described as independently reacting agents. When the user interacts with the game by means of a mouse press, the effect is to impart some energy to the cue ball, thereby forcing it to move. Thereafter the objects interact among themselves until all the balls run out of energy.

Further Information ▣

In the first two editions of the book, this case study was presented in Apple Object Pascal instead of Delphi. Those versions can still be found in the Web site ftp://ftp.cs.orst.edu/pub/budd/oopintro.

As we noted at the beginning of this chapter, our concern here is with the programming language aspects of Delphi, which are only a small part of the entire Delphi system. Further information on Delphi can be found in [Lischner 2000, Kerman 2002]. Borland also provides a wealth of online material with the Delphi integrated program development system.

Self-Study Questions ▣

1. Give some examples of how the design makes holes, walls, and balls responsible for their own behavior.
2. By making each graphical object into a separate class, and making each responsible for a different aspect of behavior, the object-oriented design is able to support a great deal of information hiding. This, in turn, leads to programs that are considerably easier to modify than when conventional techniques are used. To illustrate this, explain what sections of code would need to be modified to produce each of the following changes.

   ▪ Colored balls, rather than black and white
   ▪ Walls that absorb a bit of energy when they reflect a ball
   ▪ Holes that make a sound when they absorb a ball
   ▪ Balls that make a sound when they strike

Exercises ⊡

1. Suppose you want to perform a certain action every time the billiards program executes the event loop task. Where is the best place to insert this code?

2. Suppose you want to make the balls colored. What portions of the program do you need to change?

3. Suppose you want to add pockets on the side walls, as on a conventional pool table. What portions of the program do you need to change?

4. The billiards program uses a "breadth-first" technique, cycling repeatedly over the list of balls, moving each a little as long as any ball has energy. An alternative, and in some ways more object-oriented, approach is to have each ball continue to update itself as long as it possesses any energy and update any ball that it hits. With this technique, it is only necessary to start the cue ball moving in order to put the simulation in motion. Revise the program to use this approach. Which do you think provides a more realistic simulation? Why?

5. A hole has the same graphical representation as a ball, namely a round black spot. Similarly the algorithms used to determine if a ball has intersected are the same for balls and holes. Given this, would it make sense to declare TBall as a child class of THole? What would be the advantages of doing so? What might be some problems introduced by this modification?

CHAPTER 8

Inheritance and Substitution

The first step in learning object-oriented programming is understanding the basic philosophy of organizing the performance of a task as the interaction of loosely coupled software components. This organizational approach was the central lesson in the case studies of Chapters 6 and 7.

The *next* step in learning object-oriented programming is organizing classes into a hierarchical structure based on the concept of inheritance. By *inheritance*, we mean the property that instances of a child class (or subclass) can access both data and behavior (methods) associated with a parent class (or superclass).

8.1 ▫ An Intuitive Description of Inheritance

Let us return to Chris and Fred, the customer and florist from the first chapter. There is a certain behavior we expect florists to exhibit, not because they are florists but simply because they are shopkeepers. For example, we expect Fred to request money for a transaction and in turn give back a receipt. These activities are not unique to florists but are common to bakers, grocers, stationers, car dealers, and other merchants. It is as though we have associated certain behavior with the general category Shopkeeper, and because Florists are a specialized form of shopkeepers, the behavior is automatically identified with the subclass.

In programming languages, inheritance means that the behavior and data associated with child classes are always an *extension* (that is, a larger set) of the properties associated with parent classes. A subclass will have all the properties of the parent class and other properties as well. On the other hand, since a child class is a more specialized (or restricted) form of the parent class, it is also, in a certain sense, a *contraction* of the parent type. This tension between inheritance as expansion and inheritance as contraction is a source for much of the power inherent in the technique, but at the same time it causes much confusion as to its proper employment. We will see this when we examine a few of the uses of inheritance in a subsequent section.

Inheritance is always transitive, so a class can inherit features from superclasses many levels away. That is, if class Dog is a subclass of class Mammal, and class Mammal is a subclass of class Animal, then Dog will inherit attributes both from Mammal and from Animal.

8.1.1   The is-a test

As we noted in Chapter 2, there is a rule-of-thumb that is commonly used to test whether two concepts should be linked by an inheritance relationship. This heuristic is termed the *is-a* test. The is-a test says that to tell if concept A should be linked by inheritance to concept B, try forming the English sentence "A(n) A is a(n) B." If the sentence "sounds right" to your ear, then inheritance is most likely appropriate in this situation. For example, the following all seem like reasonable assertions.

A bird is an animal.

A cat is a mammal.

An apple pie is a pie.

A TextWindow is a window.

A ball is a GraphicalObject.

An IntegerArray is an array.

On the other hand, the following assertions seem strange for one reason or another, and hence inheritance is likely not appropriate.

A bird is a mammal.

An apple pie is an apple.

An engine is a car.

A ball is a wall.

An IntegerArray is an integer.

There are times when inheritance can reasonably be used even when the is-a test fails. Nevertheless, for the vast majority of situations, it gives a reliable indicator for the appropriate use of the technique.

8.1.2   Reasons to use inheritance

Although there are many uses for the mechanism of inheritance, two motivations far outweigh all other concerns.

- Inheritance as a means of code reuse. Because a child class can inherit behavior from a parent class, the code does not need to be rewritten for the child. This can greatly reduce the amount of code needed to develop a new idea.
- Inheritance as a means of concept reuse. This occurs when a child class overrides behavior defined in the parent. Although no code is shared between parent and child, the child and parent share the definition of the method.

An example of the latter was described in the previous chapter. The variable that was declared as holding a GraphicalObject could, in fact, be holding a Ball. When the message draw was given to the object, the code from class Ball, and not from GraphicalObject, was the method selected. Both code and concept reuse often appear in the same class hierarchies.

Public, Private, and Protected

In earlier chapters we have seen the use of the terms public and private. A public feature is accessible to code outside the class definition, whereas a private feature is accessible only within the class definition. Inheritance introduces a third alternative. In C++ (also in C#, Delphi, Ruby, and several other languages) a protected feature is accessible only within a class definition or within the definition of any child classes. Thus, a protected feature is more accessible than a private one and less accessible than a public feature. This is illustrated by the following example:

```
class Parent {
private:
  int three;
protected:
  int two;
public:
  int one;
  Parent () { one = two = three = 42; }
  void inParent ()
    { cout << one << two << three; /* all legal */ }
};

class Child : public Parent {
public:
```

continued

Public, Private, and Protected (Continued)

```
    void inChild () {
        cout << one;   // legal
        cout << two;   // legal
        cout << three; // error - not legal
    }
};

void main () {
    Child c;
    cout << c.one;   // legal
    cout << c.two;   // error - not legal
    cout << c.three; // error - not legal
}
```

The lines marked as error will generate compiler errors. The private feature can be used only within the parent class, and the protected feature only within the parent and child class. Only public features can be used outside the class definitions.

Java uses the same keyword, but there protected features are legal within the same package in which they are declared.

8.2 ▫ Inheritance in Various Languages

Object-oriented languages can be divided into those languages that require every class to inherit from an existing parent class and those languages that do not. Java, Smalltalk, Objective-C, and Delphi Pascal are examples of the former, while C++ and Apple Pascal are examples of the latter. For the former group we have already seen the syntax used to indicate inheritance—for example, in Figure 4.3 of Chapter 4. In Figure 8.1 we reiterate some of these and also show the syntax used for some of the languages in the second group.

One advantage given to those languages that insist that all classes inherit from an existing class is that there is then a single root that is ancestor to all objects. This root class is termed Object in Smalltalk and Objective-C, and it is termed TObject in Delphi Pascal. Any behavior provided by this root class is inherited by all objects. Thus, every object is guaranteed to possess a common minimal level of functionality.

The disadvantage of a single large inheritance tree is that it combines all classes into a tightly coupled unit. By having several independent inheritance hierarchies, programs in C++ and other languages that do not make this restriction are not

C++

```
class Wall : public GraphicalObject {
    .
    .
    .
}
```

C#

```
class Wall : GraphicalObject {
    .
    .
    .
}
```

CLOS

```
(defclass Wall (GraphicalObject) () )
```

Java

```
class Wall extends GraphicalObject {
    .
    .
    .
}
```

Object Pascal

```
type
    Wall = object (GraphicalObject)
        .
        .
        .
    end;
```

Python

```
class Wall(GraphicalObject):
    def __init__(self):
        .
        .
        .
```

Ruby

```
class Wall < GraphicalObject
    .
    .
    .
end
```

▢ Figure 8.1 —— Syntax used to indicate inheritance in several languages

forced to carry a large library of classes, only a few of which may be used in any one program. Of course, that means there is no programmer-defined functionality that *all* objects are guaranteed to possess.

In part, the differing views of objects are one more distinction between languages that use dynamic typing and those that use static typing. In dynamic languages, objects are characterized chiefly by the messages they understand. If two objects understand the same set of messages and react in similar ways, they are, for all practical purposes, indistinguishable regardless of the relationships of their respective classes. Under these circumstances, it is useful to have all objects inherit a large portion of their behavior from a common base class.

8.3 ▫ Subclass, Subtype, and Substitution

Consider the relationship of a data type associated with a parent class to a data type associated with a derived, or child, class in a statically typed object-oriented language. The following observations can be made.

- Instances of the child class must possess all data members associated with the parent class.
- Instances of the child class must implement, through inheritance at least (if not explicitly overridden), all functionality defined for the parent class. (They can also define new functionality, but that is unimportant for the present argument.)
- Thus, an instance of a child class can mimic the behavior of the parent class and should be *indistinguishable* from an instance of the parent class if substituted in a similar situation.

We will see later in this chapter, when we examine the various ways in which inheritance can be used, that this is not always a valid argument. Nevertheless, it is a good description of our idealized view of inheritance. We will therefore formalize this ideal in what is called the *principle of substitution*.

The principle of substitution says that if we have two classes, A and B, such that class B is a subclass of class A (perhaps several times removed), it should be possible to substitute instances of class B for instances of class A in *any situation* with *no observable effect*.

The term *subtype* is used to refer to a subclass relationship in which the principle of substitution is maintained to distinguish such forms from the general *subclass* relationship, which may or may not satisfy this principle. We saw a use of the principle of substitution in Chapter 7. Section 7.4 described the following procedure.

```
procedure drawBoard;
var
  gptr : GraphicalObject;
```

```
begin
   (* draw each graphical object *)
   gptr := listOfObjects;
   while gptr <> nil do begin
      gptr.draw;
      gptr := gptr.link;
   end;
end;
```

The global variable listOfObjects maintains a list of graphical objects, which can be any of three types. The variable gptr is declared to be simply a graphical object, yet during the course of executing the loop it takes on values that are, in fact, derived from each of the subclasses. Sometimes gptr holds a ball, sometimes a hole, and sometimes a wall. In each case, when the draw function is invoked, the correct method for the current value of gptr will be executed—not the method in the declared class GraphicalObject. For this code to operate correctly, it is imperative that the functionality of each of these subclasses match the expected functionality specified by the parent class; that is, the subclasses must also be subtypes.

All object-oriented languages will support the principle of substitution, although some will require additional syntax when a method is overridden. Most support the concept in a very straightforward fashion; the parent class simply holds a value from the child class. The one major exception to this is the language C++. In C++ only pointers and references truly support substitution; variables that are simply declared as value (and not as pointers) do not support substitution. We will see why this property is necessary in C++ in a later chapter.

*8.3.1 Substitution and strong typing

Statically typed languages (such as C++ and Object Pascal) place much more emphasis on the principle of substitution than do dynamically typed languages (such as Smalltalk and Objective-C). The reason for this is that statically typed languages tend to characterize objects by their class, whereas dynamically typed languages tend to characterize objects by their behavior. For example, a polymorphic function (a function that can take objects of various classes) in a statically typed language can ensure a certain level of functionality only by insisting that all arguments be subclasses of a given class. Since in a dynamically typed language arguments are not typed at all, the same requirement would be simply that an argument must be able to respond to a certain set of messages.

An example of this difference would be a function that requires an argument to be an instance of a subclass of Measureable, as opposed to a function that requires an argument to understand the messages lessThan and equal. The former is characterizing an object by its class, and the latter is characterizing an object by its behavior. Both forms of type checking are found in object-oriented languages.

8.4 ▫ Overriding and Virtual Methods

In Chapter 1 we noted that child classes may sometimes find it necessary to *override* the behavior they would otherwise inherit from their parent classes. In syntactic terms, what this means is that a child class will define a method using the same name and type signature as one found in the parent class. When overriding is combined with substitution, we have the situation where a variable is declared as one class but holds a value from a child class, and a method matching a given message is found in both classes. In almost all cases when this situation exists, we want to execute the method found in the child class, ignoring the method from the parent class.

In many object-oriented languages (Smalltalk, Java) this desired behavior will occur naturally as soon as a child class overrides a method in the parent class using the same type signature. Some languages, on the other hand, require the programmer to indicate that such a substitution is permitted. Many languages use the keyword virtual to indicate this. It may be necessary, as in C++, to place the keyword in the parent class[1] (indicating that overriding *may* take place; it does not indicate that it necessarily will take place) or, as in Object Pascal, in the child class (indicating that overriding *has* taken place). Or it may be required in both places, as in C# and Delphi. Figure 8.2 shows the syntax used for overriding in various languages.

C++

```
class GraphicalObject {
public:
    virtual void draw();
};

class Ball : public Graphicalobject {
public:
    virtual void draw(); // virtual optional here
};
```

▫ Figure 8.2 —— Overriding in various languages

---

1. Virtual overriding in C++ is actually more complex for reasons we will develop in the next several chapters.

C#

```
class GraphicalObject {
    public viritual void draw () { ... }
}

class Ball : Graphical Object {
    public override void draw () { ... }
}
```

Delphi

```
type
    GraphicalObject = class (TObject)
        .
        .
        .
        procedure draw; virtual;
    end;

    Ball = class (GraphicalObject)
        .
        .
        .
        procedure draw; override;
    end;
```

Object Pascal

```
type
    GraphicalObject = object
        .
        .
        .
        procedure draw;
    end;

    Ball = object (GraphicalObject)
        .
        .
        .
        procedure draw; override;
    end;
```

⊡ Figure 8.2 —— Continued

8.5 ▫ Interfaces and Abstract Classes

In Chapter 4 we briefly introduced the concept of an interface in Java and other languages. As with classes, interfaces are allowed to inherit from other interfaces and are even permitted to inherit from multiple parent interfaces. Although the specification that a new class inherits from a parent class and the specification that it implements an interface are not exactly the same, they are sufficiently similar that we will henceforth use the term *inheritance* to indicate both actions.

Several object-oriented languages support an idea, termed an *abstract method*, that is midway between classes and interfaces. In Java and C#, for example, a class can define one or more methods using the keyword abstract. No body is then provided for the method. A child class *must* implement any abstract methods before an instance of the class can be created. Thus, abstract methods specify behavior in the parent class, but the behavior itself must be provided by the child class.

```
abstract class Window {
    ⋮

    abstract public void paint ();   // draw contents of window
    ⋮

}
```

An entire class can be named as abstract, whether or not it includes any abstract methods. It is not legal to create an instance of an abstract class; it is only legal to use it as a parent class for purposes of inheritance.

In C++ the idea of an abstract method is termed a *pure virtual method* and is indicated using the assignment operator.

```
class Window {
public:
    ⋮

    virtual void paint () = 0; // assignment makes it pure virtual
};
```

A class can have both abstract (or pure virtual) methods and nonabstract methods. A class in which all methods were declared as abstract (or pure virtual) would correspond to the Java idea of an interface.

Abstract methods can be simulated even when the language does not provide explicit support for the concept. In Smalltalk, for example, programmers frequently define a method to generate an error if it is invoked, with the expectation that it will be overwritten in child classes.

```
writeTo: stream
  ↑ self error: 'subclass must override writeTo'
```

This is not exactly the same as a true abstract method, since it does not preclude the creation of instances of the class. Nevertheless, if an instance is created and this method invoked, the program will quickly fail, so such errors are easily detected.

8.6 ▫ Forms of Inheritance

Inheritance is used in a surprising variety of ways. In this section we will describe a few of its more common uses. Note that the following list represents general abstract categories and is not intended to be exhaustive. Furthermore, it sometimes happens that two or more descriptions are applicable to a single situation because some methods in a single class use inheritance in one way, while others use it in another.

8.6.1   Subclassing for specialization (subtyping)

Probably the most common use of inheritance and subclassing is for specialization. In subclassing for specialization, the new class is a specialized form of the parent class but satisfies the specifications of the parent in all relevant respects. Thus, in this form the principle of substitution is explicitly upheld. Along with the following category (subclassing for specification) this is the most ideal form of inheritance and something that a good design should strive for.

Here is an example of subclassing for specialization. A class Window provides general windowing operations (moving, resizing, iconification, and so on). A specialized subclass TextEditWindow inherits the window operations and *in addition* provides facilities that allow the window to display textual material and the user to edit the text values. Because the text edit window satisfies all the properties we expect of a window in general (thus, a TextEditWindow window is a subtype of Window in addition to being a subclass), we recognize this situation as an example of subclassing for specialization.

8.6.2   Subclassing for specification

Another frequent use for inheritance is to guarantee that classes maintain a certain common interface—that is, they implement the same methods. The parent class can be a combination of implemented operations and operations that are deferred to the child classes. Often, there is no interface change of any sort between the parent class and the child class—the child merely implements behavior described, but not implemented, in the parent.

This is in essence a special case of subclassing for specialization, except that the subclasses are not refinements of an existing type but rather realizations of an incomplete abstract specification. In such cases the parent class is sometimes known as an *abstract specification class*.

A class that implements an interface is always fulfilling this form of inheritance. However, subclassing for specification can also arise in other ways. In the billiards simulation example presented in Chapter 7, for example, the class GraphicalObject was an abstract class, since it described, but did not implement, the methods for drawing the object and responding to a hit by a ball. The subsequent classes Ball, Wall, and Hole then used subclassing for specification when they provided meanings for these methods.

In general, subclassing for specification can be recognized when the parent class does not implement actual behavior but merely defines the behavior that will be implemented in child classes.

8.6.3   Subclassing for construction

A class can often inherit almost all of its desired functionality from a parent class, perhaps changing only the names of the methods used to interface to the class or modifying the arguments in a certain fashion. This may be true even if the new class and the parent class fail to share the *is-a* relationship.

For example, the Smalltalk class hierarchy implements a generalization of an array called Dictionary. A dictionary is a collection of key-value pairs, like an array, but the keys can be arbitrary values. A *symbol table*, such as might be used in a compiler, can be considered a dictionary indexed by symbol names in which the values have a fixed format (the symbol-table entry record). A class SymbolTable can therefore be made a subclass of the class Dictionary, with new methods defined that are specific to the use as a symbol table. Another example might be forming a *set* data abstraction on top of a base class that provides *list* methods. In both these cases, the child class is not a more specialized form of the parent class because we would never think of substituting an instance of the child class in a situation where an instance of the parent class is being used.

A common use of subclassing for construction occurs when classes are created to write values to a binary file—for example, in a persistent storage system. A parent class may implement only the ability to write raw binary data. A subclass is constructed for every structure that is saved. The subclass implements a save procedure for the data type, which uses the behavior of the parent type to do the actual storage.[2]

---

2. This example illustrates the blurred lines between categories. If the child class implements the storage using a different method name, we say it is subclassing for construction. If, on the

```
class Storable {
  void writeByte(unsigned char);
  };

class StoreMyStruct : public Storable {
  void writeStruct (MyStruct & aStruct);
  };
```

Subclassing for construction tends to be frowned upon in statically typed languages, since it often directly breaks the principle of substitution (forming subclasses that are not subtypes). On the other hand, because it is often a fast and easy route to developing new data abstractions, it is widely employed in dynamically typed languages. Many instances of subclassing for construction can be found in the Smalltalk standard library.

We will investigate an example of subclassing for construction in Chapter 9. We will also see that C++ provides an interesting mechanism, *private inheritance*, which permits subclassing for construction without breaking the principle of substitution.

8.6.4 Subclassing for generalization

Using inheritance to subclass for generalization is, in a certain sense, the opposite of subclassing for specialization. Here, a subclass extends the behavior of the parent class to create a more general kind of object. Subclassing for generalization is often applicable when we build on a base of existing classes that we do not wish to, or cannot, modify.

Consider a graphics display system in which a class Window has been defined for displaying on a simple black-and-white background. You could create a subtype ColoredWindow that lets the background color be something other than white by adding an additional field to store the color and overriding the inherited window display code that specifies the background be drawn in that color.

Subclassing for generalization frequently occurs when the overall design is based primarily on data values and only secondarily on behavior. This is shown in the colored window example, since a colored window contains data fields that are not necessary in the simple window case.

As a rule, subclassing for generalization should be avoided in favor of inverting the type hierarchy and using subclassing for specialization. However, this is not always possible.

---

other hand, the child class uses the same name as the parent class, we might say the result is subclassing for specification.

8.6.5   Subclassing for extension

While subclassing for generalization modifies or expands on the existing functionality of an object, subclassing for extension adds totally new abilities. Subclassing
for extension can be distinguished from subclassing for generalization in that the
latter must override at least one method from the parent and the functionality
is tied to that of the parent. Extension simply adds new methods to those of the
parent, and the functionality is less strongly tied to the existing methods of the
parent.

An example of subclassing for extension is a StringSet class that inherits from
a generic Set class but is specialized for holding string values. Such a class might
provide additional methods for string-related operations—for example, "search
by prefix," which returns a subset of all the elements of the set that begin with a
certain string value. These operations are meaningful for the subclass but are not
particularly relevant to the parent class.

As the functionality of the parent remains available and untouched, subclassing for extension does not contravene the principle of substitution, and so such
subclasses are always subtypes.

8.6.6   Subclassing for limitation

Subclassing for limitation occurs when the behavior of the subclass is smaller or
more restrictive than the behavior of the parent class. Like subclassing for generalization, subclassing for limitation occurs most frequently when a programmer
is building on a base of existing classes that should not, or cannot, be modified.

For example, an existing class library provides a double-ended queue, or
deque, data structure. Elements can be added or removed from either end of the
deque, but the programmer wishes to write a stack class, enforcing the property
that elements can be added to or removed from only one end of the stack.

In a manner similar to subclassing for construction, the programmer can make
the Stack class a subclass of the existing Deque class and can modify or override the
undesired methods so that they produce an error message if used. These methods
override existing methods and eliminate their functionality, which characterizes
subclassing for limitation.

Because subclassing for limitation is an explicit contravention of the principle
of substitution, and because it builds subclasses that are not subtypes, it should
be avoided whenever possible.

8.6.7   Subclassing for variance

Subclassing for variance is employed when two or more classes have similar implementations but do not seem to possess any hierarchical relationships between

the abstract concepts represented by the classes. The code necessary to control a mouse, for example, may be nearly identical to the code required to control a graphics tablet. Conceptually, however, there is no reason why class Mouse should be made a subclass of class Tablet, or the other way around. One of the two classes is then arbitrarily selected to be the parent, with the common code being inherited by the other and device-specific code being overridden.

Usually, however, a better alternative is to factor out the common code into an abstract class, say PointingDevice, and to have both classes inherit from this common ancestor. As with subclassing for generalization, this choice may not be available if you are building on a base of existing classes.

8.6.8　Subclassing for combination

A common situation is a subclass that represents a *combination* of features from two or more parent classes. A teaching assistant, for example, may have characteristics of both a teacher and a student and can therefore logically behave as both. The ability of a class to inherit from two or more parent classes is known as *multiple inheritance*; it is sufficiently subtle and complex that we will devote an entire chapter to the concept.

8.6.9　Summary of the forms of inheritance

We can summarize the various forms of inheritance by the following list.

- Specialization. The child class is a special case of the parent class; in other words, the child class is a subtype of the parent class.
- Specification. The parent class defines behavior that is implemented in the child class but not in the parent class.
- Construction. The child class makes use of the behavior provided by the parent class but is not a subtype of the parent class.
- Generalization. The child class modifies or overrides some of the methods of the parent class.
- Extension. The child class adds new functionality to the parent class but does not change any inherited behavior.
- Limitation. The child class restricts the use of some of the behavior inherited from the parent class.
- Variance. The child class and parent class are variants of each other, and the class-subclass relationship is arbitrary.
- Combination. The child class inherits features from more than one parent class. This is multiple inheritance and will be the subject of a later chapter.

*8.7 ▫ Variations on Inheritance

In this section we will examine a number of mostly single-language specific variations on the themes of inheritance and overriding.

8.7.1   Anonymous classes in Java

Occasionally a situation arises where a programmer needs to create a simple class and knows there will never be more than one instance of the class. Such an object is often termed a *singleton*. The Java programming language provides a mechanism for creating such an object without even having to give a name to the class being used to define the object—hence the name for this technique, *anonymous classes*.

In order to be able to create an anonymous class, several requirements must be met.

1. Only one instance of the anonymous class can be created.
2. The class must inherit from a parent class or interface and not require a constructor for initialization.

These two conditions frequently arise in the context of user interfaces. For example, in Chapter 22 we will encounter a class named ButtonAdapter that is used to create graphical buttons. To give behavior to a button, the programmer must form a new class that inherits from ButtonAdapter and overrides the method pressed. Since there is only one such object, this can be done with an anonymous class (also sometimes termed a *class definition expression*).

Graphical elements are added to a window using the method add. To place a new button in a window, all that is necessary is the following.

```
Window p = ...;

p.add (new ButtonAdapter("Quit"){
  public void pressed () { System.exit(0); }
  }
);
```

Study carefully the argument being passed to the add operator. It includes the creation of a new value, indicated by the new operator. But rather than ending the expression with the closing parenthesis on the argument list for new, a curly brace appears as if in a class definition. In fact, this is a new class definition. A subclass of ButtonAdapter is being formed, and a single instance of this class will be created. Any methods required by this new class are given immediately in-line. In this case, the new class overrides the method named pressed. The closing curly brace terminates the anonymous class expression.

8.7.2 Inheritance and constructors

A constructor, you will recall, is a procedure that is invoked implicitly during the creation of a new object value and that guarantees that the newly created object is properly initialized. Inheritance complicates this process, since both the parent and the new child class may have initialization code to perform. Thus, code from both classes must be executed.

In Java, C++, and other languages the constructor for both parent and child will automatically be executed as long as the parent constructor does not require additional parameters. When the parent does require parameters, the child must explicitly provide them. In Java this is done using the keyword super.

```
class Child extends Parent {
  public Child (int x) {
    super (x + 2); // invoke parent constructor
    .
    .
    .
  }
}
```

In C++ the same task is accomplished by writing the parent class name in the form of an initializer.

```
class Child : public Parent {
public:
  Child (int x) : Parent(x+2) { ... }
};
```

In Delphi a constructor for a child class must always invoke the constructor for the parent class, even if the parent class constructor takes no arguments. The syntax is the same for executing the parent class behavior in any overridden method.

```
constructor TChildClass.Create;
begin
  inherited Create; // execute constructor in parent
end
```

Arguments to the parent constructor are added as part of the call.

```
constructor TChildClass.Create (x : Integer);
begin
  inherited Create(x + 2);
end
```

Similarly, an initialization method in Python does not automatically invoke the function in the parent; hence the programmer must not forget to do this task.

```
class Child(Parent):
  def __init__ (self):
    # first initialize parent
    Parent.__init__(self)
    # then do our initialization
    .
    .
    .
```

8.7.3   Virtual destructors

Recall from Chapter 5 that in C++ a destructor is a function that will be invoked just before the memory for a variable is recovered. Destructors are used to perform whatever tasks are necessary to ensure a value is properly deleted. For example, a destructor will frequently free any dynamically allocated memory the variable may hold.

If substitution and overriding are anticipated, then it is important that the destructor be declared as virtual. Failure to do so may result in destructors for child classes not being invoked. This following example shows this error.

```
class Parent {
public:
    // warning, destructor not declared virtual
  ~Parent () { cout << "in parent\n"; }
};

class Child : public Parent {
public:
  ~Child () { cout << "in child\n"; }
};
```

If an instance of the child class is held by a pointer to the parent class and subsequently released (say, by a delete statement), then only the parent destructor will be invoked.

```
  Parent * p = new Child();
  delete p;
in parent
```

If the parent destructor is declared as virtual, then both the parent and child destructors will be executed. In C++ it is a good idea to include a virtual destructor, even if it performs no action, if there is any possibility that a class may later be subclassed.

8.8 ▫ The Benefits of Inheritance

In this section we describe some of the many important benefits of the proper use of inheritance.

8.8.1   Software reusability

When behavior is inherited from another class, the code that provides that behavior does not have to be rewritten. This may seem obvious, but the implications are important. Many programmers spend much of their time rewriting code they have written many times before—for example, to search for a pattern in a string or to insert a new element into a table. With object-oriented techniques, these functions can be written once and reused.

Other benefits of reusable code include increased reliability (the more situations in which code is used, the greater the opportunities for discovering errors) and the decreased maintenance cost because of sharing by all users of the code.

8.8.2   Code sharing

Code sharing can occur on several levels with object-oriented techniques. On one level, many users or projects can use the same classes. (Brad Cox [Cox 1986] calls these software-ICs, in analogy to the integrated circuits used in hardware design.) Another form of sharing occurs when two or more classes developed by a single programmer as part of a project inherit from a single parent class. For example, a Set and an Array may both be considered a form of Collection. When this happens, two or more types of objects will share the code that they inherit. This code needs to be written only once and will contribute only once to the size of the resulting program.

8.8.3   Consistency of interface

When two or more classes inherit from the same superclass, we are assured that the behavior they inherit will be the same in all cases. Thus, it is easier to guarantee that interfaces to similar objects are in fact similar and that the user is not presented with a confusing collection of objects that are almost the same but behave, and are interacted with, very differently.

8.8.4   Software components

In Chapter 1, we noted that inheritance provides programmers with the ability to construct reusable software components. The goal is to permit the development of new and novel applications that nevertheless require little or no actual coding.

Already, several such libraries are commercially available, and we can expect many more specialized systems to appear in time.

8.8.5   Rapid prototyping

When a software system is constructed largely out of reusable components, development time can be concentrated on understanding the new and unusual portion of the system. Thus, software systems can be generated more quickly and easily, leading to a style of programming known as *rapid prototyping* or *exploratory programming*. A prototype system is developed, users experiment with it, a second system is produced that is based on experience with the first, further experimentation takes place, and so on for several iterations. Such programming is particularly useful in situations where the goals and requirements of the system are only vaguely understood when the project begins.

8.8.6   Polymorphism and frameworks

Software produced conventionally is generally written from the bottom up, although it may be *designed* from the top down. That is, the lower-level routines are written, and on top of these slightly higher abstractions are produced, and on top of these even more abstract elements are generated. This process is like building a wall, where every brick must be laid on top of an already laid brick.

Normally, code portability decreases as one moves up the levels of abstraction. That is, the lowest-level routines may be used in several different projects, and perhaps even the next level of abstraction may be reused, but the higher-level routines are intimately tied to a particular application. The lower-level pieces can be carried to a new system and generally make sense standing on their own; the higher-level components generally make sense (because of declarations or data dependencies) only when they are built on top of specific lower-level units.

Polymorphism in programming languages permits the programmer to generate high-level reusable components that can be tailored to fit different applications by changes in their low-level parts. We will have much more to say about this topic in subsequent chapters.

8.8.7   Information hiding

A programmer who reuses a software component needs only to understand the nature of the component and its interface. It is not necessary for the programmer to have detailed information concerning matters such as the techniques used to implement the component. Thus, the interconnectedness between software systems is reduced. We earlier identified the interconnected nature of conventional software as being one of the principal causes of software complexity.

8.9 □ The Costs of Inheritance

Although the benefits of inheritance in object-oriented programming are great, almost nothing is without cost of one sort or another. For this reason, we must consider the cost of object-oriented programming techniques and in particular the cost of inheritance.

8.9.1   Execution speed

It is seldom possible for general-purpose software tools to be as fast as carefully hand-crafted systems. Thus, inherited methods, which must deal with arbitrary subclasses, are often slower than specialized code.

Yet, concern about efficiency is often misplaced.[3] First, the difference is often small. Second, the reduction in execution speed may be balanced by an increase in the speed of software development. Finally, most programmers actually have little idea of how execution time is being used in their programs. It is far better to develop a working system, monitor it to discover where execution time is being used, and improve those sections, than to spend an inordinate amount of time worrying about efficiency early in a project.

8.9.2   Program size

The use of any software library frequently imposes a size penalty not imposed by systems constructed for a specific project. Although this expense may be substantial, as memory costs decrease, the size of programs becomes less important. Containing development costs and producing high-quality and error-free code rapidly are now more important than limiting the size of programs.

8.9.3   Message-passing overhead

Much has been made of the fact that message passing is by nature a more costly operation than simple procedure invocation. As with overall execution speed, however, overconcern about the cost of message passing is frequently penny-wise and pound-foolish. For one thing, the increased cost is often marginal—perhaps two or three additional assembly language instructions and a total time penalty of 10 percent. (Timing figures vary from language to language. The overhead of message passing will be much higher in dynamically bound languages, such

---

3. The following quote from an article by Bill Wulf offers some apt remarks on the importance of efficiency: "More computing sins are committed in the name of efficiency (without necessarily achieving it) than for any other single reason—including blind stupidity" [Wulf 1972].

as Smalltalk, and much lower in statically bound languages, such as C++.) This increased cost, like others, must be weighed against the many benefits of the object-oriented technique.

A few languages, notably C++, make a number of options available to the programmer that can reduce the message-passing overhead. These include eliminating the polymorphism from message passing (qualifying invocations of member functions by a class name, in C++ terms) and expanding in-line procedures. Similarly, the Delphi Pascal programmer can choose dynamic methods, which use a run-time lookup mechanism, or virtual methods, which use a slightly faster technique. Dynamic methods are inherently slower but require less space.

8.9.4   Program complexity

Although object-oriented programming is often touted as a solution to software complexity, in fact, overuse of inheritance can often simply replace one form of complexity with another. Understanding the control flow of a program that uses inheritance may require several multiple scans up and down the inheritance graph. This is what is known as the *yo-yo* problem, which we will discuss in more detail in a later chapter.

Summary ▣

In this chapter we began a detailed examination of inheritance and substitution, a topic that will be continued through the next several chapters. When a child class declares that it inherits from a parent class, code in the parent class does not have to be rewritten. Thus, inheritance is a powerful mechanism of code reuse. But this is not the only reason to use inheritance. In the abstract, a child class is a representative of the category formed by the parent class, and hence it makes sense that an instance of the child class could be used in those situations where we expect an instance of the parent class. This is known as the principle of *substitution*. But this is only an idealization. Not all types of inheritance support this ideal behavior.

We have described various forms of inheritance, noting when they seem to support substitution and when they may not.

The chapter concludes with descriptions of both the benefits of inheritance and the costs incurred through the use of the technique.

Further Reading ⊡

Many of the ideas introduced in this chapter will be developed and explored in more detail in subsequent chapters. Overriding is discussed in detail in Chapter 16. We will discuss static and dynamic typing more in Chapter 10 and polymorphism in more detail in Chapter 14.

In Section 8.1.2 we noted that inheritance is used both as a mechanism of code reuse and concept reuse. The fact that the same feature is serving two different purposes is a frequent criticism levied against object-oriented languages. Many writers have advocated separating these two tasks—for example, using inheritance of classes only for code reuse and using inheritance of interfaces (as, for example, in Java) for substitution (concept reuse). While this approach has a theoretical appeal, from a practical standpoint it complicates the task of programming and has not been widely adopted. See Exercise 5 for one way this could be accomplished.

The list describing the forms of inheritance is adopted from [Halbert 1987], although I have added some new categories of my own. The editable-window example is from [Meyer 1988a].

The principle of substitution is sometimes referred to as the *Liskov Substitution Principle*, since an early discussion of the idea was presented by Barbara Liskov and John Guttag [Liskov 1986].

Self-Study Questions ⊡

1. In what ways is a child class an extension of its parent? In what ways is it a contraction?

2. What is the is-a test for inheritance?

3. What are the two major reasons for the use of inheritance?

4. What is the principle of substitution? What is the argument used to justify its application?

5. How is a class that contains abstract methods similar to an interface? If not all methods are abstract, how is it different?

6. What features characterize each of the following forms of inheritance?

   a. Subclassing for Specialization
   b. Subclassing for Specification
   c. Subclassing for Construction
   d. Subclassing for Generalization
   e. Subclassing for Extension
   f. Subclassing for Limitation
   g. Subclassing for Variance

7. Why is subclassing for construction not normally considered to be a good idea?

8. Why is subclassing for limitation not a good idea?

9. How does inheritance facilitate software reuse?

10. How does it encourage consistency of interface?

11. How does it support the idea of rapid prototyping?

12. How does it encourage the principle of information hiding?

13. An anonymous class combines what two activities?

14. Why is the execution time cost incurred by the use of inheritance not usually important? What are some situations where it would be important?

Exercises ▫

1. Suppose you were required to program a project in a non-object-oriented language, such as Pascal or C. How would you simulate the notion of classes and methods? How would you simulate inheritance? Could you support multiple inheritance? Explain your answer.

2. We noted that the execution overhead associated with message passing is typically greater than the overhead associated with a conventional procedure call. How might you measure these overheads? For a language that supports both classes and procedures (such as C++ or Object Pascal), devise an experiment to determine the actual performance penalty of message passing.

3. Consider the three geometric concepts of a line (infinite in both directions), a ray (fixed at a point, infinite in one direction), and a segment (a portion of a line with fixed end points). How might you structure classes representing these three concepts in an inheritance hierarchy? Would your answer differ if you concentrated more on the data representation or more on the behavior? Characterize the type of inheritance you would use. Explain the reasoning behind your design.

4. The following appeared as an illustration of inheritance in a popular journal.

> Perhaps the most powerful concept in object-oriented programming systems is inheritance. Objects can be created by inheriting the properties of other objects, thus removing the need to write any code whatsoever! Suppose, for example, a program is to process complex numbers consisting of real and imaginary parts. In a complex number, the real and imaginary parts behave like real numbers, so all of the operations (+, -, /, *, sqrt, sin, cos, etc.) can be inherited from the class of objects call REAL, instead of having to be written in code. This has a major impact on programmer productivity.

    a. The quote seems to indicate that class Complex could be a child class of Real. Does the assertion that the child class Complex need not write any code seem plausible?

    b. Does this organization make sense in terms of the data members each class must maintain? Why or why not?

    c. Does this organization make sense in terms of the methods each class must support? Why or why not?

    d. Can you describe a better approach for creating a class Complex using an existing class Real? What benefit does your new class derive from the existing class?

5. In Section 8.1.2 we noted how inheritance is used for two different purposes: as a vehicle for code reuse and as a vehicle for substitution. Among the major object-oriented langauges, Java comes closest to separating these two purposes, since the language supports both classes and interfaces. But it confuses the two topics by continuing to allow substitution for class values. Suppose we took the next step and changed the Java language to eliminate substitution for class types. This could be accomplished by making the following two modifications to the language.

- A variable declared as a class could hold values of the class but not of child classes.
- If a parent class indicates that it supports an interface, the child class would not automatically support the interface but would have to explicitly indicate this fact in its class heading.

We maintain inheritance and substitution of interfaces; a variable declared as an interface could hold a value from any class that implemented the interface.

    a. Show that any class hierarchy, and any currently legal assignment, could be rewritten in this new framework. (You will need to introduce new interfaces.)

    b. Although the resulting system is much cleaner from a theoretical standpoint, what has been lost? Why did the designers of Java not follow this approach?

CHAPTER 9

A Case Study— A Card Game

In this third case study we will examine a simple card game, a version of solitaire. A slightly different rendition of this program was presented in C++ in the first edition of this book and rewritten to use the MFC library in another book [Budd 1999]. The program was translated into Java in the second edition and revised once again in Java in yet another book [Budd 1998b]. The program presented here is one more revision, this time translated into C#.

I have used this case study in so many different forms because the development of this program is a good illustration of the power of inheritance and overriding. We will get to those aspects after first considering some of the basic elements of the game. The complete source for the program can be viewed in Appendix C.

9.1 □ The Class PlayingCard

Wherever possible, software development should strive for the creation of general purpose reusable classes, classes that make minimal demands on their environment and hence can be carried from one application to another. This idea is illustrated by the first class, which represents a playing card. The class defining the playing card abstraction is shown in Figure 9.1. We have examined aspects of this class in earlier chapters.

The methods isFaceUp, rank, suit, and color have been written as *properties*. Since they include only a get clause and no set feature, they are properties that can be read and not modified. Two enumerated data types are used by the playing card class. The enumerated type Color is provided by the standard run-time system. The class Suits is specific to this project and is defined as follows.

```
public class PlayingCard
{
  public PlayingCard (Suits sv, int rv)
    { s = sv; r = rv; faceUp = false; }

  public bool isFaceUp
  {
    get { return faceUp; }
  }

  public void flip ()
  {
    faceUp = ! faceUp;
  }

  public int rank
  {
    get { return r; }
  }

  public Suits suit
  {
    get { return s; }
  }

  public Color color
  {
    get
    {
      if ( suit == Suits.Heart || suit == Suits.Diamond )
        { return Color.Red; }
      return Color.Black;
    }
  }

  private bool faceUp;
  private int r;
  private Suits s;
}
```

▢ Figure 9.1 —— The definition of the class PlayingCard

```
public enum Suits { Spade, Diamond, Club, Heart };
```

In C#, unlike C++, enumerated constants must be prefixed by their type name. You can see this in the method color through the use of names such as Color.Black or Suits.Heart, instead of simply Black or Heart.

The class PlayingCard has no information about the application in which it is developed and can easily be moved from this program to another program that uses the playing card abstraction.

9.2 □ Data and View Classes

Techniques used in the creation of visual interfaces have undergone frequent revisions, and this trend will likely continue for the foreseeable future. For this reason it is useful to separate classes that contain data values, such as the PlayingCard abstraction, from classes that are used to provide a graphical display of those values. By doing so the display classes can be modified or replaced as necessary, leaving the original data classes untouched.

The display of the card abstraction will be provided by the class CardView. To isolate the library-specific aspects of the card view, the actual display method is declared as *abstract* (see Section 8.5). This will later be subclassed and replaced with a function that will use the C# graphics facilities to generate the graphical interface.

```
public abstract class CardView
{
  public abstract void display (PlayingCard aCard, int x, int y);

  public static int Width = 50;
  public static int Height = 70;
}
```

By not only separating playing cards from card views but also separating the concept of a card view from a specific implementation, we isolate any code that is specific to a single graphics library. The effect is that the majority of the code in the application has no knowledge of the graphics library being used. This facilitates any future modifications to the graphics aspects of the application, which are the features most likely to change.

The CardView class encapsulates a pair of static constants that represent the height and width of a card on the display. The PlayingCard class itself knows nothing about how it is displayed. One abstract method is prototyped. This method will display the face of a card at a given position on the display.

It can be argued that even including the height and width as values in this class is introducing some platform dependencies, but these are less likely to change than are the libraries used to perform the actual graphical display.

9.3 ▢ The Game

The version of solitaire we will describe is known as klondike. The countless variations on this game make it probably the most common version of solitaire, so much so that when you say "solitaire," most people think of klondike. The version we will use is the one described in [Morehead 1949]; variations on the basic game are numerous.

The layout of the game is shown in Figure 9.2. A single standard pack of 52 cards is used. The *tableau*, or playing table, consists of 28 cards in 7 piles. the first pile has 1 card, the second 2, and so on up to 7. The top card of each pile is initially faceup; all other cards are facedown.

The suit piles (sometimes called *foundations*) are built up from aces to kings in suits. They are constructed above the tableau as the cards become available. The object of the game is to build all 52 cards into the suit piles.

The cards that are not part of the tableau are initially all in the *deck*. Cards in the deck are facedown and are drawn one by one from the deck and placed

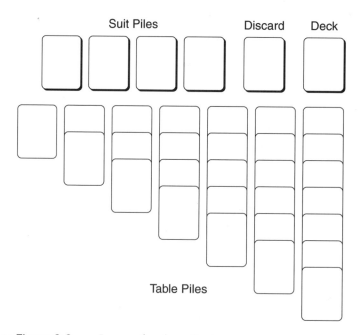

▢ Figure 9.2 —— Layout for the solitaire game

faceup on the *discard pile*. From there they can be moved onto either a tableau pile or a foundation. Cards are drawn from the deck until the pile is empty; at this point, the game is over if no further moves can be made.

Cards can be placed on a tableau pile only on a card of next-higher rank and opposite color. They can be placed on a foundation only if they are the same suit and the next-higher card or if the foundation is empty and the card is an ace. Spaces in the tableau that arise during play can be filled only by kings.

The topmost card of each tableau pile and the topmost card of the discard pile are always available for play. The only time more than one card is moved is when an entire collection of faceup cards from a tableau (called a *build*) is moved to another tableau pile. This can be done if the bottommost card of the build can be legally played on the topmost card of the destination. Our initial game will not support the transfer of a build, but we will discuss this as a possible extension. The topmost card of a tableau is always faceup. If a card is moved from a tableau, leaving a facedown card on the top, the latter card can be turned faceup.

From this short description, it is clear that the game of solitaire mostly involves manipulating piles of cards. Each type of pile has many features in common with the others and a few aspects unique to the particular type. In the next section, we will investigate in detail how inheritance can be used in such circumstances to simplify the implementation of the various card piles by providing a common base for the generic actions and permitting this base to be redefined when necessary.

9.4 □ Card Piles—Inheritance in Action

Much of the behavior we associate with a card pile is common to each variety of pile in the game. For example, each pile maintains a collection containing the cards in the pile, and the operations of inserting and deleting elements from this collection are common. Other operations are given default behavior in the class CardPile, but they are sometimes overridden in the various subclasses. The class CardPile is shown in Figure 9.3.

Each card pile maintains the coordinate location for the upper-left corner of the pile, as well as a collection that contains the card in the pile. The Stack abstraction from the standard run-time library is used to hold the cards. All these values are set by the constructor for the class. The data fields, located near the end of the declaration, are declared as protected and are thus accessible to member functions associated with this class and to member functions associated with subclasses.

The three functions top(), pop(), and isEmpty() manipulate the list of cards using functions provided by the Stack class. The remaining five operations defined in class CardPile are common to the abstract notion of our card piles, but they differ in details in each case. For example, the function canTake(PlayingCard) asks whether it is legal to place a card on the given pile. A card can be added to a foundation

```
public class CardPile {
  public CardPile (int xl, int yl )
    { x = xl; y = yl; pile = new Stack(); }

  public PlayingCard top
    { get { return (PlayingCard) pile.Peek (); } }

  public bool isEmpty
    { get { return pile.Count == 0; }  }

  public PlayingCard pop
    { get { return (PlayingCard) pile.Pop (); } }

    // the following are sometimes overridden
  public virtual bool includes (int tx, int ty ) {
    return( ( x <= tx ) && ( tx <= x + CardView.Width ) &&
        ( y <= ty ) && ( ty <= y + CardView.Height ) );
  }

  public virtual void select (int tx, int ty ) {
    // do nothing–override
  }

  public virtual void addCard (PlayingCard aCard )
    { pile.Push(aCard); }

  public virtual void display (CardView cv) {
    if ( isEmpty ) {
      cv.display(null, x, y);
    } else {
      cv.display((PlayingCard) pile.Peek(), x, y );
    }
  }

  public virtual bool canTake (PlayingCard aCard)
    { return false; }

  protected int x, y; // coordinates of the card pile
  protected Stack pile; // card pile data
}
```

☐ Figure 9.3 —— Description of the class CardPile

pile, for instance, only if it is an ace and the foundation is empty or if the card is the same suit as the current topmost card in the pile and has the next-higher value. A card can be added to a tableau pile, on the other hand, only if the pile is empty and the card is a king or if it is of the opposite color as the current topmost card in the pile and has the next-lower value.

The actions of the five virtual functions defined in CardPile can be characterized as follows.

includes   Determines if the coordinates given as arguments are contained within the boundaries of the pile. The default action simply tests the topmost card; this is overridden in the tableau piles to test all card values.

canTake   Tells whether a pile can take a specific card. Only the tableau and suit piles can take cards, so the default action is simply to return no; this is overridden in the two classes mentioned.

addCard   Adds a card to the card list. It is redefined in the discard pile class to ensure that the card is faceup.

display   Displays the card deck. The default method merely displays the topmost card of the pile but is overridden in the tableau class to display a column of cards. The top half of each hidden card is displayed. So that the playing surface area is conserved, only the topmost and bottommost faceup cards are displayed (this permits us to give definite bounds to the playing surface).

select   Performs an action in response to a mouse click. It is invoked when the user selects a pile by clicking the mouse in the portion of the playing field covered by the pile. The default action does nothing, but it is overridden by the table, deck, and discard piles to play the topmost card, if possible.

The following table illustrates the important benefits of inheritance. Given 5 operations and 5 classes, there are 25 potential methods we might have had to define. By making use of inheritance we need to implement only 13. Furthermore, we are guaranteed that each pile will respond in the same way to similar requests.

	CardPile	SuitPile	DeckPile	DiscardPile	TableauPile
includes	×				×
canTake	×	×			×
addCard	×			×	
display	×				×
select	×		×	×	×

9.4.1   The default card pile

We will examine each of the subclasses of CardPile in detail, pointing out various uses of object-oriented features. Each of the five virtual methods is first defined in the class CardPile. These implementations will represent the default behavior should they not be overridden. The implementation of these methods was shown in Figure 9.3.

9.4.2   The suit piles

The simplest subclass is the class SuitPile, which represents the pile of cards at the top of the playing surface. This is the pile being built up in suit from ace to king. The implementation of this class is as follows.

```
public class SuitPile : CardPile {
  public SuitPile (int x, int y) : base(x, y) {  }

  public override bool canTake (PlayingCard aCard ) {
    if( isEmpty )
      { return( aCard.rank == 0 ); }
    PlayingCard topCard = top;
    return( ( aCard.suit == topCard.suit ) &&
      ( aCard.rank == topCard.rank + 1 ) );
  }
}
```

The class SuitPile defines only two methods. The constructor for the class takes two integer arguments and does nothing more than invoke the constructor for the parent class CardPile.

The method canTake overrides the similarly named method in the parent class. Note the use of the keyword override that indicates this fact. This method determines whether a card can be placed on the pile. A card is legal if the pile is empty and the card is an ace (that is, has rank zero) or if the card is the same suit as the topmost card in the pile and of the next-higher rank (for example, a three of spades can only be played on a two of spades). Since the methods rank and suit were declared as properties, they can be invoked without parentheses.

All other behavior of the suit pile is the same as that of our generic card pile. When selected, a suit pile does nothing. When a card is added, it is simply inserted into the stack. To display the pile only the topmost card is drawn.

9.4.3   The deck pile

The DeckPile maintains the deck from which new cards are drawn. It differs from the generic card pile in two ways. When constructed, rather than creating an empty pile of cards, it initializes itself by first creating an array containing the 52 cards in a conventional deck, then randomly selecting elements from this collection to generate a sorted deck. The method select is invoked when the mouse button is used to select the card deck. If the deck is empty, it does nothing. Otherwise, the topmost card is removed from the deck and added to the discard pile.

```
public class DeckPile : CardPile {
  public DeckPile (int x, int y) : base(x, y) {
    // create the new deck
    // first put cards into a local array
    ArrayList aList = new ArrayList ();
    for( int i = 0; i <= 12; i++) {
      aList.Add(new PlayingCard(Suits.Heart, i));
      aList.Add(new PlayingCard(Suits.Diamond, i));
      aList.Add(new PlayingCard(Suits.Spade, i));
      aList.Add(new PlayingCard(Suits.Club, i));
    }
      // then pull them out randomly
    Random myRandom = new Random( );
    for(int count = 0; count < 52; count++) {
      int index = myRandom.Next(aList.Count);
      addCard( (PlayingCard) aList [index] );
      aList.RemoveAt(index);
    }
  }

  public override void select (int tx, int ty) {
    if ( isEmpty ) { return; }
    Game.discardPile().addCard( pop );
  }
}
```

The implementation of the select method presents us with a new problem. When the mouse is pressed on the deck pile, the desired action is to move a card from the deck pile on to the discard pile, turning it faceup in the process. The problem is that we now need to refer to a single unique card pile—namely, the pile that represents the discard pile.

One approach would be to define the various card piles as global variables, which then could be universally accessed. In fact, this approach is used in the program described in my earlier C++ version of the game in the first edition of this book. But many languages, such as Java and C#, do not have global variables. There is good reason for this. Global variables tend to make it difficult to understand the flow of information through a program, since they can be accessed from any location (that's what makes them global).

A better and more object-oriented alternative to the use of global variables is a series of static values. This reduces the number of global values to one: the class name. Static methods in the class can then be used to access further states. In our program we will name this class Game. A discussion of the details of this class will be postponed until after the description of the various card piles.

9.4.4   The discard pile

The class DiscardPile redefines the addCard and select methods. The class is described as follows.

```
public class DiscardPile : CardPile {
  public DiscardPile (int x, int y ) : base(x, y) { }

  public override void addCard (PlayingCard aCard) {
    if( ! aCard.isFaceUp )
      { aCard.flip(); }
    base.addCard( aCard );
  }

  public override void select (int tx, int ty) {
    if( isEmpty ) { return; }
    PlayingCard topCard = pop;
    for( int i = 0; i < 4; i++ ) {
      if( Game.suitPile(i).canTake( topCard ) ) {
        Game.suitPile(i).addCard( topCard );
        return;
      }
    }

    for( int i = 0; i < 7; i++ ) {
      if( Game.tableau(i).canTake( topCard ) ) {
        Game.tableau(i).addCard( topCard );
        return;
      }
    }
    // nobody can use it, put it back on our stack
    addCard(topCard);
  }
}
```

The implementation of these methods is interesting in that they exhibit two very different forms of inheritance. The select method *overrides* or *replaces* the default behavior provided by class CardPile, replacing it with code that when invoked (when the mouse is pressed over the card pile) checks to see if the topmost card can be played on any suit pile or, alternatively, on any tableau pile. If the card cannot be played, it is kept in the discard pile.

The method addCard is a different sort of overriding. Here the behavior is a *refinement* of the default behavior in the parent class. That is, the behavior of the parent class is completely executed, and in addition, new behavior is added. In this case, the new behavior ensures that when a card is placed on the discard pile it is always faceup. After satisfying this condition, the code in the parent class is invoked to add the card to the pile. The keyword base is necessary to avoid the confusion with the addCard method being defined. In Java the same problem would be addressed by sending a message to super (as in super.addCard(aCard)).

Another form of refinement occurs in the constructors for the various subclasses. Each must invoke the constructor for the parent class to guarantee that the parent is properly initialized before the constructor performs its own actions. The parent constructor is invoked by an initializer clause inside the constructor for the child class.

9.4.5   The tableau piles

The most complex of the subclasses of CardPile is that used to hold a tableau, or table pile. The implementation of this class redefines nearly all of the virtual methods defined in ClassPile. When initialized by the constructor, the tableau pile removes a certain number of cards from the deck, placing them in its own pile. The number of cards so removed is determined by an additional argument to the constructor. The topmost card of this pile is then displayed faceup.

```
public class TablePile : CardPile {
  public TablePile (int x, int y, int c) : base(x, y) {
    // initialize our pile of cards
    for(int i = 0; i < c; i++ ) {
      addCard(Game.deckPile().pop);
    }
    top.flip();
  }

  public override bool canTake (PlayingCard aCard ) {
    if( isEmpty ) { return(aCard.rank == 12); }
    PlayingCard topCard = top;
    return( ( aCard.color != topCard.color ) &&
      ( aCard.rank    == topCard.rank - 1 ) );
  }
```

```
public override bool includes (int tx, int ty) {
  return( ( x <= tx ) && ( tx <= x + CardView.Width ) &&
    ( y <= ty ) );
}

public override void select (int tx, int ty) {
  if( isEmpty ) { return; }
  // if face down, then flip
  PlayingCard topCard = top;
  if( ! topCard.isFaceUp ) {
    topCard.flip();
    return;
  }
  // else see if any suit pile can take card
  topCard = pop;
  for(int i = 0; i < 4; i++ ) {
    if( Game.suitPile(i).canTake( topCard ) ) {
      Game.suitPile(i).addCard( topCard );
      return;
    }
  }
  // else see if any other table pile can take card
  for(int i = 0; i < 7; i++ ) {
    if( Game.tableau(i).canTake( topCard ) ) {
      Game.tableau(i).addCard( topCard );
      return;
    }
  }
  addCard( topCard );
}

public override void display (CardView cv) {
  Object [ ] cardArray = pile.ToArray();
  int size = pile.Count;
  int hs = CardView.Height / 2; // half size
  int ty = y;
  for (int i = pile.Count - 1; i >= 0; i--) {
    cv.display((PlayingCard) cardArray[i], x, ty);
    ty += hs;
  }
}
}
```

A card can be added to the pile (method canTake) only if the pile is empty and the card is a king, or if the card is the opposite color from that of the current topmost card and one smaller in rank. When a mouse press is tested to determine if it covers the pile (method includes), the bottom bound is not tested, since the pile may be of variable length. When the pile is selected, the topmost card is flipped if it is facedown. If it is faceup, an attempt is made to move the card first to any available suit pile and then to any available table pile. Only if no pile can take the card is it left in place. Finally, to display a pile, all the underlying cards are displayed. The stack must be converted into an array to do this since we must access the cards top to bottom, which is the opposite of the order that stack elements would normally be enumerated.

9.5 ☐ Playing the Polymorphic Game

The need for the class Game was described earlier. This class holds the actual card piles used by the program, making them available through methods that are declared as static. Because these methods are static, they can be accessed using only the class name as a basis.

The definition of this class is shown in Figure 9.4. The game manager stores the various card piles in an array, one that is declared as CardPile, although the values are polymorphic and hold a variety of different types of card piles. These values are initialized in the constructor, which is declared as static. A static constructor will be executed when the program begins execution.

By storing the card values in a polymorphic array, the game manager need not distinguish the characteristics of the individual piles. For example, to repaint the display it is only necessary to tell each pile to repaint itself. The method display will be different, depending on the actual type of card pile. Similarly, to respond to a mouse down, the manager simply cycles through the list of card piles.

9.6 ☐ The Graphical User Interface

We have taken pains in the development of this program to isolate the details of both the graphical user interface and of the high-level program execution. This is because of all the elements of a program, the user interface is the most likely to require change as new graphical libraries are introduced or existing libraries are changed. Similarly, the way that applications are initiated using C# introduces details that would have obscured the overall design of the application.

The card images are simple line drawings. Diamonds and hearts are drawn in red, spades and clubs in black. The hash marks on the back are drawn in yellow.

```
public class Game {
  static Game () {
    allPiles = new CardPile[ 13 ];
    allPiles[0] = new DeckPile(335, 5 );
    allPiles[1] = new DiscardPile(268, 5 );
    for( int i = 0; i < 4; i++ ) {
      allPiles[2 + i] = new SuitPile(15 + 60 * i, 5);
    }
    for( int i = 0; i < 7; i++ ) {
      allPiles[6+i] = new TablePile(5+55*i, 80, i+1);
    }
  }

  public static void paint (CardView cv) {
    for( int i = 0; i < 13; i++ ) {
      allPiles[i].display(cv );
    }
  }

  public static void mouseDown (int x, int y) {
    for( int i = 0; i < 13; i++ ) {
      if( allPiles[i].includes(x, y) ) {
        allPiles [i].select(x, y);
      }
    }
  }

  public static CardPile deckPile ()
    { return allPiles[0]; }

  public static CardPile discardPile ()
    { return allPiles[1]; }

  public static CardPile tableau (int index)
    { return allPiles[6+index]; }

  public static CardPile suitPile (int index)
    { return allPiles[2+index]; }

  private static CardPile[] allPiles;
}
```

▫ Figure 9.4 —— The class Game

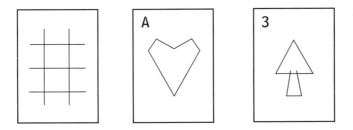

We deal first with the user interface. Recall that the display of a card was provided by a method CardView that was described as abstract. To produce actual output, we must create a subclass that implements the pure virtual methods. This class we will call WinFormsCardView:

```
public class WinFormsCardView : CardView {
  public WinFormsCardView (Graphics aGraphicsObject) {
    g = aGraphicsObject;
  }

  public override void display (PlayingCard aCard,int x,int y) {
    if  (aCard == null) {
      Pen myPen = new Pen(Color.Black,2);
      Brush myBrush = new SolidBrush (Color.White);
      g.FillRectangle(myBrush,x,y,CardView.Width,CardView.Height);
      g.DrawRectangle(myPen,x,y,CardView.Width,CardView.Height);
    } else {
      paintCard (aCard,x,y);
    }
  }

  private void paintCard (PlayingCard aCard,int x,int y) {
    String [] names = { "A","2","3","4","5",
      "6","7","8","9","10","J","Q","K" };

    Pen myPen = new Pen (Color.Black,2);
    Brush myBrush = new SolidBrush (Color.White);

    g.FillRectangle (myBrush,x,y,CardView.Width,CardView.Height);
    g.DrawRectangle(myPen,x,y,CardView.Width,CardView.Height);
    myPen.Dispose();
    myBrush.Dispose();

    // draw body of card with a new pen-color
```

```
    if (aCard.isFaceUp) {
      if (aCard.color == Color.Red) {
        myPen = new Pen  (Color.Red,1);
        myBrush = new SolidBrush (Color.Red);
      } else {
        myPen = new Pen  (Color.Blue,1);
        myBrush = new SolidBrush (Color.Blue);
      }
      g.DrawString (names[ aCard.rank ],
        new Font("Times New Roman",10),myBrush,x+3,y+7);
      if (aCard.suit == Suits.Heart) {
        g.DrawLine(myPen,x+25,y+30,x+35,y+20);
        g.DrawLine(myPen,x+35,y+20,x+45,y+30);
        g.DrawLine(myPen,x+45,y+30,x+25,y+60);
        g.DrawLine(myPen,x+25,y+60,x+5,y+30);
        g.DrawLine(myPen,x+5,y+30,x+15,y+20);
        g.DrawLine(myPen,x+15,y+20,x+25,y+30);
      } else if (aCard.suit == Suits.Spade) {
        :
        :   see code in appendix
        :
      } else if (aCard.suit == Suits.Diamond) {
        .
        .
        .
      } else if (aCard.suit == Suits.Club) {
        .
        .
        .
      }
    } else {    // face down
      myPen = new Pen (Color.Green,1);
      myBrush = new SolidBrush  (Color.Green);
        .
        .
        .
    }
  }
  private Graphics g;
}
```

This is not a text on graphics, so the actual display will be rather simple. Basically, a card draws itself as a rectangle with a textual description. Empty piles are drawn in green, the backsides of cards in yellow, the faces in the appropriate color.

Graphical output in the C# library is based around a type of object from class Graphics. This object is passed as constructor to the class and stored in the variable

9. Details of the graphical output routines provided by the Windows library will not be discussed here, although many of the names are self-explanatory. The display for our game is rather primitive, consisting simply of line rectangles and the textual display of card information.

Applications in the C# framework are created by subclassing from a system-provided class named System.WinForms.Form and overriding certain key methods. Much of the structure of the class is generated automatically if one uses a development environment, such as the Studio application. In the following we have marked the generated code with comments. The programmer then edits this code to fit the specific application. The final class is as follows.

```
public class Solitaire : System.WinForms.Form {
    // start of automatically generated code
    private System.ComponentModel.Container components;

    public Solitaire() {
      InitializeComponent();
    }

    public override void Dispose() {
      base.Dispose();
      components.Dispose();
    }

    private void InitializeComponent() {
      this.components = new System.ComponentModel.Container ();
      this.Text = "Solitaire";
      this.AutoScaleBaseSize = new System.Drawing.Size (5, 13);
      this.ClientSize = new System.Drawing.Size (392, 373);
    }
    // end of automatically generated code

    protected override void OnMouseDown (MouseEventArgs e ) {
      Game.mouseDown(e.X, e.Y);
      this.Invalidate(); // force screen redraw
    }

    protected override void OnPaint (PaintEventArgs pe ) {
      Graphics g = pe.Graphics;
      CardView cv = new WinFormsCardView(g);
      Game.paint(cv);
    }
```

```
public static void Main(string[] args)
  { Application.Run(new Solitaire()); }
}
```

The window class is responsible for trapping the actual mouse presses and repainting the window. In our application these activities are simply passed on to the game manager. As with Java, execution begins with the method named Main. This method invokes a static method from a system class named Application, passing it an instance of the game controller class.

Summary ▫

The solitaire game is a standard example program found in many textbooks. We have here used the program as a case study to illustrate a number of important concepts. In the design of the PlayingCard and CardView classes, we have separated a model from a view. This is important, since aspects of the view are likely to change more rapidly than aspects of the model. Extending this further, we have defined the view as an abstract class and thereby hidden all Windows-specific features in an implementation of this class. Moving to a different graphical library would therefore simply involve changing the implementation of this abstract class.

Probably the most notable feature of the game is the use of inheritance and overriding, exemplified by the classes CardPile and its various subclasses. Through the use of overriding we avoid having to write a large amount of code. Furthermore, the use of a polymorphic variable to reference the various classes simplifies the task of redrawing the screen or handling mouse operations.

Further Reading ▫

Source for the various earlier versions of this program can be found on my Web site, http://www.cs.orst.edu/~budd.

We have in this simple application only scratched the surface of the functionality provided by the C# system. However, the details of how Windows programs are created are complicated and beyond the issues being discussed here. A good introduction to the C# system is provided by Gunnerson [Gunnerson 2000].

Self-Study Questions ▫

1. Why should the class PlayingCard be written so as to have no knowledge of the application in which it is being used?

2. Why is it useful to separate the class PlayingCard from the class that will draw the image of the playing card in the current application?

3. Why is it further useful to define the interface for CardView as an abstract class and then later supply an implementation of this class that uses the C# graphics facilities?

4. What are the different types of card piles in this solitare game?

5. What methods in CardPile are potentially overridden? What methods are not overridden? How can you tell from the class description which are which?

6. In what way does the variable allPiles exhibit polymorphism?

7. How does the polymorphism in allPiles simplify the design of the program?

Exercises ⊡

1. The solitaire game has been designed to be as simple as possible. A few features are somewhat annoying but can be easily remedied with more coding. These include the following.

   a. The topmost card of a tableau pile should not be moved to another tableau pile if there is another faceup card below it.

   b. An entire build should not be moved if the bottommost card is a king and there are no remaining facedown cards.

   For each, describe what procedures need to be changed, and give the code for the updated routine.

2. The following are common variations of klondike. For each, describe which portions of the solitaire program need to be altered to incorporate the change.

   a. If the user clicks on an empty deck pile, the discard pile is moved (perhaps with shuffling) back to the deck pile. Thus, the user can traverse the deck pile multiple times.

   b. Cards can be moved from the suit pile back into the tableau pile.

   c. Cards are drawn from the deck three at a time and placed on the discard pile in reverse order. As before, only the topmost card of the discard pile is available for playing. If fewer than three cards remain in the deck pile, all the remaining cards (as many as that may be) are moved to the discard pile. (In practice, this variation is often accompanied by variation a, permitting multiple passes through the deck.)

   d. The same as variation c, but any of the three selected cards can be played. (This requires a slight change to the layout as well as an extensive change to the discard pile class.)

   e. Any royalty card, not simply a king, can be moved onto an empty tableau pile.

3. The game "thumb and pouch" is similar to klondike except that a card may be built on any card of next-higher rank, of any suit but its own. Thus, a nine of spades can be played on a ten of clubs but not on a ten of spades. This variation greatly improves the chances of winning. (According to Morehead [Morehead 1949], the chances of winning Klondike are 1 in 30, whereas the chances of winning thumb and pouch are 1 in 4.) Describe what portions of the program need to be changed to accommodate this variation.

CHAPTER 10

Subclasses and Subtypes

There is a paradox that lies at the heart of the way inheritance and substitution are used in statically typed object-oriented languages. This paradox derives from the twin concepts of *subclass* and *subtype*. In this chapter we will explore these concepts and this paradox.

To say that one class is a *subclass* of another is to simply assert that it has been built using inheritance. The new class is declared using an existing class as a basis, as in the following Java class declaration.

```
class Child extends Parent {
    ... // class definition
}
```

The point is that the subclass relationship is asserting a statement about definition, about how the new class was constructed. It says nothing about the meaning or purpose of the child class.

10.1 □ Substitutability

One of the more interesting features of statically typed object-oriented languages is that the type associated with a *value* held by a variable may not exactly match the type associated with the *declaration* for that variable. We saw this near the end of the billiard simulation program in Chapter 7, where a variable declared as a GraphicalObject in fact held a value of type Ball, Wall, or Hole. To appreciate how unusual this is, note that variables in conventional typed programming languages never have this property. A variable declared as a Integer, for example, can never hold a value of type String.

207

In Chapter 8 we termed this property of object-oriented languages the principle of *substitution* (sometimes called *subsumption*). A variable declared as a parent class can hold (that is, be filled with) a value that is an instance of a child class. The variable declared as pointing to a GraphicalObject in Chapter 7 could, in fact, be pointing to a Ball. Barbara Liskov described substitution this way.

> What is wanted here is something like the following substitution property: If for each object o_1 of type S there is an object o_2 of type T such that for all programs P defined in terms of T, the behavior of P is unchanged when o_1 is substituted for o_2, then S is a *subtype* of T. [Liskov 1988]

10.2 ▫ Subtypes

To understand the concept of a *subtype* and how it relates to a subclass, we must first explore how types are used in programming languages. For an idea that, at least with experience, seems so intuitive, the exact nature of types may seem surprisingly complicated.

When we say that a value, such as the number 17, has an integer type, what are we asserting? One answer is that we are asserting that the value is a member of a set of values. The name int is the handle by which we describe this set. In Java, for example, the set of integers represents the whole numbers that range from −2147483648 (which is −2^{31}) to 2147483647 (which is $2^{31} - 1$). Other primitive types denote similar sets of values.

But there is more that we know by virtue of the assertion that a value has type int. We know, for example, that we can perform a variety of *operations* on the value, such as addition, subtraction, multiplication, and division. We are not permitted to perform these operations on a value of type boolean, as the definition of the Boolean data type does not include these tasks.

So in one sense, a type is simply a set of values and a set of operations. But we know yet more about integers. We expect integers to satisfy a set of *properties*. If we add the values 3 and 5, we expect to produce the value 8. This we always expect to be true. On the other hand, if we divide the integer 8 by the integer 5, we get 1 and not the fractional value 1.6. We are not surprised at this because a property of division for integers in most languages is to truncate any fractional remainders. There are further features of type we could explore, but these three—values, operations, and properties—are sufficient for our discussion of subtypes.

Now consider how the term *type* is used when we describe an *abstract data type*, or ADT. Let us employ for our example the concept of a stack. In Java, for example, the starting place for the description of an ADT is the definition of an interface. This might be described, for example, using the following declaration.

```
interface Stack {
  public void push (Object value);
  public Object top ();
  public void pop ();
}
```

But the interface is just the beginning. Beyond the interface is the meaning, the properties that we want to associate with this data type. A Stack, for example, is characterized by the LIFO (Last-In, First-Out) property. The item retrieved by a top operation must be the most recent value pushed onto the stack. If that value is removed (by executing pop), then the next item at the top of the stack should be the item inserted prior to the removed value, and so on. A mental image, such as a stack of plates, provides a good intuition regarding the utilization of this data type.

Syntax versus Semantics

Although not an exact correspondence, the issue of subclass versus subtype is in some ways similar to the more familiar language distinction between syntax and semantics. Syntax deals with how a statement can be written, just as subclasses deal with how a class is declared. Semantics deals with what a statement means, just as subtypes deal with how a child class preserves the meaning of a parent class.

The following class definition satisfies the Stack interface but does *not* satisfy the properties we expect for a stack, since it violates the LIFO property for all but the most recent item placed into the stack.

```
class NonStack implements Stack {
  public void push (Object value) { v = value; }
  public Object top () { return v; }
  public void pop () { v = null; }

  private Object v = null;
}
```

From this example we see that the properties that are key to the meaning of the stack are not specified by the interface definition. And it is not that we were lazy; Java (like most other languages) gives us no way to specify the properties that an interface should satisfy. And thus most programmers (and most programming languages) resort to something much less formal, such as an English language description of the class requirements.

Having worked through this explanation, we are now in a position to understand how a *subtype* differs from a *subclass*. To say that a new class is a subtype of an existing class is to assert that the new class provides all of the operations of the existing class and *furthermore* satisfies the properties associated with the class. For example, any method in the new class that matches in type signature a method in the old class also satisfies the properties associated with that method. (The new class is free to add new operations, of course.)

The subtype relationship is described purely in terms of behavior; it says nothing about how the new class is defined or constructed. As the class NonStack demonstrates, it is easy for a child class to be a subclass and not a subtype. It is also easy to construct examples that represent a subtype that is not a subclass. For

Types Are a Poor Man's Specifications

The most important reason for having types in programming languages is to eliminate typing errors. Andrew Black calls types "a poor man's specification." By this he means that what we really would like to ensure, when an argument is passed to a procedure or a value is assigned to a variable, is that the argument values satisfy the requirements of the procedure and that those requirements should really be expressed in terms of specifications. Any value that satisfies the specifications (that is, any subtype) should be permitted, even if it is not formed as a subclass.

But formal specifications are both difficult to write and difficult to check or verify. Types, on the other hand, are by comparison almost trivial for a compiler to check. Therefore, even though types are not exactly what a programmer or a language designer might like, they do have the following advantages.

- They are a useful approximation.
- They are simple to explain.
- They are easy to check.

Thus, computer languages continue to treat types as a shorthand for specifications, despite their obvious shortcomings.

instance, the Smalltalk type Array defines a data type with roughly the following interface.

```
at: index put: value
at: index
size
```

The properties we associate with this data type include the fact that if a value is placed into the collection using a given index, then when the array is subsequently accessed using the same index the value will be returned. The Dictionary data type supports the same interface but does not limit the index values to being integer. Even though the class Dictionary has no inheritance relationship to the class Array because it supports the same interface, we can say that Dictionary is a subtype of Array.

Another way to look at the subclass/subtype distinction is by extending the parent/child metaphor. Parent classes provide the genetic makeup for a class. As any parent knows, genes have an influence on behavior, but they do not dictate it. The concept of subtype, on the other hand, describes behavior without reference to pedigree.

10.3 ▣ The Substitutability Paradox

Recall the argument in Chapter 8 that justified the principle of substitutability for statically typed object-oriented languages. It went something like this.

1. A child class inherits all the data fields defined in the parent class.
2. A child class must recognize all the behaviors associated with the parent class, either inheriting them directly or overriding them but preserving the type signature.
3. Therefore, an instance of a child class can be used in any situation where an instance of the parent class is expected, with no observable difference.

With the benefit of our knowledge of the subclass/subtype distinction, we see that the weak link in this argument is Step 2. Simply asserting that a child class satisfies the interface common to the parent does not ensure that it will satisfy any or all of the properties of the parent. (Remember the class NonStack.)

So why don't programming languages use the subtype relation rather than the subclass relation? Here we run into the fundamental bedrock of computer science: the *halting problem*. The halting problem asserts that there is no procedure that can, in general, tell if an arbitrary program will ever terminate. One of the classic corollaries of this principle is that there is no procedure that can determine, in general, if two programs have equivalent behavior. From this it is only a small step to showing that it is impossible to tell (again, in general) if a method in a child class matches in behavior a method in the parent class.

And so we arrive at the paradox of substitutability. In statically typed object-oriented programming languages, the veracity of substitutability for assignment is determined by ensuring that the type of a value is a *subclass* of the type of the variable being assigned. And yet such an assignment only makes logical sense if the type of the value is a *subtype* to that of the variable.

This is not to say that languages do not make some attempt to ensure that subclasses remain subtypes. Programmers are not generally permitted to delete an inherited method or hide a public data field, for example. Nor is it permitted to change the type signature of a method inherited from the parent (although this issue is subtle, as we will see in Chapter 15). But in the end all of these restrictions, while useful, are insufficient. There is simply no way that a compiler can ensure that a subclass created by a programmer is indeed a subtype.

In fact, great havoc can ensue if values are assigned through substitution that do not satisfy the subtype relationship. Imagine, for example, using an instance of NonStack in a situation where a Stack data type is expected.

10.3.1   Is this a problem?

Notice what it takes to create a subclass that is not also a subtype. To do so it is necessary to redefine an operation that is inherited from a parent class but to do so in a way that compromises some property that the parent class expects and without violating the type signature of the method. One can legitimately ask how common this problem can be. The answer is, probably not very common at all. But nevertheless when it does occur, it is almost certainly a source of annoyance, if not error. And the fact that such a fundamental problem would lie at the heart of something so basic as substitutability is a frustration to those who would aspire to place programming on a more secure theoretical foundation.

10.4 ⊡ Subclassing for Construction

A common situation where subclasses are created that are not subtypes is when inheritance is employed purely for the reuse of code. This is termed subclassing for construction, and we have discussed this idea already in Chapter 8. For example, suppose a C++ programmer needs to create a dictionary abstraction that will hold key/value pairs composed of strings and integers. The programmer decides to use the standard STL class list for the container (we will discuss the STL library in detail later in Chapter 20).

The first step is to define a small helper class for each element.

```
class association { // a single key/value pair
public:
  association (string s, int i)
    { key = s; value = i; }
  string key;
  int value;
};
```

The next step is the critical juncture. In defining the dictionary class the programmer decides to use inheritance and declare the new abstraction as a subclass of the existing list class.

```
class dictionary : public list<association> {
public:
  void add (string key, int value) {
    association ele(key, value);
    push_front(ele); // add to list
  }

  int at (string key) { // find value stored at given key
    iterator start, stop;
    stop = end();
    for (start = begin(); start != stop; ++start) {
      association ele = *start;
      if (ele.key == key)
        return ele.value;
    }
    return -1;
  }
}
```

Because the new class inherits from list, all the behaviors defined for the existing class become available to users of the new abstraction. For example, you can determine how many elements are being held by a dictionary using the list method size.

```
dictionary d;
cout << "started" << '\n';
d.add("abc", 42);
d.add("pdq", 12);
cout << "value of abc is " << d.at("abc") << '\n';
cout << "number of elements in dictionary is "
  << d.size() << '\n';
```

But for all the advantages of this arrangement, there are disadvantages as well. All of the list methods can now be used with this new class, and some of them may not be appropriate. For example, the method pop_front removes the first element from the collection. But what exactly is the first element of a dictionary?

```
d.pop_front();
cout << "number of elements in dictionary is "
   << d.size() << '\n';
```

*10.4.1   Private inheritance in C++

The problem with the dictionary abstraction is that the mechanism of inheritance is bringing with it too much semantic baggage. In this case, the programmer wants to make use of inheritance within their own class, but does not want those operations to pass through the class and be available to the world at large. In short, the programmer wants the advantages of subclassing (access to both the data and behavior defined by the parent) but does not want to assert that their new class is a subtype.

One way to do this in C++ is to use *private inheritance*. Private inheritance is indicated by using the keyword private in the class header instead of the keyword public.

```
class dictionary : private list<association> {
public:
  void add (string key, int value) { ... }

  int at (string key) { ... }

  int size () { return list<association>::size(); }
};
```

As with normal inheritance, a private inheritance makes the facilities of the parent class accessible to the new class. But unlike a public inheritance, the abilities of the parent are not accessible outside the class definition. Thus, the programmer must explicitly define whatever behavior they want associated with the new class. For example, the programmer has defined the method size so that it returns the number of elements in the list, making use of the similarly named method from the parent class. In this fashion the programmer has created a subclass of list that is not a subtype of list inasmuch as it cannot be assigned to a variable declared using the parent class.

10.5 ▫ Dynamically Typed Languages

The contrast between subclasses and subtypes takes on a slightly different form in dynamically typed languages, such as Smalltalk, because types themselves are used differently in such languages. The distinction between subclasses and subtypes is perhaps easier to appreciate if we consider argument values. For example, consider the following Smalltalk method from class Magnitude.

" *class Magnitude* "

```
between: low and: high
    ↑ (low <= self) and: [ self <= high ]
```

Although the formal arguments low and high are not typed, there are neverthe-less implicit restrictions placed on them. In particular, low must recognize the <= message (operators are simply messages in Smalltalk), and high must be usable as an argument to such a message. It is assumed, but not stated, that these messages define an ordering on their values. Thus, there is an implicit typing for these vari-ables. (The set of operations that a variable must recognize is sometimes termed its *protocol*.) Any value passed as an argument to this method must understand these messages. This assertion says nothing about the class of the arguments. While class Magnitude in Smalltalk defines these operations, nothing prevents the Smalltalk programmer from implementing the appropriate operations in an unre-lated class and thereafter using instances of the class with this method. Thus, we say that arguments for this method are expected to be of a certain subtype (the type implicitly defined by the messages it must understand) but not necessarily a specific subclass.

The disadvantage of dynamic typing is that type errors may not be caught until run time. Using an incorrect value as an argument may result in a "receiver does not understand" error, something that cannot occur in statically typed languages.

Although template or generic arguments in C++ are not dynamically typed, they have similar properties. The following is a simple but typical template function in C++.

```
template <class T>
T max (T left, T right)
{
  if (left < right)
    return right;
  return left;
}
```

It is only by examining the body of the function that the programmer can determine that the argument values must understand the < operator. One advantage of templates over dynamic typing is that errors resulting from values that do not support the required operations will be caught at compile time, although frequently the error messages that result from these situations are difficult to decipher.

*10.6 ▢ Pre- and Postconditions

One traditional way to specify the behavior of methods in an abstract data type is through pre- and postconditions. A precondition describes features of the state that must be true before a method can be executed, whereas a postcondition specifies the resulting state produced by executing a method. While most programmers use pre- and postconditions informally as comments in their code, some programming languages include formal notation for specifying these features.

The language Eiffel takes this idea one step further. It is possible to specify pre- and postconditions for methods, and these are inherited by child classes. While a child class can override the body of a method, they are not allowed to override the pre- and postconditions, and furthermore, these conditions will be tested when the method is executed in order to assure that proper state is maintained. By ensuring a minimal level of functionality, preconditions and postconditions make it harder to create a subclass that is not also a subtype.

Figure 10.1 illustrates these features in an Eiffel class that defines, but does not implement, the Stack abstraction. Preconditions are indicated by a require clause. For example, the class requires that a stack is not empty before a pop operation can be performed. Postconditions are indicated by ensure clauses. For example, when an item is pushed on the stack, the class ensures that the stack is not empty. Ensure clauses are also allowed to access the value of data fields before the method was executed, using the old notation. Notice, for example, that this class ensures the count is properly updated by checking that the count is one larger than the previous count.

The problem with formal pre- and postconditions is that they seldom can capture all the features of interest. Note that these assertions ensure that the stack does not exhibit underflow or overflow but do not guarantee that an implementation will satisfy the fundamental LIFO property. Hence, the NonStack described earlier would satisfy both the preconditions and the postconditions and yet still not be a true stack. It is for reasons such as this that formal pre- and postconditions are not widely found in programming languages.

```
class Stack [ EleType ] feature
  count : INTEGER -- number of stack elements
feature
  empty : boolean is deferred -- is stack empty
  full : boolean is deferred -- is stack full?

  push (x : EleType) is
    require
      not full
    do deferred
    ensure
      not empty
      count = old count + 1
    end

  pop () is
    require
      not empty
    do deferred
    ensure
      count = old count - 1
      not full
    end
  end
```

⊡ Figure 10.1 ——An Eiffel program showing the use of preconditions

* 10.7 ⊡ Refinement Semantics

It has been noted that one cause of the problem of subclasses that are not subtypes is the fact that a child class can override a method from a parent class and completely replace it. Thus, whatever the parent method was doing is lost entirely.

One school of language design, the so-called Scandinavian school, asserts that this problem can be avoided by *always* executing the code from the parent class. The child class can add to this behavior but cannot completely replace it. Such an overriding is termed a *refinement* instead of a *replacement*. Notable object-oriented languages based on this principle include Simula (the first object-oriented language) and Beta.

Opponents of this view assert that while it is true that refinement semantics make it more difficult to create subclasses that are not subtypes, they still cannot make it impossible, and furthermore, they also make many other useful tasks more difficult—tasks that are not dangerous and that are in fact very desirable. So-called American-style replacement semantics, while in theory more dangerous, are for this reason also more useful.

Summary ▫

- To say that one class is a subclass of another simply asserts that it was built using inheritance.
- By itself, the subclass relationship says nothing about the behavior of the child in relation to the behavior of the parent.
- The term *subtype*, on the other hand, describes the behavior of one class in relation to the behavior of another, regardless of how they were constructed.
- Most of the time the two terms intersect, although it is possible to build subclasses that are not subtypes and conversely to build subtypes that are not subclasses.

In strongly typed object-oriented languages a paradox arises around the principle of substitution. Because verifying the subclass relationship is easy and verifying the subtype relationship is impossible, languages permit substitution based on subclasses rather than subtypes. If a programmer is not careful that the subclasses are also subtypes, subtle errors that are difficult to detect can result.

Other topics we have discussed in this chapter include private inheritance in C++ (a technique for using inheritance to create child classes that are explicitly not subtypes), preconditions and postconditions in Eiffel, and refinement semantics.

Further Reading ▫

Earlier in this chapter I argued that types are not specifications but are used as the next best thing because they are sufficiently close to being specifications and are inexpensive to implement. There is a considerable body of work that has as its goal coming up with a better typing system, thereby improving the specification power of types. See, for example, [Cardelli 1985, Raj 1991, Bruce 1994].

The Liskov quote is from [Liskov 1988]. Another frequently cited paper on subtypes is Cook [Cook 1990]. The terms "American semantics" and "Scandinavian semantics" are due to a different Cook [Cook 1988].

A more theoretical analysis of the subclass/subtype distinction is presented in the previously cited paper by Cardelli and by Castagna [Castagna 1997].

We will discuss the distinction between replacement and refinement semantics in more detail in Chapter 16 when we examine overriding.

Self-Study Questions ⊡

1. What does it mean to say that one class is a subclass of another?
2. What is the principle of substitution?
3. What are the three features of a type identified in this chapter?
4. Which properties of a type are not captured in an interface definition?
5. What does it mean to say that one class is a subtype of another?
6. How can a class be a subclass of another and not a subtype?
7. How can a class be a subtype of another and not a subclass?
8. Why don't compilers use the subtype relationship to verify the validity of assignments or parameter passing?
9. What is subclassing for construction?
10. What is a private inheritance in C++? How does it differ from a normal (public) inheritance?
11. How is the association of type and parameter different in a dynamically typed language than a statically typed language?
12. What are preconditions and postconditions for a method?
13. Why are preconditions and postconditions not found in many programming languages?
14. What are refinement semantics for method overriding? How do they differ from replacement semantics?

Exercises ⊡

1. Describe some of the ways that the class NonStack fails to satisfy the properties expected of the Stack data structure.
2. Try to develop a more complete specification of the Stack data type. Can you write your specification in a formal language (such as a computer might understand), or do you need to resort to more ambiguous natural language expressions?
3. Describe as many properties as you can for the Array data abstraction. Will a Dictionary satisfy your specifications? Will a SparseArray?

4. The language Java does not support the idea of private inheritance. What are the alternatives? How can a programmer make use of the abilities provided by an existing class without creating a class that could potentially (and wrongly) be assumed to be a subtype of the class?

5. Exercise 5 in Chapter 8 proposed a change to the Java language that would separate the use of inheritance for code reuse from the issue of substitution. Would this change solve the subclass/subtype problem? Explain why or why not.

CHAPTER 11

Static and Dynamic Behavior

Much of the power of object-oriented languages derives from the ability of objects to change their behavior dynamically at run time. Understanding object-oriented programming mechanisms therefore requires an appreciation of the differences between static and dynamic behavior and the implications of this difference.

In programming languages, the term *static* almost always refers to a property or feature that is bound at compile time and cannot thereafter be modified. A statically typed variable, for example, means that the type associated with the variable is set at compile time and cannot change during the course of execution. The term *dynamic*, on the other hand, almost always refers to a property or feature that cannot be bound until run time. Thus, a dynamically typed variable will have its type determined by the value it is currently holding, which may change during the course of execution.

In this chapter we explore this static versus dynamic distinction in the context of three related concepts. First, we examine in detail static versus dynamic typing. Next, we explore the concepts of static and dynamic classes in statically typed languages. And finally, we investigate static and dynamic binding of message and methods.

11.1 ⊡ Static versus Dynamic Typing

The most obvious dichotomy in programming languages occurs between those languages that are statically typed and those that are dynamically typed. Table 11.1 describes a few of these, both object-oriented and non-object-oriented

221

	Object-Oriented	Non-Object-Oriented
Statically	C++, Delphi Pascal, Eiffel, Java, Objective-C (sometimes)	Ada, Algol, C, Fortran, Haskell, ML, Modula
Dynamically	Objective-C, Smalltalk, Dylan, Python	APL, Forth, Lisp, Prolog, Snobol

▫ Table 11.1 —— Statically typed and dynamically typed languages

languages. All programming languages incorporate the concept of *type*. The difference between static and dynamically typed languages is the question of whether types are a property of variables or of values.

In a statically typed language, a type is attached to a variable at compile time. Most often this happens through the use of declaration statements.

```
int a; // variable a will maintain integer values
double m; // while variable m holds floating point quantities
```

Some statically typed programming languages use a more subtle process of *type inference*. The (non-object-oriented) language ML is the best known example of a language that uses this technique. Here the type associated with variables is inferred from the program, thereby avoiding the requirement that the programmer provide explicit declaration statements.

```
// b must be integer, since it is being added
// to the integer constant 2.
// therefore n must also be integer,
// as must be a
val a = (b + 2) / n;
```

In contrast, there are languages that are dynamically typed. In a dynamically typed language (sometimes called an *untyped* language) types are associated with values but not with variables. A variable is simply a name. Not only may the value that a variable holds change during the course of execution, but the type of value the variable is maintaining can also change, as in the following sequences of assignments in Smalltalk.

```
a <- 2. " value is currently integer "
a <- true. " now it is boolean "
a <- 'true'   " now it is string "
```

The dichotomy between statically typed and dynamically typed languages has existed since the earliest days of programming languages. Fortran and Lisp, both created in the 1950s, were two early examples of each type. Arguments concerning the benefits of the two approaches have raged almost as long. Generally the arguments pit the competing goals of efficiency versus flexibility.

It is true that statically binding a language feature means that more can be done at compile time, and hence less work is generally required at run time. For instance, the memory layout for statically declared variables can be determined once at compile time, and this is generally more efficient than if memory requirements must be reevaluated each time the value of a variable changes. Similarly static compile time typing does allow many programming errors to be caught early, before a program begins execution.

The advocates of dynamic languages, on the other hand, assert that flexibility is more important than efficiency. Consider, for example, a simple procedure such as the following.

```
function max (left, right) {
  if  (left < right)
    then return right;
  return left;
}
```

The only requirements we need to impose on the arguments are that they understand the comparison operator. The proponents of dynamically typed languages argue that we should be able to write functions such as max and use them with a wide variety of types: integers, floats, strings, or anything else.

Both arguments have their valid points, and we are not going to take sides. Both statically typed and dynamically typed object-oriented languages exist, and both will probably continue to be used for the foreseeable future.

11.2 ▫ Static and Dynamic Classes

The introduction of object-oriented features to a statically typed programming language requires a relaxation of some of the principles of static typing. Recall the principle of substitution described in Chapter 8. This principle asserted that a variable declared as a parent class type could in fact be maintaining a value from a child class. In order to distinguish these two types we introduce a pair of terms. The *static class* of a variable is the class that was used in the declaration of the variable. The static class (as the name suggests) is fixed at compile time and does not ever change. The *dynamic class* of a variable is the class associated with the value it currently holds. Again, as the name suggests, the dynamic class can change during the course of execution as a variable is assigned new values.

```
var
  obj : GrapicalObject; (* GraphicalObject is the static class *)
begin
  obj = new Ball(); (* Ball is the current dynamic class *)
    .
    .
    .
  obj = new Wall(); (* Wall is now the dynamic class *)
end
```

The most important aspect of the distinction between static and dynamic types is the following.

In a statically typed object-oriented programming language, the legality of a message-passing expression is determined at compile time based on the static class of the receiver and not on its current dynamic value.

To see what we mean by this, consider a class hierarchy such as the set of Java classes shown in Figure 11.1. All Animals know how to speak, but only dogs and scals know how to bark. Imagine that we then have the following statements.

```
Dog fido;
fido = new Dog();
fido.speak(); // will bark
```

```
class Animal {
  public void speak () { System.out.println("Animal Speak !"); }
}

class Dog extends Animal {
  public void speak () { bark(); }
  public void bark () { System.out.println("Woof !"); }
}

class Seal extends Animal {
  public void bark () { System.out.println("Arf !"); }
}

class Bird extends Animal {
  public void speak () { System.out.println("Tweet !");
}
```

▫ Figure 11.1 ——— A Java animal class hierarchy

```
Woof !
  fido.bark();  // will bark
Woof !

  Animal pet;
  pet = fido;  // legal to assign Dog to Animal

  pet.speak();  // will work
Woof !
  pet.bark();  // error, pets do not know how to bark
```

The variable fido is declared as Dog and thus can both speak and bark. When assigned to a variable of type Animal, however, the static class changes to Animal, although the dynamic class remains Dog. Because of the change in the declared class, the variable pet is not guaranteed to understand the message bark, and thus a compile time error will be given. This is true despite the fact that the value currently being held by the variable certainly is able to understand the message.

11.2.1   Run-time type determination

The principle of substitution can be viewed as moving a value up the inheritance hierarchy. Assigning a value of type Dog to a variable of type Animal moves the presumed type from the child class to the parent.

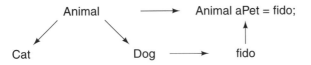

Occasionally it is necessary to do the reverse: to determine if a value currently being held by a variable declared with one class type is, in fact, derived from a class that is lower in the class hierarchy—for example, to determine if a value held by a variable of type Animal is, in fact, a Dog.

Every object-oriented language has the ability to perform such a test, but the syntax used by the various languages differs greatly. Figure 11.2 illustrates some of these facilities. These types of tests are useful even in dynamically typed object-oriented languages, and thus we have included features from those languages as well.

The functions shown in Figure 11.2 test a value to determine if it is a descendant of a given class—that is, whether it was created as an instance of the class or a child class. Some languages also provide a more precise test to determine if a value was created precisely from a given class and not from a child class. These facilities are shown in Figure 11.3.

C++

```
Animal * aPet = ...; // a pointer to an animal
Dog * d = dynamic_cast<Dog *>(aPet);
if (d != 0) { // null if not legal, nonnull if ok
    .
    .
    .
}
```

CLOS

```
(if (typep aPet 'Dog) ... )
```

Delphi Pascal

```
if (aPet is Dog) then
    .
    .
    .
```

Eiffel

```
aPet : Animal
aDog : Dog

aDog ?= aPet -- assignment attempt
if (aDog |= Void) ... -- will succeed if pet was a dog
```

Java

```
if (aPet instanceof Dog)
    .
    .
    .
```

Object Pascal

```
if Member (aPet, Dog) then
    .
    .
    .
```

Python

```
if isinstance(aPet, Dog):
    .
    .
    .
```

Ruby

```
if aPet.kind_of? Dog
```

Smalltalk

```
(aPet isKindOf: Dog) ifTrue: [ ... ]
```

◻ Figure 11.2 —— Mechanisms for testing class

Delphi Pascal

```
if aPet.classInfo = Dog then ...
```

Ruby

```
if aPet.instance_of? Dog
```

Smalltalk

```
(aPet isMemberOf: Dog) ifTrue: [ ... ]
or
(aPet class == Dog) ifTrue: [ ... ]
```

▫ Figure 11.3 —— Facilities to test for a specific class

11.2.2   Down casting (reverse polymorphism)

Once it has been determined that a value is from a given class, often the next step is to convert the value from the parent class to the child class. This process is termed *down casting*, or *reverse polymorphism* (since it reverses the effect of a polymorphic assignment). The syntax used for down casting operations in various languages is shown in Figure 11.4. Note that several languages combine down casting with type testing by having a function that returns a valid result if the conversion is proper and an empty (or null) result if the conversion cannot legally be performed.

*11.2.3   Run-time testing without language support

Before the introduction of the RTTI system (the dynamic_cast operator) to C++ it was common for programmers to simulate run-time typing using nothing more than method overriding. Although this is no longer required in C++, similar tricks may still be useful in languages that lack built-in primitives for testing the dynamic class of variables.

Imagine that we have modified our class hierarchy as follows.[1]

```
class Animal {
public:
   virtual Dog * isDog () { return 0; }
   virtual Bird * isBird () { return 0; }
   .
   .
   .
```

---

1. The meaning of the virtual keyword will be explain in the next section.

```
};

class Dog : public Animal {
public:
  virtual Dog * isDog () { return this; }
  .
  .
  .
};
```

C++

```
Animal * aPet = ... ;
Dog * d = dynamic_cast<Dog *>(aPet);
if (d != 0) { // null if not legal, nonnull if ok
   .
   .
   .
}
```

Delphi Pascal

```
var
  aPet : Animal;
  aDog : Dog;

aDog := aPet as Child
```

Eiffel

```
aPet : Animal
aDog : Dog

aDog ?= aPet -- assignment attempt
if (aDog |= Void) ... -- will succeed if pet was a dog
```

Java

```
Animal aPet;
Dog d;
d = (Dog) aPet;
```

Object Pascal

```
aDog = Dog(aPet)
```

⊡ Figure 11.4 —— Mechanisms for downcasting

```
class Bird : public Animal {
public:
  virtual Bird * isBird () { return this; }
    .
    .
    .
};
```

Imagine now that we have a variable declared as a pointer to type Animal, and we want to know if it really is maintaining a value of type Dog. If we pass it the message isDog, we will get back either a null value, if it is not a dog, or a valid pointer to a Dog. This is because the method isDog in the root class is returning a null value but has been overridden in the class Dog, to return a pointer to itself (using the pseudo-variable this to reference itself). If the value is truly a Dog the overridden method will be executed; otherwise the method in the root class will be. Thus, the message isDog is simulating the behavior of the dynamic_cast used by the RTTI system, albeit at the cost of introducing a new method.

```
Animal * aPet = ...;
Dog * aDog;
aDog = aPet.isDog(); // try the assignment
if (aDog)  ... // true if it was a dog, false otherwise
```

11.2.4 Testing message understanding

In dynamically typed object-oriented languages it is generally true that the legality of a message-passing expression cannot be known until run-time. If the receiver does not know how to respond to a message, then a run-time exception is thrown. Occasionally it is useful for the programmer to be able to test whether a receiver will understand a particular message before actually attempting to pass the message to the receiver. Mechanisms to do this are shown in Figure 11.5.

Smalltalk

```
(aPet respondsTo: #bark) ifTrue: [ ... ]
```

Ruby

```
if aPet.respond_to?("bark") ...
```

Objective-C

```
if ( [ aPet respondsTo: @selector(bark) ] ) { ... }
```

▫ Figure 11.5 —— Mechanism to determine if an object understands a message

11.3 ▫ Static versus Dynamic Method Binding

In almost all object-oriented programming languages, the binding of a method to execute in response to a message is determined by the dynamic value currently being held by the receiver. Thus, in the following Java statements the first invocation of speak will produce "woof" and in the second "tweet," as the dynamic type changes from Dog to Bird.

```
    Animal pet;
    pet = new Dog();
    pet.speak();
woof !
    pet = new Bird();
    pet.speak();
tweet !
```

In a few languages the rules for overriding are more difficult. Most notable among these is C++, although C#, Delphi Pascal, and Oberon-2 also have similar restrictions. The binding of methods to messages in C++ is complex, involving a number of choices of keywords and mechanisms for declaration. Some of these variations are shown in Figure 11.6.

```cpp
class Animal {
public:
  virtual void speak () { cout << "Animal Speak !\n"; }
  void reply () { cout << "Animal Reply !\n"; }
};

class Dog : public Animal {
public:
  virtual void speak () { cout << "woof !\n"; }
  void reply () { cout << "woof again!\n"; }
};

class Bird : public Animal {
public:
  virtual void speak () { cout << "tweet !\n"; }
};
```

▫ Figure 11.6 —— Virtual and nonvirtual overriding in C++

Let us say that a variable is *polymorphic* if the binding of message to a method is determined by the type associated with the value most recently assigned to the variable. (All variables in Smalltalk, Java, and most other object-oriented languages are, in this sense, polymorphic.) Variables in C++ that are declared with a simple type are not polymorphic, in this sense. Consider the following declarations of values and their executions in response to different messages.

```
    Animal a;
    Dog b;
    b.speak();
woof !
    a  = b;
    a.speak();
Animal speak !
    Bird c;
    c.speak();
tweet !
    a = c;
    a.speak();
Animal speak !
```

Note that in each instance, the method executed in response to the message speak when the receiver is type Animal is that found in the static class Animal. This is true even if the value held by the variable came from an assignment of a different type.

Now contrast this with what happens when pointers are used instead of simple values.

```
    Animal * d;
    d = &b; // point to the dog from earlier example
    (*d).speak();
woof !
    d = & c;
    d->speak(); // arrow is shorthand for (*).
tweet !
```

Thus, object values referenced by pointers are polymorphic in the sense that we defined the term earlier. The language C++ includes the notion of a reference, which is simply a pointer that is guaranteed to point to a valid object. References, too, are polymorphic.

```
    Animal & e = b;
    e.speak();
woof !
```

```
Animal & f = c;
   f.speak();
tweet !
```

The careful reader will have noted the presence of the keyword virtual in the declaration of the methods shown in Figure 11.6. This keyword is important. If it is left off, then even object references made by means of pointers are no longer polymorphic. This is shown by the message reply, which has not been declared as virtual.

```
Animal * g = &b;
   g.reply();
Animal reply!
   g = &c;
   g.reply();
Animal reply!
```

A nonvirtual method that is modified in the child class will be executed if the static class of the receiver is the child class and not the parent class.

```
b.reply()
woof again !
```

So polymorphic message sending is found in C++ only when using pointers or references, and even there only when the associated methods have been declared as virtual. To understand why the rules for C++ are so much more complex than the rules used by other programming languages, we need to explore the link between object-oriented polymorphic variables and memory management. We will investigate this further in the next chapter.

C# and Delphi Pascal also require the keyword virtual, although since they lack references, their rules for determining the meaning of a message expression are not as complex as those of C++. We will consider message overriding in these languages later in Chapter 16. In Oberon-2, like in C++, the meaning of a message given to a pointer variable differs from the meaning of the same message given to an ordinary variable.

Summary ▫

Static features are aspects of a program that are fixed at compile time. Dynamic features can change at run-time. The dichotomy between static and dynamic is manifested in object-oriented languages in a number of different ways. In this chapter we have considered static and dynamic typing, static and dynamic classes, and static and dynamic method binding.

- In a statically typed language, types are associated with variables. In a dynamically typed language, a variable is simply a name, and types are associated with values.
- Static typing is generally more efficient and provides better error detection. Dynamic typing is generally more flexible.
- In a statically typed object-oriented language, the static class is the class used to declare a variable, and the dynamic class is the class of the value it currently holds.
- The legality of a message expression is determined by a variable's static class. The meaning is determined by its dynamic class.
- Downcasting, or reverse polymorphism, is a conversion that moves down the class hierarchy.
- A message can be bound to a method using either the static class or the dynamic class. In some languages the programmer provides a keyword to indicate which type of binding is desired.

Further Reading ⊡

Brad Cox [Cox 1986] is one author who has explored the importance of static versus dynamic features in languages.

Self-Study Questions ⊡

1. When used to describe features of programming languages, what does the term *static* mean?
2. What does the term *dynamic* mean?
3. How does a statically typed programming language differ from a dynamically typed one?
4. What is type inference? What characterizes languages that use type inference?
5. What arguments are made in support of statically typed programming languages? What arguments are made in support of dynamically typed languages?
6. What is a static class? What is a dynamic class? How is a dynamic class different from a dynamic type?
7. How is the legality of a message-passing expression determined by a compiler in a statically typed language?
8. What is down casting?
9. What is the difference between a method that is statically bound to a message expression and one that is dynamically bound?

Exercises ⊡

1. Object Pascal uses static typing, but it also uses dynamic binding. Explain why the converse is not possible—that is, why it is not possible for a language to use dynamic typing and static binding of messages and methods.

2. Give an example that will illustrate why, in a statically typed object-oriented language (such as C++ or Object Pascal), the compiler is justified in not permitting a value associated with a variable declared as a parent class to be assigned to another variable declared as an instance of a subclass.

3. Discuss whether the error-checking facilities made possible by static typing are worth the loss in flexibility.

4. Oberon functions can use pass-by-reference. A var parameter becomes an alias for the corresponding argument, and further assignments inside the procedure alter the argument value.

```
PROCEDURE setx (VAR x : INTEGER);
BEGIN
  x := 7;
END

y := 12;
setx(y);
writeln(y);
    7
```

When object values are passed as arguments to var parameters in Oberon they are not permitted to change their type at all. That is, the static and dynamic classes must match, and this condition is checked by the run-time system. Explain why this restriction is necessary and what typing errors could otherwise arise without the limitation.

CHAPTER 12

Implications of Substitution

The introduction of inheritance and, in particular, the principle of substitution, has a subtle but pervasive impact on almost all aspects of a programming language. In this chapter, we will examine some of these effects, considering in detail the type system, the meaning of assignment, testing for equivalence, the creation of copies, and storage allocation.

We have described the is-a relationship as a fundamental property of inheritance. One way to view the is-a relationship is as a means of associating a *type*, as in a type of a variable, with a set of *values*—namely, the values the variable can legally hold. If a variable win is declared as an instance of a specific class— say, Window—certainly it should be legal for win to hold values of type Window. If we have a subclass of Window—say, TextWindow, since a TextWindow is-a Window—it should certainly make sense that win can hold a value of type TextWindow. This is the principle of substitution that we encountered in previous chapters.

While this principle makes intuitive sense, from a practical point of view there are difficulties associated with implementing object-oriented languages in a way that this intuitive behavior can be realized. These difficulties are not insurmountable, but the way various language designers have chosen to address them differs from language to language. An examination of these problems and of how they affect the language illuminates the reasons for some of the obscure features of languages over which the unwary programmer is likely to stumble.

12.1 ◻ Memory Layout

Let us start by considering a seemingly simple question, the various answers to which will lead us in different directions: How much storage should we allocate to an object instantiated from a specific class? To take a concrete example, how much storage should we allocate to the variable win that we earlier described as being an instance of class Window?

It is commonly believed that variables allocated on the stack as part of the procedure-activation process are more efficient than are variables allocated on the heap.[1] Accordingly, language designers and implementors go to great lengths to make it possible for variables to be stack-allocated. But there is a major problem with stack allocation: The storage requirements must be determined statically at compile time or, at the latest, at procedure entry time. These times are well before the values the variable will hold are known.

The difficulty is that subclasses can introduce data not present in a superclass. The class TextWindow, for example, probably brings with it data areas for character buffers, locations of the current edit point, and so on. The following might be a typical declaration.

```
class Window {
  public:
    virtual void oops();
       .
       .
       .
  private:
    int height;
    int width;
};

class TextWindow : public Window {
  public:
    virtual void oops();
       .
       .
       .
  private:
    char * contents;
    int cursorLocation;
};
```

```
Window win;   // declare a variable of type window
```

Should the additional data values (contents and cursorLocation here) be taken into consideration when space for win is allocated? There are at least three plausible answers.

---

1. But see [Appel 1987] for a dissenting opinion.

1. Allocate the amount of space necessary for the base class only. That is, allocate to win only those data areas declared as part of the class Window, ignoring the space requirements of subclasses.

2. Allocate the maximum amount of space necessary for any legal value, whether from the base class or from any subclass.

3. Allocate only the amount of space necessary to hold a single pointer. Allocate the space necessary for the value at run time on the heap, and set the pointer value appropriately.

All three solutions are possible, and two of them are found in the languages we are considering. In the following sections, we will investigate some of the implications of this design decision.

12.1.1 Minimum static space allocation

The language C was designed to be run-time efficient. Thus, given the widespread belief that stack-based allocation of memory locations results in faster execution times than are possible with dynamic variables, it is not surprising that its successor, C++, retains the concepts of both nondynamic and dynamic (run-time-allocated) variables.

In C++, the distinction is made in how a variable is declared and, accordingly, whether pointers are used to access the values of the variable. In the following, for example, the variable win is allocated on the stack. Space for it will be set aside on the stack when the procedure containing the declaration is entered. The size of this area will be the size of the base class alone. The variable tWinPtr, on the other hand, contains only a pointer. Space for the value pointed to by tWinPtr will be allocated dynamically when a new statement is executed. Since by this time the size of a TextWindow is known, there are no problems associated with allocating an amount of storage on the heap sufficient to hold a TextWindow.

```
Window win;
Window *tWinPtr;
   .
   .
   .
tWinPtr = new TextWindow;
```

What happens when the value pointed to by tWinPtr is assigned to win? In other words, what happens when the user executes this statement?

```
win = *tWinPtr;
```

The space allocated to win is only large enough to accommodate a Window, whereas the value pointed to by tWinPtr is larger (Figure 12.1). Clearly, not all of the values pointed to by tWinPtr can be copied. The default behavior is to copy

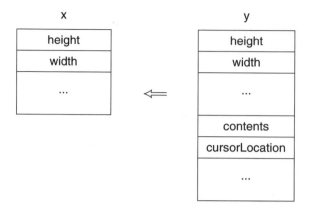

▢ Figure 12.1 —— Assigning a larger value to a smaller box

only the corresponding fields. (In C++, the user can override the meaning of the assignment operator and provide any semantics desired. Thus, we refer here only to the default behavior observed in the absence of any alternative provided by the user.) Clearly, then, some information is lost (the information contained in the extra fields of tWinPtr). Some authors use the term *slicing* for this process, since the fields in the right side that are not found in the left side are sliced off during assignment.

Is it important that this information is lost? A cynic will answer, "Only if the user can tell the difference." The question is therefore how the user might be able to notice.

The semantics of the C++ language ensure that only methods defined in the class Window can be invoked with win and no methods defined in TextWindow. Methods defined in Window and implemented in that class cannot access or modify data defined in subclasses, so no access is possible there. But what about methods defined in class Window but *overridden* in the subclass?

Consider, for example, the two procedures oops() shown here. If the user executed win.oops() and the method from class TextWindow was selected, an attempt would be made to display the data value win.cursorLocation, which does not exist in the storage assigned to win. This would either cause a memory violation or (more likely) produce garbage.

```
void Window::oops()
{
   cout << "Window oops" << endl;
}

void TextWindow::oops()
```

```
{
    cout << "TextWindow oops " << cursorLocation << endl;
}
```

The solution to this dilemma selected by the designer of C++ was to change the rules that are used to bind a procedure to the invocation of a virtual method. The new rules can be summarized as follows.

- For pointers (and references): When a message invokes a member function that could potentially have been overridden, the member function selected is determined by the dynamic value of the receiver.
- For other variables: The binding on a call of a virtual member function is determined by the static class (the class of the declaration) and not by the dynamic class (the class of the actual value).

More accurately, during the process of assignment the value is *changed* from the type representing the subclass to a value of the type represented by the parent class. This is analogous to the way an integer variable might be changed during assignment to a floating-point variable. With this interpretation, it is possible to ensure that, for stack-based variables, the dynamic class is *always* the same as the static class. Given this rule, it is not possible for a procedure to access fields that are not physically present in the object. The method selected in the call win.oops() would be that found in class Window, and the user would not notice the fact that memory was lost during the assignment.

Nevertheless, this solution is achieved only at the expense of introducing a subtle inconsistency. Expressions involving pointers bind virtual methods in the manner we described in earlier chapters. Thus, these values will perform differently from expressions using nondynamic values. Consider the following.

```
Window win;
TextWindow *tWinPtr, *tWin;
    .
    .
    .
tWinPtr = new TextWindow;
win = * tWinPtr;
tWin = tWinPtr;

win.oops( ) ;
tWin->oops( ) ;
```

Although the user is likely to think that win and the value pointed to by tWin are the same, it is important to remember that the assignment to win has transformed the type of the value. Because of this change, the first call on oops() will invoke the method in class Window, whereas the second will invoke that in class TextWindow.

Oberon-2 is another language that uses slicing on assignment, with a similar impact on semantics.

12.1.2   Maximum static space allocation

A different solution to the problem of deciding how much space to allocate to a declaration for an object is to assign the maximum amount of space used by any value the variable might hold, whether from the class named in the declaration or from any subclass. This approach is similar to the one used to lay out overlaid types in conventional languages, such as variant records in Pascal or union structures in C. On assignment, it is not possible to assign a value larger than what fits in the target destination, so the picture shown in Figure 12.1 cannot occur, and the subsequent problems described in the last section do not arise.

This would seem to be an ideal solution were it not for one small problem: The size of any object cannot be known until an entire program has been seen. Not simply a module (unit in Object Pascal, file in C++) but the entire program must be scanned before the size of any object can be determined. Because this requirement is so restrictive, no major object-oriented language uses this approach.

12.1.3   Dynamic memory allocation

The third approach does not store the *value* of objects on the stack at all. When space for an identifier is allocated on the stack at the beginning of a procedure, it is simply large enough for a pointer. The values are maintained in a separate data area, the heap, that is not subject to the first-in last-out allocation protocol of the stack. Since all pointers have a constant fixed size, no problem arises when a value from a subclass is assigned to a variable declared to be from a superclass.

This is the approach used in Object Pascal, Smalltalk, Java, and Objective-C. The reader might already have guessed by the close similarity of objects and pointers in Object Pascal. For both pointers and objects, it is necessary to invoke the standard procedure new to allocate space before the object can be manipulated. Similarly, it is necessary for the programmer to call free explicitly to release space allocated for the object.

Besides the requirement for explicit user memory allocation, another problem with this technique is that it is often tied to the use of *pointer semantics* for assignment. When pointer semantics are used, the value transferred in an assignment statement is simply the pointer value rather than the value indicated by the pointer. Consider the following program, which implements a one-integer buffer that can be set and retrieved by the user.

```
type
  intBuffer = object
    value : integer;
  end;
var
  x, y : intBuffer;

begin
  new(x);      { create a buffer }
  x.value := 5;
  writeln(x.value);
  y := x;      { y is same buffer as x }
  y.value := 7;
  writeln(x.value);
end;
```

Notice the two variables x and y declared to be instances of this class. In executing the program, the user might be surprised when the last statement prints out the value 7 rather than the value 5. The reason for this surprising result is that x and y do not just have the same value; they point to the same object. This situation is shown in Figure 12.2. The use of pointer semantics for objects in Object Pascal is particularly confusing because the alternative, *copy semantics*, is used for all other data types. If x and y were structures, the assignment of y to x would result in the copying of information from y to x. Since this would create two separate copies, changes to y would not be reflected in changes in x.

Garbage collection

Because dynamically allocated objects are stored on the heap, they will not be automatically recovered when a procedure exits. As we noted in an earlier chapter, some languages force the programmer to explicitly indicate when the memory associated with an object can be recovered. Other languages use a technique termed *garbage collection* to automatically monitor the utilization of object values

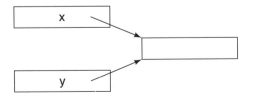

◻ Figure 12.2 —— Two object variables pointing to the same value

and reclaim them when they can no longer have any impact on the execution of a program.

Generally, the use of garbage collection systems results in fewer programming errors due to the mismanagement of memory, but it imposes a greater cost in execution time.

12.2 □ Assignment

The memory-allocation strategies used in a programming language have an effect on the meaning of assignment, so we will summarize the exact meaning of this operator in the various languages we are considering. As noted in the last section, there are two interpretations we can give to assignment.

Copy semantics. Assignment copies the entire value of the right side, assigning it to the left side. Thereafter, the two values are independent, and changes in one are not reflected in changes in the other. Copy semantics are sometimes used in C++ and sometimes not (we will explain shortly).

Pointer semantics. Assignment changes the reference of the left side to be the right side. (This approach is sometimes referred to as *pointer assignment*.) Thus, the two variables not only have the same value but also refer to the same memory location. Changes in one will alter the value held in common, which will be reflected in references obtained under either name. Pointer semantics are used in Java, CLOS, Object Pascal, and many other object-oriented languages.

(A compromise position between copy semantics and pointer semantics is found in some programming languages, although not in any of the languages we are considering in our case studies. The idea is to use pointer semantics for assignment but to convert a value into a new structure if it is ever modified. In this manner assignments are very efficient, but a value cannot be inadvertently modified by a change to an aliasing variable. This technique is often termed *copy on write*.)

Generally, if pointer semantics are used, languages provide some means for producing a true copy. Also, pointer semantics are generally more often used when all objects are allocated on a heap (dynamically) rather than on the stack (automatically). When pointer semantics are used, it is common for a value to outlive the context in which it is created.

Object-oriented languages differ in which of the two semantics they use, providing one, the other, or combinations of both.

*12.2.1   Assignment in C++

The default algorithm used in C++ to assign a class value to a variable is to copy corresponding data fields recursively. However, it is possible to overload the assignment operator to produce any behavior desired. This technique is so common that some C++ compilers issue a warning if the default assignment rule is used.

In assignment overloading the interpretation is that assignment is a message given to the expression to the left of the assignment operator, passing the expression to the right of the operator as argument. The result can be void if embedded assignments are not possible, although more typically the result is a reference to the receiver. The following example shows assignment of a string data type, which redefines assignment so that two copies of the same string share characters.

```
String & String::operator = (String& right)
{
  len = right.len;  // copy the length
  buffer = right.buffer;  // copy the pointer to values
  return (*this);
}
```

A common source of confusion for new C++ programmers is the use of the same symbol for assignment and for initialization. In conventional C, an assignment used in a declaration statement is simply a syntactic shorthand. That is, the effect of

```
int limit = 300;
```

is the same as

```
int limit;
limit = 300;
```

In C++ an assignment used in a declaration may select the constructors invoked and may not use the assignment operator at all. That is, a statement such as

```
Complex x = 4;
```

is interpreted to mean the same as the declaration

```
Complex x(4);
```

Reference variables.
Initialization is often used with reference variables and yields a situation very similar to pointer semantics. If s is a valid String, for example, the following makes t an alias for the value of s, so any change in one will be reflected in the other. As we have noted, declarations in C++ can be inserted into a program at any point.

```
... use of variable s
String & t = s;
...//  t and s now refer to the same value
```

Reference variables are most often used to implement call-by-reference parameter passing. This use can be considered a form of pointer assignment, where the parameter is being assigned the argument value. Of course, pointer semantics in C++ can also be achieved through pointer variables.

Parameter passing is in part a form of assignment (the assignment of the parameter values to the arguments), and so it is not surprising that the same issues occur here as in assignment. For example, consider the definitions shown here.

```
class Parent {
public:
  virtual void see() { cout << "In parent\n" ;}
};

class Child : public Parent {
public:
  virtual void see() { cout << "In child\n"; }
};

void f (Parent x) { x.see(); }
void g (Parent & x) { x.see(); }

Child aChild;
f(aChild);
g(aChild);
```

Both the functions f and g take as argument a value declared as the parent type, but g declares the value as a reference type. If f is called with a value of the child type, the value is converted (*sliced*) to create a value of the parent type as part of the assignment of the arguments. Thus, if see is invoked from within f, the virtual function from the base class will be used. On the other hand, this conversion, or slicing, does not occur as part of the parameter passing to g. So if see is invoked from within g, the procedure from the child class will be used. This difference in interpretation, which depends only on the one character in the function header, is sometimes known as the *slicing problem*.

The overloading of the assignment symbol and the choice of parameter-passing mechanisms provided by value and reference assignment in C++ are powerful features, but they can also be quite subtle. For example, the assignment symbol used in initialization, although it is the same as the assignment symbol used in statements, is not altered by a redefinition of the assignment operator. A good explanation of the uses and power of assignment in C++ is given by Koenig [Koenig 1989a, Koenig 1989b].

12.3 ◻ Copies and Clones

When languages use pointer semantics for assignment, they almost always provide a means to create a copy, or clone, from a value. But even in this simple task there are subtle issues that can trap the unwary. In particular, what actions should be taken when creating a copy of a value that itself points to other objects? There are two possible interpretations. A *shallow copy* shares instance variables with the original. That is, the original and the copy reference the exact same values.

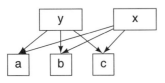

On the other hand, a deepCopy creates new copies of the instance variables, yielding a picture like this.

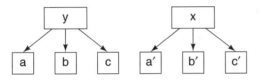

And, of course, the questions can continue recursively by asking what techniques are used to create the copies of a, b, and c.

In the following sections we will describe the facilities for creating copies in some of the languages we are considering.

12.3.1   Copies in Smalltalk and Objective-C

In Smalltalk the fundamental root class Object defines three methods: copy, shallow-Copy, and deepCopy. A deep copy recursively creates a deep copy of any instance data it may hold. Classes are themselves free to override any of these methods to exhibit different behavior. Objective-C uses methods that are analogous to those used in Smalltalk.

12.3.2   Copy constructors in C++

Copies of values are frequently produced by the C++ run-time system as temporaries or arguments to procedures. The user can control this task by defining a *copy constructor*. The argument to a copy constructor is a reference parameter of the same type as the class itself. It is considered good practice to always create a copy constructor.

```
class Complex {
public:
   .
   .
   .

   Complex (const Complex & source)
      {
         // simply duplicate fields from source
         rl = source.rl;
         im = source.im;
      }
   .
   .
   .

private:
   double rl;
   double im;
}
```

12.3.3   Cloning in Java

The class Object in Java defines a method named clone, but the method is declared as protected. To make an object that can be copied using this method the programmer must do two things. First, the programmer must declare that their class supports the Cloneable interface. Second, the method clone must be overridden and made public. This method potentially throws the error CloneNotSupportedException, which must also be part of the declaration. The method need not actually do anything other than invoke the method inherited from the parent class.

```
class PlayingCard implements Cloneable {
   .
   .
   .

   public Object clone ( ) throws CloneNotSupportedException {
      Object newCard = super.clone();
      return newCard;
   }
}
```

The default behavior creates a shallow copy. If a deep copy, or any other domain-specific behavior, is desired, the programmer can add additional code subsequent to invoking the parent method.

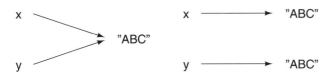

□ Figure 12.3 ——Identity and equality for character strings

12.4 □ Equality

Like assignment, deciding whether one object is equivalent to another is more subtle than it might at first appear. There are two issues to examine in relation to this problem. The first is the difference between equality and identity (Figure 12.3). The second is the paradoxes that can arise in the context of substitution if classes are allowed to redefine the meaning of equality.

12.4.1 Equality and identity

There is an old joke that goes something like this: A man walks into a pizza parlor and sits down. A waiter comes to the table and asks the man what he would like to order. The man looks around the room, then points to the woman sitting at the next table and says, "I'll have what she is eating." The waiter thereupon walks to the woman's table, picks up the half-eaten pizza from in front of her, and places it before the startled customer.

The reason this story is funny is because it confuses two related but distinct concepts: identity and equality. When we ask questions of identity, we are seeking to determine if two objects are precisely the same entity. This is what is being asked if somebody inquires, "Is the morning star the same as the evening star?" (Morning star and evening star are both common names for the planet Venus.)

On the other hand, when the man said he wanted what the woman was eating, he did not mean he wanted literally the same object she was eating but a different object that was in all important respects equivalent to what she had before her.

The question of identity versus equality did not originate with object-oriented languages, although they do seem to be more common in such languages. But strings, for example, have always needed special treatment for just this reason (Figure 12.3). Many beginning C programmers have had a program fail because they used the equality operator on two character pointers instead of the special purpose string comparison function.

```
char * a = "abc";
char * b = "abc";

if (a == b)  // will surprisingly not be true...
```

This fails because the two pointers reference different memory locations, even though the values stored at those two different locations are the same.

The double equal sign used to test identity in C and C++ is also used for the identity operator in Java, C#, and Objective-C.

12.4.2   The paradoxes of equality testing

While identity is easily defined, the meaning of equality is inherently domain specific. Should two strings, for example, be considered equal if they have the same character representation? What about two triangles? Should they be considered equal if they have the same side lengths even if they are different objects? There is no single correct answer, and every problem (and every programmer) must decide as the situation requires.

In order to accommodate this flexibility, many object-oriented languages permit the programmer to define the meaning of an equality testing operator. Equality testing is, then, nothing more than a message that is given to one value, passing the other as argument. Because message passing is not symmetric, there can be no guarantees that if a is equal to b, it follows that b will be equal to a.

In languages in which all classes descend from a common root, the equality testing operator is often defined in the root class and can be overridden in subclasses. This presents a quandary for strongly typed languages: What type should be associated with the argument value? Almost always this problem is solved by declaring the argument as the root type. Child classes are then obligated to use the same type signature, and hence the argument must be tested and cast before a meaningful comparison can be performed. For example, in the following Java class definition, the argument to equals (a method inherited from class Object) must be declared as Object. But the programmer is only concerned with testing playing cards to playing cards. Hence, a conversion is necessary before the actual test can be performed.

```java
class PlayingCard extends Object {
    .
    .
    .
    public boolean equals (Object right) {
        if (right instanceof PlayingCard) {
            PlayingCard rightCard = (PlayingCard) right;
            // do card-card comparison
            return (rank = rightCard.rank) &&
                (suit == rightCard.suit);
        }
        return false; // false on all other comparisons
    }
}
```

Because overriding of the equality operator can be performed at various levels of a class hierarchy, a number of curious paradoxes can arise. Assume, for example, that we have two classes, Parent and Child, that both provide a meaning for the equality testing message. Because each class is free to provide whatever meaning it wishes for any method, we can in general say nothing concerning the relationship between these two methods. So each of the following situations could easily occur.

- Let p be an instance of the Parent class, and c an instance of the Child class. Since testing whether p equals c is performed by the method in the parent class, while testing if c equals p is performed by the method in the child class, it can happen that one is true and the other is false.

- Similarly assume there are two instances of the child class, c1 and c2. It can happen that the method in the parent class determines that p is equal to both c1 and c2, but the comparison of c1 to c2, which uses the method in the child class, could return false.

- Conversely, assume that there is another instance of the parent class, named p2. It can happen that p is equal to c, and c is equal to p2, but p is not equal to p2.

We will return to investigate further some of the issues involved in equality testing when we take up the topic of overriding in Chapter 16.

The Eiffel Type LIKE current.

In Eiffel the problem of equality is solved in part by the ability to *anchor* a type to that of another value. Most often the anchor is the receiver pseudo-variable, which is known as Current in Eiffel. Thus, an equality method could be written in this language as follows.

```
Class PlayingCard
feature
  .
  .
  .
  equal (other : LIKE Current) is
  do
    -- compare two playing cards
    .
    .
    .
  end
end
```

The LIKE anchor continues after inheritance. Thus, if we were to form a new subclass of PlayingCard—say, PokerCard—then when an argument to PokerCard was used as the receiver, the argument would have to be of type PokerCard.

This mechanism is not without cost. In general, type correctness can only be assured by a run-time check for argument compatibility. Thus, in practice the code is no more efficient than the Java example presented earlier, where the programmer was forced to write the run-time check.

Summary ▫

In this chapter we have followed some of the language design implications that flow from the decision to support the object-oriented concept of substitution. We have examined the implications for memory management, assignment, object copies, and equality testing.

- Because a child class can introduce fields not found in the parent, the support of substitution is difficult.

- One approach is to essentially disallow substitution. This is the approach taken by C++. An assignment of a child class to a parent value slices away any data fields found only in the child.

- Most other object-oriented languages avoid the slicing problem by storing objects as pointers to heap-based memory.

- Since objects are most naturally heap based, a heap memory management system is important in object-oriented languages.

- Some languages force the programmer to manage the heap, freeing memory when it is no longer needed. Other languages include a garbage collection system that automatically detects and recovers unused memory.

- Because it is natural to implement objects as pointers to heap-based memory, most object-oriented langauges also use pointer assignment semantics.

- When a true copy of an object is needed, it can be generated either as a shallow copy (where pointer assignment is used to copy the inner state) or as a deep copy (where the inner state is copied recursively).

- Two objects can be compared either for identity or equality.

- Identity asks if two objects represent the same memory location.

- Equality asks if two objects represent the same state, even if they are different memory locations. The meaning of equality is inherently domain specific.

- Because equality can be redefined by programmers, it is difficult to ensure that basic properties are preserved, such as commutivity.

- There can be subtle interactions between equality testing and inheritance.

Further Reading ⊡

Scott [Scott 2000] presents a good introduction to the issues raised in the implementation of programming languages. Many of the issues discussed in this chapter are also explored by Joyner [Joyner 1999].

The C++ object model is explained in detail by Lippman [Lippman 1996]. The slicing of assignment in Oberon-2 is explained by Mössenböck [Mössenböck 1993].

The concept of Like Current in Eiffel is discussed by Bertran Meyer [Meyer 1994].

Self-Study Questions ⊡

1. What are the properties of a variable that is allocated on the activation record stack?
2. What are the three possible ways that memory in an activation record could be assigned to object-oriented values?
3. If the semantics of virtual functions in C++ were not changed for automatic variables, how would it be possible to tell that slicing had occurred?
4. Why is the maximum static space allocation technique not used by object-oriented languages?
5. When languages use dynamic memory allocation for objects, what is stored in the activation record?
6. What is the difference between pointer semantics for assignment and copy semantics?
7. What is the difference between a deep copy and a shallow copy?
8. What is the difference between object identity and object equality?

Exercises ⊡

1. Explain why, in statically typed object-oriented languages (such as C++ and Object Pascal), it is illegal to assign a value from a class to a variable declared as an instance of a subclass. That is, something like the following will result in a compiler error message.

```
TextWindow X;
Window Y:
   .
   .
   .
X = Y;
```

2. Assume that the C++ memory-allocation technique operates as described in Section 12.1. Explain what problems can arise if the user attempts to circumvent the problem of Exercise 1 using a cast—that is, writes the assignment as

```
x = (TextWindow) Y;
```

3. Give an example, in either Object Pascal or C++, to illustrate why an entire program, not simply a file, must be parsed before the size of any object can be determined with the approach of Section 12.1.

4. Argue why, if the principle of substitutability is to be preserved, the return type associated with an overridden method can be no more general than that associated with the parent class.

5. Suppose you did not know if your programming language used pointer semantics or copy semantics for object assignment. What experiment could you conduct to find out?

6. Suppose your programming language provided a built-in copy operation, but you did not know if this performed a shallow copy or a deep copy. What experiment could you conduct to find out?

7. Show that it is possible to define a language similar to Object Pascal that does not use pointer semantics for assignment. In other words, give an algorithm for assignment for a language that uses the approach to memory management described in Section 12.1, but that does not result in two variables pointing to the same location when one is assigned to the other. Why do you think the designers of Object Pascal did not implement assignment using your approach?

CHAPTER 13

Multiple Inheritance

At the heart of the concept of inheritance is the is-a relationship. Viewed in one way, the is-a relationship is a form of classification. For example, a *TextWindow* can be classified as a type of *Window*, and therefore it makes sense that the class TextWindow can be created by inheritance from class Window. Expressed another way, the category TextWindow is a subset of the more general category Window.

However, when we look at classifications of objects in the real world, they seldom fit the simple single parent hierarchies we have been constructing. This is because real world objects are almost always classified in multiple, mutually nonoverlapping ways. The author of this book, for example, can be described as a male, a professor of computer science, a parent, and a North American. Each of these categories reveals something about the author, and none is a proper subset of any of the others. If we try to form these categories into an inheritance hierarchy, we end up with invalid categorizations, such as asserting that all males are North American or that all professors are male or some other equally improbable classifications.

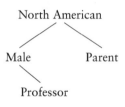

13.1   ▢   Inheritance as Categorization

The proper way to express these relationships is to assert that the author is a *combination* of many nonoverlapping categories. Each category contributes something to the result. Each relationship can legitimately be described using the is-a rule (the author is a parent; the author is a North American).

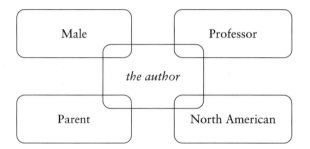

Modeling this behavior in programs seems to call for the concept of *multiple inheritance*. An object can have two or more different parent classes and inherit both data and behavior from each.

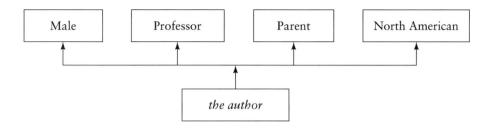

It is important to point out that we have not abandoned the is-a rule as the fundamental test for the inheritance relationship. The derived category must possess the is-a relationship to each of its parent classes, or it may have a variation in is-a: the as-a relationship.

Is-a, Has-a, and As-a

A common analogy in describing multiple inheritance is that of an actor playing many different roles, often at the same time. Likewise, multiple inheritance is not the has-a relationship, and not quite the is-a relationship (since the parent class is no longer unique) but a variation on is-a that could be described as *as-a*. The rule-of-thumb test for multiple inheritance is whether the sentence "A(n) A can be viewed as-a B" sounds right.

13.1.1 Incomparable complex numbers

Another example will illustrate the practical problems that arise from forcing concepts to fit a single inheritance hierarchy. In Smalltalk, the class Magnitude defines a protocol for objects that have measure—that is, that can be compared with one another. For example, individual characters (instances of class Char) can be compared if we use the underlying ASCII representation as a basis for measure. A more common class of objects that can be compared are numbers, which are represented as instances of the class Number in Smalltalk. In addition to being measurable, instances of class Number support arithmetic operations—addition, multiplication, and so forth. These operations do not make sense for objects of class Char. There are various number types supported by Smalltalk; examples include the classes Integer, Fraction, and Float. A portion of the class hierarchy is shown in Figure 13.1.

Now. suppose we add the class Complex, representing the complex number abstraction. The arithmetic operations are certainly well defined for complex numbers, and it is preferable to make the class Complex a subclass of Number so that,

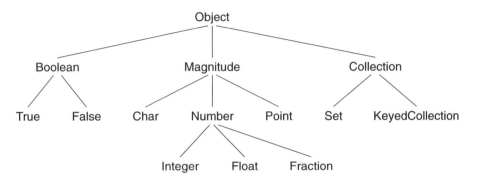

▫ Figure 13.1 —— A portion of the Smalltalk class hierarchy

for example, mixed-mode arithmetic is provided automatically. The difficulty is that comparison between two complex numbers is ambiguous. That is, complex numbers are simply not measurable.

Thus, we have the following constraints.

- The class Char should be a subclass of Magnitude but not of Number.
- The class Integer should be a subclass of both Magnitude and Number.
- The class Complex should be a subclass of Number but not of Magnitude.

It is not possible to satisfy all of these requirements in a single inheritance hierarchy. There are some alternative solutions to this problem.

1. Make Complex a subclass of Number, which is in turn a subclass of Magnitude, and then redefine the methods relating to measure in class Complex to produce error messages if they are invoked. This is subclassing for limitation, as described in Chapter 8. Although not elegant, this solution is sometimes the most expedient if your programming language does not support multiple inheritance.

2. Avoid the use of inheritance altogether and redefine every method in each of the classes Char, Integer, Complex, and so on. This solution is sometimes called *flattening the inheritance tree*. Of course, it eliminates all the benefits of inheritance described in Chapter 8—for example, code reuse and guaranteed interfaces. Furthermore, in a statically typed language, such as C++ or Object Pascal, it also prevents the creation of polymorphic objects. Thus, for example, it is not possible to create a variable that can hold an arbitrary measurable object or an arbitrary type of number.

3. Use part of the inheritance hierarchy and simulate the rest. For example, place all numbers under class Number, but have each measurable object (whether character or number) implement the comparison operations. This also eliminates many of the benefits that can be derived from inheritance.

4. Make the two classes Magnitude and Number independent of each other and thus require the class Integer to use inheritance to derive properties from *both* of the parents (Figure 13.2). The class Float will similarly inherit from both Number and Magnitude.

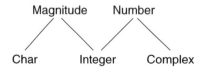

▣ Figure 13.2 —— A multiple inheritance hierarchy for complex numbers

Clearly the most elegant solution to this problem is the last. A class that inherits from two or more parent classes is said to exhibit *multiple inheritance*.

13.2 ▣ Problems Arising from Multiple Inheritance

The problems that arise from the inclusion of multiple inheritance in a language fall into two broad categories. There are problems of meaning and problems of implementation. In this chapter we will consider problems of meaning, and in Chapter 27 we will consider the impact of multiple inheritance on the implementation.

13.2.1   Name ambiguity

The most common difficulty arising from the use of multiple inheritance is that names can be used to mean more than one operation. To illustrate this, consider a programmer developing a card game simulation. Suppose there is already a data abstraction, CardDeck, that provides the functionality associated with a deck of cards (such as shuffling and being able to draw a single card from the deck) but has no graphical capabilities. Suppose further that another set of existing classes implements graphical objects. Graphical objects maintain a location on a two-dimensional display surface. In addition, graphical objects must all know how to display themselves by means of the virtual method called draw.

The programmer decides that to achieve maximum leverage from these two existing classes, he will have the class for the new abstraction, named Graphical-CardDeck, inherit from both the classes CardDeck and GraphicalObject. It is clear that conceptually the class GraphicalCardDeck is-a CardDeck and is thus logically descendant from that class and also that a GraphicalCardDeck is-a GraphicalObject. The only trouble is the clash between the two meanings of the command draw.

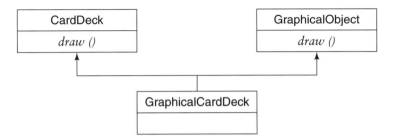

As Bertrand Meyer points out [Meyer 1988a] the problem is clearly with the child and not with the parent classes. The meaning of draw is unambiguous and meaningful in each of the parent classes when taken in isolation. The difficulty is with the combination. Since the problem arises only in the child class, the solution should also be found in that class. In this case, the child class must decide how to disambiguate the overloaded term.

One solution is to simply always use fully qualified names. Rather than asking an instance of GraphicalCardDeck to draw, the programmer specifically indicates which type of drawing is intended.

```
GraphicalCardDeck gcd;
Card * aCard = gcd->CardDeck::draw();
gcd->GraphicalObject::draw();
```

However, this solution is less than ideal, since the syntax is different from other function calls, and the programmer must remember which method comes from which parent.

The more common solution usually involves a combination of *renaming* and *redefinition*. By *redefinition* we mean a change in the operation of a command, such as what happens when a virtual method is overridden in a subclass. By *renaming* we simply mean changing the name by which a method is invoked without altering the command's functionality.

If the type signatures of the parent methods are distinguishable and our language allows overloading, then the child class can simply include both methods.

```
class GraphicalCardDeck : public CardDeck, public GraphicalObject {
public:
  virtual Card * draw () { return CardDeck::draw(); }
  virtual void draw (Graphics * g) { GraphicalObject::draw(g); }
}
```

An instance of the child can then select the appropriate method by using the correct arguments.

```
GraphicalCardDeck gcd;
Graphics g;
gcd->draw(); // selects CardDeck draw
gcd->draw(g); // selects GraphicalObject draw
```

If the type signatures are similar, or if overloading is not allowed, then the programmer is faced with a more difficult decision. The method draw can mean only one thing to the child, and the programmer must decide which of the parents interpretations it should be. In our graphical deck of playing cards, the programmer might have draw mean the process of removing a card from the deck and rename the process of drawing the image as paint.

```
class GraphicalCardDeck : public CardDeck, public GraphicalObject {
public:
  virtual void draw () { return CardDeck::draw(); }
  virtual void paint () { GraphicalObject::draw(); }
}


GraphicalCardDeck gcd;
gcd->draw(); // selects CardDeck draw
gcd->paint(); // selects GraphicalObject draw
```

13.2.2 Impact on substitutability

While the redefinition of the function name draw solves the problem locally when a GraphicalCardDeck is used in isolation, further problems arise when we consider the implications of the principle of substitution. Suppose our GraphicalCardDeck is maintained on a list of graphical objects, say for the purposes of rendering a window image. When the method draw is invoked on the graphical object, it will have the effect of executing the CardDeck method and not the graphical operation.

```
GraphicalObject * g = new GraphicalCardDeck();
g->draw(); // oops, wrong method
```

The typical way this problem is overcome in C++ is through the introduction of two new helper classes. Each of these classes inherits from one parent and redefines the draw operation to use a method of a different name.

```
class CardDeckParent : public CardDeck {
public:
  virtual void draw () { cardDeckDraw(); }
  virtual void cardDeckDraw() { CardDeck::draw(); }
};


class GraphicalObjectParent : public GraphicalObject {
public:
  virtual void draw () { goDraw(); }
  virtual void goDraw () { GraphicalObject::draw(); }
}
```

The child class can now inherit from these new parents and override the new methods, which no longer have similar names. When used by itself the new child class has access to both behaviors, and when assigned by substitution to an instance of either parent class, the expected behavior is produced.

```
class GraphicalCardDeck : public CardDeckParent, GraphicalObjectParent
{
public:
  virtual void cardDeckDraw () { ... }
  virtual goDraw () { ... }
};
```

Note that method named *draw* is still ambiguous in the child class but not when the object is referenced as an instance of either parent class. C++ does not care about this ambiguity as long as no attempt is made to use the name. An error will result if an attempt is made to reference the ambiguous method.

```
GraphicalCardDeck *gcd = new GraphicalCardDeck();
CardDeck *cd = gcd; // all three variables refer
GraphicalObject *go = gcd; // to same object
cd->draw(); // ok, will execute cardDeckDraw
go->draw(); // ok, will execute goDraw
gcd->draw(); // compiler error, ambiguous invocation
```

One might imagine that this ambiguity could be overcome by redefining draw in the child class GraphicalCardDeck and selecting one or the other meaning. However, because once a method is declared as virtual it continues to be virtual in all child classes, this cannot be done without hiding the other meaning and thus preventing substitution. However, it is still possible to use fully qualified names for the parent methods, as described earlier.

*13.2.3   Redefinition in Eiffel

The object-oriented language Eiffel allows multiple inheritance and overcomes ambiguity through a technique that permits inherited names to be redefined. The child class can therefore access inherited methods through the redefined names in an unambiguous fashion.

```
class GraphicalCardDeck
inherit
  CardDeck
    rename
      draw as cardDeckDraw
    end
  GraphicalObject
    rename
      draw as goDraw
    end
```

```
feature
  -- can use cardDeckDraw and goDraw without conflict
  -- can even override the redefined names
end
```

This solution is roughly equivalent to the earlier C++ program but avoids the need to introduce the two intermediary classes. Like the C++ program it requires that when the child class is used by itself, it must use the renamed methods. When an instance of the child class is accessed through a reference to either parent, they can use the method draw, and the correct method will be executed. However, again like the C++ solution, when the method draw is used with a child class reference, the meaning is ambiguous and will produce a compiler error.

*13.2.4 Resolution by class ordering in CLOS

While C++ and Eiffel resolve naming conflicts by insisting that the child class make the intent clear, the language CLOS takes a different approach. In CLOS conflicts are resolved by the order that parent classes are declared. For example, suppose we have two classes animated-character and movie-star, both possessing a name field and both having a method named name-of.

```
(defclass animated-character () ((name :initarg :name)))

(defmethod name-of ((self animated-character))
  (list "Animated Character" (slot-value self 'name)))

(defclass movie-star () ((name :initarg :name)))

(defmethod name-of ((self movie-star))
  (list "Movie Star" (slot-value self 'name)))
```

We can create a new class of animated movie stars by inheriting from both animated characters and movie stars.

```
(defclass animated-star (animated-character movie-star) () )
```

Note that there are two name slots in such an object, one from each parent class. If we define an instance of the child class and specify a value, both will be filled. If we print the value of the object, we can see that the method from class animated-character is selected.

```
(defvar micky (make-instance 'animated-star :name "Micky"))
(name-of micky)
("Animated Character" "Micky")
```

This is because the parent class animated-character is searched before the class movie-star. If we listed the parent classes in the reverse order, the method in class movie-star would be used.

```
(defclass star-animated (movie-star animated-character) () )
(defvar minnie (make-instance 'star-animated :name "Minnie"))
(name-of minnie)
("Movie Star" "Minnie")
```

Wrappers

Because multiple method bodies match the invocation of the name-of function, we can use the idea of *wrappers* to execute each function in turn. The method call-next-method will execute the next method that matches the given arguments. However, this can only be executed if there *is* a next method, something that can be checked using the predicate next-method-p. For example, we could rewrite both name-of methods as follows.

```
(defmethod name-of ((self animated-character))
  (list "Animated Character" (slot-value self 'name)
    (if (next-method-p) (call-next-method))))

(defmethod name-of ((self movie-star))
  (list "Movie Star" (slot-value self 'name)
    (if (next-method-p) (call-next-method))))
```

If we now execute the method, we will see that both functions have been executed and the results combined. (The if statement in the second function returns nil, since there is no next method, something we could have fixed with more programming.)

```
(name-of minnie)
("Movie Star" "Minnie" ("Animated Character" "Minnie" NIL))
```

We will examine a further use of call-next-method in Section 13.3.1.

Multiple inheritance in Python

Python is another language that resolves name conflicts that arise from multiple inheritance by performing a depth-first search of the ancestor hierarchy. Consider the following class definitions.

```
class A:
  def method1(self):
    print "method1 A"
```

```
    def method2(self)
      print "method2 A"

  class B(A):
    def method2(self)
      print "method2 B"

  class C:
    def method1(self):
      print "method1 A"
    def method2(self)
      print "method2 C"

  class D(B,C):
    def method2(self)
      C.method2(self)
```

If we create an instance of D and execute method1, it will select the method in class A.

```
    d = D()   # create a D
    d.method1()
  method1 A
    d.method2()
  method2 C
```

If inheritance had been specified as D(C,B), then the call on method1 would have found the function in class C, rather than the function in class A. Programmers can override and select the desired meaning by using the class qualified name, as show in the body of the function method2 in class D. This is similar to the use of fully qualified names in C++, which we described earlier.

13.3 □ Multiple Inheritance of Interfaces

Neither Java nor C# allow multiple inheritance of classes, but both languages permit multiple inheritance of interfaces. While sometimes used for similar purposes, there are important differences between interfaces and classes. Both mechanisms can be used for classification (the is-a relation is a valid test for both), but interfaces do not supply code to the child class. For this reason the conflict between two inherited code bodies does not arise. Either methods in the parent interfaces have the same type signature, in which case they are merged and the child need implement only one.

```
interface CardDeck {
  public void draw ();
}

interface GraphicalObject {
  public void draw ();
}

class GraphicalCardDeck implements CardDeck, GraphicalObject {
  public void draw () { ... } // only one method
}
```

Or the parent classes have different type signatures, in which case the child class must implement both.

```
interface CardDeck {
  public Card draw ();
}

interface GraphicalObject {
  public void draw (Graphics g);
}

class GraphicalCardDeck implements CardDeck, GraphicalObject {
  public Card draw () { ... } // must implement both methods
  public void draw (Graphics g) { ... }
}
```

The only restriction is similar to that encountered in simple overloading. Namely, two methods cannot differ only in their return type or in the type of exceptions they throw, since the compiler cannot determine from a function invocation which method is being called. The compiler will detect an error and issue a diagnostic message in this situation.

```
interface CardDeck {
  public void draw () throws EmptyDeckException;
}

interface GraphicalObject {
  public void draw ();
}

class GraphicalCardDeck implements CardDeck, GraphicalObject {
  public void draw () { ... } // which one is this?
}
```

In Java, interfaces are allowed to define constants (using the final modifier), and so there is the potential for two parent interfaces to define a constant using the same name and different values. However, the compiler checks for this condition and will issue an error diagnostic should it arise.

Explicit interface implementation in C#

The language C# is much more restrictive than Java with regard to the combination of methods from different interfaces. The C# compiler will report this condition as an error, even if the type signatures match. Presumably this policy is due to the assumption that if the interfaces arise from different sources they therefore most likely specify different actions.

The programmer can get around this restriction by explicitly naming the interface associated with the method being defined. If the method is to be further exposed from the child class, a third method can be defined with the same name.

```
class GraphicalCardDeck: CardDeck, GraphicalObject {
  void CardDeck.draw () {  // method number 1
    .
    .
    .
  }


  void GraphicalObject.draw () { // method number 2
    .
    .
    .
  }


  public void draw () { // method number 3
    .
    .
    .
  }
}
```

Each of these three methods can be executed, depending on the static type of a declaration.

```
GraphicalCardDeck theDeck = new GraphicalCardDeck();
theDeck.draw();   // executes method number 3
CardDeck cd = (CardDeck) theDeck;
cd.draw(); // executes method 1
GraphicalObject go = (GraphicalObject) theDeck;
go.draw(); // executed method 2
```

*13.3.1   Mixins in CLOS

CLOS programmers frequently make use of a programming idiom called a *mixin*. The concept of a mixin is in some ways almost the exact opposite of the notion of inheritance of interfaces. While interfaces specify a protocol but do not provide code, mixins provide code without changing the interface. Mixins are snippets of code that are combined precisely because of their behavior and not their type. The child class inherits a bit of code from one parent, a bit of code from the other, and combines them to form their own new behavior.

For example, suppose we have a class Person with a slot for a name and a method named title to return the name.

```
(defclass Person () ((name :initarg :name)))

(defmethod title ((self Person))
  (list (slot-value self 'name)))

(defvar tom (make-instance 'Person :name "Tom Smith"))

(title tom)
("Tom Smith")
```

We can create two mixins, one that will add the prefix "Prof." to a title, and one that will add the prefix "Dr." and tack a "PhD" on the end.

```
(defclass Prof () () )

(defmethod title ((self Prof))
  (cons "Prof." (call-next-method)))

(defclass PhD () () )

(defmethod title ((self PhD))
  (append (cons "Dr." (call-next-method)) (list "PhD")))
```

Note that these are declared as classes but do not explicitly reference the class Parent. The use of call-next-method is what distinguishes these classes as mixins. To use these, we can create a new class that uses multiple inheritance from one or more mixin before finally associating a base class. For example, we might make a simple Professor class.

```
(defclass Professor (Prof Person) () )
```

If we make an instance of this class and execute the inherited method title, we see that first the method from Prof is executed and then the method from Person.

```
    (defvar bill (make-instance 'Professor :name "Bill Jones"))
    (title bill)
("Prof." "Bill Jones")
```

A characteristic of mixins is that they can be combined in different orders. For example, we can make both classes for Professor Doctors and for Doctor Professors.

```
    (defclass ProfDr (Prof PhD Person) () )
    (defclass DrProf (PhD Prof Person) () )

    (defvar alice (make-instance 'ProfDr :name "Alice Smith"))
    (title alice)
("Prof." "Dr." "Alice Smith" "PhD")
    (defvar nancy (make-instance 'DrProf :name "Nancy Jones"))
    (title nancy)
("Dr." "Prof." "Nancy Jones" "PhD")
```

The programming language Ruby provides similar mixin facilities in the context of a language that only supports single inheritance.

13.4 □ Inheritance from Common Ancestors

By far the most subtle problems involving multiple inheritance arise when two or more classes inherit from a common parent class, such as in Figure 13.3. Scott Meyers calls this, rather melodramatically, the "diamond of death" [Meyers 1998]. The picture itself explains part of the controversy. Should it be drawn so that the common ancestors are merged or to keep them distinct?

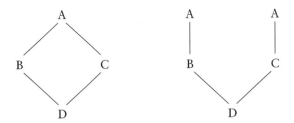

The difference between these two representations can be appreciated if we imagine that the common ancestor class defines a data member. Should the child class have one copy of this data member or two? There is no right answer to this question, since both arise in practice.

For example, suppose a programmer creates a linked list by making a parent Link class and declaring objects on the list as children of the Link class. (This is not a particularly good idea, since using standard container abstractions makes

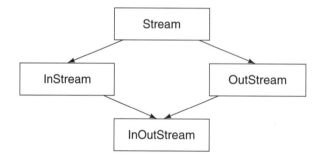

▫ Figure 13.3 ——— An inheritance graph

the code more robust, but nevertheless the technique is, perhaps unfortunately, common and is easy to understand.)

```
class Link {
public:
  Link * nextLink;
};
```

Declaring CardDeck to be a child class of Link allows the programmer to maintain a list of card decks. Similarly, declaring GraphicalObject to be a child class of Link allows the programmer to keep a list of graphical objects.

```
class CardDeck : public Link { ... };
class GraphicalObject : public Link { ... };
```

When the child class is created that inherits from both CardDeck and GraphicalObject, how many nextLink fields should it hold? Presumably the lists of card decks and graphical objects are distinct, and hence each type of list should have its own links. Therefore having two separate link fields seems appropriate.

Now imagine a different type of class hierarchy. A programmer is developing an input/output library based around the concept of *streams*. A stream is a generalization of a file, except that its elements can have more structure. We can have a stream of integers, for example, or a stream of reals. The class InStream provides a protocol for input streams. A user can open an input stream by attaching it to a file, retrieve the next element in the stream, and so on. The class OutStream provides similar functionality for output streams. Both classes inherit from a single parent class, Stream. The information that points to the actual underlying file (for example, a file pointer) is maintained in the parent class.

Now suppose the user wants to create a combined input-output stream. It makes sense to claim that an input-output stream is a descendant of both an

```
class Stream {
  File *fid;
  .
  .
  .
  };

class InStream : public virtual Stream {
  .
  .
  .
  int open(File *);
  };

class OutStream : public virtual Stream {
  .
  .
  .
  int open(File *);
  };

class InOutStream: public InStream, public OutStream {
  .
  .
  .
  };
```

▱ Figure 13.4 ——— An example of virtual inheritance

input stream and an output stream. But in this case, there is only one object, and hence we want the two file pointers (and any other common data) to refer to the same values. That is, we want only one copy of the common ancestor data.

In C++ this problem is overcome through the use of the virtual modifier in the parent class list. The virtual keyword indicates that the superclass may appear more than once in descendant classes of the current class but that only one copy of the superclass should be included. Figure 13.4 shows the declarations for the four classes.

An unfortunate consequence of the C++ approach is that, as we noted earlier, the name confusion is a problem only for the child class, but the solution (making the common ancestor virtual) involves changes to the parent classes. It is the intermediate parent classes that give the virtual designation, not the final combined class.

The fact that visibility keywords can be attached to parent classes independently means that it is possible for a virtual ancestor class to be inherited in different ways—for example, as both public and protected. In this case, the lesser

```
class D {
public:
  D() { ... }
  D(int i) { ... }
  D(double d) { ... }
};

class A : public virtual D {
public:

  A() : D(7)  { ... }
};

class B : public virtual D {
public:
  B() : D(3.14) { ... }
};

class C: public A, public B
{
public:
  C() : B(),A() { ... }
};
```

▫ Figure 13.5 —— Constructors in multiple inheritance

level of protection (for example, protected) is ignored and the more general category used.

*13.4.1   Constructors and multiple inheritance

When more than one parent class defines a constructor, the order of execution of the various constructors, and hence initialization of their data fields, may be important. The user can control this by invoking the constructors for the base classes directly in the constructor for the child class. For example, in Figure 13.5, the user explicitly directs that when an instance of class C is initialized, the constructor for B is to be invoked first, before the constructor for A. Reversing the order of invocations of the constructor in class C has the effect of reversing the order of initialization.

An exception to this rule occurs with virtual base classes. A virtual base class is always initialized once, before any other initialization takes place, by the constructor (provided by the system if not by the user), which takes no arguments. Thus, in Figure 13.5 the order of initialization when a new element of type C is constructed is first class D with the no-argument constructor, then class B, then class A. The two seeming calls on the constructor for class D that appear in the constructors for classes A and B actually have no effect, since the parent class is marked as virtual.

If it is imperative that arguments for the virtual base class be provided with the constructor, class C may legally provide these values, even though D is not an immediate ancestor for C. This is the only situation in which it is legal for a class to provide a constructor for another class that is not an immediate ancestor. That is, the constructor for class C could have been written as follows.

```
C() : D(12), B(), A() { . . . }
```

Constructors for virtual base classes must be invoked first, before the constructors for nonvirtual ancestors.

Virtual methods in the common ancestor

Virtual methods defined in virtual superclasses can also cause trouble. Suppose that each of the four classes shown in Figure 13.4 defines a method named initialize(). This method is defined as virtual in the class Stream and redefined in each of the other three classes. The initialize methods in InStream and OutStream each invoke Stream::initialize and, in addition, do some subclass-specific initialization.

Now consider the method InOutStream. It cannot call both the inherited methods InStream::initialize and OutStream::initialize without invoking the method Stream::initialize twice. The repeated invocation of Stream::initialize may have unintended effects. The way to avoid this problem is to rewrite Stream::initialize so it detects whether it has been initialized or to redefine the methods in the subclasses InStream and OutStream so they avoid the invocation of the method from class Stream. In the latter case, the class InOutStream must then invoke the initialization procedures explicitly for each of the three other classes.

13.5 ▫ Inner Classes

The ability to nest classes in Java and C++ provides a mechanism that can be used in a fashion that is very nearly equivalent to multiple inheritance but that avoids many of the semantic problems we have been discussing. A nested class in Java retains access to methods in the surrounding outer class. (This is not true in C++, but it can be simulated by passing a reference to the outer class when the inner class is constructed.) To create an object that inherits from two parents, the outer class inherits from the first parent, and the inner class inherits from the second.

```
class GraphicalCardDeck extends CardDeck {
  // outer class has access to all CardDeck behavior

  public void draw () { // can override the CardDeck methods
      .
      .
      .
  }

  private drawingClass drawer = new drawingClass();

  public GraphicalObject myDrawingObject () { return drawer; }

  private class drawingClass extends GraphicalObject {
    // inner class has access to all GraphicalObject behavior
    public void draw () {
      // can override the GraphicalObject methods
        .
        .
        .
    }
  }
}
```

The outer class can override methods from one parent, the inner class from the second. The inner class has access to methods from both parents. Seemingly the only difficulty this solution introduces is the problem of substitution. An instance of GraphicalCardDeck can be assigned to a variable of type CardDeck but not to one declared as type GraphicalObject. But even here there is an easy way to overcome this problem. The outer class can return an instance of the inner class (as is done by the method myDrawingObject) that can then be assigned to the parent class variable. There is, indeed, no way that the *same variable* can be assigned to two different parent classes, but this situation does not seem to arise in practice. The case study presented in Chapter 22 makes use of an inner class in just this fashion.

Summary ▫

One way to view the mechanism of inheritance is as a process of categorization. The child class is a more specialized form of the category defined by the parent class. However, in most real world categorizations objects fit into several mutually independent categories. This observation leads to the concept of multiple inheritance, a class that can inherit from two or more parent classes.

While multiple inheritance on the surface seems desirable, there are several pitfalls that can trap the unwary. The most important of these is the ambiguity of names that are inherited from both parents. This ambiguity can be resolved but frequently only at the cost of the elimination of polymorphic substitutability.

The problem of ambiguity becomes even more complex when one class can be reached as an ancestor along two or more paths from a child. In this situation the quandary is how many times features in the common parent class should be repeated in the child.

Further Reading ▪

A critique of multiple inheritance can be found in Sakkinen [Sakkinen 1988a], which is an abridgment and adaptation of a Ph.D. dissertation [Sakkinen 1992].

An explanation of multiple inheritance in C++ is given in Ellis [Ellis 1990]. The designer of C++ has provided a detailed history of the multiple inheritance controversy [Stroustrup 1994]. A careful explanation of implementation techniques for multiple inheritance is provided by Scott [Scott 2000].

Mixins in CLOS were first described in [Bracha 1990].

Multiple inheritance also has a reputation as being a difficult feature to implement. We will examine why this is so in Chapter 27.

Self-Study Questions ▪

1. How does multiple inheritance change the is-a rule?
2. How can name ambiguity arise in multiple inheritance? How is this ambiguity resolved?
3. How is the resolution of ambiguous names in CLOS different from the solution to the ambiguity problem in C++?
4. Why does the problem of ambiguous names not arise in the multiple inheritance of Java interfaces?
5. Explain the concept of a mixin in CLOS.
6. What problem can arise when a single ancestor class is reachable by two or more paths from a child?
7. How do inner classes in Java and C++ give the programmer some of the effect of multiple inheritance?
8. What aspect of multiple inheritance cannot be exactly realized by inner classes?

Exercises ▪

1. Cite two examples of multiple inheritance in non-computer-associated situations.

2. In [Wiener 1989], a "practical example of multiple inheritance in C++" is described that defines a class IntegerArray, which inherits from the two classes, Array and Integer. Do you think this example is a good use of multiple inheritance? Explain your answer.

3. In [Shammas 1996] another example of multiple inheritance is presented. In this example the class Distance represents an x and y coordinate pair. The class Random provides the ability to return a random number. Inheriting from both of these, the class Rescue represents a lost person with unknown coordinates. Critique this use of multiple inheritance.

4. Discuss virtual inheritance in C++ from the point of view of Parnas's principles on information hiding.

5. It is sometimes asserted that Java has multiple inheritance because it has multiple inheritance of interfaces. Explain why multiple inheritance of interfaces is not the same thing as multiple inheritance of classes.

CHAPTER 14

Polymorphism and Software Reuse

In this chapter and in the four that follow we begin an investigation of the mechanisms that are in object-oriented programming languages collectively described using the term *polymorphism*. We have seen simple examples of most of these—for example, overriding—in earlier chapters. However, an in-depth treatment will allow us to explore details that might not be obvious from a cursory explanation. After examining the various techniques denoted by this term we then examine, starting in Chapter 19, several applications of polymorphism to a range of common problems.

The term *polymorphic* has Greek roots and means, roughly, "many forms." (*poly* = many, *morphos* = form. Morphos is related to the Greek god Morphus, who could appear to sleeping individuals in any form he wished and hence was truly polymorphic.) In biology, a polymorphic species is one, such as *Homo sapiens*, that is characterized by the occurrence of different forms or color types in individual organisms or among organisms. Sponges are another polymorphic species. In chemistry, a polymorphic compound is one that can crystallize in at least two distinct forms, such as carbon, which can crystallize as graphite, diamond, or fullerenes.

14.1 ▫ Polymorphism in Programming Languages

As is perhaps appropriate, the name polymorphism means different things to different people. In part this confusion is related to language paradigms. The term originated with work in the functional language world, and only later was it adopted by designers of object-oriented languages. As a consequence the term has come to mean one thing in the object-oriented community and something slightly different when applied to functional languages.

At heart, the term means there is one name and many different meanings. But names are used for a variety of purposes (variable names, function names, class names), and meanings can be defined in a number of different ways. It is therefore useful to consider at least four different forms of polymorphism.

- The term *overloading* (also known as *ad hoc polymorphism*) is used to describe the situation where a single function name (or method name) has several alternative implementations. Typically overloaded function names are distinguished at compile time based on their type signatures.

  ```
  class OverLoader {
      // three overloaded meanings for the same name
    public void example (int x) { ... }
    public void example (int x, double y) { ... }
    public void example (string x) { ... }
  }
  ```

We will discuss overloading in Chapter 15.

- *Overriding* (or *inclusion polymorphism*) is in some sense a special case of overloading but occurs within the context of the parent class/child class relationship.

  ```
  class Parent {
    public void example (int x) { ... }
  }

  class Child extends Parent {
      // same name, different method body
    public void example (int x) { ... }
  }
  ```

Like ad-hoc polymorphism there are two definitions that use the same method name. However, unlike overloading, these two definitions must have the same type signature, and the two methods must appear in classes related by inheritance. Overriding will be described in Chapter 16.

- The *polymorphic variable* (or *assignment polymorphism*) is a variable that is declared as one type but in fact holds a value of a different type.

  ```
  Parent p = new Child(); // declared as parent, holding child value
  ```

When a polymorphic variable is used as argument, the resulting function is said to exhibit *pure polymorphism*. Both the polymorphic variable and pure polymorphism are discussed in Chapter 17.

- Finally, *generics* (or *templates*) provide a way of creating general purpose tools and specializing them to specific situations.

```
template <class T> T max (T left, T right)
{
    // return largest argument
  if (left < right)
    return right;
  return left;
}
```

A generic function or class is parameterized by a type, in much the same way that a function is parameterized by values. By leaving the type unspecified, to be filled in later, a generic allows the function or class to be used in a wider range of situations. Generics will be examined in Chapter 18.

14.1.1 Many tools, one goal

It is polymorphism more than any other feature that distinguishes object-oriented languages from other language paradigms. Each of the different polymorphic techniques permits a different form of software reuse. Each is powerful in its own way, a fact we will demonstrate in the case study chapters that will follow our investigation of the basic techniques. By facilitating the reuse of standard software components, each contributes to the goals we earlier identified as the driving forces for object-oriented programming—namely, rapid development, reliability, and ease of use.

14.2 □ Mechanisms for Software Reuse

Object-oriented programming has been billed as the technology that will finally permit software to be constructed from general-purpose reusable components. Writers such as Brad Cox have even gone so far as to describe object orientation as heralding the "industrial revolution" in software development. While the reality may not quite match the hyperbole of OOP pioneers, it *is* true that object-oriented programming makes possible a level of software reuse that is orders of magnitude more powerful than that permitted by previous software construction techniques. In this section, we will investigate and contrast the two most common mechanisms for software reuse: *inheritance* and *composition*.

To illustrate these two techniques, we will use the construction of a set abstraction by using an existing class, List, which maintains a list of integer values. Imagine we have already developed a class List with the following interface.

```
class List {
public:
    // constructor
    List ();

    // methods
    void   add        (int);
    int    firstElement ();
    int    size        ();
    int    includes    (int)
    void   remove      (int);
    .
    .
    .
};
```

That is, our list abstraction permits us to add a new element to the front of the list, to return the first element of the list, to compute the number of elements in the list, to see if a value is contained in the list, and to remove an element from the list.

We want to develop a set abstraction to perform operations such as adding a value to the set, determining the number of elements in the set, and determining whether a specific value occurs in the set.

Is-a and Has-a Revisited

It should be clear that the is-a and has-a relationships that we have been discussing since Chapter 2 correspond directly to the programming mechanisms of inheritance and composition. If class A has-a class B, then naturally a data field of class B should be part of an instance of class A. On the other hand, if class A is-a class B, then inheritance is an appropriate coding mechanism.

14.2.1   Using composition

We will first investigate how the set abstraction can be formed with composition (also sometimes called *layering*). Recall from our earlier discussion that an object is simply an encapsulation of data (data values) and behavior. When composition is employed to reuse an existing data abstraction in the development of a new data type, a portion of the state of the new data structure is simply an instance of the existing structure. This is illustrated here, where the data type Set contains an instance field named theData, which is declared to be of type List.

```
class Set {
public:
  Set  ();  // constructor

    // operations
  void  add      (int);
  int   size   ();
  int   includes  (int)

private:   // data area for set values
  List   theData;
};
```

Because the List abstraction is stored as part of the data area for our set, it must be initialized in the constructor. As with the initialization of data fields in classes (Chapter 5), the initializer clause in the constructor provides the arguments used to initialize the data field. In this case the constructor we invoke for class List is the constructor with no arguments.

```
  // initialize list
Set::Set() : theData()
{
  // no further initialization
}
```

Operations that manipulate the new structure are implemented by use of the existing operations provided for the earlier data type. For example, the implementation of the includes operation for our set data structure simply invokes the similarly named function already defined for lists.

```
int Set::size ()
{
  return theData.size();
}


int Set::includes (int newValue)
{
  return theData.includes(newValue);
}
```

The only operation that is slightly more complex is addition, which must first check to ensure that the value is not already contained in the collection (since values can appear in a set no more than once).

```
void Set::add (int newValue)
{
    // if not already in set
  if (! includes (newValue))
      // then add
    theData.add(newValue);

    // otherwise do nothing
}
```

The important point is the fact that composition provides a way to leverage an existing software component in the creation of a new application. By using the existing List class, the majority of the difficult work in managing the data values for our new component have already been addressed.

On the other hand, composition makes no explicit or implicit claims about substitutability. When formed in this fashion, the data types Set and List are entirely distinct, and neither can be substituted in situations where the other is required.

Composition in other languages

Composition can be applied in any of the object-oriented languages we consider in this book. Indeed, it can be applied in non-object-oriented languages as well. The only significant difference in the various languages is the way in which the encapsulated data abstraction is initialized.

14.2.2   Using inheritance

An entirely different mechanism for software reuse in object-oriented programming is the concept of inheritance; with inheritance a new class can be declared a *subclass*, or *child class*, of an existing class. In this way, all data areas and functions associated with the original class are automatically associated with the new data abstraction. The new class can, in addition, define new data values or new functions. It can also *override* functions in the original class, simply by defining new functions with the same names as those of functions that appear in the parent class.

These possibilities are illustrated in the class description following, which implements a different version of the Set abstraction. By naming the class List in the class heading, we indicate that our Set abstraction is an extension, or a refinement, of the existing class List. Thus, all operations associated with lists are immediately applicable to sets as well.

```
class Set : public List {
public:
    // constructor
  Set ();

    // operations
  void  add  (int);
  int   size ();
};
```

Notice that the new class does not define any new data fields. Instead, the data fields defined in the List class will be used to maintain the set elements, but they must still be initialized. This is performed by invocation of the constructor for the parent class as part of the constructor for the new class.

```
Set::Set()  : List()
{
    // no further initialization
}
```

Similarly, functions defined in the parent class can be used without any further effort, so we need not bother to define the includes method because the inherited method from List uses the same name and shares the same purpose. The addition of an element to a set, however, requires slightly more work and is handled as follows.

```
void  Set::add  (int newValue)
{
    // add only if not already in set
  if (! includes(newValue))
    List::add (newValue);
}
```

Compare this function with the earlier version. Both techniques are powerful mechanisms for code reuse, but unlike composition, inheritance carries an implicit assumption that subclasses are, in fact, subtypes. This means that instances of the new abstraction should act in a similar fashion to instances of the parent class.

14.2.3   Composition and inheritance contrasted

Having illustrated two mechanisms for software reuse, and having seen that they are both applicable to the implementation of sets, we can comment on some of the advantages and disadvantages of the two approaches.

- Composition is the simpler of the two techniques. Its advantage is that it more clearly indicates exactly what operations can be performed on a particular data structure. Looking at the declaration for the Set data abstraction, it is clear that the only operations provided for the data type are addition, the inclusion test, and size. This is true regardless of what operations are defined for lists.

- In inheritance the operations of the new data abstraction are a superset of the operations of the original data structure on which the new object is built. Thus, to know exactly what operations are legal for the new structure, the programmer must examine the declaration for the original. An examination of the Set declaration, for example, does not immediately indicate that the includes test can be legally applied to sets. It is only by examination of the declaration for the earlier List data abstraction that the entire set of legal operations can be ascertained.

   But there is a difficulty that can occur when a programmer must try to understand a class constructed using inheritance. Often the programmer must repeatedly flip back and forth between two (or more) class declarations. This has been labeled the "yo-yo" problem, due to the image of the programmer's head bobbing up and down as he (or she) moves between various class definitions.

- The brevity of data abstractions constructed with inheritance is, in another light, an advantage. Using inheritance it is not necessary to write any code to access the functionality provided by the class on which the new structure is built. For this reason, implementations using inheritance are almost always, as in the present case, considerably shorter in code than are implementations constructed with composition, and they often provide greater functionality. For example, the inheritance implementation makes available not only the includes test for sets but also the function remove.

- Inheritance does not prevent users from manipulating the new structure using methods from the parent class, even if these are not appropriate. For example, when we use inheritance to derive the class Set from the class List, nothing prevents users from retrieving the first element using the method firstElement.

- In composition the fact that the class List is used as the storage mechanism for our sets is merely an implementation detail. With this technique it would be easy to reimplement the class to use a different technique (such as a hash table) with minimal impact on the users of the Set abstraction. If users counted on the fact that a Set is merely a specialized form of List, such changes would be more difficult to implement.

- Inheritance may allow us to use the new abstraction as an argument in an existing *polymorphic* function. We will investigate this possibility in more detail in Chapter 17. Because composition does not imply substitutability, it usually precludes polymorphism.

- Understandability and maintainability are difficult to judge. Inheritance has the advantage of brevity of code but not of protocol. Composition code, although longer, is the only code that another programmer must understand to use the abstraction. A programmer faced with understanding the inheritance version needs to ask whether any behavior inherited from the parent class was necessary for proper utilization of the new class and would thus have to understand both classes.

- Data structures implemented through inheritance tend to have a very small advantage in execution time over those constructed with composition, since one additional function call is avoided (although techniques such as in-line functions in C++ can be used to eliminate much of this overhead).

Of the two possible implementation techniques, can we say which is better in this case? One answer involves the substitution principle. Ask yourself whether in an application that expected to use a List data abstraction it is correct to substitute instead an instance of class Set. While the technical answer might be yes (the Set abstraction does implement all the List operations), the more commonsense answer is no. While the type signature has been preserved, the meaning of the add operation has changed. For this reason it appears that, *in this case*, composition is the better approach.

The bottom line is that the two techniques are very useful, and an object-oriented programmer should be familiar with both of them.

14.3 ◻ Efficiency and Polymorphism

Almost all the programming techniques we will discuss in the next four chapters extract some cost in run-time efficiency. That being the case, a few words on the relative importance of efficiency in relation to other concerns is in order.

The fundamental truth is that programming always involves compromises. In particular, programming with polymorphism involves compromises between ease of development and use, readability, and efficiency. In large part, efficiency has been already considered and dismissed; however, it would be remiss not to admit that it is an issue, however slight.

A polymorphic function that does not know the type of its arguments can seldom be as efficient as a function that has more complete information. A relational test may correspond to only a few assembly language instructions if the arguments are integer, whereas much more extensive operations are necessary if the arguments are strings or dates and considerably more work if the determination of types is postponed until run time. Nevertheless, the advantages of rapid development and consistent application behavior and the possibilities of code reuse usually (but not always!) more than make up for any small losses in efficiency.

14.4 ▫ Will Widespread Software Reuse Become Reality?

In the early days of object-oriented programming, it was said that computer science had finally found a way to create software from general-purpose interchangeable parts and that programming would henceforth be more like electrical or civil engineering, where new ideas were created using a collection of standard components. Polymorphism in its various guises was the tool that would make this transformation possible.

However, while certain progress has been made (there are now a large number of commercial vendors who market general-purpose object-oriented software libraries for various applications, such as user interfaces and container classes), the overall process has not yet lived up to the early expectations. There are a variety of reasons for this.

- Inheritance and composition provide the *means* for producing reusable components, but they do not by themselves provide *guidelines* for how such a task should be performed. It turns out that producing good and useful software components is, if anything, almost always more difficult than developing special-purpose software to solve the task at hand.

- Because producing reusable components is difficult, the benefits cannot usually be realized within a single project. Indeed, they may slow down project development. Rather than creating immediate benefits, the cost of such development must be amortized over many programming projects. But as each project usually has its own budget and schedule, there is often no management mechanism to support such amortization.

- Because the benefits of developing reusable components do not immediately improve a project, there is usually little incentive for programmers to strive toward reusability.

- Because each new problem typically requires a slightly different set of behaviors, it is often difficult to design a truly useful and general-purpose software component the first time. Rather, useful reusable software components evolve slowly over many projects until they finally reach a stable state.

- Many programmers and managers are leery of software that has not been developed "in-house." This wariness is called the "not-invented-here" syndrome. Because managers pride themselves on the quality of their programmer teams, they naturally believe they can do better than whatever team developed the reusable software.
- Because many programmers have little formal training or have not kept pace with recent programming innovations (such as object-oriented techniques), they may not be aware of the mechanisms available for the development of reusable software components.

In short, development of software mechanisms for reuse does not by itself guarantee the development of a technological and management *culture* that will support and encourage reuse. Human organizations tend to move much more slowly than does technological change, so it may be many years before we see the true benefits promised by the object-oriented approach. Nevertheless, even though object reuse is probably not anywhere as frequent as claimed, it does occur and has been proven many times to be useful and cost-saving when applied correctly. For this reason it is inevitable that reuse will eventually become the norm for software development.

Summary ⊡

In this chapter we have begun our in-depth investigation of polymorphism. As is perhaps appropriate (since polymorphism means roughly "many forms") there are a variety of mechanisms that are known by this term.

- Overloading
- Overriding
- The polymorphic variable
- Generics

All the various mechanisms are united by the goal of easing software reuse and thereby promoting reliability, rapid development, and ease of use.

Further Information ⊡

Brad Cox's very readable manifesto on the software industrial revolution is [Cox 1986].

The yo-yo problem was first described in [Taenzer 1989].

Several recent books provide guidelines for developing reusable components include [Carroll 1995, McGregor 1992, Meyer 1994, Goldberg 1995].

Self-Study Questions ▫

1. What do the Greek roots of the term *polymorphic* mean?
2. What is ad hoc polymorphism?
3. In what ways is overriding similar to overloading? In what ways are they different?
4. What distinguishes a polymorphic variable from an ordinary variable?
5. How is a generic function in C++ different from an ordinary function?
6. How does composition simplify the creation of new data abstractions from existing abstractions?
7. How does inheritance simplify the creation of new data abstractions from existing abstractions?
8. In what ways does composition produce classes that are easier to understand? In what ways does inheritance achieve the same goal?
9. Why, in most cases, is efficiency not the primary concern for a programmer?
10. What are some factors that have slowed the development of large libraries of general-purpose reusable software components?

Exercises ▫

1. Do you think that the value nil in Pascal or the value NULL in C should be considered a polymorphic object? Explain your answer.
2. Other than the arithmetic operations, what operations are typically overloaded in conventional languages such as Pascal and C?
3. Chapter 10 presents another example of inheritance, the creation of a dictionary data structure using a list. Rewrite that example using composition rather than inheritance.
4. Exercise 4 in Chapter 8 criticized the suggestion that a class Complex representing complex numbers could be constructed using inheritance from a class Real. Show how Complex could be constructed using composition rather than inheritance. You can assume whatever interface you wish for the class Real.

CHAPTER 15

Overloading

We say a term is *overloaded* if it has many different meanings.[1] A glance in any dictionary will show that many words in the English language are overloaded, and the meaning of a word in a particular situation is determined by context. In programming languages it is usually function or method names that are overloaded. As with words in English, a compiler will use contextual information to determine the exact meaning.

Overloading and overriding are both techniques that take a function or method named in a specific invocation and select for execution one out of potentially many different function bodies. But the two mechanisms differ in several regards. Most importantly, overloading is performed at compile time (early binding), whereas overriding uses a run-time selection (late binding). The compiler examines the context in which an overloaded name is being used and determines the most appropriate function body. Normally the most critical feature is the type signature of the arguments being used by the call. Because the function selection is being made at compile time, it is the static (or declared) types of the arguments that are used and not their dynamic (or run-time) values.

In one sense, overloading (also called *ad hoc polymorphism*) may seem to have little to do with object-orientation, since the ability to overload function names can be found in a number of non-object-oriented languages—for example, C and Ada. But overloading is a powerful form of polymorphism, and furthermore, the interaction between overloading and other more object-oriented forms of

---

1. The term *polymorphism* is, for example, overloaded.

polymorphism, such as overriding, can be both powerful and unintuitive. In this chapter we explore some of the aspects of this idea.

15.1 ▫ Type Signatures and Scopes

A key idea necessary to understand overloading is the concept of a function (or method) *type signature*. A function type signature, you will recall, is a description of the argument types associated with a function, the order of arguments, and the return type. For methods defined within a class, it is normal to omit the type of the receiver from the type signature. This permits us to say that the type signature of a method in the parent class can be the same as the signature of a method in a child class. The following function, for example, has type signature *double × int → double*.

```
double power (double base, int exponent) {
  // raise base to exponent power
  double result = 1.0;
  for (int i = 0; i < exponent; i++)
    result = result * base;
  return result;
}
```

The second key idea needed in order to understand function overloading is the notion of a name *scope*. A scope defines the portion of a program in which a name can be used or the way in which the name can be used. Local variables, such as the identifiers result and i in the previous procedure, can only be used inside the function in which they are declared. After the final closing brace for the function, the name no longer has any meaning. Outside of a class definition, a data member name only has meaning if the name was declared as public inside the class and it is qualified by an instance of a class (or, for static features, qualified by the class name). For example, if a class defines a public data field named buffer, then outside the class definition an expression such as

```
anInstance.buffer
```

would be acceptable, but the simple name buffer would not. A class that is formed using inheritance creates a new name scope that extends the name scope of the parent. Thus, name scopes are formed in a variety of different ways in different programming languages.

At any point in the textual representation of a program there can be multiple active scopes. A method declared inside a class will have both the class scope (all the class data fields) and a local scope (local variables declared inside the method). Inheritance, nested functions, and/or nested classes introduce further layers of scope.

We can use these two concepts—type signatures and scope—to characterize two broad categories of overloading. Overloading can be based on methods having different scopes, regardless of their type signatures. For example, the same name might be used in two or more unrelated classes. Alternatively, overloading can be based on methods having different signatures, regardless of their scopes. For example, two or more functions defined in one class might have the same name but different arguments. The first form is examined in Section 15.2, and the second is described in Section 15.3.

Associated with the latter are a number of different mechanisms, each of which will be explored in a separate section. The process of coercion or conversion (Section 15.3.1) is used when the actual arguments of a method do not exactly match the formal parameter specifications, but can be converted into a form that will match. Redefinition (Section 15.4) occurs when a child class defines a method with the same name as a method in the parent class but with a *different* type signature. Polyadic functions (Section 15.5) are functions that can be invoked with varying number of parameters. Finally, in Section 15.6 we examine multi-methods, which combine features of both overloading and overriding.

15.2 ▫ Overloading Based on Scopes

A useful consequence of the division of a program into independent name scopes is that the same name can appear in different scopes with no ambiguity or loss of precision. Two different functions can have local variables of the same name, and no confusion will arise because their scopes cannot overlap. Methods can also have the same name, without introducing confusion or ambiguity. We encountered an example of this in the flower story in Chapter 1. There were two possible ways for Chris to send flowers to Robin. One solution was for Chris to give the message sendFlowersTo to the local florist; another was for Chris to give the *same* message to his friend Elizabeth. Both Chris's florist and his friend (an instance of class Friend) would have understood the message, and both would have acted on it to produce a similar result.

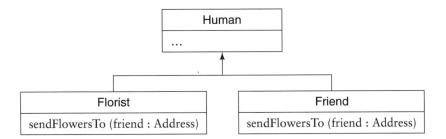

Note carefully that there is no inheritance involved in this example. The first common ancestor superclass for Friend and Florist is the category Human. But certainly the behavior sendFlowersTo is not something that is associated with all humans.

There is nothing intrinsic to overloading that requires the functions associated with an overloaded name to have any semantic similarity. Consider a program that plays a card game, such as the solitaire game we examined in Chapter 9. The method draw was used to draw the image of a card on the screen. In another application we might also have included a draw method for the pack of cards—that is, to draw a single card from the top of the deck. This draw method is not even remotely similar in semantics to the draw method for the single card, and yet they share the same name. Nor is it required that they have the same type signature. In fact, the only similarity between the two methods is their name.

Overloading of a single name with independent and unrelated meanings should *not* necessarily be considered bad style, and generally it will not contribute to confusion. In fact, the selection of short, clear, and meaningful names such as add, draw, and so on, contributes to ease of understanding and correct use of object-oriented components. It is far simpler to remember that you can add an element to a set than to recall that to do so requires invoking the addNewElement method or, worse, that it requires calling the routine Set_Module_Addition_Method.

All the object-oriented languages we are considering permit the occurrence of methods with similar names in unrelated classes. In this case the resolution of overloaded names is determined by the class of the receiver for the message. Nevertheless, this does not mean that functions or methods can be written that take arbitrary arguments. The statically typed nature of C++ and Object Pascal still requires specific declarations of all variables.

15.3 ▫ Overloading Based on Type Signatures

Another style of overloading occurs when procedures (or functions or methods) are allowed to share a name and are disambiguated by the number, order, and, in statically typed languages, the type of arguments they require. This is allowed even if the functions share the same context. This style of overloading occurs in C++, C#, Java, Delphi Pascal, and CLOS, as well as in some imperative languages (such as Ada) and many functional languages. We have already seen examples of this style in the overloading of the constructor function. C++ permits any method, function, procedure, or operator to be overloaded parametrically. The only requirement is that every implementation must have a distinctive signature. This means that the arguments must be such that the selection of the routine intended by the user can be unambiguously determined at compile time.

```
class Example {
    // same name, three different methods
  int sum (int a) { return a; }
  int sum (int a, int b) { return a + b; }
  int sum (int a, int b, int c) { return a + b + c; }
}
```

Because a single method body must be selected based only on a specific function invocation, methods are not permitted to differ only in their return types nor in other features that are not observable by examining the invocation. (An example of a feature that cannot be determined from the invocation is the type of exceptions that might be thrown.)

In Delphi Pascal two methods in the same scope can overload a common name, but the programmer must explicitly declare the fact using the overload directive.

```
type
  Example = class
  public
    function sum (a : Integer) : Integer; overload;
    function sum (a, b : Integer) : Integer; overload;
  end;
```

It is important to note that the resolution of overloading—that is, the selection of a method body to match to a particular invocation—is performed at compile time, based on the static types of the argument values. Unlike overriding, no run-time mechanism is involved. Imagine, for example, there are two methods named Test, each taking a single argument. The first requires an instance of a parent class, and the second an instance of a child class that inherits from the parent.

```
class Parent { ... };

class Child : public Parent { ... };

void Test(Parent * p) { cout << "in parent" << endl; }
void Test(Child * c) { cout << "in child" << endl }
```

The following would, perhaps surprisingly, execute the first method and not the second.

```
Parent * value = new Child();
    // resolution based on static type,
    // not dynamic value in parent
Test(value);
```

Stream output in C++.   The stream output facility in C++ is an excellent case study that illustrates how overloading can be used to solve the problem of extending a library to new user-defined data types. A problem with traditional output libraries is that they are designed to work only with the built-in types. Consider the printf facility in C. A printf statement is easy to write if the output consists of the basic data types provided as part of the language.

```
printf("average of %d and %d is %g", 3, 5, (3+5)/2.0);
```

But what happens when a programmer creates a new data type? Imagine, for example, that a programmer has defined a Fraction data abstraction, where fractions are represented by two integer data fields.

```
class Fraction {
public:
  Fraction (int top, int bottom) { t = top; b = bottom; }

  int numerator() { return t; }
  int denominator() { return b; }

private:
  int t, b;
};
```

The only way to print a fractional value is to break it into the two parts and print them each independently.

```
Fraction f(3,4);
printf("The value of f is %d/%d", f.numerator(), f.denominator());
```

The designers of C++ realized that an alternative could be found by using the ability to overload operators with several different meanings. They selected the left shift operator, <<, as the output operator. An abstraction termed an *output stream* (or ostream) represents an entity that will accept a sequence of characters. Writing to a stream thus generalizes such activities as writing to a file, a window, or a network. The stream output library provides a collection of overloaded definitions for the left shift operator.

```
ostream & operator << (ostream & destination, int source);
ostream & operator << (ostream & destination, short source);
ostream & operator << (ostream & destination, long source);
ostream & operator << (ostream & destination, char source);
ostream & operator << (ostream & destination, char * source);
//  :  and so on
    :
```

Each operator takes a stream as the left argument and another value as the right argument. When executed, each operator will, as a side effect, write the right argument to the stream, then return the stream value as the result. The latter action allows a complex stream expression to be built out of parts. For example, consider the evaluation of the statement.

```
double d = 3.14;
cout << "The answer is " << d << '\n';
```

The output statement would be evaluated in stages, as follows.

```
cout << "The answer is "   << d   << '\n'
           cout            << d   << '\n'
               cout               << '\n'
```

First, the operator overloaded to work with a stream and a character array would be executed. After printing the string, this operator returns the stream. Next, the operator overloaded to work with a stream and a double precision value would be executed. Once more, after printing the number, the stream is returned. Finally, the operator overloaded to work with a stream and a single character would be executed. The character would be printed, and the stream value returned. The final value is then discarded, since the purpose of printing has been achieved as a side effect.

Using overloaded operators makes it simple to extend the output library to new user-defined data types. All that is needed to add the ability to output fractional values, for example, is to define yet another overloaded meaning for the output stream operator.

```
ostream & operator << (ostream & destination, Fraction & source)
{
    destination << source.numerator() << "/" << source.denominator();
    return destination;
}
```

With this new ability the output of fractions can be intermixed with the output of other data types.

```
Fraction f(3, 4);
cout << "The value of f is " << f << '\n';
```

15.3.1   Coercion and conversion

Overloading based on type signatures occurs frequently in all programming languages, not simply object-oriented languages. Perhaps the most common example is the overloading of the addition operator, +. The code generated by a compiler

Coercion, conversion, and casts

The meanings of the terms *coercion* and *conversion* are easily confused, since both represent a change in type. A *coercion* is an *implicit* change in type, one that occurs without overt reference in the program. The canonical example of this is the addition of two variables, one declared as real and one declared as integer. The value of the integer variable will be converted to real before the addition.

```
double x = 2.8;
int i = 3;
x = i + x; // integer i will be converted to real
```

In contrast, the term *conversion* usually represents a change in type that is explicitly requested by the programmer. In many languages the operator used to perform this change is termed a *cast*. A cast in C++ or Java would be written as follows.

```
x = ( (double) i ) + x;
```

Parentheses surround the expected type following the conversion, in this case double.

Casts, and conversions in general, can either change the underlying representation (such as when an integer is converted into a real) or simply change the type without changing the representation (such as when a pointer to a child class is changed into a pointer to the parent class).

for an integer addition is often radically different from the code generated for a floating-point addition; yet programmers tend to think of the operations as a single entity, the "addition" function.

In this example it is important to point out that overloading may not be the only activity taking place. A semantically separate operation, *coercion*, is also usually associated with arithmetic operations. It occurs when a value of one type is converted into one of a different type. If mixed-type arithmetic is permitted, the addition of two values may be interpreted in at least three different ways.

- There may be four different functions, corresponding to integer + integer, integer + real, real + integer, and real + real. In this case, there is overloading but no coercion.

- There may be two different functions for integer + integer and real + real. In integer + real and real + integer, the integer value is coerced by being changed into a real value. In this situation there is a combination of overloading and coercion.

- There may be only one function for real + real addition. All arguments are coerced into being real. In this case there is coercion only, with no overloading.

Substitution as conversion. If we interpret the word *coercion* broadly as "a change in type," then the principle of substitution introduces a form of coercion not found in conventional languages. This occurs when a value from a child class is used as an actual parameter in a method that is defining the corresponding formal parameter with the parent class type. A similar change in type can occur with an interface and an instance of a class that implements the interface.

The following example from Java illustrates some of the subtle interactions between overloading and inheritance. In Java, if two or more methods have the same name and the same number of parameters, the compiler uses the following algorithm to determine the match.

1. Find all the methods that could possibly apply to the invocation—that is, all methods for which the arguments could legally be assigned to the parameter types. If one method exactly matches the argument types used in the invocation, then execute that method.

2. If any method in the set identified in Step 1 has parameter types that are *all* assignments to any other method in the set, then remove the second method from the set. Repeat until no further eliminations can be performed.

3. If exactly one method remains, that method is the most specific and will be invoked. If more than one method remains, the invocation is ambiguous, and a compiler error will be reported.

To illustrate this process, imagine we have five classes structured in the following inheritance hierarchy.

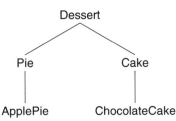

Now suppose some scope includes the following three overloaded methods, each taking a pair of Dessert parameters.

```
void order (Dessert d, Cake c);
void order (Pie p, Dessert d);
void order (ApplePie a, Cake c);
```

Imagine that we have a set of variables, each representative of a different class. Variable aCake holds a value of type Cake, anApplePie a value of type ApplePie, and so on. Finally, consider a series of invocations, both legal and illegal.

```
order (aDessert, aCake); // example 1, legal
order (anApplePie, aDessert); // example 2, legal
order (aDessert, aDessert); // example 3, illegal
order (anApplePie, aChocolateCake); // example 4, legal
order (aPie, aCake); // example 5, illegal
```

The first invocation is legal because Dessert and Cake match the type signature of the first method directly. The second invocation similarly matches the second overloaded method, since it is the only method for which the arguments could legally be assigned to the parameters. (Assigning the Dessert argument to the Cake parameter is illegal in both the first and third methods.)

The third example is illegal. After Step 1 the set of possible candidate methods is empty, since a Dessert value cannot be arbitrarily downcast to a more specific type. Therefore, a compiler error will be reported.

The forth invocation is more subtle. Initially all three methods are candidates for execution. So the method selection algorithm moves to Step 2. In this step the first overloaded method would be eliminated, since ApplePie is a more specific class than Dessert (an ApplePie can be assigned to a Dessert, but not vice-versa), and the second argument is the same. The second method would be removed for the same reason (both arguments are less specific; Pie is less specific than ApplePie and Dessert less specific than Cake). This leaves one candidate, and the fourth example will execute the third method.

Like the third example, the final invocation is also invalid. After Step 1 only the last method has been eliminated, leaving two elements in the set of possible candidates. But the first method cannot be subsumed by the second, since a Dessert cannot be assigned to a Pie. But neither can the second method be subsumed by the first, since a Dessert cannot be converted into a Cake. Thus, two methods remain after Step 2, and with the compiler unable to decide between them, an error will be reported.

Conversion operators in C++.   The language C++ gives the programmer a great deal of control over how an instance of a class can be implicitly converted from or to another type. We consider first the conversion to an object type. A constructor that takes a single argument will be interpreted by the compiler as a rule for converting from the argument type to the class type. We could incoporate this into the Fraction data type discussed earlier by, for example, defining a constructor that takes a single integer argument.

```
class Fraction {
public:
    Fraction (int top, int bottom) { t = top; b = bottom; }
```

```
Fraction (int top) { t = top; b = 1; }

int numerator() { return t; }
int denominator() { return b; }

Fraction operator * (Fraction & right)
{
    Fraction result (numerator() * right.numerator(),
        denominator() * right.denominator());
    return result;
}

private:
    int t, b;
};
```

We have also given the implementation of the operator that will handle the multiplication of two fractional values. In an expression that involves the multiplication of a fraction and an integer, a temporary value will be formed that represents the conversion of the integer into a fraction. The constructor will be used to initialize this temporary object.

```
Fraction a(2, 3);
```

```
a = a * 3; // right argument will become 3/1
```

In the other direction is the conversion of an object value into a different type. Here C++ has an interesting feature that gives the programmer the ability to explicitly state how the conversion should be performed. A type name can be used as an operator. As with all operators in C++, the programmer can provide a new meaning by defining the operator as a method. For instance, suppose the programmer is continuing to develop the Fraction data type. The following class definition shows a new operator being defined. The "operator" double is invoked when a Fraction must be converted into a double precision value.

```
class Fraction {
public:
    Fraction (int top, int bottom) { t = top; b = bottom; }

    Fraction (int top) { t = top; b = 1; }

    int numerator() { return t; }
    int denominator() { return b; }

    Fraction operator * (Fraction & right)
```

```
{
  Fraction result (numerator() * right.numerator(),
    denominator() * right.denominator());
  return result;
}

operator double ()
{
  // cast is necessary to make double precision division
  return numerator() / (double) denominator();
}

private:
  int t, b;
};
```

The following example illustrates the use of the conversion operator. Two declaration statements are used to construct two fractional values. In the third statement a fraction is formed using the multiplication operator defined in the class. In the fourth and final statement a multiplication is performed using a fraction and a double precision number. Since the fraction does not define a method for this situation, the fraction is converted into a double, using the conversion method supplied by the class, and the normal double precision multiplication is performed.

```
Fraction one(2,3);
Fraction two(3,4);
Fraction three = one * two; // multiply two fractions
double four = one * 3.14159; // multiply fraction and double
```

Needless to say, when implicit conversion, explicit conversion, and the substitution of object-oriented values are all combined in one statement, the algorithm used to resolve an overloaded function name can become quite complex. Typically it must include at least the following steps.

1. If there is a method with an exact match for the actual arguments, then call that version.
2. Otherwise, see if there is a match that uses standard type promotions (such as converting a short integer to a standard integer).
3. Otherwise, see if there is a match that uses standard conversions (such as interpreting a child type as an instance of the parent type).
4. Otherwise, see if a match can be found using user-supplied conversions.

5. Otherwise, if no match can be found or if more than one method seems to match, then issue a compile time error.

15.4 ▫ Redefinition

A *redefinition* occurs when a child class defines a method using the same name as a method in the parent class but with a different type signature. The change in type signature is what differentiates redefinition from simple overriding. Redefinition would not be notable, except that languages use two different techniques to resolve a redefined name, and thus the unwary programmer can easily be surprised if they are not cognizant of the differences. These two models might be termed the *merge* model of redefinition and the *hierarchical* model.

The programming language Java uses the merge model. Here the various different meanings found in all currently active scopes are merged together to form a single collection. To match an invocation that uses an overloaded method name to a specific method body, all the possible alternatives are examined, and the closest match is the one selected.

The programming language C++ uses a different approach. In this language each surrounding scope is maintained on its own separate list. To match a name to a method, each scope will be examined in turn—hence the designation *hierarchical*. However, when a scope is found in which the name is defined, the closest match *in that scope* will be the one selected.

An example will help illustrate this distinction. Suppose a parent class defines a method with one integer argument, and the child class redefines the method using the same name but this time with two integer arguments.

```
class Parent {
  public void example (int a)
    { System.out.println("in parent method"); }
}

class Child extends Parent {
  public void example (int a, int b)
    { System.out.println("in child method"); }
}
```

Now imagine we create an instance of the child and try to execute the method using only one argument.

```
Child aChild = new Child();
aChild.example(3);
```

In the programming language Java, the method from the parent class will be selected as the best fit. The same is true in C#. The equivalent program in

C++, on the other hand, will produce a compilation error. This is because the scope corresponding to the child class is examined first, before the scope for the parent class. A method with the given name is found in the child scope, but upon examination the arguments for this method do not match those of the invocation. The C++ programmer can achieve the same effect as the Java model but only by redefining both methods in the child class.

```
class Child : public Parent {
  public void example (int a) { Parent::example(a); }
  public void example (int a, int b)
    { cout << "in child method"; }
};
```

The Delphi Pascal language offers the programmer control over which model to use. If a child class declares a method and uses the overload modifier, then the definitions in the child class will be merged with those inherited from the parent class. If the modifier is omitted, then the child class definition replaces that of the parent class. The following example illustrates this behavior. One child class redefines the method as an overloading, and the second does not. When an attempt is made to invoke the method from the parent, one class will produce a compile time error, but the second will not.

```
type
  Parent = class
  public
          procedure Example(A: Integer);
  end;

  ChildWithOneMethod = class (Parent)
  public
    procedure Example(A, B: Integer);
  end;

  ChildWithTwoMethods = class (Parent)
  public
    procedure Example(A, B: Integer); overload;
  end;

var
  C1: ChildWithOneMethod;
  C2: ChildWithTwoMethods;
begin
  C1 := ChildWithOneMethod.Create;
  C2 := ChildWithTwoMethods.Create;
```

```
C1.Example(42); // error: not enough parameters
C2.Example(42); // okay
end
```

*15.5 ▫ Polyadicity

A *polyadic* function is one that can take a variable number of arguments. In CLOS, for example, the addition operator is polyadic, so each of the following will evaluate to an integer value.

```
(+ 2 3)
(+ 2 3 4 5 6 7)
(+ 2)
```

Polyadic functions are found in a large number of different languages. The built-in function writeln in Pascal or the library function printf in C and C++ are examples.

```
printf("2 + 5 is %d", (2+5));
printf("the average of %d and %d is %g", 3, 7, (3+7)/2.0);
```

While it is easy to write an invocation of a polyadic function, it is much more difficult to write the body of the function itself. For example, how do you name an indefinite number of arguments? The language C++ uses a somewhat *ad hoc* device consisting of an ellipsis, a data type named va_list (for *variable argument list*), and a trio of methods va_start, va_arg, and va_end. The following example illustrates their use, defining a function that will return the sum of a list of integer values, where the first argument must represent the number of integers in the list.

```
# include <stdarg.h>
int sum (int argcnt, ...)
{
  va_list ap;
  int answer = 0;
  va_start(ap, argcnt);
  while (argcnt > 0) {
    answer += va_arg(ap, int);
    argcnt--;
  }
  va_end(ap);
  return answer;
}
```

The language C# provides a more elegant solution to this problem. The keyword params can be used in conjunction with an array argument. If no other matching method can be found, as a final alternative the compiler will check to see if all remaining values can be assigned as array elements. If so, then a temporary internal array is created and passed as parameter to the method.

```
class ParamsExample {
  public void Write (int x) {
    // use this with one argument
    WriteString("Example one ");
    WriteString(x.ToString());
  }

  public void Write (double x, int y) {
    // use this with two arguments
    WriteString("Example two ");
    WritoString(x.ToString());
    WriteString(y.ToString());
  }

  public void Write (params object [ ] args) {
    // use this with any other combination of arguments
    WriteString("Example three ");
    for (int i = 0; i < args.GetLength(0); i++)
      WriteString(args[i].ToString());
  }
}
```

Here are some example invocations and their associated results:

```
  ParamsExample p;
  p.Write(42);
Example one 42
  p.Write(3.14,159);
Example two 3.14159
  p.Write(1,2,3,4);
Example three 1234
  p.Write(3.14);
Example three 3.14
  p.Write(3,"abc");
Example three 3abc
```

15.5.1   Optional parameters

A slightly easier to understand technique for writing polyadic functions is found
in C++ and also in Delphi Pascal. This is the concept of an optional or default
parameter. The basic idea is to provide an implicit value for one or more parameters. If the invoking expression explicitly provides a value for these parameters,
then the default values are ignored; otherwise, if the invoking expression omits
them, the default values will be used. Optional parameters must appear at the end
of the argument list.

The following simple program illustrates this technique being used in a Delphi
Pascal procedure.

```
function Count (A, B : Integer; C : Integer = 0; D : Integer = 0);
begin
    (* Result is a pseudo-variable used *)
    (* to represent result of any function *)
  Result := A + B + C + D;
end


begin
  Writeln (Count(2, 3, 4, 5)); // can use four arguments
  Writeln (Count(2, 3, 4)); // or three
  Writeln (Count(2, 3)); // or two
end
```

C++ and Ada have similar facilities. Judicious use of optional parameters can
often eliminate the need to write multiple overloaded methods. This is particularly
useful with constructors. When optional parameters are used with a function
that is itself overloaded, the type signatures of all functions must be such that a
unique function body can be determined once the argument values used by a call
are known. (Note that a function that uses optional parameters will have several
different type signatures.)

* 15.6 ▢ Multi-Methods

Both overloading and overriding match an invocation by selecting one method
out of many. But as we noted at the beginning of the chapter, overloading
is performed at compile time, whereas overriding is performed at run time.
Overriding, you will recall, uses the dynamic (or run-time) type of the receiver to
determine which method should be executed. The types of any other arguments
passed along with a message generally play no part in the overriding selection
mechanism.

Many people have wondered whether it would be possible to combine these two techniques, allowing an overloaded function to be selected based on the types of all arguments and not just the receiver. The situations where this would be useful are common. Unfortunately, the problems that such a mechanism would introduce, particularly for statically typed languages, are difficult to solve. In this section we will illustrate these problems by means of a simple example.

Imagine that we have a statically typed object-oriented language in which Integers and Real numbers are both child classes of a more general class Number.

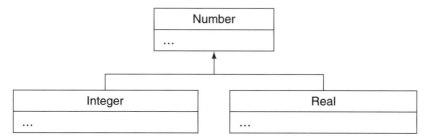

To implement addition as a function it is necessary to overload the add function with four different definitions.

```
function add (Integer a, Integer b) : Integer { ... }
function add (Integer a, Real b) : Real { ... }
function add (Real a, Integer b) : Real { ... }
function add (Real a, Real b) : Real { ... }
```

Notice that the return type for the first definition is different from the return type for the remaining three.

The basic idea of a multi-method is that any argument, and not just the receiver, should be allowed to be polymorphic. Furthermore, it should be the run-time value and not the static compile-time value of this variable that determines which function to execute. For example, consider the following execution sequence.

```
Number x = ...; // variable x and y are given
Number y = ...; // some unknown values
Real r = 2.134;

Real r2 = add(r, x); // which method to execute?
Real r3 = add(x, y); // is the assignment type-safe?
```

Variables x and y are numbers. By the principle of substitution, they could be assigned values that are either Integer or Real. Variable r, on the other hand, is known to be an instance of class Real. Now consider the first execution of the method add. We know the type of the first argument, but that still leaves two potential candidates for execution, depending on whether the variable x is integer or real. Which one should be selected? A run-time test must be performed to determine the most appropriate function.

Now consider the second invocation. This one is much more difficult to handle. Here, any of the four candidate function bodies can be selected, based on the run-time types of the variables x and y. But only three of these return a value that can be assigned to a variable of type Real. If x and y are both integer, then the assignment is not type-correct, and an error should be reported. So it is necessary to perform a run-time test on both the arguments (in order to select the correct function to execute) and the result (in order to ensure type safety in the assignment).

So arguments against multi-methods are based on two complaints. The first is that the execution time cost of the function selection algorithm is too high, and second, in a statically typed language the typing issues introduce too many complications. It should be noted that the only widely used language to incorporate multi-methods is CLOS, a dynamically typed language in which the second issue is not important.

Double dispatch.   One common solution to the problem just described is a technique termed *double-dispatch*. The key insight behind the double-dispatch approach is that a message can be used to determine the type of the receiver, since each object knows its own type. Determining the type of two independent values can therefore be accomplished by using each value as receiver in turn.

Imagine, for example, that the classes Integer and Real are written in Smalltalk, and each implements three methods. In Integer we have the following:

```
" class Integer "
{add:} arg
   ↑ arg addToInteger: self

{addToInteger:} anInteger
   ... " whatever is necessary to add two integers "

{addToReal:} aReal
   ... " whatever is necessary to add an integer and a real "
```

In class Real the methods are similar, except that the add: method turns around and passes the message addToReal: to its argument. Now imagine we are adding two variables, anInteger and aReal, with the types indicated by their name. The message add: given to anInteger will take its argument (which at this point is of indeterminent type) and pass it the message addToInteger. The class Real, receiving this message, knows that it is holding a real value and that the argument is integer, and it can act accordingly.

15.6.1   Overloading Based on Values

There is another curious language feature that, like multi-methods, appears to be found only in Lisp-based languages (such as CLOS or Dylan). This is the ability to overload a function based on argument values and not just types. A parameter specifies that its argument must be exactly the value specified in the function definition. For example, we could see the following two function definitions.

```
function sum (a : integer, b : integer) { return a + b; }

function sum (a : integer = 0, b : integer) { return a; }
```

The second function will only be invoked if the first argument is the constant value zero; otherwise, the more general function will be executed. Value constraints on parameters can be a very useful programming language feature. However, like multi-methods, they increase significantly the run-time execution overhead involved in method selection.

Summary ▫

Overloading is the compile time matching of a function invocation to one of many similarly named methods. There are two major categories of overloading. Overloading can be based on different scopes, where the class of the receiver determines the function to execute. Alternatively, overloading can be based on type signatures, where the type associated with the parameters that accompany the invocation is used to determine the correct method. Overloading should not be confused with the similar concepts of conversion or redefinition. An alternative to overloading is the creation of polyadic functions, functions that can take a variable number of arguments.

Further Information ▫

More detailed information regarding the conversion rules used by C++ can be found in [Ellis 1990] and [Stroustrup 1986].

Craig [Craig 2000] provides an analysis of polyadicity in various languages.

The designer of C++ has discussed his reasons for rejecting multi-methods in [Stroustrup 1994]. Castagna [Castagna 1997] describes an algorithm that could be used in the implementation of multi-methods for a dynamically typed language.

Double dispatching was first described in Ingalls [Ingalls 1986], who called the technique multiple polymorphism. Later authors have preferred the term *double dispatching*, both because it is more accurate and because it avoids confusion with multiple inheritance.

Self-Study Questions ▣

1. What does it mean to say that a word is overloaded?
2. What is a type signature?
3. What is a scope?
4. What are the two major types of overloading?
5. Why is overloading of simple names not necessarily a bad idea?
6. When overloading is based on type signatures, how is the meaning of a function invocation resolved?
7. When a C++ programmer creates a new data type, what do they need to do in order to allow instances of the data type to be printed on streams?
8. What is the difference between overloading and coercion?
9. What is a method redefinition? How is it different from an overriding?
10. What is a polyadic function?
11. How do optional parameters reduce the need for overloading?
12. What do multi-methods differ from overloaded functions?

Exercises ▣

1. Suppose a programmer wanted to take a data type such as the Set abstraction defined in the previous chapter and allow the stream output operator to be used with this data type. Explain the steps required to accomplish this.
2. Some languages, such as Java, allow the + operator to be used with strings. Two strings combined using this operator are catenated to form a new string. Is this an example of overloading or coercion?
3. Which of the following are legal invocations of the Java functions described in Section 15.3.1?

   ```
   order (aChocolateCake, anApplePie);
   order (aChocolateCake, aChocolateCake);
   order (aPie, aChocolateCake);
   ```

4. Suppose a strongly typed language has two classes: the class Rectangle that represents rectangular objects with horizontal and vertical sides, and triangle that represents a three-sided figure. Imagine that a programmer wished

to create overloaded copies of a procedure named intersection, which determines the intersection of two such objects. For which combinations can the resulting type be determined?

5. Show that double dispatching described in Section 15.6 correctly handles the four possible types of addition (that is, integer + integer, integer + real, real + integer, and real + real).

6. Explain why the double dispatching technique described in Section 15.6 would not solve the problem of addition in a strongly typed language. Where does the approach break down?

7. Imagine that you have two independent class hierarchies. A class of Shapes, consisting of Triangle and Square, and a class of OutputDevice, consisting of Printer and Terminal. Each of the four possible combinations of shape and output device requires a different algorithm for display. You have two variables, a Shape and an OutputDevice. Show how double dispatching can be used to correctly match a specific shape to a specific output device.

CHAPTER 16

Overriding

We say that a method in a child class *overrides* a method in the parent class if the two methods have the same name and type signature.[1]

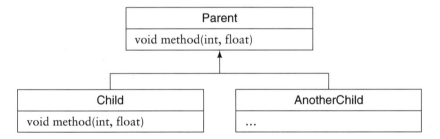

Overriding (also called *inclusion polymorphism*) is important when it is combined with substitution. Recall that a polymorphic variable can, using the principle of substitution, be declared as one type (for example, the parent type) but in reality hold a value of another type (typically a child type). When a message that corresponds to an overridden method is passed to such a value, the procedure that will be executed is that given by the child class and not by the parent.

In a certain sense, method overriding might be considered to be a special case of overloading, since as with overloading we again have one method name and two or more method bodies. But having made that observation we reach the end

---

1. As we will note in a moment, some languages require an additional keyword before overriding will take place. The feature common to all languages, however, is the parent/child relationship and the matching type signatures.

of the similarities. On the other hand, the differences between overloading and overriding include the following.

- In method overriding the classes in which the methods appear must stand in a parent/child inheritance relationship to each other, something that was not a requirement for simple overloading.
- For overriding to occur, the method type signatures must match.
- Overloaded methods are always separate, but when overriding, two methods are sometimes combined to perform the actions of both together.
- And finally, and most importantly, while overloading is typically resolved at compile time, overriding is a run-time mechanism. This means it may not be possible to predict what actions it will perform in response to any specific message until a program is actually executing.

Overriding in Smalltalk class Magnitude. An interesting example of overriding occurs in the class Magnitude in the Little Smalltalk system. Magnitude is an abstract superclass dealing with quantities that possess at least a partial, if not a total, ordering. Numbers are perhaps the most common example of objects that have magnitude, although time and date can also be ordered, as can characters, points in a two-dimensional coordinate plane, and words in a dictionary.

The six relational operators are defined in the class Magnitude as follows.

```
<= arg
    ↑ self < arg or: [ self = arg ]

>= arg
    ↑ arg <= self

< arg
    ↑ self <= arg and: [ self ~= arg ]

> arg
    ↑ arg < self

= arg
    ↑ self == arg

~= arg
    ↑ (self = arg) not
```

Note that the definitions appear to be circular, each one depending on some number of the others. How, then, is an infinite loop to be avoided if any of them are invoked? The answer is that subclasses of class Magnitude must override and redefine at least one of the six relational messages. We leave it as an exercise for the reader to show that if the message = and either < or <= are redefined, all the remaining operators can be executed without falling into an infinite loop.

Overriding of a method contributes to code sharing, insofar as instances of the classes that do *not* override the method can all share one copy of the original. It is only in situations where this method is not appropriate that an alternative code fragment is provided. Without overriding, it would be necessary for all subclasses to provide their own method to respond to the message, even though many of these methods are identical.

16.1 ▫ Notating Overriding

Languages differ in how they require the possibility of overriding to be documented in the code itself. Some languages, such as Smalltalk, Java, or Objective-C, say nothing at all. In these languages it is only the similarity of type signatures between the parent and child classes that indicates overriding. In other languages, such as C++, a notation must be placed in the parent class to indicate that overriding can potentially take place (although the mark does not guarantee that overriding *must* take place). In other languages, such as Object Pascal, the documentation is placed in the child class. In Delphi Pascal and in C# a keyword is required in both parent and child. These differences are described in more detail in Figure 16.1.

Overriding cannot change the accessibility of a method. If the method is public in the parent, it cannot be made private in the child or vice-versa. (An exception to this rule is the use of private inheritance in C++, where public features in a parent become private in the child.)

C++ Keyword required in parent class.

```
class Parent {
public:
    virtual int example(int a) { ... }
};


class Child : public Parent {
public:
    int example(int a) { ... }
};
```

▫ Figure 16.1 —— Different ways to describe overriding

C# Keyword required in both parent and child classes.

```
class Parent {
   public virtual int example (int a) { ... }
}
class Child : Parent {
   public override int example (int a) { ... }
}
```

Delphi Pascal

```
type
  Parent = class (TObject)
     function example (int) : integer; virtual;
  end;

  Child = class (Parent)
     function example (int) : integer; override;
  end;
```

Java No keyword in either parent or child. Smalltalk, Objective-C are similar.

```
class Parent {
   public void example(int a) { ... }
}

class Child extends Parent {
   public void example(int a) { ... }
}
```

Object Pascal Keyword in child class, not in parent class.

```
type
  Parent = object
     function example (int) : integer;
  end;

  Child = object (Parent)
     function example (int) : integer; override;
  end;
```

▫ Figure 16.1 ——— Continued

16.2 ▫ Replacement versus Refinement

While we have talked about a child class overriding the method in a parent class, in actual fact there are two different ways to interpret the process of overriding:

Replacement   A method *replacement* totally overwrites the method in the parent class during execution. That is, the code in the parent class is never executed when instances of the child class are manipulated.

Refinement   A method *refinement* includes, as part of its behavior, the execution of the method inherited from the parent class. Thus, the behavior of the parent is preserved and augmented.

The first interpretation of the meaning of overriding is often called *American semantics* because it is usually associated with languages of American origin (such as Smalltalk and C++). The second is known as *Scandinavian semantics* because it is most frequently associated with Simula, the original object-oriented language, and with the later language Beta, both of Scandinavian origin.

In reality, both forms of overriding are useful, and often both can be found in the same programming language. For example, almost all languages (even those solidly in the American school) use refinement semantics for constructors. That is, a constructor for a child class will *always* invoke the constructor for the parent class, thereby insuring that the data fields for both the parent and child will be properly set.

We will give two examples to illustrate the concepts of replacement and refinement. The replacement example uses Smalltalk, whereas the refinement example will be based on Beta.

16.2.1 Replacement in Smalltalk

Replacement is used in many different places in the standard Smalltalk class library. The two major reasons for using replacement are in support of code reuse and as a technique for optimization. We will illustrate both.

First consider code reuse. In Smalltalk, integers and floating-point numbers are objects; they are instances of class Integer and class Float, respectively. In turn, both of these classes are subclasses of a more general class, Number. There are several other types of objects that are also numbers, such as class Fraction.

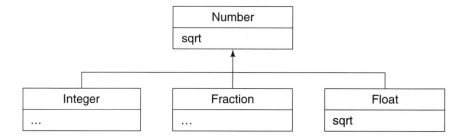

Now suppose we have a variable, aNumber, that currently contains a Smalltalk integer, and we send to aNumber the square-root-generating message sqrt. There is no method corresponding to this name in class Integer, so class Number is searched, and the following method is discovered.

```
"class Number"
  {sqrt}
    " convert to float then compute square root "
    ↑ self asFloat sqrt
```

This method passes the message asFloat to self, which, as you will recall from Chapter 5, represents the receiver for the sqrt message. The asFloat message results in a floating-point value with the same magnitude as that of the integer number. The message sqrt is then passed to this value.

This time, the search for a method begins with class Float. It so happens that class Float contains a different method named sqrt, which for floating-point values *overrides* the method in class Number. That method (which is not shown here) computes and returns the expected floating-point value.

The ability to override and totally *replace* the method sqrt means that many kinds of numbers can share the single default routine found in class Number. This sharing avoids the need to repeat this code for each of the different subclasses of Number (which includes not only integers and floats but infinite-precision integers and fractions). Classes, such as Float, that require a behavior different from the default can simply override the method and substitute the alternative code.

Another Smalltalk example illustrates using overriding as a means of optimization. The Boolean constants true and false are instances of the classes True and False, respectively. These, in turn, are both subclasses of Boolean.

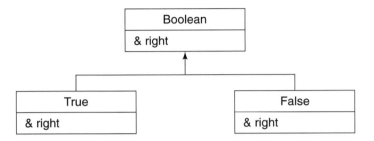

The methods & (logical *and*) and | (logical *or*) are implemented in the parent class with a general mechanism that defines the Booleans using conditional statements. This technique is correct for any combination of values.

```
"class Boolean"
  {&} right
    self ifTrue: [ right ifTrue: [ ↑ true ] ].
    ↑ false

  {|} right
    self ifTrue: [ ↑ true ].
    right ifTrue: [ ↑ true ].
    ↑ false
```

Of course, in the child classes the implementation can take advantage of additional information. That is, we know the truth or falsity of the left argument; we can therefore use this information to define much more efficient implementations of these operations. For example, here is the code for the logical operators in class True.

```
"class True"
  {&} right
    ↑ right

  {|} right
    ↑ true
```

In the case of the logical *and* operator, the entire condition depends only on the right argument. In the case of the logical *or* operator, there is no need to even consider the right argument, since a true value *or* anything else is also true. Here are the definitions of the same operations in class False.

```
"class False"
  {&} right
      ↑ false

  {|} right
      ↑ right
```

In both the classes True and False, the child classes have an implementation that is much more efficient than is possible in the parent class.

16.2.2   Refinement in Beta

A refinement occurs when the code in the child class is combined with the code in the parent class, and both are ultimately executed. As we have previously noted, in almost all object-oriented languages that support the mechanism, constructors perform a refinement even if other methods use replacement semantics. This is because it is important that any initialization required by the parent class be included as part of the process of initializing an instance of the child class.

Refinement can be simulated in those languages that use replacement semantics by having the child class explicitly invoke the method in the parent. Various different notations are used for this purpose, as illustrated in Figure 16.2.

Refinement semantics occur in the earliest object-oriented language, Simula, which was developed in the early 1960s. This idea was carried forward into the later language Beta, also of Scandinavian origin. In both these languages, code from the parent class is always executed *first*, before any code from the child class. If the code in the parent class includes the special statement

```
inner;
```

then at that point in execution the code from the child class will be executed.

We will illustrate how this mechanism works with an example modeled on Beta. The syntax we will use is different from Beta in order to more clearly point out the role of refinement. However the basic underlying principles are the same. Imagine a class includes a method designed to print out a World Wide Web anchor.

```
class Anchor {
  public void printAnchor () {
    print('<A href="http:');
    inner;
    print('">');
  }
}
```

C++ Qualified name formed using class name, two colons, then method name.

```
void Parent::example (int a) {
    cout << "in parent code\n";
}

void Child::example (int a) {
    Parent::example(12); // do parent action
    cout << "in child code\n"; // then child action
}
```

Java Pseudo-variable super refers to parent class. Smalltalk and Objective-C use a similar idea. C# uses keyword base.

```
class Parent {
    void example (int a) {
        System.out.println("in parent");
    }
}

class Child {
    void example (int a) {
        super.example(12);
        System.out.println("in child");
    }
}
```

Object Pascal and Delphi Pascal Keyword inherited invokes method in parent class.

```
procedure Parent.example (int a);
begin
    writeln("in parent code");
end;

procedure Child.example (int a);
begin
    inherited example(12); (* do parent action *)
    writeln("in child code"); (* then child action *)
end;
```

▫ Figure 16.2 —— Simulation of refinement using replacement

The inner keyword does not indicate that a subclass *must* be formed. If no subclass is present, the inner statement performs no operation.

```
Anchor anAnchor = new Anchor();
anAnchor.printAnchor();
<A href=http:"">
```

Note carefully that some operations have occurred before the call on inner, and some have occurred after the call.

Now imagine that we create a subclass—say, a class that will print an anchor for Web pages on a specific machine.

```
class OSUAnchor extends Anchor {
  public void printAnchor () {
    print('//www.cs.orst.edu/');
    inner;
  }
}
```

If we now create an instance of the child class and execute the method, the code for the parent class will be executed first, and only when the inner statement is encountered will the code from the child class be executed.

```
Anchor anAnchor = new OSUAnchor();
anAchor.printAnchor();
<A href=http:"//www.cs.orst.edu/">
```

We can continue this process indefinitely. Imagine we create a third class that will print pages in an individual's personal Web directory.

```
class BuddAnchor extends OSUAnchor {
  public void printAnchor () {
    print('~budd/');
    inner;
  }
}
```

Creating an instance of this class and executing the method will then have the effect of first invoking the code from the "grandparent" class Anchor, then from the parent class OSUAnchor, and only last from the class BuddAnchor.

```
Anchor anAnchor = new BuddAnchor();
anAnchor.printAnchor();
<A href=http:"//www.cs.orst.edu/~budd/">
```

Note that in Beta it is the parent that is first given control, and behavior in the parent can wrap around the code provided by the child. When simulating refinement in American languages (as shown in Figure 16.2), it is the child's code that is executed first, and this can wrap around the code in the parent. It is surprisingly difficult to simulate the Beta-style behavior using the mechanism of replacement. (We explore this in an exercise at the end of the chapter.)

16.2.3 Refinement and the subclass/subtype distinction

Advocates for those languages that use refinement argue that the mechanism is conceptually elegant in that it makes it almost impossible to write a subclass that is not also a subtype. This is because refinement guarantees that the behavior of the parent will be preserved, and thus whatever actions the parent performs must also be part of the child. In a language that uses replacement there is no such guarantee. An extreme illustration, but one that is not prohibited by the language definitions, would be for a parent class to use the message sqrt to compute a square root of a number and the child class overriding the message to compute a logarithm.

Advocates for replacement semantics argue that such errors are not common and are easily detected. Adopting replacement semantics as the default means you cannot use the mechanism to support code reuse or optimization of the form described by the earlier examples in Smalltalk. Furthermore, it is easy to simulate at least the most important parts of refinement using replacement (as shown in Figure 16.2), but the reverse is not true.

16.2.4 Wrappers in CLOS

Another interesting variation on refinement semantics occurs in the Lisp dialect, CLOS. In CLOS a subclass may override a method in a parent class and specify a *wrapping method*. A wrapping method can be a *before method*, an *after method*, or an *around method*. According to the type, the method is executed before, after, or surrounding the method in the parent class.

For example, suppose we define the following parent and child classes with three methods named atest, btest, and rtest. In the parent class these simply print out a message.

```
(defclass parent () () )

(defclass child (parent) () )

(defmethod atest ((x parent)) (print "atest parent"))
(defmethod btest ((x parent)) (print "btest parent"))
(defmethod rtest ((x parent)) (print "rtest parent"))
```

In the child class, we redefine the methods, one as a before method, one as an after method, and one as an around method. In the last case, a special statement, call-next-method, invokes the method in the parent class. This is similar to the way in which refinement is simulated in languages such as C++ and Object Pascal.

```
(defmethod atest :after ((x child)) (print "atest child"))
(defmethod btest :before ((x child)) (print "btest child"))
(defmethod rtest :around ((x child))
  (list "rtest child before" (call-next-method) "rtest child after"))
```

If we make an instance of the child class and execute the three methods, we see the before methods execute the child class before the parent, the after methods execute the child class after the parent, and the around methods do both.

```
(defvar aChild (make-instance 'child))
(atest aChild)
"atest child"
"atest parent"
(btest aChild)
"btest parent"
"btest child"
(rtest aChild)
("rtest child before" "rtest parent" "rtest child after")
```

16.3 ▫ Deferred Methods

We say a method is *deferred* if in the parent class the method is defined but not implemented. Deferred methods are also sometimes called *abstract* methods, and in C++ they are usually called a *pure virtual method*.

One advantage of deferred methods is conceptual in that their use allows the programmer to think of an activity as associated with an abstraction at a higher level than may actually be the case. For example, in a collection of classes representing geometric shapes, we can define a method to draw the shape in each of the subclasses Circle, Square, and Triangle. We could have defined a similar method in the parent class Shape, but such a method cannot, in actuality, produce any useful behavior, since the class Shape does not have sufficient information to draw the shape in question. Nevertheless, the mere presence of this method permits the user to associate the concept *draw* with the single class Shape and not with the three separate concepts Square, Triangle, and Circle.

There is a second, more practical reason for using deferred methods. In statically typed object-oriented languages, such as C++ and Object Pascal, a programmer is permitted to send a message to an object only if the compiler can

C++

```
class Shape {
public:
    virtual void draw () = 0;
};
```

Java (C# and Delphi are similar.)

```
abstract class Shape {
    abstract public void draw ();
}
```

Smalltalk (Objective-C is similar.)

```
draw
    " child class should override this "
    ^ self subclassResponsibility
```

▫ Figure 16.3 —— Syntax for deferred classes

determine that there is in fact a corresponding method that matches the message selector. Suppose the programmer wishes to define a polymorphic variable of class Shape that will, at various times, contain instances of each of the different shapes. Such an assignment is possible, according to our rule of substitutability. Nevertheless, the compiler will permit the message draw to be used with this variable only if it can ensure that the message will be understood by any value that may be associated with the variable. Assigning a method to the class Shape effectively provides this assurance, even when the method in class Shape is never actually executed.

Figure 16.3 illustrates some of the ways that deferred methods are documented in various languages. In both Java and C# a deferred method is declared as abstract. In C++ the notation looks like one is assigning the method the value zero. In Smalltalk and Objective-C the parent class implements the deferred method but invokes an error message generating routine (subclassResponsibility). The child class overrides the method, thereby avoiding calling the error message.

Deferred methods are almost always found in conjunction with other methods that are not intended to be overridden. The idea is to balance code reuse (the non-overridden methods) with specialization (the overridden methods). The non-overridden methods (sometimes called *foundational* methods) provide functionality that is modified for different situations by means of the deferred methods. We will see several examples of this when we explore the idea of software Frameworks in Chapter 21.

16.4 ▫ Overriding versus Shadowing

Because they have superficial syntactic similarities, it is easy to confuse the mechanism of overriding and the related programming language concept of shadowing. To explain this, let us first examine a slightly simpler form of shadowing. Consider the following class and method.

```
class Silly {
  private int x; // an instance variable named x

  public void example (int x) { // x shadows instance variable
    int a = x+1;
    while (a > 3) {
      int x = 1; // local variable shadows parameter
      a = a - x;
    }
  }
}
```

In this example class definition there are three different variables named x. The first is an instance variable. This variable is normally accessible from within any method defined as part of the class. However, in the method example there is a parameter defined using the same name. The parameter name hides, or shadows, access to the instance variable. This means that within the method, the name x is matched to the parameter and not to the instance variable. (In this case the instance variable can still be accessed using the construct this.x.)

Within the while loop another variable named x is declared. This is a local variable, and it again shadows access to the parameter x. Declaring variables in this fashion is not something to be encouraged, but nothing in the language definition prohibits it. (Some compilers will issue warning messages.)

Keep this simple example in mind when we next consider how shadowing can occur in conjunction with inheritance. A good example is with instance variables. The following is legal in Java, although it is probably not something to be encouraged.

```
class Parent {
  public int x = 12;
}

class Child extend Parent {
  public int x = 42; // shadows variable from parent class
}
```

The declaration of x in the child class will shadow that of the parent. The most important feature that distinguishes shadowing from overriding is that, like overloading, shadowing is resolved at compile time based on static types and does not require any run-time mechanism.

```
Parent p = new Parent();
System.out.println(p.x);
12
  Child c = new Child();
  System.out.println(c.x);
42
  p = c; // be careful here!
  System.out.println(p.x);
12
```

Many of those languages in Figure 16.1 that require an explicit indication of overriding will perform a shadowing if no keyword is provided. This can be illustrated by the following classes in C++.

```
class Parent {
public:
    // note, no virtual keyword here
    void example () { cout << "Parent" << endl; }
};

class Child : public Parent {
public:
    void example () { cout << "Child" << endl; }
};
```

As was true with the Java example of instance variables, a match of message to method is determined by the static declaration and not by a dynamic value.

```
Parent * p = new Parent();
p->example()
Parent
  Child * c = new Child();
  c->example()
Child
  p = c; // be careful here!
  p->example()
Parent
```

Like C++, Delphi will shadow a method if the override directive is omitted, but the compiler will issue a warning. This warning can be eliminated by using the

reintroduce directive, which explicitly indicates that the programmer intended the
new method to shadow the earlier one.

```
type
  TParent = class
    public
      procedure example (); virtual;
    end;

  TChild = class (TParent)
    public
      procedure example (); reintroduce;
    end;
```

The ideas of overriding, shadowing, and redefinition (discussed in the previous
chapter) should not be confused. The following table summarizes the differences.

overriding	The type signatures are the same in both parent and child classes, and the method is declared as virtual in the parent class.
shadowing	The type signatures are the same in both parent and child classes, but the method was not declared as virtual in the parent class.
redefinition	The type signature in the child class differs from that given in the parent class.

16.5 ▫ Covariance and Contravariance

Frequently it seems as if it would be useful if overriding could be used but the
type signature of a method in a child class could be different from that found in
the parent class. A common example (one we will explore in another section) is a
method equals used to compare two objects. Since normally one is only interested
in comparing objects of the same type, it would seem to make sense that the
argument in the child class should be the child class type. Unfortunately, the whole
concept of changing type signatures is fraught with subtle difficulties, as we will
explore in this section.

One seldom wants to change the type signatures arbitrarily but typically move
either up or down the type hierarchy. The term *covariant* change is used when
a type moves down the type hierarchy in the same direction as the child class.
The term *contravariant* is used for the opposite—when a type moves up the class
hierarchy in the opposite direction from subclassing. These two are shown in the
following class hierarchy, where in the child class the first argument (named covar)

moves from Mammal to the more specific type Cat, while the second argument is changed in a contravariant fashion to the more general type Animal.

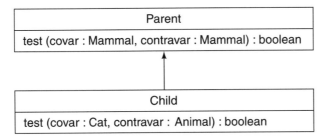

The impact of covariant or contravariant change is complicated by the fact that types can be used in a variety of different ways. The effect of changing a pass-by-value parameter is different from the effect of changing a pass-by-reference parameter, which is in turn different from the effect of changing the return type for a procedure. For this reason it is slightly easier to think about the problem using sets and consider the relationships between the set of values that are acceptable (for example, as an argument) to the parent in relationship to the set of values that are acceptable to the child.

We first consider what can happen if the set of values acceptable to the child is smaller than the set of values acceptable to the parent. This can happen, for example, in a covariant change to a pass-by-value parameter. (The parent class has a parameter of type Mammal, and the child class restricts the same parameter to the type Cat.)

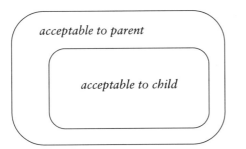

A problem occurs when this covariant change runs into the principle of substitution. According to the principle of substitution, we should be able to declare a variable using the parent type but assign it a value from the child class.

```
Parent aValue = new Child();
aValue.test(new Dog(), new Mammal()); // note type of first argument
```

As far as the compiler is concerned, the first argument is perfectly acceptable, since the declaration insists only that the value be type Mammal. But the invocation will bind the message to the method in the child class, which is prepared only to accept values of type Cat. The consequence will almost certainly be a completely erroneous and catastrophic outcome.

It is occasionally proposed that run-time checks could be used to detect this condition, allowing at least a graceful error reporting, albeit at run time rather than at compile time. However, note that such checks are never necessary when the child is being used as an instance of the child class, but only when the child is being used as an instance of the parent class. Thus, in a large percentage, perhaps the majority, of cases such run-time checks would be superfluous.

An error will not occur in the opposite case, where a contravariant change to a by-value parameter increases the range of values the child class is willing to handle. In this case neither the parent class nor the child class can pass an unacceptable value to the method.

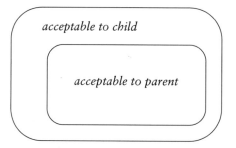

However, that is only true for pass-by-value parameters. When we consider a change to the result type of a method, the situation is exactly the reverse. Suppose a method in the parent class returns a value of type Mammal, and the child class includes a contravariant change that extends this to Animal, thereby making the set of values acceptable to the child *larger* than the set of values acceptable to the parent. Once again we run into problems with the principle of substitution. It would be perfectly legal for the child class to return a value of type Bird, since locally a bird satisfies the typing restrictions.

```
class Parent {
  Mammal test ( ) {
    return new Cat();
  }
}

class  Child extends Parent {
  Animal test () {
    return new Bird();
  }
}
```

But it is also legal for a variable of the parent class to hold an instance of the child class and for the result of executing the method in question to be assigned to a variable of type Mammal, since as far as the compiler is concerned, the result of the method fits that class designation.

```
Parent aValue = new Child();
Mammal result = aValue.test();   // error—a bird is not a mammal
```

The consequence will be the variable of type Mammal holding a non-mammal value, with no typing error having been reported.

A pass-by-reference parameter can be used to pass information both into and out of a procedure. Therefore, both of these errors could arise if any change whatsoever is permitted in such a value.

It is possible to specify a language so that both covariant and contravariant overriding is permitted in certain situations. Examples of languages that permit this include Eiffel and Sather. (See Section 12.4.2 for a discussion of LIKE CURRENT, which is one approach to covariant overriding.) C++ allows a covariant change in signature on the return types. This is typically used in a method such as the following.

```
class Parent {
public:
   Parent * clone () { return new Parent(); }
};

class Child : public Parent {
public:
   Child * clone () { return new Child(); }
};
```

As we noted earlier, the restriction of the set of types the child can return cannot result in a type error, since any value the child can yield will still match the specifications of the parent.

However, most language designers have opted to avoid this problem altogether by using a rule that might be termed *novariance*—namely, that a child class is not allowed to change the type signature of an overridden method in any fashion.

Equality testing.   The example where covariant modification of type signatures often seems most compelling is in the implementation of equality and comparison tests. Examining this situation will provide a concrete illustration of the problems that can arise.

Imagine we have the following class hierarchy where the equals method in the parent class always returns false, whereas the overridden method in the child classes correctly handles the comparison of triangles to triangles and of squares to squares.

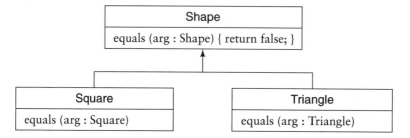

In the imaginary language we envision here, consider what meaning might be assigned to an attempt to compare a triangle to a square.

```
Triangle aTriangle;
Square aSquare;

if aTriangle.equals(aSquare) ...
```

There are two possibilities.

- The search for a method is based solely on the receiver, a triangle, and yields the triangle method, which requires a triangle as argument. Thus, the use of a square as argument results in a compiler error.
- The search for a method is based both on the receiver and on the argument type signatures. Since the argument does not match the method in class Triangle, the method in the parent class Shape is then invoked.

Selecting either interpretation leads to trouble as soon as we consider the principle of substitution. Suppose we create a shape variable and assign it the triangle value. Comparing the triangle and the shape is then effectively comparing a value to itself. But the first interpretation results in an error, and the second interpretation results in the nonsensical result that the value is not equal to itself.

```
Shape aShape = aTriangle;
if aTriangle.equals(aShape) ...
```

A similar incongruity occurs if the parent variable is used as the receiver. Since the only reasonable method to use is the one defined in the parent class, the test yields an unexpected false value.

```
if aShape.equals(aShape) ...
```

Both because the implementation of either covariant or contravariant overriding is complex and because the semantics are cloudy, almost all object-oriented languages prohibit any modification of argument types in overridden methods. To get around this restriction, programmers most often resort to explicit tests and casts, as in the following C++ example.

```
bool Triangle.equals (Shape * aShape)
{
   Triangle * right = dynamic_cast<Triangle *>(aShape);
   if (right) { // it was a triangle
      // :  do triangle comparison
   } else // it was not a triangle
      return false;
}
```

Again it is important to note that we here are discussing only overloading. Equality can be implemented using a redefinition (as described in the previous chapter), but redefinition is resolved at compile time based on static types and not at run time using dynamic values.

*16.6 □ Variations on Overriding

In this section we will explore a few of the language-specific variations on the theme of overriding.

16.6.1 Final methods in Java

While the virtual keyword *permits* overriding, and the abstract keyword *requires* it, it is sometimes desirable to *prohibit* overriding. That is, the programmer might like to insist that the method defined in a parent class is the final and definitive version and no further changes can be made by a child class. In Java this can be accomplished through the use of the final modifier.

```
class Parent {
   public final void aMethod (int) { ... }
}

class Child extends Parent {
      // compiler error, not allowed to override final method
   public void aMethod (int) { ... }
}
```

Java also permits the keyword to be applied to an entire class, in which case the class cannot be subclassed.

The language C# has a similar keyword, sealed, that can be applied to classes but not to individual methods.

```
sealed class Parent {
  .
  .
  .
}


class  Child : Parent { // generates a compiler error
  .
  .
  .
}
```

Final methods and sealed classes can be exploited by an optimizing compiler, since the use of such features will often eliminate the need for a run-time message resolution.

16.6.2   Versioning in C#

As software changes over time, it is not uncommon for new methods to be introduced into class hierarchies. Sometimes this can have unfortunate consequences. For example, suppose that a child class implements a virtual method on its own—that is, one that is not inherited from its parent.

```
class Parent {
  .
  .
  .
}


class Child : Parent {
  public virtual void aMethod(int) { ... }
}
```

Later a new revision of the parent class is released, and this new revision (which may have been created in an entirely different organization from that developing the child class) includes a method using the same name.

```
class Parent {
  public virtual void aMethod(int) { ... }
}


class Child : Parent {
  public virtual void aMethod(int) { ... }
}
```

Almost all object-oriented languages will consider these to be the same method. However, the original intent was for them to be different. In C# the programmer can add the new keyword in the child class. The presence of this keyword changes an overloading into a redefinition. (That is, the method in the child class is considered to be independent of the method in the parent class.)

```
class Parent {
   public virtual void aMethod(int) { ... }
}

class Child : Parent {
   public new virtual void aMethod(int) { ... }
}
```

A difficulty in using this feature is that the programmer cannot predict ahead of time which methods should be declared as new, since it is only necessary after a change has been introduced in the parent.

Summary ⊡

- An *override* occurs when a method in a child class uses the same name and type signature as a method in the parent class.

- While technically an override is an overloading (there are two method bodies with the same name), overriding is resolved at run time, whereas overloading is resolved at compile time.

- The effect of an override can be handled in two possible ways. A *replacement* completely replaces the code in the parent class; a *refinement* combines the code in the child with that of the parent.

- A *deferred method* is a form of overriding where the parent provides no implementation and the child is solely responsible for implementing the specified behavior.

- A name can *shadow* another use of the same name if it temporarily hides access to the previous meaning. Some languages permit both shadowing and overriding.

- A covariant change in parameter or return type is a change the moves down the class hierarchy in the same direction as the child class. A contravariant change moves a parameter or return type up the class hierarchy in the opposite direction from the child class. The semantics of both types of changes can be subtle.

Further Information ▫

Introductions to the first object-oriented language, Simula, can be found in [Dahl 1966, Birtwistle 1979, Kirkerud 1989]. Beta is described in [Madsen 1993]. I have always thought that Beta is an extremely interesting language that has been overlooked because it has such an obscure syntax. The terms "American Semantics" and "Scandinavian Semantics" are due to Cook [Cook 1988].

Wrappers in CLOS are discussed in [Keene 1989].

Contravariance in Eiffel is discussed in [Rist 1995]. The rationale for not allowing any covariant or contravariant change in C++ except in return types is discussed by the designer of the language in [Stroustrup 1994].

Versioning in C# is discussed in [Gunnerson 2000].

Self-Study Questions ▫

1. What are the key features necessary to say that one method overrides another?

2. In what ways is overriding similar to overloading? In what ways are they different?

3. What is the difference between an overriding that uses replacement and one that uses refinement?

4. Why do constructors in most languages use refinement even if other method overriding uses replacement?

5. Why are refinement semantics for overriding sometimes called Scandinavian semantics?

6. What is the effect of the inner statement in Beta or Simula?

7. Is a wrapper in CLOS an example of a replacement or a refinement?

8. What is a deferred method?

9. What does it mean to say that a declaration of a name shadows a previous declaration?

10. What is a covariant change in a parameter type? What is a contravariant change?

11. In Java what is the effect of declaring a method as final?

Exercises ▫

1. By following the execution of each of the other five, show that if either < or <= is redefined by a subclass of Magnitude in Little Smalltalk that all relational operators will produce the correct result.

2. Suppose we want to add a third subclass of Boolean to the two classes described in Section 16.2.1. The class Unknown represents values with an unknown truth value. Without redefining any methods in class Unknown, what is the meaning of any operation that uses these quantities? (Assume that an if statement will only execute the true block if a conditional is true.) For both the and and or operators, draw a three by three truth table that describes the result of each possible combination of values.

3. Show how to simulate the refinement example described in Section 16.2.2, using an American semantics language such as C++ or Java. Make sure you support the principle of substitution so an instance of a child class can be assigned to a variable declared using the parent class, and executing the printAnchor method will have the desired effect. You will probably need to introduce additional methods. Does your scheme allow the class hierarchy to be extended arbitrarily?

4. Show that even if an instance of a child class is substituted where a parent class value is expected, no error can result from the covariant change in result type that is allowed by C++.

CHAPTER 17

The Polymorphic Variable

A *polymorphic variable* is a variable that can reference more than one type of object. As a consequence, such a variable can maintain values of different types during the course of execution. In a dynamically typed language all variables are potentially polymorphic. In a statically typed language the polymorphic variable is the embodiment of the principle of substitution, a topic we examined in Chapter 8. Many of the examples we've seen that discussed the principle of substitution have used a simple assignment.

```
//  assign a child value to a parent variable
Parent variable = new Child();
```

However, such examples are, in fact, relatively rare in practice. Most commonly, substitution comes about through the binding of values to arguments during the process of function or method invocation.

In this chapter we examine the various different forms that the polymorphic variable can take. In Section 17.1 we examine simple variables. In Section 17.2 we consider the polymorphic variable that represents the receiver during the course of method execution. In Section 17.3 we will investigate downcasting, which is sometimes called *reverse polymorphism*. Finally, in Section 17.4 we consider *pure polymorphism*, which is the term used to describe a polymorphic variable being used as an argument.

17.1 ▫ Simple Polymorphic Variables

A good example of a polymorphic variable is the array allPiles in the Solitaire game presented in Chapter 9. The array was declared as maintaining a value of type

CardPile, but in fact it maintains values from each of the different subclasses of the parent class. A message presented to a value from this array, such as display in the example code shown here, executes the method associated with the dynamic type of the variable and not that of the static class.

```
public class Solitaire {
    .
    .
    .
    static CardPile allPiles [ ];
    .
    .
    .
    public void paint(Graphics g) {
        for (int i = 0; i < 13; i++)
            allPiles[i].display(g);
    }
    .
    .
    .
}
```

Another example of a simple polymorphic variable occurs in the Java abstract windowing toolkit, or AWT. (We will examine many different features of the AWT in Chapter 22.) In the AWT the placement of graphical elements such as buttons, scroll bars, labels, and the like is determined by an object called the *Layout Manager*.

In fact LayoutManager is not a class but an interface. There are several different implementations of this interface provided in the standard library, but the user is free to implement his or her own.

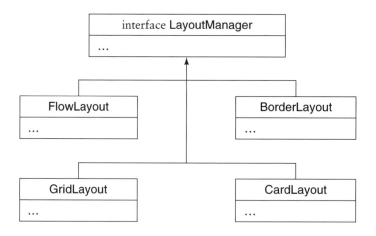

To select the layout manager, the programmer simply invokes the method setLayoutManager inherited from class Component (a parent class to all windows). This method in turn simply assigns the argument to a polymorphic local variable.

```
class Component {
   .
   .
   .
   void setLayoutManager (layoutManager mgr)
     { layoutMgr = mgr; }

   LayoutManager layoutMgr;
}
```

Later, when it is necessary to determine the location of each graphical element, the class Component uses the services of whatever layout manager the user has provided.

Now one can argue that it is not the ability to assign the variable layoutMgr a variety of different values that is important here, but the fact that subsequently each of those different values can tailor its effect by the way it implements methods to match the LayoutManager interface. Therefore (it might be argued), it is overriding that is important and not the polymorphic variable. However, we see throughout the discussion of polymorphic techniques that it is the *combination* of tools in a variety of ways that produces the greatest effect.

17.2 □ The Receiver Variable

It is perhaps ironic that the most common place that a polymorphic variable is used is the one place where it is not normally visible at all. This form is as the value that represents the receiver inside an executing method.

The variable that maintains the receiver is not normally declared, and for this reason it is often termed a *pseudo-variable*. It goes by a number of different names in different languages. It is termed self in Smalltalk and Object Pascal; this in C++, C#, and Java; and current in Eiffel.

The major role for this variable is to act as the basis for access to data fields and to serve as the receiver when methods are passed to "oneself." In both of these roles the variable is normally implicit and does not appear in the code, although nothing prevents the explicit naming. Consider, for example, the following simple class in Java.

```
class ThisExample {
  public void one (int x) {
    value = x*4;
    two (x + 3);
  }
```

```
    private int value;

    private void two (int y) {
      System.out.println("value is " + (value + y));
    }
  }
```

The access to the data member named "value" inside method one could be considered ambiguous, since there are many different data fields with this name, one in each instance of the class. Similarly, the invocation of the method two appears to occur without a receiver having been named. But in both of these cases the disambiguation comes from the implicit use of the receiver value. In fact, this program could have been written in an entirely unambiguous fashion as follows.

```
class ThisExample {
  public void one (int x) {
    this.value = x*4; // explicitly name which value
    this.two (x + 3); // give explicit receiver
  }

  private int value;

  private void two (int y) {
    System.out.println("value is " + (this.value + y));
  }
}
```

There are some coding conventions that encourage the use of the explicit qualifier on data access, particularly in constructors. One advantage is that this eliminates the need to think of two different variable names in those situations where an argument is being used simply to initialize a local data field.

```
class ThisExample {
  public ThisExample (int value) {
      // the use of "this" here is needed in order to
      // disambiguate the two uses of the same name
    this.value = value;
  }

  private int value;
  .
  .
  .
}
```

17.2.1 The role of the polymorphic variable in frameworks

The true power of the polymorphic receiver comes when message passing is combined with overriding. As we will see in Chapter 21, this combination is the key to the development of software frameworks. Consider, for example, a typical windowing system. An example might be the Java AWT, although the same principle is found in almost all frameworks. Methods in such a system can be divided into two major categories. There are the foundational methods defined in the parent class. These are inherited by child classes and are not overridden. Then there are activity methods that are defined in the parent class but deferred to child classes. In the following hierarchy, repaint is a foundational method, while paint is deferred.

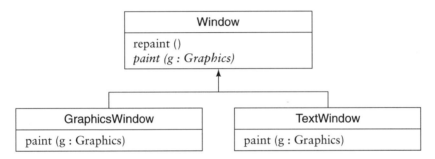

Because the foundational methods are inherited, they can be used by instances of subclasses. It is here that the receiver variable shows its polymorphic colors. When the foundation method is executed, the receiver is actually maintaining a *value* that is an instance of the child class. Thus, when an overridden method is executed, it is the method in the child class that is executed, not the method in the parent class.[1]

```
class Window {
    public void repaint () {
        // invoke the deferred method paint.
        // Because the implicit receiver, this,
        // is polymorphic, the method from the
        // child class will be executed
        paint (graphicsContext);
    }
```

---

1. This simple example should not be taken to be accurate with regards to the AWT. In fact, a repaint in the AWT schedules a painting event for a later execution. But the relationship between foundation methods and deferred methods remains the same.

```
abstract public void paint (Graphics g); // deferred

private Graphics graphicsContext;
}

class GraphicsWindow extends Window {
  public void paint (Graphics g) {
    // do the appropriate painting job
  }
}
```

This pattern of a foundation method executing a deferred method is repeated countless times in all types of software frameworks. As we noted in Chapter 15, this combination of foundation and deferred methods is the key to unlocking the power of software reuse, since it permits the foundation methods to be tailored to new situations without the need to modify the original code. Such specialization-without-modification is extremely difficult without object-oriented techniques.

17.2.2   Endpoint comparisons in Smalltalk

Another example will illustrate how the polymorphic receiver is used in an untyped programming language. As we noted in Chapter 16 on overriding, the class Magnitude in Smalltalk is an abstract superclass that deals with quantities that possess at least a partial, if not a total, ordering. Consider the method called between:and: shown here.

```
{between:} low {and:} high
  " test to see if the receiver is between two endpoints "
  ↑ (low <= self) and: [ self <= high ]
```

This method occurs in the class Magnitude and presumably (according to the comment) tests whether the receiver is between two endpoints. It performs this test by sending the message <= to the lower bound with the receiver as argument and to the receiver with the upper bound as argument. (Remember, in Smalltalk all operators are treated as messages.) Only if both of these expressions yield true does the method determine that the receiver is between the two endpoints.

Once again, we see the conjunction of a foundation method (between:and:) working in combination with a deferred method (<=). After the message (between:and:) has been sent to an object with a pair of arguments, what happens next depends on the particular meaning given to the message <=. This message is overridden in many of the subclasses. For integer values, the meaning is that of integer comparison; thus, between:and: can be used to test whether an integer value is between two other integer values. Floating-point values define < similarly, with similar results.

```
anInteger between: 7 and: 11
```

```
aFloat between: 2.7 and:   3.5
```

For characters, the relation <= is defined in terms of the underlying ASCII collating sequence; thus, between:and: tests whether a character is between two other characters. To see whether a variable aChar contains a lowercase letter, for example, we can use the following expression (a is the token denoting the literal character a in Smalltalk).

```
aChar between: $a and: $z
```

For Points, the relation <= is defined as being true if the receiver is above and to the left of the argument (that is, both the first and second components of the point are less than or equal to their corresponding part in the other point). Point objects are a basic data type in Smalltalk; numbers respond to the @ operator by constructing a point with their own value as the first coordinate and the argument as the second coordinate. Note that the definition of < for points provides only a partial order, since not all points are thereby commensurate. Nevertheless, the expression

```
aPoint between: 2@4 and: 12@14
```

is true if aPoint is in the box defined by the coordinates (2,4) in the upper left and (12,14) in the lower right corner.

The important feature to note is that in all of these cases there is only *one* method being used for between:and:. This method is polymorphic; it works with a number of argument types. In each case, the redefinition of the messages involved in the polymorphic routine (in this case, the message <=) tailors the code to specific circumstances.

17.2.3   Self and super

In the languages Smalltalk and Java there is another pseudo-variable named super. Like self (in Smalltalk and Objective-C) or this (in C++, C#, and Java), the name super refers to the receiver for the method currently being executed. But a message passed to super is interpreted differently from a message passed to self.

A message passed to self will begin the search for a corresponding method with the class of the receiver. A message passed to super, on the other hand, looks for a method to match the message starting from the parent class for the class in which the currently executing method resides. This is illustrated by the following example. The code is shown in Java, but the concept would be the same in Smalltalk, although the syntax would be different.

```java
class Parent {
  void exampleOne () {
    System.out.println("In parent method");
  }

  void exampleTwo () {
    System.out.println("In parent method");
  }
}

class Child extends Parent {
  void exampleOne () {
    System.out.println("In child method");
    super.exampleOne();
  }

  void exampleTwo () {
    System.out.println("In child method");
    this.exampleTwo(); // infinite loop
  }
}
```

The child class overrides both methods inherited from the parent. In the method named exampleOne the child class explicitly invokes the method defined in the parent. As we noted in Chapter 16, this is the way that methods in Java can achieve a refinement of the parent, as opposed to a replacement. The method named exampleTwo is similar, only it uses the pseudo-variable this instead of super. The result is an infinite loop, since the method invoked will be the same method in class Child.

Note that method binding for a message passed to super can be performed at compile time, since both the class and the parent must be known. Thus no run-time message resolution mechanism is necessary. A good optimizing compiler can exploit this fact and produce more efficient code for messages passed to super than for messages in general.

In C# the pseudo-variable base is used for this purpose, but otherwise it is the same as the use of super in Java. The previous example would be written in C# as follows.

```
public class Parent {
  public void exampleOne () {
    Console.WriteLine("In parent method");
  }
}

public class  Child : Parent {
  public void exampleOne () {
    Console.WriteLine("In child method");
    base.exampleOne();
  }
}
```

17.3 ▫ Downcasting

Downcasting is the process of taking a polymorphic variable and, in a sense, undoing the process of substitution. That is, the polymorphic variable, while declared as the parent class, is actually holding a value derived from a child class. Can we therefore assign it to a variable that is declared as the child class? Since it is undoing the polymorphic assignment, this process is also sometimes described as *reverse polymorphism*.

There are actually two related problems involved in this operation. To illustrate, suppose we define a class, Ball, and two subclasses, BlackBall and WhiteBall. Next, we construct the software equivalent of a box into which we can drop two instances of class Ball, and one of those instances (selected randomly) will fall out and be returned (Figure 17.1). We drop a BlackBall and a WhiteBall into the box and recover the result.

Now, the resulting object can certainly be considered a Ball and can thus be assigned to a variable declared as that type. But is it a BlackBall? We can ask these two questions.

- Can I tell whether or not it is a BlackBall?
- What mechanisms are necessary to assign the value to an instance of the child class?

Although the BlackBall/WhiteBall example may seem contrived, the underlying problem is quite common. Consider the development of classes for frequently used data structures, such as sets, stacks, queues, lists, and the like. Containers of this nature are used to maintain collections of objects. A touted benefit of object-oriented programming is the production of reusable software components, and collection containers are candidates for such components. However, a collection

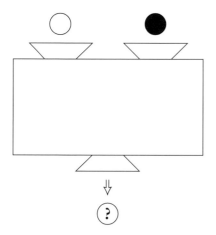

▫ Figure 17.1 ——A ball losing its identity

container is in some circumstances exactly like the ball machine. If a programmer places two different objects in a set and later takes one out, how does he or she know which type of object will result?

In practice, the problem of identification and the problem of assignment are almost always solved in combination. This is because the assignment mechanism will almost always fail if a proper identification has not been made. For this reason some languages combine these two features, while others keep them separate. The various different techniques are illustrated in Figure 17.2.

17.4 ▫ Pure Polymorphism

Many authors reserve the term *polymorphic method* (or *pure polymorphism*) for situations where one function can be used with a variety of arguments, and the term *overloading* for situations where there are multiple functions all defined with a single name.[2] Such facilities are not restricted to object-oriented languages. In Lisp or ML, for example, it is easy to write functions that manipulate lists of arbitrary elements. Such functions are polymorphic because the type of the argument is not known at the time the function is defined. The ability to form polymorphic functions is one of the most powerful techniques in object-oriented

---

2. The extreme cases may be easy to recognize, but discovering the line that separates overloading from polymorphism can be difficult. In both C++ and ML a programmer can define a number of functions, each having the same name but different arguments. Is it overloading in C++ because the various functions sharing the same name are not defined in one location, whereas in ML-style polymorphism they must all be bundled together under a single heading?

C++

```
Child * c = dynamic_cast<Child *>(aParentPtr);
if (c != 0) { // null if not legal, nonnull if ok
    .
    .
    .
}
```

Delphi Pascal

```
if (aVariable is Child) then
    childVar := aVariable as Child
```

Java

```
Child aChild;
if (aVariable instanceof Child)
    aChild = (Child) aVariable;
```

Oberon-2

```
IF aVariable IS Child THEN
    aChild := aVariable(Child)
END
```

Object Pascal

```
if Member (aVariable, Child) then
    aChild = Child(aVariable)
```

Python

```
if isinstance(aVariable, Child):
    .
    .
    .
```

Smalltalk

```
(aVariable class == Child) ifTrue: [ ... ]
or
(aVariable isKindOf: Child) ifTrue: [ ... ]
```

▢ Figure 17.2 —— Mechanisms for downcasting

programming. It permits code to be written once, at a high level of abstraction, and to be tailored as necessary to fit a variety of situations. Usually, the programmer accomplishes this tailoring by sending deferred messages to the receiver for the method.

A simple example of pure polymorphism is the method append in the Java class StringBuffer. The argument to this method is declared as Object and thus can be any object type. The method has roughly the following definition.

```java
class StringBuffer {
  String append (Object value)
    { return append(value.toString()); }
  .
  .
  .
}
```

The method toString is deferred. It is defined in class Object and redefined in a large number of different subclasses. Each of these definitions of toString will have a slightly different effect: A Double will produce a textual representation of its numeric value; a Color will generate a string that describes the red, green, and blue values in the color; a Button will create a string representing the class name followed by a hexadecimal number that represents the location of the object in memory; and so on.

Because these various versions of toString produce a variety of different effects, the method append will similarly produce a number of different results. This variety of effects is achieved despite the fact that there is only one definition of method append.

In a certain sense the polymorphic receiver discussed in Section 17.2 is simply a special case of pure polymorphism. As we will see in Chapter 27 when we discuss the implementation of object-oriented languages, when a method is invoked, the receiver is actually passed as a "hidden parameter." For example, consider the method named one in the following class definition.

```java
class Test {
  void one (int x) { ... }
};
```

When it comes time to generate code for the method, it is internally translated into the following.

```java
void Test_one (Test this, int x) { ... }
```

Note that two changes have been made. The name of the method has been altered to make it unique (by prepending the class name), and an additional first argument has been inserted. This additional argument is the polymorphic receiver we discussed in Section 17.2.

Similarly, the Smalltalk example in Section 17.2.2 also illustrates features of pure polymorphism. Differences in execution depend both on the arguments low and high, as well as on the receiver.

Summary ▫

- A *polymorphic variable* is a variable that can reference more than one type of object.
- Polymorphic variables derive their power from an interaction with inheritance and overriding. When a method is overridden, the code executed will be determined by the current value of a polymorphic variable, not its declared type.
- The most common polymorphic variable is the one that represents the receiver within the body of a method. This value is named this in Java and C++, and self in many other languages.
- The polymorphic variable that represents the receiver has an important part to play in the development of software frameworks. In a framework, methods are divided into *foundation* methods, which are implemented in the framework itself, and *deferred* methods, which are defined in the framework but implemented by the programmer using the framework.
- Downcasting is the process of undoing a polymorphic assignment—that is, assigning a value being held by a variable to a more specialized type than that used in creating the variable.
- Pure polymorphism occurs when a polymorphic variable is used as argument in a method.

Further Information ▫

Palsberg and Schwartzbach [Palsberg 1994] present an algorithm for performing type inference on polymorphic methods.

For years people have argued whether the latest version of the programming language Ada (Ada 95) is an object-oriented language. Although it does not have classes, it does have packages that can be used in much the same way. It does support inheritance, and polymorphism of a sort. But what makes Ada 95 most difficult to use in the object-oriented way is the near complete absence of anything similar to a polymorphic variable. Further information on Ada 95 can be found in [Feldman 1997].

Self-Study Questions ⊡

1. What is a polymorphic variable?
2. Explain why the receiver variable (this, self, or current) can be considered polymorphic.
3. Under what circumstances will the receiver variable hold a value that is not an instance of the class in which the method appears?
4. In Smalltalk, how is the meaning of super different from self?
5. What is reverse polymorphism?
6. What is pure polymorphism?

Exercises ⊡

1. In many object-oriented languages, all classes descend from a common parent class. In Java, for example, all classes descend from Object, whereas in Delphi they all descend from TObject. In such languages it is common for data structure classes to maintain their values by holding them in variables declared as the root class (e.g., in a variable declared as Object). Explain how such a strategy naturally leads to the downcasting problem described in Section 17.3.

CHAPTER 18

Generics

Yet another form of polymorphism is provided by the facility known as a *generic* (in C++, a *template*). Generics provide a way of parameterizing a class or a function by use of a *type*, just as normal parameters to a function provide a way to define an algorithm without identifying specific values.

With generics, a name is defined as a type parameter. This parameter can then be used within the class definition just as if it were a type, although no properties of the type are known when the class description is being read by the compiler. At some later point the type parameter is matched with a specific type and a complete declaration can be formed.

Among object-oriented languages generics are best known in C++, Beta, and Eiffel. There are proposals to add generic facilities to Java and C#, but these features are not at present found in those languages. Generics are also found in functional languages, such as ML or Haskell, and in other non-object-oriented languages, such as Ada.

18.1 □ Template Functions

To illustrate the idea of a generic, let us first consider how they can be used with stand-alone functions and then move on to consider generic classes. Consider the following definition of a C++ function.

```
template <class T>
T max(T left, T right) {
    // return largest argument
  if (left < right)
```

```
      return right;
   return left;
}
```

The name T is a parameter, but it is different from the two value parameters in the function. Most importantly, T must be a type. (The keyword class is actually, for this reason, a misnomer, since T can also be replaced with primitive, nonclass types such as int. For this reason a recent change to C++ allows the keyword typename to be used in place of class in this situation.) Within the body of the function, T can be used wherever a type would be appropriate.

There are limits that constrain what types can be used in place of T, but these limits are not imposed by the function header but instead by the function body. In particular, note that whatever type T might be, it must be possible to compare two instances of the type using the less-than operator. But any types that satisfy this property can be used. In particular, the primitive types recognize the relational operators.

To invoke a templated function, the programmer simply writes an ordinary function call. The template argument is inferred from the argument types.

```
int a = max(3, 27); // inferred type for T is integer
double d = max(3.14159, 2.753); // inferred type for T is double
```

Since the same type is used for both arguments, a compiler error is reported if the arguments do not have the same type or if the type does not support the less-than operator.

```
double d = max(3, 4.8); // error, types don't match
string x = "abc";
string y = "def";
string z = max(x, y); // error, string doesn't support less than
```

Template functions can be applied to programmer-defined types as long as the argument types support the operations required by the body of the method. For example, suppose the programmer has created the following Fraction abstraction.

```
class Fraction {
public:
   Fraction (int top, int bottom) { t = top; b = bottom; }

   int numerator() { return t; }
   int denominator() { return b; }

   bool operator < (Fraction & right)
      { return t * right.b < right.t * b; }
```

```
private:
  int t, b;
};
```

It would then be perfectly acceptable to use the max function with two fraction values.

```
Fraction x(3, 4);
Fraction y(7, 8);
Fraction z = max(x, y);
```

18.2 ☐ Template Classes

While template functions are useful, it is more common to see template arguments applied to entire classes. Here is a template class that defines a generic box, suitable for holding almost any type of value.

```
template <class T> class Box {
public:
  Box (T initial) : value(initial) { }
  T getValue() { return value; }
  setValue (T newValue) { value = newValue; }
private:
  T value;
};
```

Notice how the identifier T can be used anywhere a type name can appear. For example, one can declare data fields of type T, arguments of type T, and so on. To create an instance the template argument must be associated with a type.

```
  Box<int> iBox(7);
  cout << iBox.getValue();
7
  iBox.setValue(12);
  cout << iBox.getValue();
12
```

Arguments must match the appropriate type for the receiver.

iBox.setValue(3.1415); // *ERROR - invalid type*

Using a different type with a template class creates a different new class.

```
  Box<double> dBox(2.7);
  cout << dBox.getValue();
2.7
```

```
dBox.setValue(3.1415);
cout << dBox.getValue();
3.1415
iBox = dBox; // ERROR - mismatched types
```

Template classes are commonly used to develop container classes, a problem we will consider in more detail later in the next chapter. For example, a linked list in C++ could be declared in the following fashion.

```
template <class T> class List {
public:
  void add(T);
  T firstElement();
    // data fields
  T value;
private:
  List<T> * nextElement;
};
```

Just as in the function example, here T is being used as a type parameter. Each instance of class List holds a value of type T and a pointer to the next link. The add member function adds a new element to the list, and the value of the front of the list is returned by the function firstElement.

To create an instance of the class, the user must provide a type value for the parameter T. The following declares both a list of integer values and a list of floating-point values.

```
List<int> aList;
List<double> bList;
```

Functions, including member functions, can also have template definitions. Here is the definition of a function for determining the number of elements in a list regardless of the list type.

```
template <class T> int length(List<T> & aList)
{
  if (aList == 0)
    return 0;
  return
    1 + length(aList.nextElement);
}
```

*18.2.1   Bounded genericity

Templates, as they are implemented in C++, do not place any explicit restriction on the template argument values; instead, type restrictions are defined implicitly by the method body. This is illustrated by the following example.

```
template <class A, class B>
int countAll (A value, B collection)
{
  int count = 0;
  A element = B.firstValue();
  while (element != null) {
    if (value.equals(element))
      count++;
    element = B.nextValue();
  }
}
```

A careful examination of the body of the function will reveal that instances of the class A need to understand the method equals, while instances of the class B need to implement the methods firstValue and nextValue. However, it is only the statements in the code and nothing in the function header that indicates this fact.

Other programming languages that support genericity, such as the programming language Eiffel, allow the programmer to place restrictions on the type parameters in much the same way that value parameters can be typed. For example, in Eiffel a hash table might be described as follows.

```
class
  HASH_TABLE [ H -> HASHABLE ]
  .
  .
  .
```

The arrow indicates that the argument can only be filled with a subtype of HASHABLE (that is, a class that inherits from HASHABLE if it is a class or implements the HASHABLE interface if it is an interface). Bounding the type arguments allows for slightly better type checking, since the legality of argument values can be determined at compile time.

*18.3 ▫ Inheritance in Template Arguments

If Box is the templated class shown earlier, and we create a new class Box[Integer] by filling in the template value, is the new class a child class of the parent? Some languages, such as Beta, say yes to this question. In Beta this is termed a *virtual binding*. But Palsberg and Schwartzbach show that this can lead to type inconsistencies.

To see why, consider the following definitions. These have been rewritten from Beta to a more general pseudo-code so as to bring out the relevant features.

```
class Box [ T : Object ] {
  public T value;
  public void set (T arg) { value = arg; }
}


class IntBox extends Box[Integer] { }
```

Class IntBox does nothing but fill in the generic argument. It does not define any new behavior.

Now consider a class DoubleBox that wants to take a generic argument of type Box.

```
class DoubleBox [ R : Box ] {
  public R dboxValue;
  public void set (Object arg) { dboxValue.set(arg); }
}
```

The instance value dboxValue must represent something of type Box. And a Box requires the argument to set to be an Object. Since the template parameter to Box was also required to be a subtype of Object, there seem to be no obvious type errors.

But what happens now if we try to create a DoubleBox by filling in the generic parameter with a value of type IntBox?

```
class TroubleBox extends DoubleBox[IntBox] { }
```

On the face of it, there should be no problem. But if we now create an instance of TroubleBox, the only requirement on the method set is that the argument is an Object. A String, for example, should certainly suffice. But if you trace the execution, you will find that this ultimately ends by assigning the string to an instance variable we have assumed to hold only integers.

```
TroubleBox bigTrouble;
bigTrouble.set("Hi there"); // oops!
```

The only weak link in this argument seems to be the assertion that Box[Integer] was a subclass of Box, and hence an instance of the former could be substituted for the latter. Therefore, we are led to the conclusion that the question of whether Box[Integer] is a subclass of Box is either meaningless or false but certainly not true.

But what about when the generic parameter has been filled with two actual class values? If Box is the templated class shown earlier, and class Child is a subclass of Person, then is there any inheritance relationship between Box[Person] and Box[Child]? Unless one is willing to perform run-time checks, the answer, in general, is that there is no relationship at all. (That is, there can be no relationship without the possibility of type errors that cannot be detected at compile time.)

To see why, imagine that instead of one, there are two child classes—say, BoyChild and GirlChild. If we imagine that Box[BoyChild] is a subclass of Box[Person], then an instance of the latter should be permitted to be substituted for the former. But then look what problems can arise.

```
Box[Person] aBox = new Box[BoyChild]; // permitted by our assumption
Person aGirl = new GirlChild; // permitted by substitution
aBox.set(aGirl); // boychild box now holds a girl
```

A similar argument can be used to show that the inverted inheritance cannot be permitted either. This problem is a notable error in the Eiffel type system, which is otherwise quite secure.

18.3.1 Inheritance and arrays

Although Java does not support generics, it comes close to it with the class Array. An array can be created using any type as a base.

```
int [ ] intArray = new int[10];
BoyChild [ ] boys = new BoyChild[10];
```

There are a number of situations where it could be argued that the Java semantics are an improvement over the C++ semantics, most often because the C++ semantics are incomplete or undefined. However, there is one curious situation where the Java semantics seem more confused than their C++ counterpart. This concerns an interaction between inheritance and arrays. Assume we have declared an array of BoyChild values. Java permits this array to be assigned to a variable that is declared as an array of the parent class.

```
Person [ ] people = boys; // legal
```

In effect, Java is asserting that the type BoyChild[ ] (that is, array of boy children) is a subtype of the type Person[ ]. To see what confusion can then arise, imagine the following assignment.

```
GirlChild sally = new GirlChild;
people[2] = sally; // is this legal?
```

On the face of it, it would seem to certainly be legal to reassign an element in the array to now hold a GirlChild value. After all, the array is declared as an array of people, and a GirlChild is a subclass of Person. But remember that the array in question shares a reference with an array of boy child values, and by performing this assignment we actually convert one element in the boy array into a girl.

To prevent this, Java actually performs a run-time check on assignments to arrays of objects. C++, on the other hand, takes a simpler approach and simply asserts that even though a BoyChild or a GirlChild may both be a Person, there is no inheritance or subtype relationship between an array of BoyChild and an array of Person.

18.4 ▫ Case Study—Combining Separate Classes

In Chapter 19 we will consider the use of generics in the development of container classes, which is probably the most common use for the feature. In Chapter 20 we will examine the STL, the standard library in C++ that makes extensive use of templates. In this section we examine a slightly different problem, but one that illustrates the combination of many different forms of polymorphism.

A common problem encountered in practice is how to combine elements from two or more different classes when you are not permitted to make changes to the original classes. For example, the original classes may be distributed in binary form by two separate vendors. Nevertheless, you would like to maintain these values in a common representation and perform common tasks on them. Solving this problem is an excellent illustration of the different uses for inheritance, templates, overloaded functions, and the interactions between these mechanisms.

Suppose, for example, that you have Apples and Oranges, both products of different companies. Apples (Figure 18.1) can print themselves on an output stream using the method printOn(ostream &), whereas Oranges (Figure 18.2) perform a similar operation but using a method named writeTo(ostream &). You want to keep both Apples and Oranges on the same list and write them out to an output stream using a single polymorphic function.

We can address this problem in a sequence of small steps. Since the class descriptions for Apples and Oranges are distributed only in binary form, we cannot add a new member function to these classes. However, nothing prevents us from writing new ordinary functions that take their respective types as arguments. By doing so, we can use a single name, print, for the operation of printing to a stream.

```
// class Apple
// created 1987 by Standard Apple of Ohio
class Apple {
public:
    // constructors
  Apple () : variety("generic") { }
  Apple (string & v) : variety (v) { }
  Apple (const Apple & r) : variety (r.variety) { }

    // apple operations
  ostream & printOn (ostream & out)
    { return out << "Apple: " << variety; }
private:
  string variety;
};
```

□ Figure 18.1 —— Class description for Apple

```
// Orange code
// written by Chris (Granny) Smith, 1992
// House of Orange
class Orange : public Produce {
public:
    // constructor
  Orange ();
  void writeTo (ostream & aStream)
    { aStream << "Orange"; }
};
```

□ Figure 18.2 —— Class description for Orange

```
void print (const Apple & a, ostream & out)
{
  a.printOn(out);
}

void print (const Orange & a, ostream & out)
{
  a.writeTo(out);
}
```

This is a small step toward combining Apples and Oranges. We now have a single common function name, print, that can be used for both data types.

```
Apple anApple("Rome");
Orange anOrange;


  // can print both Apples and Oranges
print (anApple, cout);
print (anOrange, cout);
```

Unlike Java containers, containers in C++ are homogeneous—they can only hold values of one type. Thus, to combine Apples and Oranges in the same container, we need an adapter that will convert the type into a more suitable data value. We do this first by defining a common parent class that will describe the behavior we wish all fruit to possess.

```
class Fruit {
public:
  virtual void print (ostream &) = 0;
};
```

Because the specific implementation of the behavior will be different for each fruit, we make the description of this function into a pure virtual method.

Using a template method, we can create a fruit adapter that will take either an Apple or an Orange and satisfy the fruit interface.

```
template <class T>
class FruitAdapter : public Fruit {
public:
  FruitAdapter (T & f) : theFruit(f) { }

  T & value () { return theFruit; }

  virtual void print (ostream & out) { print(theFruit, out); }

public:
  T & theFruit;
};
```

The template argument allows us to use the adapter with both Apples and Oranges but always yields a new value that is a subclass of Fruit.

```
Fruit * fruitOne = new FruitAdapter<Apple> (anApple);
Fruit * fruitTwo = new FruitAdapter<Orange> (anOrange);
```

Since we now have a common representation for Apples and Oranges, it is easy to create containers that will hold fruit values.

```
list<Fruit *> fruitList; // make a list of fruits
fruitList.insert(fruitOne); // add an Apple
fruitList.insert(fruitTwo); // add an Orange
```

A template function can simplify the creation of the adapter, since the template argument types are inferred from the parameter values and need not be specified when a template function is invoked.

```
template <class T>
Fruit * newFruit (T & f)
{
    return new FruitAdapter<T>(f);
}
```

Using the newFruit function, the fruit types will be inferred from the function arguments and need not be specified explicitly by the programmer.

```
Fruit * fruitThree = newFruit (anApple);
Fruit * fruitFour = newFruit (anOrange)
```

Now we have all the elements necessary to maintain both Apples and Oranges in the same collection—for example, in a list, and to perform polymorphic operations on these values.

```
Apple anApple("Rome");
Orange anOrange;

list<Fruit *> fruitList; // declare list of pointers to fruits

fruitList.insert(newFruit(anApple));
fruitList.insert(newFruit(anOrange));

list<Fruit *>::iterator start = fruitList.begin();
list<Fruit *>::iterator stop = fruitList.end();

// loop over and print out all fruits in container
for ( ; start != stop; ++start) {
    Fruit  & aFruit = *start; // get current fruit
    aFruit.print(cout);
}
```

Notice how this solution uses all the polymorphic mechanisms we have discussed: overloaded functions, template classes, template functions, inheritance, and overriding.

Summary ⊡

A *generic* is a class or function that is parameterized by a type. In C++ generics are termed *templates*. Generics provide a powerful alternative to object-oriented style polymorphism in the development of reusable abstractions. We will see examples of such abstractions in later chapters.

Further Reading ⊡

The history of the introduction of templates into the programming language C++ is recounted in [Stroustrup 1994]. The use of generics in Eiffel is described in [Meyer 1994] or [Joyner 1999]. Generics in Ada 95 are described in [Feldman 1997]. Another non-object-oriented language that includes generics is CLU [Liskov 1977]. A good discussion of the theoretical underpinnings of generics is [Palsberg 1994].

Virtual binding in Beta is explained in [Madsen 1993]. The type conflict in Beta virtual binding is adapted from [Palsberg 1994].

The major application of templates is in the development of reusable container classes. We will examine this topic in Chapters 19 and 20.

There are proposals to add generics to Java, but as of this writing (July 2001) none have been formally approved by Sun.

Self-Study Questions ⊡

1. How is the parameterization used by a generic in C++ different from a parameter to a function?

2. In C++, how are the requirements for a template parameter determined?

3. How does the bounded genericity in Eiffel differ from template mechanism in C++?

Exercises ⊡

1. Give an argument similar to that presented in Section 18.3 to show that if BoyChild and GirlChild are subclasses of Person, Box<Person> cannot be considered to be a subclass of either Box<BoyChild> or Box<GirlChild>.

2. Suppose a data structure library contains a linked list abstraction consisting of a series of links, such as the following.

```
template <class T> class Link {
public:
   Link (T v, Link<T> * n) : value(v), next(n) { }

   T value;
   Link<T> * next;
};
```

A lazy student thinks that they might save typing by creating a subclass that does nothing more than fill in this template argument.

```
class StringLink : public Link<string> { };
```

Explain what will happen the first time the student tries to iterate down the list of elements in a collection.

```
StringLink * s;
StringLink * p;
for (p = s; p != null; p = p->next) ...
```

CHAPTER 19

Container Classes

Simple data structures are found at the heart of almost all nontrivial computer programs. Example data structures include vectors, linked lists, stacks, queues, binary trees, sets, and dictionaries. Because data structures are so common, one would expect them to be ideal for development as reusable components. Indeed, it *is* possible to create such components, but there are subtle issues involved that can trap the unwary programmer.

An exploration of the problems in developing reusable container classes is, for this reason, a good illustration of how the features of a programming language influence the style of development, as well as a demonstration of some of the powers and some of the limitations of object-oriented techniques.

19.1 □ Containers in Dynamically Typed Languages

Producing reusable container abstractions is considerably easier in a dynamically typed language, such as Smalltalk, CLOS, or Objective-C, than it is in a statically typed language. Indeed, dynamically typed languages usually come with a large collection of data abstractions already developed—thus freeing the programmer from having to address the container problem.

As we saw in our earlier discussion on binding times, in a dynamically typed language it is a value itself that retains knowledge of its type, not the variable by which it is accessed. Thus, any object can be placed into a container, and when it is removed, it can be assigned to any variable. The following, for example, shows an integer and a string being placed into a Smalltalk array and later removed.

```
anArray <- Array new: 2.
anArray at: 1 put: 'abc'.
anArray at: 2 put: 12.3.
theString <- anArray at: 1.
theNumber <- anArray at: 2.
theString <- theString characterAt: 2.
theNumber <- theNumber * 7.
```

Notice how a dynamic language permits values of different classes to be held in the same container. Such a collection is sometimes termed a *heterogeneous* collection, as opposed to a *homogeneous* collection where values are all of the same type. Statically typed languages have difficulty forming truly heterogeneous collections, although they can approximate them through the use of the principle of substitution.

19.1.1   Containers in Smalltalk-80

The software reuse techniques of inheritance and composition can be used to advantage in the creation of collection classes. To illustrate, consider the Smalltalk-80 classes Collection, Set, Bag, and Dictionary. These four classes are linked in the inheritance hierarchy shown in Figure 19.1.

The parent class Collection is shown as abstract, since some of the methods (those shown in italics) must be redefined in child classes. The subclass Set represents an unordered collection of unique elements. It redefines the abstract methods for addition and removal that were inherited from Collection, as well as adding new functionality (not shown).

The class Dictionary represents a collection of key/value pairs. Elements can be inserted into the dictionary using a specific key, and the user can search for the element associated with a key. The dictionary is implemented as a Set where each element of the set is an Association representing a single key/value pair. By defining Dictionary as a subclass of Set, the methods that do not deal with the keys directly can be inherited without change from the parent. (Using the categories from Chapter 8, this is subclassing for construction.)

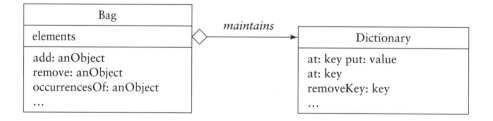

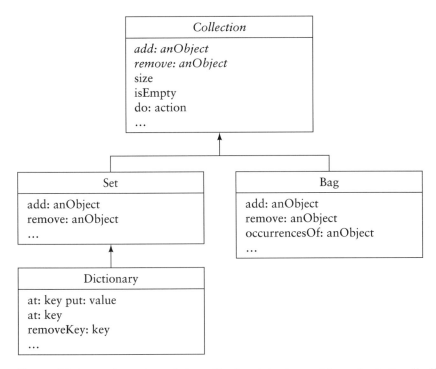

□ Figure 19.1 —— A portion of the collection inheritance hierarchy in Smalltalk-80

A third type of collection is a Bag. Conceptually, a Bag is similar to a Set, only values are allowed to be entered into the collection more than once. To implement this behavior, the class Bag uses composition, maintaining an internal value of type Dictionary. The keys in the dictionary represent the elements inserted into the Bag, whereas the value associated with the key is the number of times the item appears in the Bag. In this fashion only one instance of each element is actually stored in the container, but as items are inserted and removed, the counts are updated appropriately.

Note the variety of techniques that are being used in just these four classes. We have inheritance as a mechanism of specialization (Set from Collection and Bag from Collection), the use of deferred methods (such as add:), inheritance as a mechanism of construction (Dictionary from Set), and composition (Bag and Dictionary).

19.2 □ Containers in Statically Typed Languages

It is clear from the countless data structure textbooks that have appeared over the years that container abstractions can be written in almost any language, including statically typed languages. The problem with statically typed languages is not that they preclude the development of container classes but that static typing interferes with software reuse. That is, it is difficult to write a container class in such a way that it can be easily carried from one project to the next and still retain the benefits of static typing.

In the following section we first describe in detail the origin of this tension between static typing and software reuse. After considering the problem, we then explore how object-oriented software techniques have been used to overcome this difficulty. In particular, we will consider three different solutions.

- Using the principle of substitution to store values in a container and combine with downcasting (reverse polymorphism) when values are removed
- Again using the principle of substitution but avoiding downcasting through the use of overriding
- Using generics or templates

19.2.1   The tension between typing and reuse

To place the problem in perspective, we must first consider how data structures are typically implemented in a conventional language, such as C or Pascal. We will use a linked list of integers as our example abstraction. In Pascal a linked list might be formed out of two types of records. The first is the list header itself, which maintains a pointer to the first link.

```
type
  List = Record
      firstLink : ↑ Link;
      end;
```

A list header can be statically allocated, since the amount of storage it maintains (namely, one pointer) remains fixed throughout execution. The second record is used to maintain the actual values themselves. Each Link node maintains one integer value and a pointer to the next link.

```
type
  Link = Record
      value : integer;
      nextElement : ↑ Link;
    end;
```

Link nodes must be dynamically allocated and released, although such details can be largely hidden from the user of the list abstraction through the development of functions, such as a function to add a new value to the front of the list, return and remove the first element in a list, and so on.

```
procedure addToList (var aList : List; newVal : integer);
var     (* add a new value to a list *)
  newLink : ↑ Link;
begin
   (* create and initialize a new link *)
  new (newLink);
  newLink ↑.value := newVal;
   (* place it at the front of the list *)
  newLink ↑.nextElement := aList.firstLink;
  aList.firstLink = newLink;
end;


function firstElement (var aList : List) : integer;
var     (* remove and return first element from a list *)
  firstNode : ↑ Link;
begin
  firstNode := aList.firstLink;
  firstElement := firstNode ↑.value;
  aList.firstLink := firstNode ↑.nextElement;
  dispose (firstNode);
end;
```

Our concern here is not with the details of how a linked list might be implemented (such details can be found in any data structure textbook) but with the question of reusability. Suppose our programmer has implemented the preceding linked-list abstraction and now wishes to maintain, in addition to a linked list of integers, a linked list of real numbers.

The problem is that the programming language is *too* strongly typed. The data type integer used for the value being held by the link is an intrinsic part of the definition. The only way it can be replaced by a different type is through the creation of a totally new data type—for example, RealLink—as well as a totally new list header, RealList, and totally new routines for accessing and manipulating the data structures (addToRealList and firstElementInRealList, for example).

Now, it is true that something like a variant record (called a *union* in C) could be used to permit a single list abstraction to hold both integers and real numbers. Indeed, a variant record would permit one to define a heterogeneous list that contains both integers *and* real numbers. But variant records solve only part of the problem. It is not possible to define a function that returns a variant record, for example, so one still needs to write separate functions for returning the first element in a list. Furthermore, a variant record can have only a finite number of possible alternatives. What happens when the next project requires a totally new type of list, such as a list of characters?

In short, a language that is too strongly typed does not provide the facilities necessary to create and manipulate truly reusable container abstractions.[1] The question, then, is do the additional facilities provided by object-oriented languages yield any new way to overcome this problem? The principal new tool found in an object-oriented language that is not found in a conventional language is the principle of substitution. And indeed, the principle of substitution can be used in at least two different ways to overcome the problem of overly strong typing.

19.2.2   Substitution and downcasting

It is tempting to think that substitutability by itself can solve the container class problem for statically typed languages. Recall from Chapter 6 that the principle of substitution claims that a variable declared as maintaining some object type can, in fact, be assigned a value derived from a subclass of the variable's declared class.

The principle of substitution is most valuable in languages that have a single class at the root of the inheritance hierarchy. Recall that this was true for both Java (the root class is Object) and Delphi (the root class is TObject). So we see that in both of these languages containers are provided that store elements in variables declared as the root class. A Java Vector, for example, stores its elements in an array of Object values.

While this purposeful suppression of typing information solves one problem, it comes only at the cost of introducing another. As we have noted, any value can be assigned to a variable of type Object (in Java) or TObject (in Delphi). But when values are removed from the container, the programmer typically wants them restored to their original type. Since the removal method can only declare its result as an Object, a casting expression must be used to restore the original data type, as in the following code fragment in Java.

```
Vector aVector = new Vector();
Cat Felice = new Cat();
aVector.addElement(Felice);
     .
     .
     .

     // cast used to convert Object value to Cat
Cat animal = (Cat) aVector.elementAt(0);
```

A problem with this approach is the detection of typing errors. Suppose a programmer creates a container that he or she thinks will maintain values of a certain type—for example, class Cat. By accident a value of the wrong type—

---

1. There are those who argue that it is not strong typing that is at fault here but the outmoded type systems found in languages such as Pascal and C. More recent languages such as ML have found a way to preserve strong typing and still allow the creation of container classes.

for example, a Dog—is placed into the container. The error cannot be discovered by any static compile time analysis of the program. Worse, the resulting run-time error will not be discovered at the point of insertion (which is where the logic error is being committed) but at the point of removal, when the attempt to perform the downcast will result in an casting exception being thrown.

```
// make a collection of Cat values
Vector catCollection = new Vector();
Cat aCat = new Cat();
Dog aDog = new  Dog();
catCollection.addElement(aCat); // no problem
    // although the following incorrectly inserts
    // a value of type Dog into the collection,
    // no compiler error will ensue
catCollection.addElement(aDog);
    .
    .
    .
    // it is only here, when the element is removed and an
    // attempt is made to convert to type Cat, that
    // a run-time error is detected.
Cat newCat = (Cat) catCollection.elementAt(1);
```

Heterogeneous collections

Because Java collections store their values in variables declared as type Object, in principle it is easy to create heterogeneous collections. But in practice the problem is not placing the values into the collections but taking them back out again. As we have noted, normally a value must be downcast to a more specific type after it is removed from the container. In a heterogeneous collection this type must first be tested before it can be cast, as shown in the following example.

```
// make a stack that contains both cats and dogs
Stack stk = new Stack();
stk.addElement(new Cat());
stk.addElement(new Dog());
    .
// :   adding more values
    .
// now do something with Cat values
if (stk.peek() instanceof Cat) {
    // do conversion to Cat
  Cat aCat = (Cat) stk.pop();
    .
// :   also do something with cat values
    .
// now do something with Dog values
} else if (stk.peek() instanceof Dog) {
```

```
    //  do conversion to Dog
  Dog aDog = (Dog) stk.pop();
    //  :   do something with Dog value
}
```

While the use of instanceof is legal, it is often considered bad form or an indication of design flaws, since most uses can be better served by overridden methods.

In certain situations, an alternative is to try the conversion and use the fact that Java will throw an exception if the cast is illegal.

```
try {
  Cat aCat = (Cat) stk.pop();
    //  :   handle case where it is a cat
} catch (ClassCastException e) {
    //  :   handle non-cat case
}
```

Container classes in Delphi

A popular container collection in Delphi, the Spider classes marketed by Interval Software, has an interesting solution to the error detection problem. Although values are still stored internally in variables of type TObject, a class value can be given as argument to the constructor when the collection is created. As each element is inserted, the class value is used to ensure the element matches the desired type. If it is not, an error exception is raised. Since this error occurs at the point of insertion, not at the point of removal, it makes the discovery of logic errors much easier.

```
var
  stack : TStack;
  aCat : TCat;
  aDog : TDog;

begin
    // create a stack that can hold only TCat values
  stack := TStack.Create (TCat);
  stack.push (aCat); // ok
  stack.push (aDog); // will raise exception
  .
  :
  .
end
```

Heterogeneous collections can be accommodated by using a more general class value. For example, if both cats and dogs must be held in the same list, the collection can be created using the class value TMammal (or TAnimal).

Although a check was performed as the value was inserted into the container, it is still necessary to cast the value back to the correct type when it is accessed or removed, since the declared results of these operations is only TObject. As we saw in Chapter 17, Delphi provides two different ways to perform this operation. The as operator performs a check to ensure that the conversion is valid.

```
aCat := stack.Pop as TCat;
```

The alternative syntax uses the name of the child class as if it were a function call. This form, however, does not check the veracity of the cast and so should only be used when you are absolutely certain no errors can occur.

```
aCat := TCat(stack.Pop);
```

Storing non-object data in containers

Java containers can store any value that is ultimately derived from class Object. The Spider container classes in Delphi can store any value that is ultimately derived from TObject. Unfortunately, in both of these languages the primitive values, such as integers and floating point numbers, are not objects in the technical sense. Thus, primitive values cannot be stored directly in a container in these languages.

In both cases the solution is to provide a series of auxiliary classes that do little more than act as a box that can hold a single primitive value. In Java these are called wrapper classes, and in the Spider Delphi containers they are called bucket classes. The following illustrates how a double precision number can be stored and later removed from a Java Vector.

```
Vector aVector = new Vector();
    // create a wrapper to hold a real number
aVector add: (new Double(12.34));

    // :
    // :

    // later we first find the Double object
Double dwrap = (Double) aVector.elementAt(0);
    // then unwrap to get original value
double dval = dwrap.doubleValue();
```

Table 19.1 gives the wrapper classes for Java and for the Spider data structure classes in Delphi associated with the more common primitive types. (The use of the term *wrapper* in this context should not be confused with wrappers in CLOS, which we discussed in Chapter 16, or with the wrapper design pattern, which we will discuss in Chapter 24.)

	Java	Delphi
boolean	Boolean	TBooleanBucket
byte	Byte	TByteBucket
char	Character	TCharBucket
double	Double	TRealBucket
int	Integer	TIntegerBucket
long integer	Long	TLongIntBucket
short integer	Short	TShortIntBucket

▫ Table 19.1 —— Auxiliary classes used to store primitive types

The C# language uses wrappers but hides them from the programmer. When a primitive type is assigned to an object value, an implicit internal wrapper is created through a process known as *boxing*. When the resulting object value is once more used as a primitive type, it is automatically *unboxed*. The result is that as far as the programmer is concerned, it appears that primitive values are simply objects.

19.2.3   Using substitution and overriding

A cast expression is often considered to be not truly object-oriented, since it requires the programmer to name an explicit type in the code. In many situations explicit casts can be avoided through the use of substitution combined with method overriding. However, in the case of container classes this is possible only when the original developer knows how an object will be used, even if they do not know what type of value will be stored in the container. Thus, this technique is applicable only in a few restricted situations.

One example is found in the code in Java used to respond to user initiated events, such as mouse presses. In Java, events are handled by creating a *listener* object and attaching it to a window. When an event occurs in the given window, all the registered listeners are notified of the event. A listener must match a fixed specification. There are a number of different types of specifications corresponding to the variety of events that can occur.

ActionListener	Change in graphical component state
ItemListener	Changes to selected item component
KeyListener	Key press events
MouseListener	Mouse presses and releases
MouseMotionListener	Mouse motions
TextListener	Text component changes
WindowListener	Window actions

Because many listeners are used for a large number of different actions, the Java library also provides a collection of *adapters* that implements the interface and defines an empty action for each possibility. To create a listener the Java programmer defines a class that implements this interface and overrides key methods. An example is the following, which subclasses from the WindowAdapter class (which in turn implements the WindowListener interface) and overrides the method windowClosing.

```
public class CloseQuit extends WindowAdapter {
    // execute when the user clicks in the close box
  public void windowClosing (WindowEvent e) {
    System.exit(0); // halt the program
  }
}
```

All the listeners attached to a window are stored in a linked list. The Window class maintains the view that these values are all instances of WindowListener (or one of the other listener hierarchies). In reality, they are instances of user-defined classes that implement the WindowListener interface and are only stored on the list through the principle of substitution. When an event occurs, the Window passes a message to each listener, "thinking" that it is an instance of WindowListener. But the method is overridden, and the message is actually handled by the user defined class.

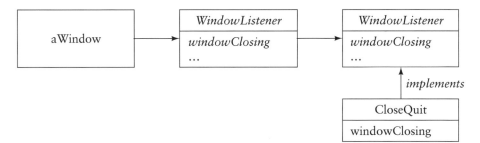

Notice how this achieves the desired effect without the need to explicitly cast the listener value to a new type. On the negative side, this technique is only applicable when the programmer has precise information concerning how a value stored in the container will be used, even if the programmer does not know the type for the value.

Common link classes

A technique that has features in common with both of the two previous approaches involves the creation of a linked list data abstraction in which elements must subclass themselves from a fixed Link class.

```
class Link { // all elements must subclass link
public:
  Link * next;
  Link () : next(0) { }
  Link (Link * n) : next(n) { }
}

class RealLink : public Link { // link containing a number
public:
  RealLink (double r) : Link(), value(r) { }
  double value;
}
```

We examined some of the implications of this design in Chapter 13. The Link class does not include the data values, and hence we avoid the problem of the Pascal abstraction described at the beginning of this chapter. Nevertheless, to do almost anything with a container developed using this technique requires downcasting a link to find the actual child class. Since so many standard data abstraction classes are available, nowadays it seems better to avoid this approach to implementing lists.

19.2.4   Parameterized classes

The previous two solutions to the container abstraction problem both employed the principle of substitution. However, this technique is only suitable if there is a parent class that can be used as the basis for the substitution. If a language has a single root as the ultimate ancestor of all classes, as does Java, then that is the logical candidate for the parent type. But what about a language such as C++, where there is no single root class?

The language C++ gets around this difficulty by introducing a new language feature, which in turn permits an entirely different solution to the container class problem. This new feature is the ability to define classes that are *parameterized* by type arguments. As we saw in Chapter 17, such classes are called *templates* in C++.

A class template gives the programmer the ability to define a data type in which some type information is purposely left unspecified, to be filled in at a later time. One way to think of this is that the class definition has been parameterized in a manner similar to a procedure or function. Just as several different calls on the same function can all pass different argument values through the parameter list, different instantiations of a parameterized class can fill in the type information in different ways.

A parameterized class definition for a linked list abstraction might be written in C++ in the following way.

```
template<class T> class List {
public:
  void  addElement (T newValue);
  T  firstElement ();

private:
  Link<T> * firstLink;

  private class Link { // nested class
  public:
    T  value;
    Link *  nextLink;

    Link (T v, Link * n) : value(v), nextLink(n) { }
  };
};
```

Within the class template, the template argument (T, in this case) can be used as a type name. Thus, one can declare variables of type T, have functions return values of type T, and so on.

Member functions that define template operations must also be declared as template.

```
template<class T>
void List<T>::addElement (T newValue)
{
  firstLink = new Link<T> (newValue, firstLink);
}

template<class T>
T List<T>::firstElement ()
{
  Link * first = firstLink;
  T result = first->value;
  firstLink = first->nextLink;
  delete first;
  return result;
}
```

The user creates different types of lists by filling in the parameterized type values with specific types. For example, the following creates a list of integer values as well as a list of real numbers.

```
List<int>     integerList;
List<double>  doubleList;
```

In this fashion, homogeneous lists of any type can be created.

A template is an efficient solution to the container class problem. It allows truly reusable, general-purpose components to be created and manipulated and yet still retain the type safety, which is the goal of statically typed languages. On the other hand, there are drawbacks to the use of templates. They do not permit the definition of heterogeneous lists, since all elements must match the declared type. More importantly, implementations of the template mechanism vary greatly in their ease of use and the quality of code they generate. Most implementations act as little more than sophisticated macros, generating for each new type of element an entirely new class definition as well as entirely new method bodies. Needless to say, if several different element types are used in the same program, this can result in a considerable growth in code size.

Nevertheless, because templates free the programmer from so much conceptual drudgery (namely, rewriting data structure classes in every new program), their appeal is widespread. In the next chapter we will examine one such library.

*19.3 ⊡ Restricting Element Types

Container classes can be divided into three major groups that are differentiated by the requirements they place on their element types. The simplest are containers such as linked lists or vectors. These require only that elements have the ability to be compared against other elements for equality. Slightly more complicated are the ordered containers, such as binary search trees or sorted lists. These require that elements have the ability to be compared against other elements for ordering. A third category of container are hash tables. These require that every element have the ability to determine an integer value, called the hash of the element.

Once again we have the situation where there is a simple interface (the relational test or the hash function) and a wide range of implementations (the technique used to determine a hash value for a character, for example, will be very different from that used to compute the hash value for a complex number). Languages and libraries exhibit a wide range of solutions to this problem.

In languages that have a single root class at the top of the inheritance hierarchy, such as Smalltalk or Java, it is common for operations to have a default implementation in the root class and allow for this default implementation to be overridden in child classes. Thus, in Smalltalk, for example, the class Object contains the methods == and hash. In Java the corresponding methods are equals and hashValue. Since these methods are defined in Object, they can be applied to every object value. Since they can be overridden, classes can supply their own specialized meaning.

Nevertheless, it is useful to allow the programmer to supply their own comparison algorithm for sorting elements in an ordered container. In Smalltalk this is accomplished by passing a block to the instance creation method.

```
aCollection <- SortedCollection sortBlock: [ :a :b | a <= b ]
```

In Java, the programmer can specify ordering by defining a class that implements the Comparator interface.

```
public interface Comparator {
    public int compare (Object left, Object right);
}
```

The method compare returns the integer −1 if the left argument is smaller than the right, 0 if they are equal, and 1 if the left is larger than the right. The user must create a class that implements this interface. The following, for example, is a comparator that will test two instances of the wrapper class Double. Note how the arguments are declared as Object and must be downcast to the appropriate type before the actual comparison can be performed.

```
public class DoubleCompare implements Comparator {
    public int compare (Object left, Object right) {
        // first downcast the arguments
        Double dleft = (Double) left;
        Double dright = (Double) right;
        // then do the comparison
        if (dleft.doubleValue() == dright.doubleValue())
            return 0;
        if (dleft.doubleValue() < dright.doubleValue())
            return -1;
        return 1;
    }
}
```

A comparator object is then passed to the constructor when an ordered collection is created.

```
// create a new ordered collection
SortedSet aCollection = new TreeSet(new DoubleCompare());
```

The Delphi Spider classes use a similar technique.

In the previous section we saw how template container classes also restrict the type of values they can handle. Unbounded template classes, such as those found in C++, define implicitly the requirements for element types. This implicit requirement derives from the functions used in the body of the methods for the container. Bounded generics, such as are found in Eiffel, explicitly place restrictions on the types of elements that containers can hold.

Some developers of data structure classes prefer to place responsibility for comparisons and hash values in the objects themselves rather than in the container. This is made more difficult if there is no single root class or if, as in Delphi, the root class does not provide all the necessary functionality. A developer of data structure classes in Delphi, for example, might insist that to be held, elements must implement an interface such as the following.

```
type
  TContainable = interface
    public
      function compareTo (const right : TContainable) : integer;
      function hashValue : integer;
  end;
```

This is in some respects a combination of the techniques described in Sections 19.2.2 and 19.2.3. The container itself can invoke the methods compareTo and hashValue without needing to execute a cast. However, the user must still cast values to their correct type when they are accessed or removed from the container.

19.4 ▫ Element Traversal

Regardless of whether a language is statically typed or dynamically typed, another difficult problem that must be handled in order to create truly useful container abstractions is the task of element traversal. The problem of element traversal is best understood in the context of a multiperson development project. Suppose there are two programmers named Alice and Bob. Alice must create a data abstraction—for example, a set implemented using a red-black tree—and Bob is going to use the abstraction. Bob need only know the interface in order to add elements to the container and remove elements from the container. But now imagine that Bob wants to write a loop that will iterate over the elements of the container. How can Bob perform this task without any explicit knowledge of the internal structure of the container class?

We can see the problem in concrete terms by again considering the Pascal linked list data type we introduced in Section 19.2.1. A typical loop that prints the values in a list might be written as follows.

```
var
  aList : List;  (* the list being manipulated *)
  p : Link;  (* a pointer for the loop *)

begin
  .
  .
  .
  p := aList.firstLink;
  while (p <> nil) do begin
    writeln (p.value);
    p := p↑.nextElement;
  end;
```

Note that to create a loop it was necessary to introduce an extraneous variable, here named p. Furthermore, this variable had to be of type Link, a data type we were taking pains to hide, and the loop itself required access to the link fields in the list, which we were also attempting to hide.

Once again we can ask whether the new mechanisms provided by object-oriented languages permit a solution to this problem that was not available in more conventional languages. And once again, the answer is yes. There are two solutions we will examine.

- An *iterator* uses the property that in an object-oriented language it is possible to have many different implementations for the same interface. An iterator is an object that implements an interface designed specifically for forming a loop.
- A *visitor* is an alternative approach that is possible when the programming language provides an easy way to encapsulate a series of actions and hand them to the container.

19.4.1   Iterator loops

The concept of an iterator relies on the ability to have many different implementations match the same interface. The iterator interface is designed to be easy to remember and flexible enough to work with a wide variety of containers. In Java, for example, the iterator interface (called an Enumeration) consists of just two methods.[2] The method hasMoreElements returns true if the loop should continue,

---

2. Java version 1.2 introduced a new class Iterator. This class adds a third method that removes the current element from the container.

and the method nextElement yields the next element in the sequence. A typical loop looks like the following.

```
// create the iterator object
Enumeration e = aList.elements();
  // then do the loop
while (e.hasMoreElements()) {
  Object obj = e.nextElement();

  // ⋮  do something with obj

}
```

Every container class in the Java library implements a method named elements, which returns a value that matches the specification defined by the class Enumeration. In fact, however, the actual value returned will differ from one collection to another, since each different type of collection requires its own set of actions to perform an enumeration. Thus, a LinkedList, for example, will return a ListIterator, which is a data type that is derived from Enumeration. Because many different implementations can match the same specification, the loop used to access the elements in a container will look exactly the same, regardless of the type of container being examined.

The language C++ also uses the concept of an iterator. However, iterators in C++ are manipulated in pairs, in much the same fashion as pointers. (This is perhaps to be expected, since pointers are such an important part of the language.) The first iterator value specifies the current element, while the second iterator specifies the end of the loop. The interface for iterators includes the following three operators.

Operation	Purpose	Example
==	Compare two iterators for equality	start == stop
++	Advance iterator to next element	start++
*	Return value referenced by iterator	*start

A typical iterator loop looks something like the following.

```
// create starting and stopping iterators
list<string>::iterator start = aList.begin();
list<string>::iterator stop  = aList.end();
  // then do the loop
for ( ; start != stop; start++ ) {
  string value = *start; // get the value

  // ⋮  do something with the value

}
```

Although the interfaces are different, in both languages the key idea is that each container can provide an implementation of the iterator interface that is specific to the container. A method in the container class returns a value that is more specialized than its type signature might indicate. The methods begin and end in each of the C++ STL containers return an iterator appropriate to the container.

The language C# adds a further layer of syntax on top of the enumeration. A foreach statement that will cycle through the elements of a container can be written as follows.

```
foreach (value in container)
{
    :   // do something with value
    :
}
```

Internally the compiler converts the statement into the following:

```
IEnumerator enumerator = container.GetEnumerator();
while (enumerator.GetNext())
{
    value = (ElementType) enumerator.Current;
    :   // do something with value
    :
}
```

The statement will work with programmer-defined container classes as well as those in the system library. The programmer must define the method GetEnumerator that will return a value that satisfies the IEnumerator interface. The methods GetNext and Current in this interface are similar to the methods hasMoreElements and nextElement in the Java class Enumeration.

It is indeed true that in all of these examples the enumerator classes must have intimate knowledge of the container over which they are looping. An iterator for a linked list, for example, must know about the link classes that are used in the implementation. But since the iterator classes are written by the same programmer who developed the abstraction, and these internal details are not exposed by the interface, the key principle of information hiding is not being violated. (Frequently techniques such as friends or inner classes, both of which are discussed in Chapter 23, are necessary in order to link a container and its iterator.)

19.4.2 The visitor approach

An alternative solution to the problem of iteration is possible if the programming language provides a way to bundle a sequence of actions and hand them to the container—for example, in the form of a function. The container can then take the bundle and execute the actions on each element of the collection in turn.

This technique is used in the language Smalltalk. A Block in Smalltalk is a series of statements enclosed in square brackets, which can optionally begin with a sequence of argument values. In essence, a block is a simple way to create an unnamed function. To iterate over a collection, the programmer uses the method do:, passing as argument a one-argument block containing the action to be performed.

```
aList do: [ :x | ('element is ' + x) print ]
```

The container executes the block repeatedly, passing each element in the collection as argument in turn.

The same idea is also possible in C++ as an alternative to the use of iterators in that language. A *function object* is an object that implements the parentheses operator and hence can be used both as an object (for example, it can be stored in a variable) and as a function. For example, a simple function object might just print its argument.

```
class printingObject {
public:
  void operator () (int x)
  {
    cout << "value is " << x << endl;
  }
};
```

The generic function for_each takes a pair of iterators and a function object. It executes the function object on each element specified by the iterator.

```
printingObject printer;  // create an instance of the function object
for_each (aList.begin(), aList.end(), printer);
```

Often the argument will be specified by a nameless temporary, using the ability in C++ to create a new value by simply naming the class.

```
for_each (aList.begin(), aList.end(), printingObject());
```

In the Spider classes in Delphi, looping is performed in a similar fashion using the method ForEachCallMethod. The following is an example.

```
var aList : LinkedList;

procedure PrintingObject
    (const Obj : TObject, const additionalData : LongInt);
begin
```

```
    writeln("Value is ", Obj);
  end

  begin
    .
    .
    .
    aList.ForEachCallMethod (PrintingObject, 0);
  end;
```

The second argument can be used to pass additional data from one invocation to the next. Use of this argument frequently eliminates the necessity of introducing global variables.

Premature termination and parallel looping

It is natural to compare the two different approaches to looping (iterators and visitors) and to ask if there are problems that are more easily addressed using one form instead of the other. And indeed, two common problems can be identified that are both more easily addressed using the iterator approach than using the visitor technique.

The first situation arises when it is desirable to halt a loop before it has enumerated the entire range of values. This might occur, for example, if one wanted to find the first element in a collection that satisfied a given condition. Such a loop is easy to write using an enumerator and the ability to break a loop before it has completed.

```
Enumeration e = aList.elements();
while (e.hasMoreElements()) {
  Object obj = e.nextElement();
  if (... obj satisfies condition ...)
    break; // break out of loop
}
```

None of the visitor mechanisms allow the user to halt an iteration prematurely, although the C++ STL library does provide a specialized form of visitor designed for just this type of search (see the next section).

The second common situation in which iterators seem to have an edge over visitors occurs when it is necessary to iterate over two collections in parallel, operating on them element by element. This is easily accomplished by simply combining the ending conditions for two iterators.

```
Enumeration e = listOne.elements();
Enumeration f = listTwo.elements();
while (e.hasMoreElements() && f.hasMoreElements()) {
```

```
Object objOne = e.nextElement();
Object objTwo = f.nextElement();
//  :   operate on objOne and objTwo
    :
}
```

The equivalent action cannot be achieved using visitors without writing a special-purpose parallel visitor routine.

Other loop-like activities

Languages that use the visitor mechanism, such as Smalltalk and C++, frequently extend the model to provide other functionality that is based on looping. For example, in Smalltalk it is simple to create a computation in which every element is operated on in turn to produce a single final result. An example of such a computation might be a summation of the elements of the collection. To form this expression, the base element (the identity, such as zero for a summation) is combined with a two-argument block that defines the computation used to generate the intermediate values.

```
sum <- aList inject: 0 into: [:x :y | x + y ].
```

Each element if the collection (here, a list) is considered in turn. The block is evaluated using the current result (initially, the identity argument) and the collection element. The final result will be the value yielded by the block after the last element is considered.

Another example, this time from C++, is the generic function find_if. Just as with for_each, this function takes as argument a pair of iterators and a function object. With this function, however, the function object must return a Boolean (true/false) value. Each element of the collection is tested in turn. When the first element for which the function object returns true is encountered, the function will halt, and the corresponding iterator will be returned. In this way the first element that satisfies a property can be found. If no element satisfying the property is found, the ending iterator is returned.

```
class BiggerThan12 {
// function object that finds a value larger than 12
public:
  bool operator () (int x)
  {
    return x > 12;
  }
}
```

```
list<int>::iterator start = aList.begin();
list<int>::iterator stop = aList.end();
start = find_if (start, stop, BiggerThan12());
if (start != stop) // found it
   .
   .
   .
```

Summary ▫

The development of reusable container abstractions illustrates both the power and the limitation of object-oriented techniques. Container classes are relatively easy to define in dynamically typed languages, but as is true of many other features of such languages, the dynamic typing hinders the detection of typing errors at compile time. Statically typed languages have better static error detection abilities, but the static typing interferes with the development of reusable abstractions.

	Advantages	Disadvantages
Dynamically Typed Language	Easy to define reusable classes	Poor static error detection
Statically Typed Language	Good static error detection	Strong typing complicates developing reusable abstractions

One way to resolve the conflict between static typing and reusability is to use the principle of substitution. In this chapter we examined two different approaches that both use this mechanism. The first stores values in variables of type Object (or TObject in Delphi), which is the root of the inheritance hierarchy. By the principle of substitution any object value can be stored in such a variable but must be downcast to the correct type when it is accessed or removed from the container. The second approach stores elements in a specific class type and uses substitution combined with method overriding to specialize the behavior.

	Advantages	Disadvantages
Substitution and Downcasting	Works for most objects	Specific types required in cast expressions
Substitution and Method Overriding	No cast expressions	Only works with methods known in advance

There are negatives to both approaches. Cast expressions, required for downcasting, require putting explicit types into code. Having to name explicit types is often considered to violate the spirit of the object-oriented philosophy. On the other hand, using method overriding is only possible if the developer of the container abstraction can predict ahead of time how the objects stored in the container will be used.

An alternative approach that does not use the principle of substitution is the mechanism of template, or generic, classes. A template can be thought of as a type parameter. When using templates, the developer of a container abstraction need not know the type of elements that will be stored in the container. The final element types must then be specified by the user of the containers. Conceptually templates provide an elegant solution to the container class problem, but in practice the implementation of the template mechanism tends to be exceedingly complex, and the error messages that result from incorrect usage are often cryptic and misleading.

	Advantages	Disadvantages
Template (**or Generic**)	Works with all data types	Implementation is complex Error messages often cryptic

An entirely different problem that must be addressed in the creation of reusable container abstractions is the issue of iteration. How can the developer of a container class allow users to form a loop that will iterate over the elements in the container without exposing the inner implementation details for the container?

In the object-oriented languages we are considering, there are two broad categories of solution to this problem. The first is to form iterators. An iterator is a specialized object whose sole purpose is to provide a means of forming a loop. Using the fact that many different implementations can be provided for the same interface, containers can each define a specialized iterator that implements a common interface in a unique way. The same type of loop can then be written for any container.

An alternative to an iterator is a visitor. The visitor mechanism bundles the actions to be performed and passes them to the container, which in turn executes the actions using each element as argument in turn. The visitor is not as general as an iterator and requires the ability to encapsulate a sequence of statements into a bundle.

Further Reading ▫

The data structure textbooks in C++ and Java with which I am most familiar are [Budd 1998] and [Budd 2000], respectively. Collection classes in Smalltalk-80 are described in [Goldberg 1983]. A discussion of how bounded generics are used in Eiffel data structures is presented in [Meyer 1994]. Kerman [Kerman 2002] is one of the few data structures textbooks to use Delphi.

The term *visitor* is from the *design pattern* of the same name. We will examine design patterns in Chapter 24.

As I noted in the Chapter 10 Further Reading section, many see the container problem not as a failure of strong typing, but as a weakness in the typing systems for conventional languages. More modern languages, such as Haskell [Thompson 1996] or ML, permit types such as "list of α," where α is left unspecified. This solves the container problem while preserving strong typing.

Self-Study Questions ▣

1. What is the difference between a homogeneous collection and a heterogeneous collection?
2. Explain the conflict that arises between static typing and the creation of reusable container abstractions.
3. One solution to the container class problem is to store values using variables declared with a common ancestor type, such as Object. What problems can arise from this approach?
4. Another approach is to use the principle of substitution, passing messages to a parent class that are then overridden in child classes. Why does this approach have only limited utility?
5. What is a parameterized class?
6. What is the problem presented by the creation of loops for containers? How is this problem addressed using an iterator?
7. What is a visitor? How does the visitor approach address the problem of looping?

Exercises ▣

1. Argue whether container classes represent a success or a failure of object-oriented programming techniques.
2. Data structures can be divided into those that are characterized by their implementation (linked lists, trees) and those that are characterized by their purpose (stacks, sets). Describe how object-oriented programming techniques can be used to simplify the latter, hiding the implementation details. Give an illustration of a data structure with one interface and two very different implementations.
3. Suppose a programmer creates a linked list abstraction using the technique described in the section "Common Link Classes" on page 373. The programmer successfully creates a linked list of real numbers by forming a link of

RealLink values. What surprise are they going to find when they try to execute the following loop?

```
for (RealLink * p = theList; p != null; p = p->next)
    . . .
```

4. Java has classes as a data type (an instance of class Class) and the ability to test an object to see if it is an instance of a class. Show how these can be combined to create containers that can trap the insertion of an illegal value in the same manner as the Spider collections described in this chapter.

5. Give an example application of a heterogeneous container—that is, one with many different types of values.

6. The Smalltalk approach to iteration is to bundle the action to be performed and hand it to the data structure. In contrast, an iterator is a data structure that hands values one by one back to a statement performing a certain action. Would it be possible to implement the Smalltalk approach in a different programming language such as Object Pascal or C++? Does static typing get in the way?

7. Give an example application for templates that is not associated with container classes.

CHAPTER 20

A Case Study: The STL

A rich collection of template data structures was recently added to the definition of the C++ standard library. These data structures include classes for vectors, lists, sets, maps (dictionaries), stacks, queues, and priority queues. As implementations of this standard become more widespread, the C++ programmer will become increasingly free from the need to constantly redefine and reimplement the standard set of data structure classes.

The design of the Standard Template Library (STL) is the result of many years of research conducted by Alexander Stepanov and Meng Lee of Hewlett-Packard and David Musser of Rensselaer Polytechnic Institute. STL development drew inspiration not only from previous object-oriented libraries but from the creators' many years of experience in functional and imperative programming languages such as Scheme and Ada.

One of the more unusual design ideas in STL, *generic algorithms*, deserves discussion because it seems to fly in the face of the object-oriented principles we have been describing, and yet it is the source of a great deal of STL's power. The implementation of generic algorithms in STL uses the ability not only to create a template container *class* but also to make template definitions of individual *functions*. To understand the concept of generic algorithms, we must first describe how encapsulation is used in most object libraries.

Object-oriented programming holds *encapsulation* and *data hiding* as a primary ideal. A well-designed object will try to encapsulate all the state and behavior necessary to perform whatever task it is designed for and at the same time hide as many of the internal implementation details as possible. In many previous object-oriented data structure libraries this philosophical approach was manifested by container classes with exceedingly rich functionality and, consequently, with large interfaces.

The designers of STL moved in an entirely different direction. The behaviors provided in their standard components are minimal, almost spartan. Instead, each component is designed to operate in conjunction with a rich collection of *generic algorithms*, also provided. These generic algorithms are independent of the containers and can therefore operate with many different container types.

By separating the functionality of the generic algorithms from the container classes themselves, the STL realizes a great savings in size in both the library and the generated code. Instead of duplication of algorithms in each of the dozen or so different container classes, a single definition of a library function can be used with any container. Furthermore, the definition of these functions is so general that they can be used with ordinary C-style arrays and pointers as well as with other data types.

An example will illustrate some of the basic features of the standard template library. A generic algorithm, find, locates the first occurrence of a given value in a collection. Iterators in the standard library consist of *pairs* of values, marking the beginning and end of a structure. The find algorithm takes an iterator pair and searches for the first occurrence. It is defined as follows.

```
template<class InputIterator, class T >
InputIterator
  find (InputIterator first, InputIterator last, const T& value)
{
    while (first != last && *first != value)
      ++first;
    return first;
}
```

The algorithm will work with any type of structure, even regular C-style arrays. To find the location of the first occurrence of the value 7 in a vector of integers, for example, the user executes the following.

```
int data[100];
    .
    .
    .
int * where;
where = find(data, data+100, 7);
```

Finding the location of the first occurrence of the value 7 in a list of integers is hardly more difficult.

```
list<int> aList;
   .
   .
   .
list<int>::iterator where;
where = find(aList.begin(), aList.end(), 7);
```

In a single chapter we can only describe the most basic features of the STL. The following sections present two basic concepts used by the library, namely iterators and function objects. Then three case studies will illustrate the STL's use of containers and generic algorithms.

20.1 □ Iterators

Iterators are fundamental to the use of the container classes and the associated algorithms provided by the standard library. Abstractly, an iterator is simply a pointer-like object used to cycle through all the elements stored in a container.

Just as pointers can be used in a variety of ways in traditional programming, iterators are also used for a number of purposes. An iterator can denote a specific value, just as a pointer can reference a specific memory location. On the other hand, a *pair* of iterators can describe a *range* of values analogously to two pointers describing a contiguous region of memory.

Imagine, for example, an array that is being used to represent a deck of playing cards. Two pointer values can be used to denote the beginning and end of the deck.

If we need to represent the beginning and end of the memory space, we can use the values cards and cards+52. Note that the latter value is not actually describing an element in the array, but it is one *past* the final element in the collection.

In the case of iterators the values being described are not necessarily physically in sequence but rather are logically in sequence because they are derived from the same container, and the second follows the first in the order elements are maintained by the collection, regardless of their physical locations in memory.

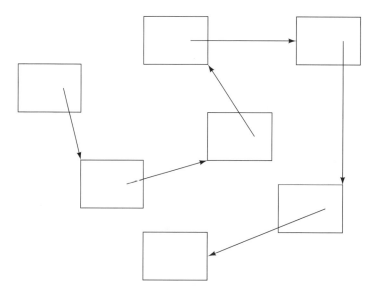

Conventional pointers can sometimes be *null*—that is, they point at nothing. Iterators, as well, can fail to denote any specific value. Just as it is a logical error to dereference and use a null pointer, it is an error to dereference and use an iterator that is not denoting a value. When two pointers that describe a region in memory are used in a C++ program, it is conventional that the ending pointer is *not* considered to be part of the region. We see this in the picture of the cards array, where the array is described as extending from cards to cards+52, even though the element at cards+52 is not part of the array. Instead, the pointer value cards+52 is the *past-the-end* value—the element that is the next value *after* the end of the range being described.

Iterators are used to describe a range in the same manner. The second value is not considered to be part of the range being denoted. Instead, the second value is a *past-the-end* element, describing the next value in sequence after the final value of the range. Sometimes, as with pointers to memory, this will be an actual value in the container. Other times it may be a special value specifically constructed for the purpose. The value returned by the member function end() is usually of the latter type, being a special value that does not refer to any element in the collection. In either case, it is never legal to try to dereference an iterator that is being used to specify the end of a range. (An iterator that does not denote a location, such as an end-of-range iterator, is often called an *invalid* iterator.) In the standard containers, the beginning iterator is returned by the function begin(), and the ending iterator is returned by the function end().

Just as with conventional pointers, the fundamental operation that modifies an iterator is the increment operator (operator ++). When the increment operator is applied to an iterator that denotes the final value in a sequence, it is changed to the past-the-end value. The dereference operator (operator *) accesses the value being denoted by an iterator.

20.2 ▫ Function Objects

A number of the generic algorithms provided in the STL require functions as arguments. A simple example is the generic algorithm for_each(), which invokes a function, passed as argument, on each value held in a container. The following, for example, might be used to produce output describing each element in a list of integer values.

```
void printElement (int value)
{
  cout << "The list contains " << value << endl;
}


main () {
  list<int> aList;
      .
      .
      .

  for_each (aList.begin(), aList.end(), printElement);
}
```

Functions have been generalized to include *function objects*. A function object is an instance of a class that defines the parentheses operator as a member function. There are a number of situations where it is convenient to substitute function objects for functions. When a function object is used as a function, the parentheses operator is invoked whenever the function is called.

To illustrate, we will consider the following class definition.

```
class biggerThanThree {
  public:
    bool operator () (int v )
      { return v > 3; }
};
```

If we create an instance of the class biggerThanThree, every time we reference this object using the function call syntax, the parentheses operator member function will be invoked. The next step is to generalize this class by adding a constructor and a constant data field, which is set by the constructor.

```
class biggerThan {
  public:
    biggerThan (int x) : testValue(x) { }
```

```
   const int testValue;
   bool operator () (int val)
     { return val > testValue; }

};
```

The result is a general "bigger than X" function, where the value of X is determined when we create an instance of the class. If we wanted to find the first occurrence of a value larger than 12 in a list of numbers, we could write this as follows.

```
biggerThan tester(12); // create our function object
list<int>::iterator firstBig = find_if (aList.begin(),
     aList.end(), tester);
```

Often we have no further use for the function object once the value is returned. For this reason C++ allows the creation operation to be used as an expression. A temporary expression will be formed and passed as argument to the function, then deleted once the function returns. Using this mechanism the statement could be more concisely written as follows.

```
list<int>::iterator firstBig =
   find_if (aList.begin(), aList.end(), biggerThan(12));
```

20.3 ▫ Example Program—An Inventory System

Our first example uses a simple inventory management system to illustrate the creation and manipulation of containers in the STL. We will assume that a business named WorldWideWidgetWorks requires a software system to manage its widget supply. Widgets are simple devices distinguished by different identification numbers.

```
class  Widget {
public:
  Widget(int a) : id(a) { }
  Widget() : id(0) { }
  int id;
};

ostream & operator << (ostream & out, Widget & w)
  { return out << "Widget " << w.id; }
```

```
bool operator == (const Widget & lhs, const Widget & rhs)
  { return lhs.id == rhs.id; }

bool operator < (const Widget & lhs, const Widget & rhs)
  { return lhs.id < rhs.id; }
```

The state of the inventory is represented by two lists. One represents the stock of widgets on hand; the other represents the type of widgets that customers have back-ordered. The first is a list of widgets, and the second is a list of widget identification types. To handle our inventory we have two commands: The first, order(), processes orders, and the second, receive(), processes the incoming shipment of a new widget.

```
class inventory {
public:
   void order (int wid);   // process order for widget type wid
   void receive (int wid); // receive widget of type wid
private:
   list<Widget> on_hand;
   list<int> on_order;
};
```

When a new widget arrives in a shipment, we compare its identification number with the list of widget types on back order. We use find() to search the back-order list, immediately shipping the widget if necessary. Otherwise, it is added to the stock on hand.

```
void inventory::receive (int wid)
{
  cout << "Received shipment of widget type " << wid << endl;
  list<int> ::iterator weNeed =
      find (on_order.begin(), on_order.end(), wid);
  if (weNeed != on_order.end()) {
    cout << "Ship " << Widget(wid)
      << " to fill back order" << endl;
    on_order.erase(weNeed);
    }
  else
    on_hand.push_front(Widget(wid));
}
```

When a customer orders a new widget, we scan the list of widgets in stock, using the function find_if() to determine if the order can be processed immediately. To do so we need a unary function that takes as its argument a widget and determines whether the widget matches the type requested. We write this as a function object as follows.

```
class WidgetTester {
public:
  WidgetTester (int t) : testid(t) { }
  const int testid;
  bool operator () (const Widget & wid)
    { return wid.id == testid; }
};
```

The widget order function is then as follows.

```
void inventory::order (int wid)
{
  cout << "Received order for widget type " << wid << endl;
  list<Widget>::iterator weHave =
    find_if(on_hand.begin(), on_hand.end(), WidgetTester(wid));
  if (weHave != on_hand.end()) {
    cout << "Ship " << *weHave << endl;
    on_hand.erase(weHave);
    }
  else {
    cout << "Back order widget of type "  << wid  << endl;
    on_order.push_front(wid);
    }
}
```

20.4 ☐ Example Program—Graphs

The second and third example programs both use the map data type. A map is an indexed dictionary, a collection of key and value pairs.

Imagine that we have a weighted graph that represents, for example, the cost to travel between pairs of cities. The graph is directed, meaning that travel can be made in one direction but not the other. An example graph is shown in Figure 20.1. The task is to determine not only the minimum cost to travel from one city to each of the others but also the path to follow in making the journey.

To see how we could represent a graph internally, consider first the information we need to maintain for a single city in isolation. If we consider just one city—Phoenix, for example—we need to know the names of the cities that can be reached starting from Phoenix, and the cost of each journey. This information could be maintained by a *map*, which is an indexed dictionary structure. The keys in the map will be the destination cities, and the value fields will be the cost.

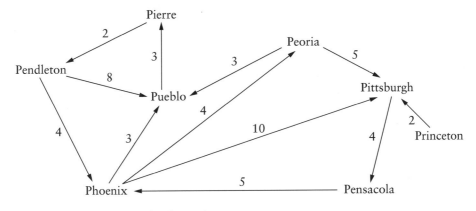

▢ Figure 20.1 ——— A Weighted Graph

Phoenix: [Peoria, 4]
            [Pittsburgh, 10]
            [Pueblo, 3]

Let us call this information a cityInfo. In terms of the STL data structures, this could be represented by a map in which the keys are represented by constant character pointers (the common representation for strings in C++) and the value fields by integers. To use the map data type, we need a *function object* that defines the ordering on keys. Since the default ordering on pointer values (ordering by location in memory) is not appropriate, we must create a new data type. We do this as follows.

```
class charCompare {
public:
   bool operator () (const char * left, const char * right) const
   {
     return strcmp(left, right) < 0;
   }
};
```

An instance of charCompare is a function object, an object that can be used like a function. The behavior we desire is a simulation of the less-than operator applied to our key values. When invoked as a function it takes two arguments, which are pointers to character arrays. Using the standard library routine strcmp, it compares the two string texts. A negative value indicates that the first is lexicographically smaller than the second and hence that the less-than operator should return a true value.

Using charCompare, the cityInfo data type could be defined as follows.

```
typedef map <const char *, unsigned int, charCompare> cityInfo;
```

That is, we declare the name cityInfo to be a synonym for a type of map in which the key field is a character pointer and the value field is an unsigned integer. The third argument represents the comparison algorithm that will be used to determine the ordering of the keys. We have chosen to use a typedef to declare the new name, rather than defining a new class. This is because all the behavior we need is provided already by the map data type when properly parameterized. The typedef creates a *synonym* name for the new structure but does not create any new class structure. We can use this synonym name in our later programs to help simplify the code and make it more readable.

To represent the entire graph, we need only maintain the city information for each city. We can again use a map for this purpose. The key field in the map will once again be a city, and the value field will be a cityInfo that encodes the information associated with the city. Let us use the name graph to represent the entire data structure.

```
typedef map <const char *, cityInfo, charCompare> graph;
```

Once more we have used a typedef, since all the functionality we desire is provided already by the map data abstraction. We can, as follows, create an instance of graph and initialize it with the information described in the graph in Figure 20.1.

```
graph cityMap;

cityMap["Pendleton"]["Phoenix"] = 4;
cityMap["Pendleton"]["Pueblo"] = 8;
cityMap["Pensacola"]["Phoenix"] = 5;
cityMap["Peoria"]["Pittsburgh"] = 5;
cityMap["Peoria"]["Pueblo"] = 3;
cityMap["Phoenix"]["Peoria"] = 4;
cityMap["Phoenix"]["Pittsburgh"] = 10;
cityMap["Phoenix"]["Pueblo"] = 3;
cityMap["Pierre"]["Pendleton"] = 2;
cityMap["Pittsburgh"]["Pensacola"] = 4;
cityMap["Princeton"]["Pittsburgh"] = 2;
cityMap["Pueblo"]["Pierre"] = 3;
```

The first subscript indexes the graph and returns a cityInfo, creating a new cityInfo if no such value exists already. The second subscript is then applied to the cityInfo, creating a new position for an unsigned integer value. The assignment then changes the association in the cityInfo map. The type graph is, in effect, a two-dimensional sparse array, indexed by strings and holding integer values.

20.4.1   Shortest path algorithm

We now turn our attention to the problem of finding the shortest path to each reachable city, starting from a given initial location. The algorithm we use is a well-known technique named *Dijkstra's Algorithm* in honor of the computer scientist credited with its discovery.

The idea of Dijkstra's algorithm is to start with a city of origin and make a list of the cities that can be reached in one step. Order this list by cost, with the least costly city listed first.

Remove the first element from this list. This cannot help but be the least costly way to reach this first city, since any other path to the city would have to be along a path that begins in another reachable city, and we know that all other reachable cities are more costly.

Now comes the key insight. Determine the cities that are reachable from this first destination, and add the costs of travel for each to the cost of making the first leg. Using these combined cost figures, add these new destinations to our list of reachable locations, once more keeping the list ordered by the total cost.

To complete the algorithm (Figure 20.2), we need only put a loop around this operation and note that we need not consider a city when it reaches the top of the list if we have already discovered a less costly way to reach the city.

20.4.2   Developing the data structures

The final result we desire is the cost to travel to each city on our list. We can use the cityInfo data type defined earlier to hold this information. Let us use the name travelCosts for this data structure.

The list discussed in the informal description consists of entries that hold two values: a name and a cost. There is no ready-made data type for this structure, so we are forced to define a new class. The constructor for the class will take a city name and a cost. Because some of the data structures in the STL require elements to have a default constructor, we provide one, although it will never be used in our algorithm. Because we want to be able to compare two such values, we override the comparison operator.

```
class Destination {
public:
  Destination () : distance(0) { }
  Destination (const char * dt, unsigned int ds)
    : distance(ds), destination(dt)  { }

  bool operator < (const Destination & right) const
    { return distance < right.distance; }
```

```
    unsigned int distance;
    const char * destination;
};
```

We have here overloaded the comparison operator as a member function. Note that when a binary operator is implemented in this fashion, only the right argument is specified as an argument. Binary operators can also be overloaded as ordinary functions, in which case both the right and left values are treated as arguments.

Remember that we wanted to keep the list ordered by cost, least to first. This action will be performed for us automatically if we use a *priority queue*. The priority_queue data type in the STL requires two template arguments, the first indicating an underlying container to use for holding the actual values and the second indicating the operation used in comparing values. We can use a vector for the first and a library provided function object named lesser for the second. (lesser is a function object that invokes the comparison operator for our data type and eliminates the need to define a special function object.) The queue is initialized with a single entry, corresponding to a "trip" with no cost to the initial city.

```
priority_queue< vector<Destination>, lesser<Destination> > que;
    // put starting city in queue
que.push (Destination(startingCity, 0));
```

At each step of the algorithm we pull an entry from the priority queue and ask whether or not we have yet visited this city. There is no direct way to determine if a map has an entry under a given key, but the information can be indirectly inferred. We do this by counting the number of entries in the cost map that have the new city as a key. If this count is zero, then we have not yet visited the city.

```
    // remove top entry from queue
char * newCity = que.top().destination;
int cost = que.top().distance;
que.pop();
if (travelCosts.count(newCity) == 0) {
    // :  have not seen it yet
    // :
}
```

If we have not been to the city, an entry is made in the travelCosts map.

```
travelCosts[newCity] = cost;
```

Next we want to add to the priority queue the cities that are reachable from the new city. To do that, we create iterators that cycle over the city information map associated with the new city. Recall that iterators for a map data type yield values of type Pair. The key field in such a value is obtained as the field named first, while the value portion is found in a field named second. At each step of the iteration we add the cost to date to the new cost and create a new destination entry:

```
cityInfo::iterator start = cityMap[newCity].begin();
cityInfo::iterator stop = cityMap[newCity].end();
for (; start != stop; ++start) {
  const char * destCity = (*start).first;
    // make the new routine
  unsigned int destDistance = (*start).second;
  que.push(Destination(destCity, cost + destDistance));
}
```

We can put everything together in the algorithm shown in Figure 20.2. Note how, in this one algorithm, we have made use of the following STL collections: map, vector, priority_queue, as well as the function object lesser.

To complete the program we need a main procedure. The following double-nested loop will print the cost of travel from each city to every other reachable city.

```
int main()
{

  graph cityMap;
  //  :  initialization of the map
  //  :

  graph::iterator start = cityMap.begin();
  graph::iterator stop = cityMap.end();
  for ( ; start != stop; ++start) {
    const char * city = (*start).first;
    cout << "\nStarting from " << city << "\n";
    cityInfo costs;
    dijkstra(cityMap, city, costs);
    cityInfo::iterator cstart = costs.begin();
    cityInfo::iterator cstop = costs.end();
    for ( ; cstart != cstop; ++cstart) {
      cout << "to " << (*cstart).first <<
          " costs " << (*cstart).second << '\n';
    }
  }
  return 0;
}
```

```
void dijkstra
  (graph cityMap, const char * start, cityInfo & travelCosts)
  // dijkstra's single source shortest path algorithm
{
    // keep a priority queue of distances to cities
  priority_queue < vector<Destination>, lesser<Destination> > que;
  que.push (Destination(start, 0));

    // while queue not empty
  while (! que.empty() ) {
      // remove top entry from queue
    const char * newCity = que.top().destination;
    int cost = que.top().distance;
    que.pop();
      // if so far unvisited,
    if (travelCosts.count(newCity) == 0) {
        // visit it now
      travelCosts[newCity] = cost;
        // add reachable cities to list
      cityInfo::iterator start = cityMap[newCity].begin();
      cityInfo::iterator stop = cityMap[newCity].end();
      for (; start != stop; ++start) {
        const char * destCity = (*start).first;
        unsigned int destDistance = (*start).second;
        que.push(Destination(destCity, cost + destDistance));
      }
    }
  }
}
```

▣ Figure 20.2 —— Dijkstras shortest path algorithm

20.5 ▣ A Concordance

Our final example program to illustrate the use of the STL collection data abstractions will be a concordance. A concordance is an alphabetical listing of words in a text that indicates the line numbers on which each word occurs. The data values will be maintained in the concordance by a map, indexed by strings (the words), and holding sets of integers (the line numbers). A set is employed for the value stored under each key because the same word will often appear on multiple different lines. Indeed, discovering such connections is one of the primary purposes of a concordance.

```
class concordance {
    typedef set<int, less<int> > lineList;
    typedef map<string, lineList, less<string> > wordDictType;
public:
    void readText (istream &);
    void printConcordance (ostream &);

protected:
    wordDictType wordMap;
};
```

Note that the class definition does not include a constructor function. In such situations a default constructor will be automatically created, and this will in turn invoke the default constructor for the wordMap data field. The default constructor for a map creates a collection with no entries.

The creation of the concordance is divided into two steps: First, the program generates the concordance (by reading lines from an input stream), and then the program prints the result on the output stream. This is reflected in the two member functions readText() and printConcordance(). The first of these, readText(), is written as follows.

```
void concordance::readText (istream & in)
    // read all words from input stream, entering into concordance
{
    string line;
    for (int i = 1; getline(in, line); i++) {
        // translate into lowercase, split into words
        allLower(line);
        list<string> words;
        split(line, " ,.;:", words);
        // enter each word on line into concordance
        list<string>::iterator wptr;
        for (wptr = words.begin(); wptr != words.end(); ++wptr)
            wordMap[*wptr].insert(i);
    }
}
```

Lines are read from the input stream one by one. The text of the line is first converted into lowercase, and then the line is split into words, using the function split().

```
void split (const string & text, const string & separators,
            list<string> & words)
    // split a string into a list of words
    // text and separators are input,
```

```
    // list of words is output
{
    int textLen = text.length();

        // find first non-separator character
    int start = text.find_first_not_of(separators, 0);
        // loop as long as we have a non-separator character
    while ((start >= 0) && (start < textLen)) {
            // find end of current word
        int stop = text.find_first_of(separators, start);
            // check if no ending character
        if ((stop < 0) || (stop > textLen)) stop = textLen;
            // add word to list of words
        words.push_back (text.substr(start, stop - start));
            // find start of next word
        start = text.find_first_not_of (separators, stop+1);
        }
}
```

Each word is then entered into the concordance. Subscripting the map creates an entry for the line list if one does not already exist. Using the insert method for sets, the word is then entered into the container.

The final step is to print the concordance. This is performed in the following fashion.

```
void concordance::printConcordance (ostream & out)
    // print concordance on the given output stream
{
    string lastword = "";
    wordDictType::iterator pairPtr;
    wordDictType::iterator stop = wordMap.end();
    for (pairPtr = wordMap.begin(); pairPtr != stop; ++pairPtr) {
        out << (*pairPtr).first << " ";
        lineList & lines = (*pairPtr).second;
        lineList::iterator wstart = lines.begin();
        lineList::iterator wstop = lines.end();
        for ( ; wstart != wstop; ++wstart)
            out << *wstart << " ";
        cout << endl;
    }
}
```

An iterator loop is used to cycle over the elements being maintained by the word list. Each new word generates a new line of output; thereafter, line numbers appear separated by spaces. For each word, a nested iterator loop cycles over the line numbers.

If, for example, the input was the text

It was the best of times,
it was the worst of times.

the output, from best to worst, would be

best: 1
it: 1 2
of: 1 2
the: 1 2
times: 1 2
was: 1 2
worst: 2

20.6 ▫ The Future of OOP

We have noted that in many ways the design of the STL is not object-oriented at all, drawing inspiration instead from techniques used in functional programming languages. Does the introduction of the STL into the standard C++ library imply that OOP is now outmoded and obsolete?

Absolutely not. Object-oriented design and programming techniques are almost without peer as guideposts in the development of large complex software. For the majority of programming tasks, OOP techniques will remain the preferred approach, but the development of software such as the STL indicates a welcome realization within the object-oriented community that not *all* ideas should be expressed in object-oriented fashion nor all problems solved with purely object-oriented techniques.

Speaking about another language and a different application, Mössenböck makes the following observation [Mössenböck 1993].

Object-oriented programming has given rise to a certain euphoria. Advertisements promise incredible things, and even some researchers seem to consider object-oriented programming to be the panacea that will solve all the problems of software development. This euphoria will subside. After a period of disillusionment, people will perhaps cease to speak about object-oriented programming, just as hardly anybody speaks about structured programming anymore. But classes will be used quite naturally then and will be seen as what they are: components that help to build modular and extensible software.

Summary ▫

The standard template library is an extensive collection of data structures that has in recent years been incorporated into the C++ standard library. The standard template library is interesting because by eschewing encapsulation, the algorithms in the library integrate both with object-oriented data types and with traditional C-style data values.

Further Reading ▫

Further information on the standard template library can be found in [Musser 1996, Glass 1996]. The author has also written an introductory data structures textbook that uses the STL [Budd 1998].

Self-Study Questions ▫

1. What do the letters STL stand for?
2. What is a generic algorithm?
3. Why do some people consider the philosophy of generic algorithms to be counter to that of object-oriented programming?
4. What is an iterator? What problem is it solving?
5. What is a function object?

Exercises ▫

1. Assume a straightforward implementation of a linear data structure class, such as the linked-list class we described in Chapter 19. Outline the major features of an iterator class for this structure. What information does your iterator need to maintain?
2. Consider next a nonlinear data structure—for example, a binary tree. What information does an iterator need to maintain to traverse the elements being held in the container?

CHAPTER | **21**

Frameworks

The concept of an object-oriented *software framework* illustrates the powers that derive from the application of the ideas of inheritance and overriding and the difference between software reuse in the object-oriented world and the more limited form of software reuse that is possible with conventional languages. Expressed in the most basic terms, a software framework is nothing more than a skeleton solution to a class of similar problems. The structure for the framework is formed by a set of classes that cooperate closely with each other and together embody a reusable solution to a problem.

The most widely used application frameworks are employed in the creation of graphical user interfaces, or GUIs. We will examine one such framework in detail in Chapter 22. However, the concept has applicability beyond the development of user interfaces. For example, frameworks exist that are geared to building editors for various domains, for compiler construction, and for financial modeling applications.

21.1 ◻ Reuse and Specialization

The key insight behind the development of a framework is that inheritance can be used in two very different ways. First, it can be employed as a vehicle for software reuse, carrying code abstractions from one project to another. Second, at the same time that inheritance is providing the ability to share code between parent and child, overriding can be used as a vehicle for specialization—that is, fitting a general purpose tool to a specific task.

To fit these pieces together to form a framework, we can divide the methods in a class into two broad categories.

407

> **Reuse of code, reuse of concept**
>
> The distinction between foundation methods and specialization methods is just another aspect of the various uses for inheritance. Recall that in Chapter 8 we noted the two major motivations for the technique of inheritance were the reuse of code and the reuse of concept. Foundation methods are those that get inherited from the parent and thus reflect the reuse of code supplied by the parent. Specialization methods are those defined in the parent but implemented in the child. These are thus an example of reuse of concept.

- The *foundation* methods embody the solution to the problem at hand. They are defined in a parent class and become part of a child class through inheritance but are not overridden.

- The *specialization* methods are those that change the behavior of the parent class to fit the particular circumstances of the child. These methods are generally *deferred*, in the sense we discussed in Chapter 16. It is these methods that change a general purpose solution into a solution to a specific application.

For example, a GUI framework might be structured as shown in Figure 21.1. (The specific methods in this framework are not taken from any particular GUI but are common to similar systems.) A general parent class Window has methods for setting a title, setting a size, moving around on the display surface, setting menu categories and menu items, and so on. These foundational methods are inherited untouched by child classes.

On the other hand, there is some information that the parent class cannot know. What should be displayed in the content portion of a window? What does a mouse click within the bounds of a window mean? How should a keypress be interpreted? To answer these specific types of question, a child class must override key methods from the parent. In Figure 21.1 the child class overrides the methods paint, mouseDown, and keyPress.

These deferred methods must be part of the parent class definition, since the framework must be assured that all instances of the class will respond to the appropriate messages. As we have seen earlier, in statically typed languages the *legality* of a message is determined by a static declaration. Therefore, if the framework is going to pass the message mouseDown to a window, the message must be defined in the parent class. But because the class Window does not know how to handle the message, it must be overridden in the child class. Thus, the parent class

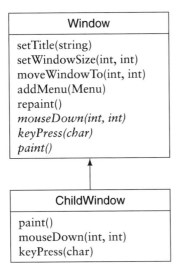

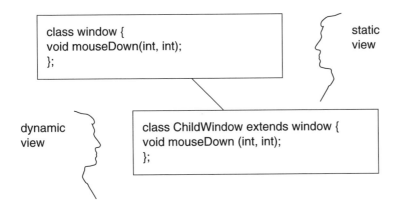

□ Figure 21.1 —— A GUI class from a typical framework

in the framework is viewing the class in one way and the child class in another (Figure 21.2).

Frameworks need not be just a single class. Generally a framework will consist of a number of classes designed to work together. Some classes may be intended to be subclassed in the fashion we are describing, and some may be intended to be used directly. For example in a GUI framework there may be classes that correspond to graphical items such as buttons, where the user provides specialized behavior by overriding key methods. The combination of defined behavior versus

□ Figure 21.2 —— Two views of the same class.

specialized behavior in the relationship between parent and child in the button is exactly the same as that of the window, only operating on a smaller scale.

21.1.1   High- and low-level abstractions

One way to contrast the style of code reuse found in frameworks with that found in conventionally designed software is to examine the differences in how they are applied to a simple problem. Let us take the problem of sorting a set of records. Suppose for some application we have defined an employee record consisting of a name, a department, and the year the employee joined the company.

```
class Employee {
public:
  string name;
  int salary;
  int startingYear;
}
```

If we have an array of such records, we can sort them—for example, using an insertion sort.

```
void sort (Employee * data[ ], int n) {
  for (int i = 1; i < n; i++) {
    int j = i-1;
    while (j >= 0 &&
        v[j+1]->startingYear < v[j]->startingYear) {
      // swap elements
      Employee * temp = v[j];
      v[j] = v[j+1];
      v[j+1] = temp;
      j = j - 1;
    }
  }
}
```

Now suppose we want to use this same function for a slightly different purpose. Imagine first that we want to sort not by starting year but by salary. It is simple enough to do: We simply edit the method and change startingYear to salary—but make sure you get both occurrences of the field. If you change one and not the other, there will be no compiler error, just the wrong answer. Now imagine that in the next project you aren't sorting employee records but an array of floating point numbers. To provide this functionality you need to change the function heading, the internal data value named element, and the access used in the comparison.

The key feature to note is that both of these changes required *source code* level modifications to the original program. In reality, all that we were able to reuse was the *idea* of insertion sort and not the actual implementation.[1]

Now let us imagine an object-oriented solution to the same problem. The features that are likely sources of change include the element types, the number of elements, the comparison between two element values, and the process of swapping two elements. Since we want these features to change, we encapsulate them in methods.

```
class InsertionSorter {
public:
  void sort () {
    int n = size();
    for (int i = 1; i < n; i++) {
      int j = i - 1;
      while (j >= 0 && lessThan(j+1, j)) {
        swap(j, j+1);
        j = j - 1;
      }
    }
  }

private:
  virtual int size() = 0; // abstract methods
  virtual boolean lessThan(int i, int j) = 0;
  virtual void swap(int i, int j) = 0;
}
```

To adapt the code to a specific problem requires building a subclass and implementing the deferred methods. We could solve our employee seniority sorting problem as follows.

```
class EmployeeSorter : public InsertionSorter {
public:
  EmployeeSorter (Employee * d[], int n)
    { data = d; sze = n; }
private:
  Employee * data[];
  int sze = n;
```

---

1. C programmers will at this juncture point to the method qsort in the standard C library. But to anybody who has used it, the difficulty in fitting qsort to any particular situation is itself a testimony to the limitations of software reuse in the conventional setting.

```
virtual int size () { return sze; }

virtual bool lessThan (int i, int j)
  { return data[i]->startingYear < data[j]->startingYear; }

virtual void swap (int i, int j) {
  Employee * temp = v[i];
  v[i] = v[j];
  v[j] = temp;
}
}
```

Changing the problem to sorting on salary would involve changing the child but not the parent. Similarly, an entirely different problem, such as sorting floating point numbers, would involve creating a new child but no change to the parent. So the key difference is that inheritance allows us not only to encapsulate high-level algorithmic details but to modify or specialize those details *without modification to the original code*. This is almost never possible using conventional techniques.

21.1.2   An upside-down library

The use of an application framework usually leads to an inversion of control between the new application-specific code and the library-supplied code. In a traditional application, application-specific code defines the overall flow of execution through the program, occasionally invoking library routines in order to execute some specific function (such as a mathematical routine or an input/output operation).

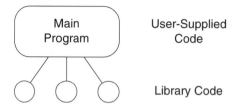

In an application framework, on the other hand, the flow of control is dictated by the framework and is the same from application to application. The creator of a new application merely changes the routines invoked by the framework but does not change the overall structure. Thus, the framework has the dominant position, and the application-specific code is reduced to a secondary position.

> **Anticipating changes**
>
> As the example problem shows, part of the art of object-oriented design is to anticipate the set of changes that will at some future time be needed to customize an application. This is not always an easy task. Frequently it is only after the fact that a programmer realizes that a new problem can be viewed in a fashion that makes it similar to a previously solved problem or that an existing software system can be generalized to permit it to cover a wider range of applications.
>
> In languages such as C++ that require the programmer to distinguish which methods can be overridden (by means of the virtual keyword) and which methods cannot, it can happen that a framework, even if well structured, is too rigid because the original programmer did not anticipate the need to override a key method.

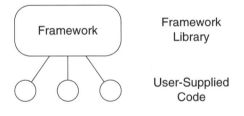

Framework Library

User-Supplied Code

Because a framework inverts this relationship between application-developer-defined code and library code, it is sometimes described as an *upside-down library*.

21.2 ⊡ Example Frameworks

Let us look at several examples that illustrate the concept of a software framework.

21.2.1 The Java Applet API

The first is the framework used for the control of applets in the language Java. Applets in Java are intended to be run inside a Web browser. They are one of two different forms of Java program, the other form being an application.

The fundamental class for every Java applet is the class Applet. This class defines the overall structure of the application through a method, main, that is normally not overridden by programmers. This method invokes a number of other methods, which are overridden to provide application-specific behavior. A few of these methods are summarized here.

init()	Invoked when the applet is initialized
start()	Invoked when the application is started
paint(Graphics)	Invoked when the window is to be redrawn
stop()	Invoked when the window is removed
destroy()	Invoked when the applet is about to be terminated

In addition, the framework provides a rich collection of classes for constructing items such as buttons and menus, displaying text in a variety of fonts, dealing with colors, using mathematical operations, and much more. This framework, the AWT, will be the topic of Chapter 22.

21.2.2   A Simulation Framework

To illustrate that not all frameworks need be associated with user interfaces, we will sketch the design of a framework that can be used to drive simulations, such as the billiard ball illustration presented in Chapter 7. As described in the latter part of that chapter, we might start by defining all objects in the simulation as subclasses of a general class for graphical objects, such as the following.

```
GraphicalObject = object
   (* data fields *)
  link : GraphicalObject;
  region : Rect;

   (* initialization function *)
  procedure setRegion (left, top, right, bottom : integer);

   (* operations that graphical objects perform *)
  procedure draw;
  procedure erase;
  procedure update;
  function intersect (anObj : GraphicalObject) :  boolean;
  procedure hitBy (anObj : GraphicalObject);
end;
```

Graphical objects have a region, they know how to draw themselves, and they can tell when they intersect. Thus, the framework for the simulation can be provided by a general purpose class for managing graphical objects, such as the following.

```
GraphicalUniverse = object
   (* data fields *)
  moveableObjects : GraphicalObject;
  fixedObjects : GraphicalObject;
```

```
  continueUpdate : boolean;
    (* methods *)
  procedure initialize;
  procedure installFixedObject (newObj : GraphicalObject);
  procedure installMovableObject (newObj : GraphicalObject);
  procedure drawObjects;
  procedure updateMoveableObjects;
  procedure continueSimulation;
end;
```

The heart of the framework is the routine to update all movable objects. This procedure simply cycles through the list of movable objects, asking each to update itself. If any object requests the update cycle to continue (by invoking the routine continueSimulation, which in turn sets the data field continueUpdate), the update cycle continues; otherwise, the simulation halts.

```
procedure GraphicalUniverse.updateMoveableObjects;
var
  currentObject : GraphicalObject;
begin
  repeat
    continueUpdate := false;
    currentObject := moveableObjects;
    while currentObject <> nil do begin
      currentObject.update;
      currentObject := currentObject.link;
    end
  until not continueUpdate
end;
```

The resulting framework knows nothing of the particular application in which it will be used and therefore can be applied to the simulation of billiard balls, the simulation of fish in a fish tank, an ecological simulation of rabbits and wolves, and many other applications.

21.2.3 An event-driven simulation framework

The billiards game can be considered to be a special case of a more general class of simulations, called *event-driven* simulations. In this style of programming the computation proceeds as a series of *events*. These *events* are stored in a priority queue ordered by their time of execution. Values are removed from the queue and executed one by one. Each event may spawn new events, which are then added to the queue.

User-defined events are subclassed from the framework class Event, which has the following definition.

```
class Event {
public:
  Event (unsigned int t) : time(t) { }

  const unsigned int time;
  virtual void processEvent () = 0;
};
```

The abstract method processEvent must be overridden in each defining subclass. This method provides the behavior that the simulation should exhibit when the event occurs.

Events are stored in a standard STL container, a priority queue. Because the container must hold a variety of different types of events, it will actually maintain pointers to events, rather than events themselves. (See the comments on heterogeneous collections in Chapter 19.) Events are ordered by their time. When using the standard library, this is accomplished by defining a new structure, the sole purpose of which is to define the function invocation operator (the () operator) in the appropriate fashion.

```
class eventComparison {
public:
  bool operator () (event * left, event * right)
    { return left->time > right->time; }
};
```

The basic functions of the simulation framework are found in the class Simulation. There are two functions. The first is used to insert a new event into the queue, and the second runs the simulation. A data field is also provided to hold the current simulation "time."

```
class Simulation {
public:
  Simulation () : eventQueue(), currentTime(0) { }

  void scheduleEvent (event * newEvent)
    { eventQueue.push (newEvent); }

  void run();

  unsigned int currentTime;

protected:
```

```
    priority_queue<vector<event *>, eventComparison> eventQueue;
};
```

The heart of the simulation is the member function run(), which defines the event loop. This method is implemented as follows.

```
void Simulation::run()
    // execute events until event queue becomes empty
{
    while (! eventQueue.empty()) {
        event * nextEvent = eventQueue.top();
        eventQueue.pop();
        time = nextEvent->time;
        nextEvent->processEvent();
        delete nextEvent;
    }
}
```

Ice cream store simulation

Imagine you are thinking about opening an ice cream store on a popular beach location. You need to decide how large the store should be and how many tables there should be. If you plan too small, customers will be turned away when there is insufficient space, and you will lose profits. On the other hand, if you plan too large, most of the seats will be unused, and you will be paying useless rent on the space and still lose profits. So you need to choose approximately the right number—but how do you decide?

You decide to do a simulation. You first examine similar operations in comparable locations and form a model that includes, among other factors, an estimation of the number of customers you can expect to arrive in any period of time, the length of time it will take a customer to choose a flavor and the length of time the customer will then sit at a table and eat the ice cream. Based on this, you can design a simulation.

Objects in the simulation represent objects in the real world, and are programmed to react as much as possible as the real objects would react. A priority queue is used to store a representation of "events" that are waiting to happen. This queue is stored in order, based on the time the event should occur, so the smallest element will always be the next event to be modeled. As an event occurs, it can spawn other events. These subsequent events are placed into the queue as well. Execution continues until all events have occurred or until a preset time for the simulation is exceeded.

To see how we might design a simulation of the ice cream store, consider a typical scenario. A group of customers arrive at the ice cream store. From the measurements of similar stores we derive a probability that indicates how frequently this occurs. For example, suppose we assume that groups will consist of from one to five people, selected uniformly over that range. (In actual simulations the distribution would seldom be uniform. For example, groups of size two and three might predominate, with groups of size one and groups larger than three being relatively less frequent. The mathematics involved in forming nonuniform distributions is subtle and not particularly relevant to our discussion. We will therefore use uniform distributions throughout.) These groups will arrive at times spaced from one to ten minutes apart, again selected uniformly. Once they arrive, a group will either be seated or see that there are no seats and leave. If seated, they will take from 2 to 10 minutes to order, and once they order, they will remain from 15 to 35 minutes in the store. We know that every customer will order from one to three scoops of ice cream and that the store makes a profit of 35 cents on each scoop.

The primary object in the simulation is the store itself. It might seem odd to provide "behavior" for an inanimate object such as a store, but we can think of the store as a useful abstraction for the servers and managers who work in the store. The store manages two data items: the number of available seats and the amount of profit generated. The behavior of the store can be described by the following list.

- When a customer group arrives, the size of the group is compared to the number of seats. If insufficient seats are available, the group leaves. Otherwise, the group is seated and the number of seats decreased.
- When a customer orders and is served, the amount of profit is computed.
- When a customer group leaves, the seats are released for another customer group.

A class description for `IceCreamStore` is shown in Figure 21.3. The implementation of the methods is shown in Figure 21.4.

An instance of class `simulation` is defined as a global variable, called `theSimulation`. An instance of `iceCreamStore` is accessible via the name `theStore`.

As we noted already, each activity is matched by a derived class of event. Each derived class of event includes an integer data field, which represents the size of a group of customers. The arrival event occurs when a group enters. When executed, the arrival event creates and installs a new order event.

```
class arriveEvent : public event {
public:
   arriveEvent (unsigned int time, unsigned int gs)
     : event(time), groupSize(gs) { }
   virtual void processEvent ();
protected:
   unsigned int groupSize;
};
```

```
class IceCreamStore {
public:
  IceCreamStore()
    : freeChairs(35), profit(0.0) { }

  bool canSeat (unsigned int numberOfPeople);
  void order(unsigned int numberOfScoops);
  void leave(unsigned int numberOfPeople);

  unsigned int freeChairs;
  double profit;
};
```

▫ Figure 21.3 —— The class `IceCreamStore`

```
void arriveEvent::processEvent()
{
  if (theStore.canSeat(groupSize))
    theSimulation.scheduleEvent
      (new orderEvent(time + randBetween(2,10), groupSize));
}
```

An order event similarly spawns a leave event.

```
class orderEvent : public event {
public:
  orderEvent (unsigned int time, unsigned int gs)
    : event(time), size(gs) { }
  virtual void processEvent ();
protected:
  unsigned int groupSize;
};
```

```
void orderEvent::processEvent()
{
    // each person orders some number of scoops
  for (int i = 0; i < groupSize; i++)
    theStore.order(1 + rand(3));
  theSimulation.scheduleEvent
    (new leaveEvent(time + randBetween(15,35), groupSize));
};
```

Finally, leave events free up chairs but do not spawn any new events.

```
bool IceCreamStore::canSeat (unsigned int numberOfPeople)
  // if sufficient room, then seat customers
{
  cout << "Time: " << time;
  cout << " group of " << numberOfPeople << " customers arrives";
  if (numberOfPeople < freeChairs) {
    cout << " is seated" << endl;
    freeChairs -= numberOfPeople;
    return true;
    }
  else {
    cout << " no room, they leave" << endl;
    return false;
    }
}


void IceCreamStore::order (unsigned int numberOfScoops)
  // serve ice cream, compute profits
{
  cout << "Time: " << time;
  cout << " serviced order for " << numberOfScoops << endl;
  profit += 0.35 * numberOfScoops;
}


void IceCreamStore::leave (unsigned int numberOfPeople)
  // people leave, free up chairs
{
  cout << "Time: " << time;
  cout << " group of size " << numberOfPeople << " leaves" << endl;
  freeChairs += numberOfPeople;
}
```

▫ Figure 21.4 —— The methods implementing the class IceCreamStore

```
class leaveEvent : public event {
public:
  leaveEvent (unsigned int time, unsigned int gs)
    : event(time), groupSize(gs) { }
  virtual void processEvent ();
protected:
  unsigned int groupSize;
};
```

```
void leaveEvent::processEvent ()
{
  theStore.leave(groupSize);
}
```

The main program simply creates a certain number of initial events, then sets the simulation in motion. In our case we will simulate two hours (120 minutes) of operation, with groups arriving with random distribution between two and five minutes apart.

```
void main() {
    // load queue with some number of initial events
    unsigned int t = 0;
    while (t < 120) {
      t += randBetween(2,5);
      theSimulation.scheduleEvent
        (new arriveEvent(t, randBetween(1,5)));
      }

    // then run simulation and print profits
    theSimulation.run();
    cout << "Total profits " << theStore.profit << endl;
}
```

An example execution might produce a log such as the following:

```
customer group of size 4 arrives at time 11
customer group of size 4 orders 5 scoops of ice cream at time 13
customer group size 4 leaves at time 15
customer group of size 2 arrives at time 16
customer group of size 1 arrives at time 17
customer group of size 2 orders 2 scoops of ice cream at time 19
customer group of size 1 orders 1 scoops of ice cream at time 19
customer group size 1 leaves at time 22
        .
        .
        .
customer group of size 2 orders 3 scoops of ice cream at time 136
customer group size 2 leaves at time 143
total profits are 26.95
```

Summary ▫

A framework is a set of classes that creates a skeleton application without providing any of the application-specific details needed to realize a working program. Classes in the framework are then modified through subclassing in order to fill in the details. The most common frameworks are involved in graphical user interfaces, but frameworks can be created for almost any type of problem.

A characteristic of frameworks is the interaction of two types of methods. Foundation methods are defined in parent classes and not generally overridden. Deferred methods are specified in parent classes but must be overridden in application-specific child classes.

The use of a well-designed framework can significantly reduce the development time for an application, while providing more robust and reliable performance.

Further Reading ▫

Examples of frameworks that have been described in the literature include [Gamma 1995, Deutsch 1989, Weinand 1988]. The description of a framework as an upside-down library is due to Wilson [Wilson 1990].

I have used the ice cream store framework in several previous books in several languages [Budd 1987, Budd 1994, Budd 2000].

Self-Study Questions ▫

1. What is a software framework?
2. What are the two different ways that inheritance is used in a software framework?
3. Why in a statically typed language are methods that must be overridden even defined in a parent class?
4. Explain the idea of high-level versus low-level abstractions? How do frameworks permit the reuse of higher-level abstractions that is possible in non-object-oriented languages?
5. Explain the reasoning behind the description of a framework as an upside-down library.

Exercises ▫

1. Extract a graphical simulation framework from the billiard game in Chapter 7, and rewrite the program to use your simulation.

CHAPTER 22

An Example Framework: The AWT and Swing

The AWT (the *Abstract Windowing Toolkit*) and the newer *Swing* library extensions are the portions of the Java run-time library that are involved with creating, displaying, and facilitating user interaction with window objects. The AWT is an example of a software *framework*. As we noted in Chapter 21, a framework is a way of structuring generic solutions to a common problem, using polymorphism as a means of creating specialized solutions for each new application. Examining the AWT will illustrate how polymorphism is used in a powerful and dynamic fashion in this library.

22.1 □ The AWT Class Hierarchy

In Java, the class Frame represents the Java notion of an application window, a two-dimensional graphical surface that is shown on the display device, and through which the user interacts with a computer program.[1] Applications are formed by subclassing from Frame, overriding various methods, such as the paint method for repainting the window. In actuality, much of the behavior provided by class Frame is inherited from parent classes (see Figure 22.1). Examining each of these abstractions in turn helps to illustrate the functioning of the Java windowing system, as well as illustrating the power of inheritance as a mechanism for code reuse and sharing.

---

1. The Swing library, which was added to Java in version 1.2 of the language, uses JFrame. Applets, which we discussed briefly in Chapter 21, subclass from Applet. However, both JFrame and Applet are subclasses of Frame. We will discuss the Swing library in Section 22.6.

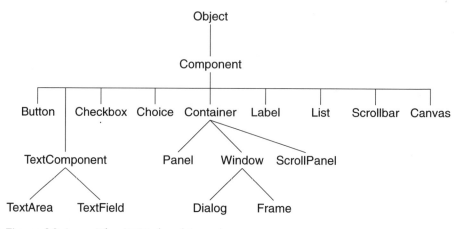

◻ Figure 22.1 —— The AWT class hierarchy

The class Object is the parent class of all classes in Java. It provides the ability to compare two objects for equality, compute a hash value for an object, and determine the class of an object. Methods defined in class Object include the following.

equals (anObject)	Returns true if object is equal to argument
getClass ()	Returns the class of an object
hashCode ()	Returns a hash value for an object
toString ()	Returns a string representation of an object

A Component is something that can be displayed on a two-dimensional screen and with which the user can interact. Attributes of a component include a size, a location, foreground and background colors, whether or not it is visible, and a set of listeners for events. Methods defined in class Component include the following.

enable(), disable()	Enable/disable a component
setLocation(int,int), getLocation()	Set and get component location
setSize(int,int), getSize()	Set and get size of component
setVisible(boolean)	Show or hide the component
setForeground(Color), getForeground()	Set and get foreground colors
setBackground(Color), getBackground()	Set and get background colors
setFont(Font), getFont()	Set and get font
repaint(Graphics)	Schedule component for repainting
paint(Graphics)	Repaint component appearance
addMouseListener(MouseListener)	Add a mouse listener for component
addKeyListener(KeyListener)	Add a keypress listener for component

Besides frames, other types of components include buttons, checkboxes, scroll bars, and text areas.

A Container is a type of component that can nest other components within it. A container is the way that complex graphical interfaces are constructed. A Frame is a type of Container, so it can hold objects such as buttons and scroll bars. When more complicated interfaces are necessary, a Panel (another type of container) can be constructed, which might hold, for example, a collection of buttons. Since this Panel is both a Container and a Component, it can be inserted into the Frame. A container maintains a list of the components it manipulates, as well as a layout manager to determine how the components should be displayed. Methods defined in class Container include the following.

setLayout (LayoutManager)	Set layout manager for display
add (Component), remove (Component)	Add or remove component from display

A Window is a type of Container. A window is a two-dimensional drawing surface that can be displayed on an output device. A window can be stacked on top of other windows and moved either to the front or back of the visible windows. Methods defined in class Window include the following.

show()	Make the window visible
toFront()	Move window to front
toBack()	Move window to back

Finally, a Frame is a type of window with a title bar, a menu bar, a border, a cursor, and other properties. Methods defined in class Frame include the following.

setTitle(String), getTitle()	Set or get title
setCursor(int)	Set cursor
setResizable()	Make the window resizable
setMenuBar(MenuBar)	Set menu bar for window

If we consider a typical application, we see that it uses methods from a number of different levels of the class hierarchy.

setTitle(String)	Inherited from class Frame
setSize(int, int)	Inherited from class Component
show()	Inherited from class Window
repaint()	Inherited from class Component
paint()	Inherited from Component, overridden in application class

The code in the parent classes (Component, Container, Window, and Frame) has all been written without reference to any particular application. Thus, this code can be easily carried from one application to the next. To specialize the design framework to a new application it is only necessary to override the appropriate

⊡ Figure 22.2 —— Locations recognized by border layout manager

methods (such as paint or event listeners) to define application-specific behavior. Thus, the combination of inheritance, overriding, and polymorphism permits design and software reuse on a grand scale.

In the remainder of this chapter we will examine various aspects of the AWT framework and illustrate how the basic concepts of inheritance and overriding are used to solve various problems.

22.2 ⊡ The Layout Manager

A typical user interface may hold a variety of buttons, slide bars, text windows, and selection boxes, in addition to application-specific graphical elements. The layout manager is the portion of the AWT charged with determining where each graphical element should be placed. This task is complicated by the ability of end-users to alter and resize windows, and therefore the layout manager cannot simply place elements at fixed locations specified by the programmer, since these locations would change as the window sizes changes.

There are a variety of standard layout managers, each of which will place components in a slightly different way. For example, the BorderLayout places up to five elements around the edges of the display (Figure 22.2). A GridLayout places components in a rectangular grid. Other layout managers allow components to be placed one on top of another (with only the topmost element showing) and in a variety of other ways.

The programmer developing a graphical user interface creates an instance of a layout manager and hands it to a container. Generally, the task of creation is the only direct interaction the programmer will have with the layout manager, since thereafter all commands will be handled by the container itself.

The connections between the application class, the container, and the layout manager illustrate the ways that inheritance, composition, and interfaces can be combined in order to achive an extremely loose coupling and a high degree of flexibility in design. The heart of the problem is that the framework code, the

AWT, does not know how the layout should be structured; only the programmer creating the application has that information. Therefore, the AWT cannot itself specify the layout strategy. However, the algorithms and techniques required to program a layout manager are complex, and the developers of the framework cannot realistically expect that the application programmers will have the ability to write a new manager for each class. To circumvent this quandary, the class LayoutManager is defined as an interface, and the framework library provides several alternative implementations.

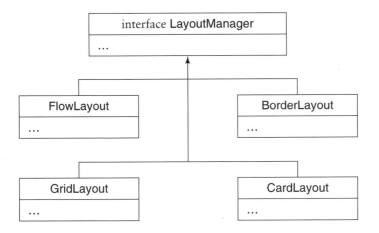

The selection of the layout manager is placed in the hands of the application programmer and not the framework developer. (The application programmer is even free to develop his or her own layout manager if desired, although few will be this ambitious.) As noted in Chapter 17, the application programmer simply creates an instance of layout manager and hands it to the framework by means of the inherited method setLayoutManager. Later, when the framework finds it necessary to determine the location of each graphical element, the framework simply invokes methods in the layout manager.

The relationship between the application class, the framework class, the layout manager interface, and the actual layout manager is shown in Figure 22.3. Note how flexible the connections are between these elements. There are three different mechanisms at work here: inheritance, composition, and implementation of an interface. Each is serving a slightly different purpose. Inheritance is the is-a relation and links the application class to the parent window class. This allows the code written in the AWT class Window to perform application-specific actions by invoking methods in the application class that override methods in the parent class (paint(), for example). The fact that composition is used to link the container with the layout manager makes the link between these two items very flexible and dynamic—the programmer can easily change the type of layout manager

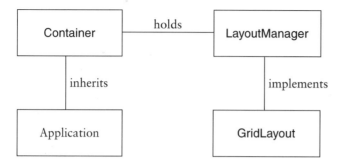

▫ Figure 22.3 —— Relationships between layout manager components

being used by a container. This dynamic behavior is very difficult to achieve using inheritance alone, since the inheritance relationship between a parent and child is established at compile time. Finally, the fact that LayoutManager is simply an interface, and that various different classes of objects implement this interface means that the programmer is free to develop alternative layout managers using a wide variety of techniques. This freedom would be much more constrained if, for example, LayoutManager was a class that alternative layout managers needed to extend.

22.3 ▫ Listeners

As we have noted several times, a fundamental feature of software frameworks is a tension between software reuse and specialization, and that in a framework this tension is resolved by the twin mechanisms of inheritance (for providing reusable algorithms) and overriding (for specializing the algorithms to new situations).

To handle features such as repainting, setting the title, setting menu categories, and other similar operations, the window class uses simple inheritance; the application class simply inherits from Frame and invokes the right methods. To handle end-user-generated events, such as mouse motions and key presses, the AWT uses a slightly more complex arrangement.

A *listener* is an object whose sole purpose is to sit and wait (to listen) for an event to occur. Each of the graphical elements that can generate an event, such as a window, a button, or a slide bar, will maintain its own collection of listeners. When an event occurs, the listeners are notified, and they take the appropriate action.

Once again we have the fundamental problem that the framework is defining the structure in which the events are to be handled, but the framework does not know the specific details concerning *how* these events should be handled. Only the application programmer knows what a mouse press or a key press should mean. And once again the solution is to use a combination of inheritance and overriding.

The AWT framework defines a series of interfaces, one for each category of event. For example, the interface actionListener is associated with items such as buttons. It is defined as follows.

```
public interface ActionListener extends EventListener {
    public void actionPerformed (ActionEvent e);
}
```

The application programmer, who knows what a button press should mean, must create a class that implements this interface. An object that performs this implementation is then handed to the slider object by means of the method setActionListener. So we have the following structure.

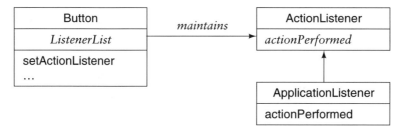

Note carefully the source of and role played by each of the three elements. The button class and the interface are part of the AWT framework and must be very general and know nothing of the specific application. The implementation of the interface is provided by the application programmer, who is the only one who knows what the action should mean in the context of the final application. By separating the listener from the button, this structure allows several components to be handled by a single listener object. By combining the listener and its interface through inheritance, the framework provides a way to handle events that is very flexible and easy to modify.

22.3.1 Adapter classes

Many events have several different but related manifestations. A mouse, for example, can be moved, can enter the portion of a window covered by a component, can exit this space, or can be pressed. Thus, the framework class to handle mouse activities has several different parts.

```
public interface MouseListener extends EventListener {
    public void mouseClicked (MouseEvent e);
    public void mouseEntered (MouseEvent e);
    public void mouseExited (MouseEvent e);
```

```
    public void mousePressed (MouseEvent e);
    public void mouseReleased (MouseEvent e);
}
```

More often than not the application programmer is interested in only one or two of these events and not the entire suite of methods. To accommodate this, the AWT framework provides a number of *adapter* classes. These implement the interface but do nothing in response to each of the methods.

```
public class MouseAdapter implements MouseListener {
    public void mouseClicked (MouseEvent e) { }
    public void mouseEntered (MouseEvent e) { }
    public void mouseExited (MouseEvent e) { }
    public void mousePressed (MouseEvent e) { }
    public void mouseReleased (MouseEvent e) { }
}
```

If the application programmer is interested only in mouse presses, it is easier to subclass from MouseAdapter and override only one method than it is to implement MouseListener and give an implementation to all five methods. The application class listener is then handed to a window (for example), which maintains a list of all the listeners waiting on mouse events. So we have the following picture.

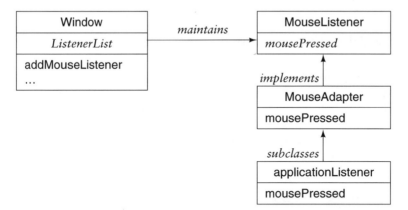

The window "thinks" that it is maintaining a list of MouseListener objects. In fact, the listener is a child class created by subclassing from MouseAdapter.

22.4   ◻   User Interface Components

The variety of user interface components in the Java AWT library provides, once again, a good illustration of the power of polymorphism. With the exception of menu bars, all the user interface components are subclassed from the parent class

Component (Figure 22.1). Containers assume only that the elements they will hold are instances of class Component. In fact, the values they maintain are polymorphic and represent more specialized values, such as buttons or scroll bars. Thus, the design of the user interface construction system depends on the mechanisms of inheritance, polymorphism, and substitutability. We will consider only a few examples that illustrate the general character of the AWT components.

A Button (or JButton in the Swing library) is a labeled component represented by a rounded box that can respond to user interaction. The application programmer places a button in a specific location. In the following example we will place the button at the top (or north) part of the screen. Interaction with a button is achieved by attaching an ActionListener object to the button. The ActionListener object is then notified when the button is pressed.

```
Button butn = new Button ("do it!");
add("North", butn); // place at top of screen
butn.addActionListener (new doIt()); // add listener
  ..
private class doIt implements ActionListener {
  public void actionPerformed (ActionEvent e) {
    // whatever do it does
      .
      .
      .
  }
}
```

In this example an inner class defines whatever actions should be taken when the button is pressed. A useful technique is to combine the button object and the button listener in one new class. This new class both subclasses from the original Button class and implements the ActionListener interface. For example, in the case study that is presented in Section 22.5, we create a set of buttons for different colors. Each button holds a color value and when pressed, invokes a method using the color as argument. This class is written as follows.

```
class ColorButton extends Button implements ActionListener {
  private Color ourColor;

  public ColorButton (Color c, String name) {
    super (name); // create the button
    ourColor = c; // save the color value
    addActionListener (this); // add ourselves as listener
  }

  public void actionPerformed (ActionEvent e) {
```

```
   //  set color for middle panel
   setFromColor (ourColor);
}
}
```

Notice how the object registers *itself* as a listener for button actions. When pressed, the button will invoke the method actionPerformed, which will then invoke the procedure setFromColor that is found in the surrounding class.

We can take this technique one step further and define a generic ButtonAdapter class that is both a button and a listener. The actions of the listener will be encapsulated by an abstract method, which must be implemented by a subclass.

```
abstract class ButtonAdapter extends Button implements ActionListener
{
  public ButtonAdapter (String name) {
    super (name);
    addActionListener (this);
  }

  public void actionPerformed (ActionEvent e) { pressed(); }

  public abstract void pressed ();
}
```

To create a button using this abstraction, the programmer must subclass and override the method pressed. This, however, can be done easily using a class definition expression. The following, for example, creates a button that when pressed will halt the application.

```
p.add (new ButtonAdapter("Quit"){
  public void pressed () { System.exit(0); }});
```

A ScrollBar is a slider used to specify integer values over a wide range. Scroll bars can be displayed in either a horizontal or a vertical direction. The maximum and minimum values can be specified, as well as the line increment (the amount the scroll bar will move when it is touched in the ends) and the page increment (the amount it will move when it is touched in the background area between the slider and the end). Like a button, interaction is provided for a scroll bar by defining a listener that will be notified when the scroll bar is modified.

The case study at the end of this chapter uses a technique similar to the one described earlier in the discussion of buttons. Figure 22.4 shows a snapshot of this application, which includes three vertical scroll bars. The class ColorBar represents a scroll bar for maintaining colors. The constructor for the class creates a vertical scroll bar with an initial value of 40 and a range between 0 and 255.

▣ Figure 22.4 —— Snapshot of ColorTest application

The background color for the scroll bar is set using a given argument. Finally, the object itself is made a listener for scroll bar events. When the scroll bar is changed, the method adjustmentValueChanged will be executed. Typically, within this method the current value of the scroll bar would be accessed using getValue(). In this particular application, a bank of three scroll bars will be created, and the value of all three will be recovered in a shared procedure named setFromBar.

```
private class ColorBar extends Scrollbar implements AdjustmentListener
{
  public ColorBar (Color c) {
    super (Scrollbar.VERTICAL, 40, 0, 0, 255);
    setBackground (c);
    addAdjustmentListener (this);
  }

  public void adjustmentValueChanged (AdjustmentEvent e) {
    // method setFromBar will get scroll bar
    // value using getValue ();
    setFromBar ();
  }
}
```

22.5 ▣ Case Study: A Color Display

A simple test program will illustrate how panels and layout managers are used in developing user interfaces. The application will also illustrate the use of scroll bars and the use of methods provided by the class Color. Finally, we can also use this program to illustrate how nested classes can be employed to combine the actions of creating a new graphical component (such as a button or a slider) and listening for actions relating to the component.

The class ColorTest (Figure 22.5) creates a window for displaying color values. The window, shown in Figure 22.4, is divided into four separate regions. These four regions are managed by the default layout manager for class Frame. This layout manager is a value of type BorderLayout.

At the top (the "north" side) is a text region, a component of type TextField, that describes the current color. To the left (the "west" region) is a trio of sliders that can be used to set the red, green, and blue values. To the right (the "east" region) is a 4 × 4 bank of 16 buttons. These are constructed on a Panel that is organized by a GridLayout manager. Thirteen of the buttons represent the predefined color values. Two more represent the actions of making a color brighter and darker. The final button will halt the application. Finally, in the middle will be a square panel that represents the specified color.

The class ColorTest holds six data fields. The first represents the current color in the middle panel, and the remaining five represent different graphical objects. Three represent the slider, one represents the text field at the top of the page, and one represents the color panel in the middle.

The three sliders use the class ColorBar described in Section 22.4. The argument used with the constructor for each class is the color to be used in painting the buttons and background for the scroll bar. You will recall that when adjusted, the scroll bar will invoke its listener, which will execute the method adjustmentValueChanged. This method will then execute the procedure setFromBar.

Complex graphical layouts can be created by composing one type of layout on top of another. For example, the three scroll bars are themselves stored in a Panel (another type of component) that is organized using a BorderLayout. This is performed in the following method.

```
private Panel makeScrollBars () {
  Panel p = new Panel();
  p.setLayout (new BorderLayout());
  p.add("West", redBar);
  p.add("Center", greenBar);
  p.add("East", blueBar);
  return p;
}
```

The idea of combining inheritance and implementation of an interface is used in creating the buttons that represent the 13 predefined colors. Each instance of ColorButton, shown in Section 22.4, both extends the class Button and implements the ActionListener interface. When the button is pressed, the method setFromColor

```
class ColorTest extends Frame {
  static public void main (String [ ] args)
    { Frame window = new ColorTest(); window.show(); }

  private TextField colorDescription = new TextField();
  private Panel colorField = new Panel();
  private Color current = Color.black;
  private Scrollbar redBar = new ColorBar(Color.red);
  private Scrollbar greenBar = new ColorBar(Color.green);
  private Scrollbar blueBar = new ColorBar(Color.blue);

  public ColorTest () {
    setTitle ("color test"); setSize (400, 600);
    add("North", colorDescription);
    add("East", makeColorButtons());
    add("Center", colorField);
    add("West", makeScrollBars());
    setFromColor (current);
  }

  private void setFromColor (Color c) {
    current = c; colorField.setBackground (current);
    redBar.setValue(c.getRed());
    greenBar.setValue(c.getGreen());
    blueBar.setValue(c.getBlue());
    colorDescription.setText(c.toString());
  }

  private void setFromBar () {
    int r = redBar.getValue();
    int g = greenBar.getValue();
    int b = blueBar.getValue();
    setFromColor (new Color(r, g, b));
  }

  private Panel makeColorButtons () { ... }
  private Panel makeScrollBars () { ... }
private class BrightenButton extends Button implements
    ActionListener ...
private class ColorButton extends Button implements ActionListener ...
private class ColorBar extends Scrollbar implements
    AdjustmentListener ...
}
```

▢ Figure 22.5 —— The class ColorTest

will be used to set the color of the middle panel, using the color stored in the button.

The class BrightenButton is slightly more complex. An index value is stored with the button. This value indicates whether the button represents the "brighten" button or the "darken" button. When pressed, the current color is modified by the appropriate method, and the new value is used to set the current color.

```
private class BrightenButton extends Button implements ActionListener
{
  private int index;
  public BrightenButton (int i) {
    super ( i == 0 ? "brighter" : "darker");
    index = i;
    addActionListener(this);
  }

  public void actionPerformed (ActionEvent e) {
    if (index == 0)
      setFromColor (current.brighter());
    else
      setFromColor (current.darker());
  }
}
```

A panel is used to hold the 16 button values. In this case the layout is described by a 4 × 4 grid pattern. Thirteen represent the predefined buttons, 2 represent the brighter and darker buttons, and the last creates a button that when pressed exits the application.

```
private Panel makeColorButtons () {
  Panel p = new Panel();
  p.setLayout (new GridLayout(4,4,3,3));
  p.add (new ColorButton(Color.black, "black"));
  p.add (new ColorButton(Color.blue, "blue"));
  p.add (new ColorButton(Color.cyan, "cyan"));
  p.add (new ColorButton(Color.darkGray, "darkGray"));
  p.add (new ColorButton(Color.gray, "gray"));
  p.add (new ColorButton(Color.green, "green"));
  p.add (new ColorButton(Color.lightGray, "lightGray"));
  p.add (new ColorButton(Color.magenta, "magenta"));
  p.add (new ColorButton(Color.orange, "orange"));
  p.add (new ColorButton(Color.pink, "pink"));
  p.add (new ColorButton(Color.red, "red"));
```

```
      p.add (new ColorButton(Color.white, "white"));
      p.add (new ColorButton(Color.yellow, "yellow"));
      p.add (new BrightenButton(0));
      p.add (new BrightenButton(1));
      p.add (new ButtonAdapter("Quit"){
        public void pressed() { System.exit(0); }});
      return p;
   }
```

22.6 ▫ The Swing Component Library

As we noted earlier, the Java user interface library underwent a major revision between Java version 1.1 and version 1.2. The newer Swing library promised greater platform independence and a consistency of appearance between components. On the negative side, the newer library tends to run more slowly than the older AWT library.

Depending on what platform is being used, readers may encounter either the earlier or the later libraries. If applets are being developed, then the programmer should be aware that many Web browsers do not yet support the Java 1.2 libraries. In the next section we describe the most important differences between the two systems.

22.6.1 Import libraries

To use the older AWT library it was only necessary to import java.awt.* and java.awt.event.* To include the newer Swing libraries it is necessary to import javax.swing.* and javax.swing.event.* Since Swing is built on top of AWT, it is usually necessary to import both sets of libraries.

22.6.2 Different components

The AWT components had names like Button and Scrollbar. The Swing components have for the most part simply prepended the letter J to the name, as in JButton. (Although there are exceptions to this rule—for example, Scrollbar became JScrollBar, with a capital B.)

There are minor differences in the methods supported by the two sets of components, and the Swing library has introduced many new components not found in AWT. But generally backwards compatibility has been preserved, so methods that formerly worked with the AWT should still work with the Swing library.

22.6.3   Different paint protocol

In the Swing library it is almost always necessary to invoke the parent class paint method from inside an overridden paint method. This is accomplished by calling super.paint.

```
public class BallWorld extends JFrame {
    .
    .
    .

    public void paint (Graphics g) {
        super.paint(g); // first call parent, then do
        aBall.paint(g); // class-specific painting
    }
    .
    .
    .

}
```

22.6.4   Adding components to a window

In the AWT library the user generally attached a component to a window by issuing an add method in the constructor for an application class. In the Swing library it is necessary to first invoke the method getContentPane, then add the component to the value returned by this method.

```
public class CannonWorld extends JFrame {

    public CannonWorld () {
        .
        .
        .

        getContentPane().add("East", scrollbar);
    }
}
```

Summary ▫

The Abstract Windowing Toolkit, or AWT, is the portion of the Java library used for the creation of graphical user interfaces. The design of the AWT is an excellent illustration of the power of object-oriented techniques in the creation of an application framework. In this chapter we described the varous AWT components and the way they are used to created user interfaces.

Further Reading ⊡

A good introduction to the AWT under Swing is [Walrath 1999].

Self-Study Questions ⊡

1. What do the letters AWT stand for?
2. Explain the relationships between the various parts in the manipulation of a layout manager.
3. What is a listener? When does a listener get invoked?
4. What purpose is being addressed by the mouse adapter?

Exercises ⊡

1. Explain why MouseListener can be represented as an interface, but MouseAdapter must be a class.

CHAPTER 23

Object Interconnections

Starting with this chapter we step back and move up a level of abstraction. In Chapter 1 we presented the idea that an object-oriented program should be viewed as a community of agents working together to address a common purpose. Rather than considering the structure of individual classes in isolation (as we have done in previous chapters) or the parent class/child class relationship, starting with this chapter we will examine the relationships between groups of classes or objects working together. In particular, in this chapter we will consider the nature of the connections that can bind one object to another.

One way to look at interconnections between objects is to examine the concepts of *visibility* and *dependency*. The software engineering term visibility describes a characterization of *names*—the handles by which objects are accessed. An object is visible in a certain context if its name is legal and denotes the object. A related term frequently used to describe visibility is the *scope* of an identifier.

Visibility is related to connectedness in the sense that, if it is possible to control and reduce the visibility of names for an identifier, we can more easily characterize how the identifier is being used. In Smalltalk, for example, instance variables have their visibility restricted to methods; they cannot be accessed directly except within a method. This does not mean that such values cannot be accessed or modified outside of the class; all such uses, however, must be mediated by at least one method. In Apple Object Pascal, on the other hand, instance variables are visible wherever a class name is known. Thus, the language provides no mechanisms to ensure that instance variables are modified only by methods; instead, we must rely on the appropriate conduct of users.

The concept of *dependency* relates one object or class to another. If an object cannot meaningfully exist without another object, it is said to be *dependent* on the second. A child class is almost always dependent on its parent, for example. Dependencies can also be much more subtle, as we will discover in the next section.

23.1 ▫ Coupling and Cohesion

The idea of *coupling* and *cohesion* provides a framework for evaluating effective use of objects and classes. As we noted in Chapter 3, coupling describes the relationships *between* classes, and cohesion describes the relationships *within* them. A reduction in interconnectedness between classes is therefore achieved via a reduction in coupling. On the other hand, well-designed classes should have some purpose; all the elements should be associated with a single task. This means that in a good design the elements within a class should have internal cohesion.

23.1.1   Varieties of coupling

Coupling between classes can arise for different reasons, some of which are more acceptable, or desirable, than others. A list ranked from worst to better might look something like the following.

- Internal data coupling
- Global data coupling
- Control (or sequence) coupling
- Component coupling
- Parameter coupling
- Subclass coupling

Internal data coupling occurs when instances of one class can directly modify the local data values (instance variables) in another class.

```
class  SneakyModifier {           class Person {
public:                            public:
   void sneaky () {                Person () {
     // change my friends name      name = "Larry";
     myFriend->name = "Lucy";       }
   }                                string name;
   Person * myFriend;             };
};
```

The reason why internal data coupling is so insidiously bad is that it complicates the ability to understand classes in isolation. If one examines only the class on the right-hand side, how is one to know that an internal data field can magically be modified by a force working external to the class? This activity makes understanding and reasoning about programs difficult and should be avoided whenever possible. In a later section, we will explore one heuristic used to reduce internal data coupling in object-oriented systems.

Global data coupling occurs when two or more classes are bound together by their reliance on common global data structures.

```
double todaysDow;
```

```
class One {                    class Two {
public:                        public:
   void setDow () {               void printDow () {
     todaysDow = 9473;               cout << "Today the Dow hit "
   }                                 << todaysDow;
};                               }
                               };
```

Once more, the reason why this form of coupling is bad is that it complicates the understanding of classes taken in isolation. Each class by itself is incomplete, and understanding the interaction between them is possible only when one examines both class definitions at once. Nevertheless, sometimes global data coupling is unavoidable.

In practice, it is important to distinguish between two varieties of global variables. In multifile programs some global variables have *file scope*, which means they are used only within one file. Other global variables have *program scope*, which means they can potentially be modified anywhere in a program. Understanding the use of global variables that possess program scope can be much more difficult than understanding the manipulation of variables that have only file scope.

Many languages provide techniques to control the visibility of names that are between individual classes and complete programs. Examples are name spaces in C++, packages in Java, or units in Object Pascal. These features allow some names to have a scope that is larger than an individual class and yet smaller than the entire program. Objects that interact with each other by means of such values are slightly better than objects that interact through true global variables, since the portion of the program where interactions can occur is reduced. However, such coupling can still be difficult to understand, and it should be avoided wherever possible.

In an object-oriented framework, a possible alternative to global data coupling is to make a new class that is charged with "managing" the data values and to route all access to the global values through it. (This approach is similar to our use of access functions to shield direct access to local data within an object.) This technique reduces global data coupling to parameter coupling, which is easier to understand and control. In Java there are no global variables, and all values must be managed by some class.

```
class MyClass {
public:
  void mustDoFirst() { ... }

  void doSecond () { ... }

  void doThird () { ... }
};
```

Control or sequence coupling occurs when one class must perform operations in a certain fixed order but the order is controlled elsewhere. A database system might go through, in order, the stages of performing initialization, reading current records, updating records, deleting records, and generating reports. However, each stage is invoked by a different routine and the sequencing of the calls can be dependent on code in a different location. The presence of control coupling indicates that the designer of a class was following a lower level of abstraction than was necessary (each of the various steps versus a single directive, "process a database"). Even when control coupling is unavoidable, prudence usually dictates that the class being sequenced assures itself that it is being processed in the correct order, rather than rely on the proper handling of the callers.

```
class Set {
  .
  .
  .
private:
  List data;
};
```

Component coupling occurs when one class maintains a data field or value that is an instance of another class. Ideally the relationship in a component coupling is one way. The container clearly has knowledge of the class of value it maintains, but the element being held should have no knowledge of the container in which it is being used. The Set abstraction that used a List to maintain elements described in Chapter 14 was an example of component coupling.

```
class MyClass {
public:
  void doSomething (Set aSet) {
    // do something using the argument value
    .
    .
    .
  }
}
```

Parameter coupling occurs when one class must invoke services and routines from another and the only relationships are the number and type of parameters supplied and the type of value returned. This form of coupling is common, easy to see, and easy to verify statically (with tools that check parameter calls against definition, for example); therefore, it is the most benign option.

```
class Parent {
  .
  .
  .
}


class Child extends Parent {
  .
  .
  .
}
```

Subclass coupling is particular to object-oriented programming. It describes the relationship a class has with its parent class (or classes in the case of multiple inheritance). Through inheritance, an instance of a child class can be treated as though it were an instance of the parent class. As we have seen in several case studies in this book, this feature permits the development of significant software components (such as windowing systems) that are only loosely related, via subclass coupling, to other portions of an application.

23.1.2 Varieties of cohesion

The internal cohesion of a class is a measure of the degree of binding of the various elements within the structure. As with coupling, cohesion can be ranked on a scale of the weakest (least desirable) to the strongest (most desirable) as follows.

- Coincidental cohesion
- Logical cohesion
- Temporal cohesion
- Communication cohesion
- Sequential cohesion
- Functional cohesion
- Data cohesion

Coincidental cohesion occurs when elements of a class are grouped for no apparent reason—often the result of someone "modularizing" a large program by arbitrarily segmenting it into several small units. It is usually a sign of poor design. In an object-oriented framework, we say that coincidental cohesion occurs when a class consists of methods that are not related.

Logical cohesion occurs when there is a logical connection among the elements of the class but no actual connection in either data or control. A library of mathematical functions (sine, cosine, and so on) might exhibit logical cohesion if each of the functions is implemented separately without reference to any of the others.

Temporal cohesion occurs when elements are bound together because they all must be used at approximately the same time. A class that performs program initialization is a typical example. Here, a better design would distribute the various initialization activities over the classes more closely charged with subsequent behavior.

Communication cohesion occurs when methods in a class are grouped because they all access the same input/output data or devices. The class acts as a "manager" for the data or the device.

Sequential cohesion occurs when elements in a class are linked by the necessity to be activated in a particular order. It often results from an attempt to avoid sequential coupling. Again, a better design can usually be found if the level of abstraction is raised. (Of course, if it is necessary for actions to be performed in a certain order, this sequentiality must be expressed at some level of abstraction. The important principle is to hide this necessity as much as possible from all other levels of abstraction.)

Function cohesion is a desirable type of binding in which the elements of a class all relate to the performance of a single function.

Finally, data cohesion is when a class defines a set of data values and exports routines that manipulate the data structure. Data cohesion occurs when a class is used to implement a data abstraction.

One can often estimate the degree of cohesion within a class by writing a brief statement of the classe's purpose and examining the statement (similar to the CRC card description we used in Chapter 3). The following tests are suggested by Constantine.

1. If the sentence that describes the purpose of a class is a compound sentence containing a comma or more than one verb, the class is probably performing more than one function; therefore, it probably has sequential or communicational binding.

2. If the sentence contains words relating to time, such as "first," "next," "then," "after," "when," or "start," the class probably has sequential or temporal binding. An example is "Wait for the instant teller customer to insert a card, then prompt for the personal identification number."

3. If the predicate of the sentence does not contain a single, specific object following the verb, the class is probably logically bound. For example, "Edit all data" has logical binding; "Edit source data" may have functional binding.

4. If the sentence contains words such as "Initialize" or "Clean up," the class probably has temporal binding.

23.1.3   The Law of Demeter

Style guidelines for program coding range from the abstract, such as the directive "Modules should exhibit internal cohesion and minimize external coupling," to the concrete, such as "No procedure should contain more than 60 lines of code." Concrete guidelines are easy to understand and apply, but often they lull programmers (and managers) into a false sense of security and may direct attention away from the real problem. As an aid in reducing complexity, the rule banning all procedures of more than 60 lines is an approximation at best. A short procedure with complicated control flow may be much more difficult to understand and code correctly than a far longer sequence of straight-line assignment statements.

Similarly, the fanatical attempt some people made a few years back to ban goto statements was often misguided. The goto itself was merely a symptom of a disease, not the disease itself. The assertion was not that goto statements are intrinsically bad and programs that avoid them are uniformly improved but rather that it is more difficult to produce an easily understood program using goto statements. It is the understandability of programs that is important, not the use or nonuse of goto statements. Nevertheless, we cannot overlook the utility of a simple rule that is easy to apply and that is effective *most* of the time in achieving some desirable end, and we may ask whether any such guidelines might be developed specifically for object-oriented programs.

One such guideline has been proposed by Karl Lieberherr as part of his work on an object-oriented programming tool called Demeter: the Law of Demeter. There are two forms of the law, strong and weak. Both strive to reduce the degree of coupling between objects by limiting their interconnections.

The Law of Demeter.   In any method, M, attached to a class, C, only methods defined by the following classes may be used.

- The instance-variable classes of C
- The argument classes of method M (including C); note that global objects or objects created inside the method M are considered arguments to M.

If we rephrase the law in terms of instances (or objects) instead of methods, we arrive at the following.

The Law of Demeter–weak form.   Inside a method, data can be accessed in and messages can be sent to only the following objects.

1. The arguments associated with the method being executed (including the self object)
2. Instance variables for the receiver of the method
3. Global variables, both with file scope and with program scope
4. Temporary variables created inside the method

The strong form of the law restricts access to instance variables only to those variables defined in the class in which the method appears. Access to instance variables from superclasses must be mediated through accessor functions.

The Law of Demeter—strong form.   Inside a method it is permitted to access or send messages only to the following objects.

1. The arguments associated with the method being executed (including the self object)
2. Instance variables defined in the class containing the method being executed
3. Global variables
4. Temporary variables created inside the method

It is instructive to consider what forms of access are ruled out by the law of Demeter and to relate the law to the concepts of coupling and cohesion described earlier. The major style of access eliminated by programs that satisfy the rule is the direct manipulation of instance variables in another class. Permitting access in this form creates a situation where one object is dependent on the internal representation of another—a form of internal data coupling. On the other hand, satisfaction of this rule means that classes generally can be studied and understood in isolation from one another, since they interact only in simple, well-defined ways. Some have even gone further than the Law of Demeter and suggested that references to instance variables from within a method should always be mediated by accessor functions. Their argument is that direct references to variables severely limit the ability of programmers to refine existing classes.

23.1.4   Class-level versus object-level visibility

The idea that a class can have multiple instances introduces a new dimension in the control of coupling. Two general models are used in object-oriented languages to describe the visibility of names. These can be described as *class-level visibility* and *object-level visibility*. The distinction can be summarized as the answer to a simple question: Is an object allowed to examine the inner state of a sibling object?

Languages that control visibility on the class level, such as C++, treat all instances of a class in the same manner. As we will see shortly, C++ permits a wide range of possibilities in controlling the visibility of identifiers. Yet even in the most restrictive case—so-called "private" data fields—an instance of a class is always permitted access to the data fields of other instances of the same class. In short, objects are permitted complete access to their sibling objects' internal state.

Object-level control of visibility, on the other hand, treats the individual object as the basic unit of control. Languages that exhibit object-level control include Smalltalk, in which no object is permitted access to the inner state of another object, even if both are instances of the same class.

23.1.5 Active values

An active value is a variable for which we want to perform some action each time its value changes. An active-value system illustrates why parameter coupling is preferable to other forms of coupling, particularly in object-oriented languages. Suppose a simulation of a nuclear power plant includes a class Reactor that maintains various pieces of information about the reactor state. Among these values is the temperature of the coolant (the water that surrounds the fuel rods). Further suppose that this value is modified, in good object-oriented fashion, via a method, setHeat, and access is achieved through the function getHeat. This class is pictured below.

```
@interface Reactor : Object
{ ...
   double heat; ...
}
- (void)  setHeat: (double) newValue;
- (double) getHeat;
@end
```

Imagine the program has been developed and is working when the programmer decides it would be nice to have a visual display that continuously shows the current temperature of the moderator as the simulation progresses. It is desirable to do this as noninvasively as possible. In particular, the programmer does not want to change the Reactor class. (This class may have been written by another programmer, for example, or it may be used in other applications where this new behavior is not desired.)

A simple solution is to make a new subclass of Reactor—say, GraphicalReactor—that does nothing more than override the setHeat method, updating the graphical output before invoking the superclass methods (see following). The programmer thus needs only to replace the creation of new Reactor objects with the creation of GraphicalReactor objects. This creation probably takes place once during initialization. As long as all changes to the Reactor value are mediated through the method setHeat, the gauge will reflect the value accurately.

```
@implementation GraphicalReactor : Reactor
- (void) setHeat: (double) newValue
  {
    /* code necessary to */
    /* update gauge */
    [ super setHeat: newValue ];
  }
@end
```

Smalltalk and Objective-C both support a more generalized concept called *dependency*. We will discuss this in Section 23.4.

23.2 ⊡ Subclass Clients and User Clients

We have noted several times that an object, like a module, has both a public and a private face. The public side encompasses all features, such as methods and instance variables, that can be accessed or manipulated by code outside the module. The private face includes the public face, as well as methods and instance variables accessible only within the object. The user of a service provided by a module (the client) needs to know the details only of the public side of a module. Details of implementation, and other internal features not important for module utilization, can be hidden from view.

Inheritance in an object-oriented language means that classes have yet a third face—namely, those features accessible to subclasses but not necessarily to other users. The designer of a subclass for a given class will probably need to know more internal implementation details of the original class than will an instance-level user but may not need as much information as the designer of the original class.

We can think of both the designer of a subclass and a user of a class as "clients" of the original class, since they use the facilities it provides. Because these two groups have different requirements, however, it is useful to distinguish them as *subclass clients* and *user clients*. User clients create instances of the class and pass messages to these objects. Subclass clients create new classes based on the class.

In the classes we developed as part of our solitaire game in Chapter 9, the class PlayingCard declares the variables r and s to be private. The variables maintain the rank and suit of the card. Only methods associated with class PlayingCard can access or modify these values. The data associated with class CardPile, on the other hand, are divided into three categories: private, protected, and public. The private variable firstCard can be accessed only within the class CardPile, while the protected fields x and y can be accessed either in this class or by subclasses. The only public interface is through methods; there are no publicly accessible instance variables. By eliminating publicly accessible instance variables, the language ensures that no data coupling is permitted between this class and other software components. (However, the language only provides the mechanism. It is still the responsibility of the programmer to use the features properly—for example, by declaring all data members as private or protected.)

We can think of software evolution and modification in terms of user and subclass clients. When a class designer announces the public features of a class, he is making a contract to provide the services described. He can consider and implement changes in the internal design freely as long as the public interface remains unchanged (or perhaps only grows). Similarly, although perhaps less common and less obvious, the designer of a class is specifying an interface to subclasses. A common and subtle source of software errors is created when the internal details of a class are changed and subclasses cease to operate. By dividing the private internal details of a class from the various levels of public interface, if only by convention, the programmer sets the boundaries for acceptable change and modification. The ability to make changes to existing code safely is critical in the maintenance of large and long-lived software systems.

The notion of a subclass client may strike some readers as odd, since when an instance of the subclass is created, the class and the subclass are melded into one object. Nevertheless, the notion makes good sense when we consider the creators or designers of the class. Often, the designer of a subclass and the designer of the original class are not the same. It is thus good OOP practice for the designer of any class to consider the possibility that at some future point, the class may be subclassed, and to provide adequate documentation and software connections to facilitate this process.

23.3 ▫ Control of Access and Visibility

In this section, we briefly outline some of the various information-hiding features found in a few of the object-oriented languages we are considering, and we note how each language supports the concepts discussed in earlier sections of this chapter.

23.3.1 Visibility in Smalltalk

The Smalltalk system provides few facilities for the protection and hiding of either data or methods. Instance variables are always considered private and are accessible only within the methods associated with the class in which the variables are defined or in subclasses. Access to them from outside the object must be accomplished indirectly through access functions.

Methods, on the other hand, are always considered public and can be accessed by anybody. Just as there are no facilities for making instance variables public, there are no facilities for enforcing the hiding of methods. It is common, however, for certain methods to be labeled "private," meaning that they should be used only by the class itself and should not be invoked by user clients. It is good practice to respect these suggestions and to avoid using private methods.

23.3.2   Visibility in Object Pascal

Apple Object Pascal provides weak facilities for managing the visibility of object fields. All fields—data and methods—are public and are accessible to both user and subclass clients. It is only by convention or agreement that data fields are restricted to subclass clients and that methods are open to user clients. Even though style guidelines such as the Law of Demeter cannot be strictly enforced by the system, they are still valuable and should be respected by programmers. It is helpful, too, if programmers use comments to indicate those methods in a class that they expect to be overridden in subclasses.

The Borland version of the language is slightly more powerful. Delphi supports the keywords public, protected, and private in a fashion very similar to that in C++. However, within the implementation section of a unit, all fields are treated as public. This allows sibling instances to access the private data fields of sister objects.

23.3.3   Visibility in C++

Of the languages we are considering, C++ provides by far the most complete range of facilities for controlling access to information. As we noted in earlier chapters, these facilities are provided through three new keywords: public, protected, and private.

When these keywords are used in the field-definition part of class descriptions, their effect can be described almost directly in terms of the concepts from Section 23.2. The data that follow the public: access specifier are available to subclass and user clients alike. The data that follow the protected: access specifier are accessible only within the class and subclasses and so are intended for subclass clients, not for user clients. Finally, the private: designator precedes fields that are accessible only to instances of the class itself and not to subclass or user clients. In the absence of any initial designation, fields are considered private.

Philosophically, the C++ access-control mechanisms are intended to protect against accident, not to guarantee security from malicious users. There are several ways to defeat the protection system. Probably the most direct involves the use of functions that return pointer or reference values. Consider the class shown following.

```
class Sneaky
{
  private:
    int safe;
  public:
      // initialize safe to 10
    Sneaky() { safe = 10; }
    int &sorry() { return safe; }
}
```

Although the field safe is declared private, a reference to the value is returned by the method sorry. Thus, in an expression such as

```
Sneaky x;
x.sorry() = 17;
```

the value of the data member safe will be changed from 10 to 17, even if the call to sorry takes place in user (client) code.

A more subtle point is that access specifiers in C++ control not visibility but the access of members. The classes shown below illustrate this.

```
int i;    // global variable

class A {
private:
  int i;
};

class B : public A {
  void f();
};

B::f()
{ i++;}        // error - A::i is private
```

An error occurs because the function f attempts to modify the variable i, which is inherited from class A, although it is inaccessible (because it is declared private:). If the access modifiers controlled visibility rather than accessibility, the variable i would be invisible, and the global variable i would have been updated.

Sibling instances.   Access modifiers define properties of a class, not of instances. Thus, private fields in C++ do not correspond exactly to the concept developed in our earlier general discussion of visibility. In that discussion, private data were accessible only to an object itself, whereas in C++ the private fields are accessible to any object of the same class. That is, in C++, an object is permitted to manipulate the private members of another instance of the same class.

As an example, consider the class declaration shown here. Here the rp and ip fields, representing the real and imaginary parts of a complex number, are marked as private.

```
class Complex {
public:
  Complex (double a, double b) { rp = a; ip = b; }
  Complex operator + ( Complex & x)
    { return Complex(rp + x.rp, ip + x.ip); }
private:
  double rp;
  double ip;
};
```

The binary operation + is overridden to provide a new meaning for the addition of two complex numbers. Despite the private nature of the rp and ip fields, the operator function is permitted to access these fields in the argument x because the argument and the receiver are of the same class.

Constructor and destructor functions, such as the constructor function Complex (just shown) are usually declared public. Declaring a constructor as protected implies that only subclasses or *friends* (see the subsequent discussion) can create instances of the class, while declaring it as private restricts creation only to friends or other instances of the class.

The weak form of the Law of Demeter can be enforced in part by declaration of all data fields as protected. The strong form is enforced by declaration of such fields as private.

While the access modifiers in C++ provide power and flexibility far in excess of the other languages we are considering, making effective use of these features requires foresight and experience. As with the question of whether to make a method virtual, one serious problem with the degree of control provided by C++ or Delphi Pascal is that the ease with which a subclass can be formed is often dependent on how much thought the designer of the original class gave to the possibility of subclassing. Being overly protective (declaring information private that should be protected) can make subclassing difficult. Problems arise if the subclass designer cannot modify the source form of the original class—for example, if the original is distributed as part of a library.

Private inheritance.   The keywords public and private also preface the name of a superclass in a class definition. When they are used in this fashion, the visibility of information from the superclass is altered by the modifier. A subclass that inherits publicly from another class corresponds to the notion of inheritance we have used up to this point—namely, that a subclass is also a subtype. If a subclass inherits privately, the public features of the superclass are reduced to the level of the modifier. In effect, this indicates that inheritance is being used only for construction and that the resulting class should not and cannot be considered a subtype of the original class.

When a class inherits privately from another class, instances of the subclass cannot be assigned to identifiers of the superclass type, as is possible with public inheritance. An easy way to remember this limitation is in terms of the is-a relationship. Public inheritance is an overt assertion that the is-a relationship holds, and thus an instance of the subclass can be used when the superclass is called for. A Dog is-a Mammal, for example, and so a Dog can be used in any situation in which a Mammal is called for. Private inheritance does not maintain the is-a relationship, since instances of a class that inherits in such a manner from a parent class cannot always be used in place of the parent class. Thus, it would not make sense to use a SymbolTable where an arbitrary type of Dictionary was required. If a variable is declared to be a type of Dictionary, we cannot assign a value of type SymbolTable to it (whereas we could if the inheritance were public).

Friend functions. Another aspect of visibility in C++ is a *friend function*. This is simply a function (not a method) that is declared by the friend modifier in the declaration of a class. Friend functions are permitted to read and write the private and protected fields within an object.

Consider the class declaration that follows, which extends the earlier complex-number class description.

```
class Complex {
public:
  Complex(double, double);
  friend double abs(Complex&);
private:
  double rp;
  double ip;

};

Complex::Complex(double a, double b)
{
  rp = a; ip = b;
}

double abs(Complex& x)
{   return sqrt(x.rp * x.rp + x.ip * x.ip); }
```

The fields rp and ip of the data structure representing complex numbers are declared to be private and thus are generally not accessible outside of methods associated with the class. The function abs—which, incidentally, overloads a function of the same name defined for double precision values—is not a method but simply a function. However, since the function has been declared a friend of the complex class, it is permitted to access all fields of the class, even private fields.

It is also possible to declare classes, and even individual methods in other classes, as friends. The most common reasons for using friend functions are that they require access to the internal structure of two or more classes or that it is necessary for the friend function to be invoked in a functional, rather than a message-passing, style (that is, as abs(x) instead of as x.abs()).

Friend functions are a powerful tool, but they are easy to abuse. In particular, they introduce exactly the sort of data couplings that we identified in the beginning of this chapter as detrimental to the development of reusable software. Whenever possible, more object-oriented encapsulation techniques (such as methods) should be preferred over friend functions. Nevertheless, there are times when no other tool can be used, such as when a function needs access to the internal structure of two or more class definitions. In these cases, friend functions are a useful abstraction.

Name spaces.   Yet another recent change in C++ is the introduction of *name spaces.* The namespace facility helps reduce the proliferation of global names. While the static keyword can limit the scope of a name to a single file, previously if a name needed to be shared between two or more files the only choice was to make the name global. Such values can now be enclosed within a name-space definition.

```
namespace myLibrary {
  int x;
  class A {
    .
    .
    .
  };
  class B : public A {
    .
    .
    .
  };
}
```

The variables defined within the name space are not global. If a programmer wishes to include the name space, he or she issues an explicit directive, which then places all top-level names defined in the name space in the current scope.

```
using namespace myLibrary;
```

Individual items can also be imported from a specific name space, either by explicitly naming the space or by importing just the single item.

```
myLibrary::A anA;  // explicitly name the name space
```

```
using myLibrary::B;  // import only the class B
B aNewB;     // B is now a type name
```

23.3.4   Visibility in Java

As we have seen in the examples of Java code in this book, in Java the modifiers public and private are placed individually on each data field and member function.

Java introduces an interesting new modifier named final. A final class cannot be subclassed, a final method cannot be overridden, and a final instance variable cannot be assigned to. Use of the final keyword permits the compiler to perform a number of optimizations.

As in C++, the private modifier in Java refers to classes, not instances. Sibling members of the same class are permitted access to each other's private data fields.

Another name-scoping facility provided by Java is the *package*—a group of classes and interfaces that serve as a tool for managing large name spaces and avoiding conflicts. A package is specified by the package statement, which must be the first statement in a file.

```
package packageName;
```

Code in one package can specify classes or interfaces from another package either by explicitly naming the package in which the object is found or by importing one package into another. The following illustrates the first mechanism.

```
// get type foo from package bar
bar.foo newObj = new bar.foo();
```

The importing of a package makes the names of all its public classes and interfaces available, just as if they were defined in the present file.

```
// import all objects and interfaces
// from package named bar
import bar.*;
foo newObj  = new foo();
```

If desired, individual objects or interfaces can be specified by use of a name in place of the wild-card character.

```
// import the name foo
// from the package bar
import bar.foo;
```

graphical ball object. The location of the ball, represented by the coordinates in the x and y fields, are publicly accessible, whereas the direction and energy of the ball are protected.

```
@interface Ball : Object
{
   double direction;
   double energy;
@public
   double x;
   double y;
}
@end
```

Unlike in instance-variable fields, it is possible to define methods in the implementation section of a class that are not declared in the interface section. Such methods are visible and can be invoked only within that portion of the program that follows the definition of the new method.

There is no way to create a method that can be invoked by subclass clients but not by user clients, and there is no way to create truly private instance-variable values.

23.4 ▫ Intentional Dependency

Although most often programmers attempt to avoid dependency in their code, there are situations where it is an essential component. A simulation, for example, might include a model that changes over time as the simulation progresses. Features of the model might be displayed graphically in one or more windows, and as the model changes, the windows should be continuously updated.

Yet a concern for reducing the coupling within the program should lead the programmer to avoid making too tight a connection between the model and the windows. In particular, there is no reason for the model to know the type or even the number of views in which it might be displayed. (There may be more than one view—for example, both a numeric or a graphical representation of a variable numeric quantity.) How can the model alert the views to update their displays without an explicit connection between the two?

One way to avoid a tight interconnection between dependent components is to use a *dependency manager*. Such a feature is a standard part of the Smalltalk and Objective-C run-time library but can be easily constructed in other languages, such as C++. The basic idea is for the dependency manager to act as the intermediary, maintaining a list of objects and the other components that depend on them. The model need know only about the dependency manager. The view objects "register" themselves with the dependency manager by indicating that they depend on the model object. Subsequently, when the model object changes, it sends a single message to the dependency manager, saying that it has changed and that all of its dependents should be notified. The dependents will then receive a message, sent by the dependency manager, indicating that the model has been modified and they should take appropriate action.

The dependency system works well at isolating components from each other, reducing the number of explicit links within a program. However, unlike the scheme described in Section 23.1.5, it works only when dependents know that someone may be waiting on their change. This scheme will not work when, as in the Reactor example, it is necessary to be as noninvasive of the original code as possible.

Summary ▫

Starting with this chapter we begin the investigation of the relationships between general objects—and not just those in a parent class/child class relationship. These connections can be described by the software engineering terms *coupling* and *cohesion*. We have examined a variety of different forms of coupling and how they affect the ability to form abstractions that are reusable and understandable.

The parent class/child class relationship means that there are two categories of clients that a class designer needs to consider. These two categories are clients formed by child classes and clients formed by more general users.

The chapter concluded by examining the features used to control visibility and coupling in the various languages.

Further Reading ▫

The issues of coupling and dependency have been investigated for many years by researchers in the software engineering community. See, for example [Gillett 1982, Fairley 1985].

The concepts of coupling and cohesion were introduced by Stevens, Constantine, and Myers [Stevens 1981].

The Law of Demeter was originally described in [Lieberherr 1989a, Lieberherr 1989b]. A detailed analysis of the Law of Demeter for C++ can be found in [Sakkinen 1988b].

The assertion that references to instance variable from within a method should always be mediated by accessor functions was presented by Wirfs-Brock and Wilkerson [Wirfs-Brock 1989a].

The categories of coupling presented in Section 23.1.1 are adapted from Fairley [Fairley 1985], although he does not discuss subclass coupling, and other terms have been changed slightly to make them more language independent.

The active value discussion is adapted from [Stefik 1986].

The observation that the mechanisms of inheritance and overriding mean that objects really have three faces was first made by Alan Snyder [Snyder 1986].

A good description of the importance of friend functions in C++ has been given by Andrew Koenig [Koenig 1989c].

The concept of intentional dependency is generalized to the observer design pattern, which we will discuss in Chapter 24.

Self-Study Questions ⊡

1. How are object connections related to name visibility?
2. What does the term *coupling* mean?
3. Why is internal data coupling a bad idea?
4. What is the difference between file scope (package scope in some languages) and program scope?
5. What is sequence coupling?
6. What is component coupling? Why do we say that this coupling is only one way?
7. What is parameter coupling?
8. What is the term used for the relationship between a parent class and a child class?
9. What is cohesion?
10. What are the varieties of cohesion?
11. What type of data access is ruled out by the Law of Demeter?
12. What is the difference between class level and object level visibility?
13. What is the distinction between a subclass client and a user client?
14. What capabilities is a friend permitted in C++ that other objects are not?

Exercises ⊡

1. Design a tool that can examine programs written in your favorite object-oriented language and report violations of the Law of Demeter.

2. The strong form of the Law of Demeter prevents access to inherited instance variables. Describe the advantages and disadvantages of this restriction. Consider issues such as the coupling between classes and the effect on the understandability of code.

3. Do you think the strong form of the Law of Demeter also should have restricted access to global variables? Support your opinion by well-reasoned arguments. You might want to look at the article by Wulf and Shaw [Wulf 1973] in preparing your answer.

4. What other concrete rules, similar to the Law of Demeter, can you think of in which (1) the satisfaction of the law usually leads to systems with fewer interconnections and more cohesion and (2) exceptions in which the rule must be violated are rare. In particular, the Law of Demeter addresses coupling between different objects. Can you think of a guideline that encourages greater cohesion within an object?

5. There is an alternative level of visibility that, like protected (subclass client) data, is also more restrictive than public information and less restrictive than information to which access is permitted only inside an object. Under this alternative, instances of the same class have access to the internal state of an object even when such access is denied to all others. In C++, for example, an object can access any field in another instance of the class, even if those fields are private or protected. In other languages, such as Smalltalk, this style of access is not permitted. Discuss the advantages and disadvantages of each approach.

6. Another possible variation on visibility rules for subclass clients is to permit access to an immediate ancestor class but not to more distant ancestors. Discuss the advantages and disadvantages of this rule. (This issue is presented in [Snyder 1986].)

7. Of the languages we are considering, only C++ and Delphi Pascal have explicit facilities for distinguishing features accessible to subclass clients from those accessible to user clients. Nevertheless, all languages have some mechanism for describing the programmer's intent through the use of comments. Often, structured comments, such as compiler directives, are used to provide optional information to a language system. Describe a commenting convention that could denote levels of visibility. Then outline an algorithm that could be used by a software tool to enforce the visibility rules.

CHAPTER 24

Design Patterns

When faced with the task of solving a new problem, most people will consider first previous problems they have encountered that seem to have characteristics in common with the new assignment. These previous problems can be used as a model, and the new problem can be attacked in a similar fashion, making changes as necessary to fit the different circumstances.

This insight lies behind the idea of a software *design pattern*. A pattern is really nothing more than an attempt to document a proven solution to a problem so that future problems can be more easily handled in a similar fashion.

Patterns have become important in the development of object-oriented programming because they aid in discussing structures and relationships at a different and higher level of abstraction than do classes, instances, or components. Recall the presentation of levels of abstraction from Chapter 2. At the highest level of abstraction an object-oriented program is viewed as a community of interacting agents.

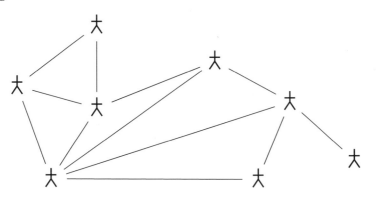

Certain types of relationships appear over and over in many different object-oriented applications. A pattern attempts to distill the essential features of these associations. The practice of collecting and recording patterns serves two important purposes:

- It speeds the process of finding a solution when the next problem comes along with similar characteristics (eliminating the need to "reinvent the wheel").
- Almost as important, the *naming* of patterns gives programmers a common vocabulary with which to discuss design alternatives. This vocabulary is often termed a *pattern language*.

Since patterns deal with connections and relationships among parts, it is perhaps not surprising that the idea was first adapted from techniques developed by architects. In fact, many people continue this analogy, declaring that design patterns are used to document software architecture.

24.1 ▫ Controlling Information Flow

Many design patterns deal with managing the information that must flow across a client/server boundary.[1] Normally one wants to reduce as far as possible the information that must pass over this boundary and to make the process of connecting as simple as possible.

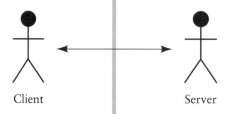

Client   Server

This idea of a pattern is perhaps best illustrated by an example. One of the easiest patterns to describe is the adapter. Suppose you have one object in your community (a client) that needs a service and requires a specific interface. Imagine you have another object that provides the functionality you need but does not happen to support the desired interface. Rather than rewriting either the client or the service provider, you can get the two to communicate with each other by creating an *adapter*. The adapter simply speaks the language of the requester, but

---

1. Again, we are using the term *server* in the sense of an object that provides a service and not necessarily in the sense of a file or Web server. We will briefly look at network servers in Chapter 26.

rather than doing the work itself, it translates into the interface used by the service provider.

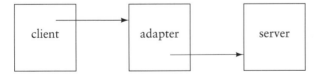

The following is an example of an adapter. The client has an interface named Collection that is described by the methods isEmpty, size, addElement, containsElement, and findElement. The server has a data structure that will hold the values but uses the interface count, add, and find. The adapter connects the two, translating requests from one language into the other.

```
class MyCollection implements Collection {

  public boolean isEmpty ()
    { return data.count() == 0; }
  public int size ()
    { return data.count(); }
  public void addElement (Object newElement)
    {data.add(newElement); }
  public boolean containsElement (Object test)
    { return data.find(test) != null; }
  public Object findElement (Object test)
    { return data.find(test); }

  private DataBox data = new DataBox();
}
```

The characteristic of the adapter is the change in the interface and the fact that the adapter itself does little work, but for the most part passes requests along to the service provider.

24.2 □ Describing Patterns

In their application to computer science, design patterns have evolved their own special format. A pattern will typically be described by a narrative that includes some or all of the following parts.

name   The term that will be used to describe the pattern. By means of these names a collection of patterns creates a vocabulary with which various different design alternatives can be discussed.

synopsis A short description of the problem the pattern is designed to solve.

forces A description of the requirements for a pattern or the considerations that must be taken into account in the use of the pattern.

solution The essence of the solution.

counterforces A description of reasons that might need to be considered in deciding to *not* use a pattern.

related patterns This section describes related patterns the user might want to consider in the solution to their problem.

Not all sections need be found in all pattern descriptions. The following describes an adapter in pattern format.

name The adapter pattern. (The term is derived from a comparison to electrical outlet adapters, such the type one might use when traveling abroad.)

synopsis Used to connect a client who needs a service described using one interface with a provider who implements the desired functionality but uses a different interface.

solution The adapter implements the interface as specified by the client, but rather than performing the given operations, passes the work on to the service provider.

counterforces Adds one layer of indirection between the client and provider and also introduces another class of object.

In the sections that follow we will describe some of the more common patterns and how they relate to object-oriented systems. Many of these patterns have already been encountered elsewhere in this book.

24.3 ▫ Iterator

The idea of an iterator was introduced in Chapter 19. The iterator is sometimes also termed an enumerator or an enumeration (although technically the enumeration is the sequence that is produced using an enumerator). An iterator is used when a server is maintaining a collection of values for a client. The iterator is used to reduce the amount of information that a client must know in order to have access to the elements in the collection.

Imagine an object that is maintaining a simple data structure, such as a sorted list. There are various different ways to maintain such a collection—for example, a linked list, a vector, or a binary tree. In general, the client need not have any information regarding the implementation technique being used by the service provider.

Now imagine that the client desires to create a loop that will iterate over the elements in the collection. The exact sequence of operations needed to do this is very different for a vector than for a binary tree. But the server seeks to keep this information hidden from the client.

The solution to this problem involves the server first publishing the interface it will use. For example, iterators in Java use the following interface.

```
interface Enumerator {
  public boolean hasMoreElements();
  public Object nextElement();
}
```

The server then provides the client with an implementation that matches the interface. The details of how the iterator operates need not concern the client, who can simply use the published interface to access the elements.

```
Enumerator e = ...;
while (e.hasMoreElements) {
  Object val = e.nextElement();
    .
    .
    .
}
```

Note that the iterator and the data structure from which it obtains values will almost always have to share detailed information with each other, but this is acceptable because both live on the same side of the client/server division.

24.4 □ Software Factory

The technique described in the previous section that allowed the data structure to interact with a client can be generalized and is found in a number of other situations. It is applicable whenever there are a variety of alternative implementations for a particular task and the client need not have precise knowledge of the implementation being used.

Let us describe the features that are characteristic of the factory method as it is embodied in the iterator problem. First, there was a simple interface that was shared between the client and server.

```
interface Enumerator {
  public boolean hasMoreElements();
  public Object nextElement();
}
```

Next, the server included as part of its interface a method that would yield an instance of this class. This method is the "factory" in the name of the pattern.

```
class SortedList {
   .
   .
   .
   public Enumerator elements();
   .
   .
   .
}
```

But while the factory method claims to be returning an instance of the interface, in reality it returns a subclass that implements the interface. It is returning a more specialized form—for example, a BinaryTreeEnumerator. Different objects might return instances of other child classes while preserving the same interface. In fact, in some cases the same factory might return different child values in response to different circumstances. It is the fact that the server returns a more specialized class than the method signature would indicate that is indicative of the factory method.

24.5 ⊡ Strategy

Closely related to the factory method is the structure described as the *strategy* design pattern. An example of this pattern is found in the AWT user interface system. In that example the server (the AWT system) is assisting in the presentation of graphical information. The server, however, does not know exactly how the client wishes to display the various graphical elements. There are a number of alternatives. Components can be laid out in the four edges of a window, laid out in a grid, or in a variety of other possibilities. But the knowledge of exactly how to create a layout is complex, certainly not something we can expect the client to do.

The solution is that the server prepares a number of alternative implementations of a common interface. In the AWT the interface is termed a LayoutManager, and the various alternatives go by names such as GridLayout, BorderLayout, and so on. The client then selects from among the choices and hands it back to the server. In this fashion the client has control over the appearance without needing to know exactly how the display is being implemented.

The characteristic feature of the strategy pattern is that the server presents the client with a number of choices, typically expressed as different implementations of a common interface. The client selects one of the alternatives and gives it back to the server.

24.6 ▫ Singleton

Not all design patterns deal with client/server interactions. Another common pattern is the *singleton*. In this pattern the developer of a class wants to ensure that there will never be more than one instance of the class created. This objective can be realized in various different ways in different languages.

In C++ (or Java or C#) a singleton can be created by declaring a constructor as private. Because the constructor is private, no object outside the class definition is permitted to access it, and hence no instances can be formed. But a static data field that is created within the class can be initialized using the constructor. By making the field public, the programmer permits access to the one and only instance of the class.

```
class SingletonClass {
public:
   static SingletonClass * oneAndOnly () { return theOne; }
private:
   static SingletonClass * theOne;
   SingletonClass () { ... }
};

   // static initialization
SingletonClass * SingletonClass::theOne = new SingletonClass();
```

In Smalltalk and Objective-C a singleton can be created by redefining the operator new as a class method. An example is the boolean value true, which is an instance of the class True. The class method new in class True is defined as follows.

```
"class method True"
  {new}
    ↑ true
```

Any attempt to create another instance of the class will simply yield the existing value.

Another way to create singleton objects in Java is through the use of anonymous classes (Section 8.7.1).

24.7 ▫ Composite

The problem addressed by the composite design pattern is how to permit the creation of complex objects using only simple parts. The solution is to provide a small collection of simple components but also allow these components to be nested arbitrarily. The resulting composite objects allow individual objects and compositions of objects to be treated uniformly. Frequently, an interesting feature

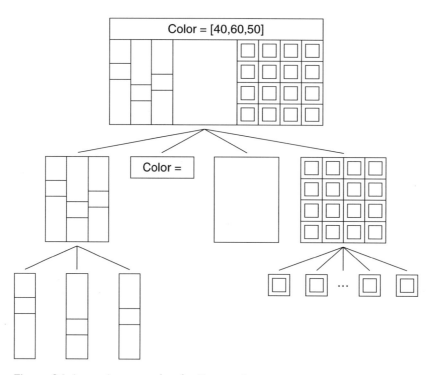

⊡ Figure 24.1 ——An example of a Composite

of the composition pattern is the merging of the is-a relation with the has-a relation.

A good example of composition in the Java library is the creation of design layouts through the interaction of Components and Containers. There are only five simple types of layouts provided by the standard library, and of these five only two, border layouts and grid layouts, are commonly used. Each item in a layout is a Component. Composition occurs because Containers are also Components. A container holds its own layout, which is again one of only a few simple varieties. Yet the container is treated as a unit in the original layout.

The structure of a composite object is often described in a tree-like format. Consider, for example, the layout of the window shown at the top of Figure 24.1. (A screen shot of this application was given in Chapter 22, Figure 22.4.) At the application level there are four elements to the layout. These are a text area, a simple blank panel, and two panels that hold composite objects. One of these composite panels holds three scroll bars, and the second is holding a grid of 16 buttons. By nesting panels one within another, arbitrarily complex layouts can be created.

Another example of composition is the class SequenceInputStream, which is used to catenate two or more input streams so that they appear to be a single input source. A SequenceInputStream is-an InputStream (meaning it extends the class InputStream). But a SequenceInputStream also has-an InputStream as part of its internal state. By combining inheritance and composition, the class permits multiple sequences of input sources to be treated as a single unit.

This pattern is useful whenever it is necessary to build complex structures out of a few simple elements. Note that the merging of the is-a and has-a relations is also characteristic of the *Decorator* pattern (see next section), although decorators can be constructed that are not composites.

24.8 ▫ Decorator

A *decorator* (also sometimes termed a *filter* or a *wrapper*[2]) is one of a number of patterns that deal with how new functionality can be attached to existing objects. The inheritance relationship is one way to do this, since child classes can add new behavior to that provided by their parent classes. But inheritance is a very static and heavyweight technique and does not permit values to change their behavior dynamically during execution. A decorator wraps around an existing object and satisfies the same requirements (for example, is subclassed from the same parent class or implements the same interface). The wrapper delegates much of the responsibility to the original but occasionally adds new functionality.

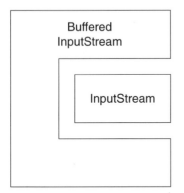

An example of the decorator is found in the Java I/O library. The class InputStream provides a way to read bytes from an input device, such as a file. The class BufferedInputStream is a subclass of InputStream, adding the ability to buffer the

2. The wrapper design pattern should not be confused with the use of the term *wrapper* in CLOS, which we described in Chapter 16, or the wrapper classes for primitive data types, which we discussed in Chapter 19.

input so that it can be reset to an earlier point and values can be reread two or more times. Furthermore, a BufferedInputStream can take an InputStream as argument in its constructor.

```
// a buffered input stream is-an input stream
class BufferedInputStream extends InputStream {

    public BufferedInputStream (InputStream s) { data = s; }
    .
    .
    .


    // and a buffered input stream has-an input stream
    private InputStream data;
}
```

Because a BufferedInputStream both *is* an InputStream and *has* an input stream as part of its data, it can be easily wrapped around an existing input stream. Due to inheritance and substitutability, the BufferedInputStream can be used where the original InputStream was expected. Because it holds the original input stream, any actions unrelated to the buffering activities are simply passed on to the original stream.

A decorator, or wrapper class, is often a flexible alternative to the use of subclassing. Functionality can be added or removed simply by adding or deleting wrappers around an object.

24.9 ◻ The Double-Dispatching Pattern

The double-dispatching pattern occurs when there are two or more sources of variation in an exchange. Suppose, for example, that we have a variety of polygon shapes represented by a general class Shape and various subclasses (Triangle, Square, and the like). We also have two types of output devices—say, a printer and a terminal—represented by subclasses of Device. The graphics commands necessary to perform printing operations for these devices are sufficiently different that no general interface is possible. Instead, each shape itself encapsulates information concerning how to display on a printer and how to display on a terminal.

```
class Triangle : public Shape {
public:
    Triangle (Point, Point, Point);
        .
    // :
        .
    virtual void displayOnPrinter (Printer);
    virtual void displayOnTerminal (Terminal);
```

```
// :
private:
  Point p1, p2, p3;
};
```

The question is how to handle two polymorphic variables: one a Shape (which could be any subclass of class Shape) and the other a Device. The clue to this pattern is that message passing can be used to "tie down" one of the two values. To determine both, we simply make each value a receiver for a message in turn. (The extension of the idea to three or more variables is then obvious—simply make each unknown a receiver in turn.)

For example, we first pass the device a command and then pass the shape as argument. This command is deferred and redefined in each of the subclasses of Device. Message passing therefore selects the right function to be executed. An example might be the following.

```
function Printer.display (Shape aShape)
begin
   aShape.displayOnPrinter (self);
end;


function Terminal.display (Shape aShape)
begin
   aShape.displayOnTerminal (self);
end;
```

Note that the display method has no idea what type of form is being generated. But each of the methods—displayOnPrinter and displayOnTerminal—is itself deferred, defined in class Shape and redefined in every subclass. Suppose that the shape is indeed a triangle. By the time the method in class Triangle is executed, both sources of variation—the shape and the printing device—have been bound to specific quantities.

```
void Triangle.displayOnPrinter (Printer p)
{
   // :  printer-specific code to display triangle

}


void Triangle.displayOnTerminal (Terminal t)
{
   // :  terminal-specific code to display triangle

}
```

The major difficulty with this technique is the large number of methods it requires. Notice, for example, that every shape must have a different method for every printing device. Nevertheless, it is very efficient for handling variability in two or more quantities.

24.10 ▫ Flyweight

How can one reduce the storage costs associated with a large number of objects that have similar state? A solution is to share state in common with similar objects, thereby reducing the storage required by any single object.

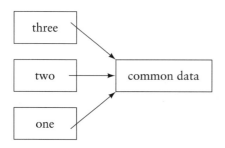

For example, in many languages all instances of a class point to a common data value. This data value maintains information concerning the class, such as the class name and the description of the methods to which instances of the class will respond. If this information were to be duplicated in each object, the memory costs would be prohibitive. Instead, this information is defined once by an object of type Class, and each instance of the class points to this object.

The objects that share common information are known as *flyweights*, since their memory requirements are reduced (often dramatically) by moving part of their state to the shared value. The flyweight pattern can be used whenever there are a large number of objects that share a significant common internal state.

24.11 ▫ Proxy

A proxy is very similar to the adapter pattern we discussed at the beginning of the chapter. An example problem that might be addressed using the proxy design pattern is how to hide details such as transmission protocols when communicating over a network to remote objects. Like the adapter the proxy is not actually doing the major part of the work. However, rather than simply changing the interface, the proxy is maintaining the interface but hiding some of the work. It does this by acting as a surrogate or placeholder for another object—the object that is really doing the work.

The idea of a proxy is that one object is standing in place of another. The first object receives requests for the second and generally forwards the requests to the second, after processing them in some fashion.

An example proxy in the Java Library is the RMI, or Remote Method Invocation system. The RMI is a mechanism that can be used to coordinate Java programs running on two or more machines. Using the RMI, a proxy object is created that runs on the same machine as the client. When the client invokes a method on the proxy, the proxy transmits the method across the network to the server on another machine. The server handles the request, then transmits the result back to the proxy. The proxy hands the result back to the client. In this fashion, the details of transmission over the network are handled by the proxy and the server and are hidden from the client.

24.12 ▫ Facade

A facade is similar to a proxy, but the actual work involved in servicing requests from the client is not done by a single object, but rather by a collection of interacting objects. The intermediary acts as a focal point, handing off requests to the appropriate handler. It hides the need to remember all the objects performing the actual service by providing a single simple interface.

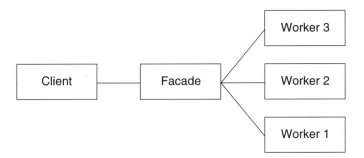

24.13 ▫ Observer

The last pattern we will describe is the observer. The problem addressed by the observer pattern is how two objects can stay synchronized with each other without having direct knowledge of each other. This may be desirable if, for example, one or both parties to this transaction are dynamically created and destroyed during the course of execution.

For example, a simulation might have a *model*, a part that is doing the actual work of the simulation, and a *view*, the portion of the program charged with displaying the results of the simulation. There might even be more than one view, and the user might be allowed to select views dynamically. Therefore, the designer of the system does not want to have the model cluttered with details such as all the current views. On the other hand, when the model changes, we certainly want the view or views to be updated as well.

This loose coupling between the two parties is achieved by creating an intermediary, the ObserverManager. The ObserverManager communicates with both the model (the object being observed) and the observers. The model and the observers need not, then, have any direct interaction with each other.

The ObserverManager maintains a list of objects being observed and their observers. Observers register themselves with the manager and can remove themselves if they no longer wish to be notified (for example, if they represent a window that is being deleted). When the model changes, it tells the ObserverManager that all its observers should be notified. The ObserverManager then cycles through the list of observers and passes to each of them a message that the model has changed. The result is a very loose and flexible connection between the model and the elements watching the model.

Summary ⊡

A design pattern captures the salient characteristics of a solution to a commonly observed problem, hiding details that are particular to any one situation. By examining design patterns, programmers learn about techniques that have proven to be useful in previous problems and are therefore likely to be useful in new situations.

As illustrated by these examples, an important aspect of design patterns is that they provide a vocabulary for discussing solutions to problems. This common vocabulary allows groups of programmers to share ideas in an application-independent fashion, and it provides a means by which to codify and pass on knowledge and tradition from one project to the next.

In this chapter we examined the following design patterns.

iterator   Used when a server wants to provide a client with access to elements in a collection without exposing the internal organization of the container.

software factory   Used when a client needs only a very general description of a task and the server must provide a more specialized implementation of the task.

strategy Used when a server seeks to provide a client with a choice of alternative techniques but the details of how each choice is implemented need not be a concern to the client.

singleton Used when for one reason or another a class should have at most one instance.

composite Permits the creation of complex objects by allowing simple parts to be combined in a variety of different ways.

decorator An alternative to inheritance, allows new functionality to be dynamically added to an existing object.

double-dispatch Uses inheritance as a means to classify along two or more sources of variation.

flyweight Allows the burden of sharing common information to be amortized over a number of objects.

proxy Allows certain information, such as a network protocol, to be hidden from the end client.

facade Combines the effort of a number of workers behind a single interface.

observer Provides a framework that permits two objects to observe each other without having direct connections.

Finally, it should be emphasized that though patterns may be useful in exposing the developer of an application to many alternative design possibilities, selecting a pattern is not a substitute for developing a solution. That is, the pattern simply lays out the broad outlines of a solution; filling in the details may still require considerable effort.

Further Reading ▫

The origin of the idea of patterns in architecture is the book by Christopher Alexander [Alexander 1977].

The most important reference for design patterns is [Gamma 1995], by Erich Gamma, Richard Helm, Ralph Johnson, and John Vlissides (commonly known as the Gang of Four, or GOF). Another recent book on patterns is by Richard Gabriel [Gabriel 1996]. Design patterns in Java are discussed in the two-volume collection by Mark Grand [Grand 1998, Grand 1999]. An entertaining introduction to patterns in Java is the book by Felleisen and Friedman [Felleisen 1998].

Double dispatching was first described by Dan Ingalls [Ingalls 1986], who called the technique *multiple polymorphism*. The alternative term *double dispatching* has come to be more widely used to avoid confusion with *multiple inheritance*. Double dispatching is also discussed in [Ingalls 1986, Budd 1991, LaLonde 1990a, Hebel 1990].

While individual patterns may be relatively easy to describe, a more complicated problem is developing a categorization technique that can be used to record and recall patterns in later projects. Much of the current work in this area involves creating such knowledge bases [Gamma 1995, Coplien 1995, Pree 1995, Rising 2000].

The idea of a design pattern has been applied to many other areas. A recent catalog by Linda Rising [Rising 2000] presents literally hundreds of patterns from all different problem domains.

Self-Study Questions ▫

1. What is the most important purpose of a design pattern?
2. What is a pattern language?
3. What are the characteristic features of the adapter design pattern?
4. In a pattern description, what are forces and counterforces?
5. What problem is addressed using an iterator?
6. What is the characteristic feature of the software factory design pattern?
7. In the strategy design pattern, why does the server provide a number of alternative objects that each implement the same interface?
8. What is a singleton object?
9. Explain why both the is-a and has-a relationships are intrinsic features in forming a composite.
10. In what ways does the decorator design pattern have features in common with a composite? In what ways are they different?
11. What does the word "double" refer to in the title of the double dispatching pattern?
12. What are the characteristics of a flyweight object?
13. How is a proxy similar to an adapter? How is it different?
14. How is a facade similar to a proxy? How is it different?
15. What problem is being addressed by the observer design pattern?

Exercises ▫

1. Some implementations of Smalltalk use double dispatching to resolve the conflict between integer and floating point arithmetic in expressions such as x + y. Sketch the methods needed in order to do this.
2. In Chapter 19 we described two approaches to looping: the use of iterators and the idea of visitors. Extract the key ideas, and rewrite the concept of a visitor as a design pattern.
3. In what ways is a design pattern similar to a software framework? In what ways are they different?

CHAPTER 25

Reflection and Introspection

The terms *reflection* and *introspection* refer to the ability of a program during execution to "learn" something about itself. The first term suggests the mental image of a program examining itself in a mirror, which is a useful metaphor. The mechanisms for reflection allow the program to examine its own internal state in more detail than is possible in languages that do not have reflection facilities. In some languages, the program can even add new behavior to itself as it is executing.

We can divide the mechanisms used in reflection and introspection into two broad categories. The first group are features designed to gain *understanding* concerning the current state of computation. These mechanisms yield information but do not add any new behavior to the program. The second group consists of features intended for *modification*. These add new behavior to the program as it is executing. We will examine the tools provided for understanding in Section 25.1 and the tools for modification in Section 25.3.

25.1 ▫ Mechanisms for Understanding

25.1.1 Class objects

Almost all reflection facilities begin with an *object* that is the dynamic (run-time) embodiment of a *class*. We have examined class objects several times since we first encountered them in Chapter 4. Such a class object is not an instance of the class it is defining, although instances are often linked to their associated class objects. The class object is instead an instance of a more general class, often called Class. The information held by and the behavior exhibited by class objects differ from

Language	Example	Type
C++	`typeinfo aClass = typeid(aVariable);`	typeinfo
CLOS	`(class-of aVariable)`	standard-class
Delphi Pascal	`aClass := aVariable.ClassType;`	TClass
Java	`Class aClass = aVariable.getClass();`	Class
Smalltalk	`aClass <- aVariable class`	Class

▫ Table 25.1 —— Accessing class objects in various languages

language to language but typically include the name of the class, the amount of memory occupied by instances of the class, and the ability to create new instances.

Table 25.1 illustrates how class objects can be obtained starting from a generic object named aVariable and yielding a value named aClass. The table also provides the class (or type) that aClass represents. (The idea that a class object must itself be an instance of a class is something we will take up further in Section 25.4.)

Generally the variable used in expressions such as those shown in Table 25.1 is a polymorphic variable, in the sense of Chapter 17. It would make little sense for the programmer to ask for the class of a nonpolymorphic variable, since he or she would already know all there is to know about the value. In Java the class value for a known class, such as String, can be accessed using the following notation.

```
Class aClass = String.class;
```

One common operation that can be performed with a class object is to retrieve its parent class.

CLOS
```
(class-precedence-list aClass)
```

Java
```
Class parentClass = aClass.getSuperclass();
```

Smalltalk
```
parentClass <- aClass superclass
```

In some languages the objects that represent subclasses are also maintained by their parent class. These can be returned in the form of a collection.

CLOS
```
(subclasses aClass)
```

Smalltalk
```
aSet <- aClass subclasses
```

In some languages it is possible to obtain a class object from the textual string name for the class.

Java

```
Class aClass = Class.forName("ClassName");
```

In the following sections we will describe some of the information that can be obtained using a class value.

25.1.2 The class name as string

A fundamental bit of information that is often useful in debugging is the class name represented as a string. This is easily obtained from the class object. In some languages this information can also be obtained from the original variable itself. In Delphi it can only be obtained from the original variable. Example statements that illustrate these facilities are shown following.

C++

```
char * name = typeinfo(aVariable).name();
```

CLOS

```
(class-name aClass)
```

Delphi Pascal

```
     (* result is a ShortString *)
aString := aVariable.ClassName;
```

Java

```
String internalName = aClass.getName();
String descriptiveName = aClass.toString();
```

Smalltalk

```
name <- aClass asString
```

25.1.3 Testing the class of an object

In the discussion of reverse polymorphism in Chapter 17, we mentioned how it is possible to determine if a polymorphic variable is actually holding an instance of a specific child class. The details of this test are shown following.

C++

```
Child * c = dynamic_cast<Child *>(aParentPtr);
if (c != 0) { // null if not legal, nonnull if ok
    .
    .
    .
```

```
}
```

Delphi Pascal

```
if (aVariable is Child) then
    childVar := aVariable as Child
```

Java

```
if (aVariable instanceof Child) ...
      or
if (aClass.isInstance(aVariable)) ...
```

Obcron-2

```
IF aVariable IS Child THEN
    aChild := aVariable(Child)
END
```

Object Pascal

```
if Member (aVariable, Child) then
    aChild = Child(aVariable)
```

Python

```
if isinstance(aVariable, Child):
    .
    .
    .
```

Smalltalk

```
(aVariable isMemberOf: aClass) ifTrue: [ ... ]
```

However, it should be noted that the inappropriate use of this type of test is often a sign of a poorly designed class structure. More often than not an explicit test can be replaced by an invocation of an overridden method. To illustrate, assume we have a class hierarchy with an ancestor class and two child classes.

Suppose next that it is necessary to perform different actions, depending on the specific type being held by a polymorphic variable. Testing the class directly, this could be performed as follows.

```
Pet p = ...;
if (p instanceof Cat) {
    // do Cat specific actions
```

.
.
.

```
} else if (p instanceof Dog) {
  // do Dog specific actions
```

.
.
.

```
} else {
  System.err.println("value is unknown class");
}
```

A better solution would be to create a new method and move the child-specific actions to the child classes. The default action can be moved to the parent class. The same effect as the switch can then be achieved with a single statement.

```
Pet p = ...
p.newMethod(); // do the appropriate action
```

Not only is this code shorter, it is also less error prone. Suppose a new child class is added. It is only necessary to ensure the class implements the correct interface. In the code written using conditional statements, it would be necessary to track down every occurrence of the conditional switch and add a new if statement.

Testing the ancestry of an object. Although less common than testing if an object is an instance of a specific class, it is occasionally necessary to determine if an object is an instance of a class that descends from a given parent class. Techniques for doing this are shown following.

C++

```
if (typeid(aVariable).before(typeid(anotherVariable)))
```

Delphi Pascal

```
if (aVariable.InheritsFrom(AncestorClass)) ...
```

Python

```
if issubclass(Child, Parent):
```

.
.
.

Smalltalk

```
(aVariable isKindOf: AncestorClass) ifTrue: [ ... ]
```

25.1.4 Creating an instance from a class

In many languages it is possible to pass a message to a class object that will have the effect of creating a new instance of the class.

CLOS

```
(make-instance aClass)
```

Java

```
Object newValue = aClass.newInstance();
```

Smalltalk

```
newValue <- aClass new
```

In Java the method will only work if the given object can be initialized by a constructor with no arguments. However, it is possible to retrieve a list of all constructors for a given class, and with this, one can execute a constructor method, passing it a list of arguments.

25.1.5　Testing if an object understands a message

In some languages you can determine whether an object understands a message, independently of the class of the object. Techniques for doing this are shown following.

Delphi Pascal

```
if (aVariable.MethodAddress("message") <> null) ...
```

Smalltalk

```
(aVariable respondsTo: #message) ifTrue: [ ... ]
```

25.1.6　Class behavior

Class methods in Java.　Here are a few of the methods defined for class Class in Java.

Class	forName (String)
Class	getSuperclass ()
Constructor [ ]	getConstructors ()
Field	getField (String)
Field [ ]	getFields ()
Method [ ]	getDeclaredMethods ()
boolean	isArray()
boolean	isAssignableFrom (Class cls)
boolean	isInstance (Object obj)
boolean	isInterface ()
Object	newInstance ()

Methods such as isArray or isInterface can be used to determine properties of a class. The method newInstance can be used to create an instance of the class. The constructor with no arguments is used to initialize the object, throwing an exception if an object cannot be constructed in this fashion. Methods exist to return an array of methods for a class, or an array of data fields, or an individual field given its name.

Class behavior in Smalltalk.   In a very early chapter we described how classes were defined by passing a message to the class object that would ultimately be the parent class.

```
Object subclass: #PlayingCard
  instanceVariableNames: 'rank suit'
  classVariableNames: ' '
  category: 'Playing Card Application'
```

A table describing the behavior of Class in Smalltalk would include the following.

subclasses	immediate subclasses
superclass	parent class
inheritsFrom:	test ancestry
instSize	number of instance variables
instVarNames	variables defined in class
allInstVarNames	includes those inherited
selectors	methods defined in class
allSelectors	includes inherited methods
respondsTo:	test for message selector

Using these methods the user can discover all the methods a class defines (stored as a Dictionary), all the instance variables, and various other facts about a class.

25.2 □ Methods as Objects

Both Smalltalk and Java, and a few other object-oriented languages, treat methods as objects that can be accessed and manipulated. For example, a method in Java is an instance of class Method, a class that defines the following operations.

String	getName ()
Class	getDeclaringClass ()
int	getModifiers ()

Class   getReturnType
Class [ ]   getParameterTypes ()
 Object   invoke (Object receiver, Object [ ] args)

The latter definition can be used to execute a method, passing it as argument to the receiver and any arguments. The following illustrates this use. First, the class in which the method is declared is captured as a variable of type Class. Next, an array of parameter types for the method must be constructed. The method we seek, concat, requires a single value of type String. Using the method getMethod we find the code we want. We then construct an array of arguments and pass the argument array along with a receiver to the method, using the message selector invoke.

```
Class sc = String.class;
Class [ ] paramTypes = new Class[1];
paramTypes[0] = sc;
try {
  Method mt = sc.getMethod("concat", paramTypes);
  Object mtArgs [ ] = { "xyz" };
  Object result = mt.invoke("abc", mtArgs);
  System.out.println("result is " + result);
} catch (Exception e) {
  System.out.println("Exception " + e);
}
```

The result is the catenation of the two strings.

```
result is abcxyz
```

25.3 ⊡ Mechanisms for Modification

Mechanisms that allow a running program to modify itself are much less common in object-oriented languages, and so we will describe such facilities in longer, language-specific sections.

25.3.1   Method editing in Smalltalk

The user edits the string representation of a method. When the user is finished with edits, the following message is given to a class.

```
aClass compile: methodString
```

If compilation is successful, the method is entered into the class method dictionary and becomes part of the class behavior.

New classes are similarly formed by means of a message. The message is given to the parent class, instructing it to create a new child class. The child class object is returned as the result.

```
ParentClass subclass: 'ClassName'
   instanceVariableNames: #(a b c)
   classVariableNames: #(x y z)
```

Facilities also exit to read from a file (to *file in*) a textual description of classes and methods and to create and compile the appropriate objects.

25.3.2 Dynamic class loading in Java

The Java standard library defines a class named ClassLoader that can be used to load a class from a description stored in a file. The class is declared as abstract, so to use this facility the programmer must first define a new loader that subclasses from ClassLoader. The following is a simple example.

```java
import java.io.*;

class SimpleClassLoader extends ClassLoader {
   public Class getClass (String name) {
     Class theClass = null;
     try {
       File f = new File(name);
       InputStream is = new FileInputStream(f);
       int bufsize = (int) f.length();
       byte buf [] = new byte[bufsize];
       is.read(buf, 0, bufsize);
       is.close();
       theClass = defineClass (null, buf, 0, buf.length);
     } catch (Exception e) {
       System.err.println("Error during load " + e);
       System.exit(1);
     }
     return theClass;
   }
}
```

The class opens a file from the argument string, reads the contents, then uses the inherited method defineClass to construct a class object.

Using some of the reflection features described in Section 25.1.6, we could create the following simple program.

```
import java.io.*;
import java.lang.reflect.*;

class Main {
  public static void main (String [ ] args) {
    SimpleClassLoader simpload = new SimpleClassLoader();
    Class newClass = simpload.getClass(args[0]);
      // first print class name
    System.out.println("class name " + newClass.getName());
      // now print some of the features of the class
    Field [ ] fields = newClass.getFields();
    for (int i = 0; i < fields.length; i++) {
      System.out.println("field " + fields[i].getName() +
        " " + fields[i].getType());
    }
      // now print out the methods
    Method [ ] methods = newClass.getMethods();
    for (int i = 0; i < methods.length; i++) {
      Method aMethod = methods[i];
      System.out.println("method " + aMethod.getName() +
        ":" + aMethod.getReturnType());
      Class [ ] ptypes = aMethod.getParameterTypes();
      for (int j = 0; j < ptypes.length; j++) {
        System.out.println("parameter " + j +
          " type " + ptypes[j].getName());
      }
    }
  }
}
```

Assume, for example, that the programmer has created the following class definition.

```
class Sample {
  public int a;
  public int b;
  private Double c;

  public Sample () { a = 3; }

  public void setA (int ia) { ia = a; }

  public void setBC (int ib, Double ic)
    { b = ib; c = ic; }
}
```

Executing the main program with the file name Sample.class yields the following output.

```
class name Sample
field a int
field b int
method equals:boolean
parameter 0 type java.lang.Object
method getClass:class java.lang.Class
method hashCode:int
method notify:void
method notifyAll:void
method toString:class java.lang.String
method wait:void
method wait:void
parameter 0 type long
method wait:void
parameter 0 type long
parameter 1 type int
method setA:void
parameter 0 type int
method setBC:void
parameter 0 type int
parameter 1 type java.lang.Double
```

Notice that the list of methods includes those inherited from the parent class Object.

25.4 ◻ Metaclasses

If an object-oriented language upholds the following two principles

- All objects are instances of some class
- A class is an object

then it is reasonable to ask what is the class of a class object. In some languages the answer is relatively simple. In Java, for example, a class is an instance of Class—that is, an instance of itself. This can be easily verified by a simple program, such as the following.

```
class Test {
  static public void main (String [ ] args) {
    Test a = new Test();
    Class b = a.getClass();
    System.out.println("a class is " + b);
```

```
    Class c = b.getClass();
    System.out.println("b class is " + c);
    Class d = c.getClass();
    System.out.println("c class is " + d);
    if (c == d) System.out.println("They are the same");
  }
}
```

The output will show that variable a is of type (that is, class) Test, whereas variable b is of type Class. Variable c is also type Class. In fact, b is the same object as c, indicating that Class is an instance of itself.

The situation in Smalltalk is similar but more subtle. In Section 5.8 we introduced the concept of metaclasses. Recall that metaclasses gave the language a way to solve the problem of how to incorporate class specific behavior without moving outside the object-oriented model. Rather than being an instance of Class, a class was first an instance of its metaclass, which ultimately descended from Class. By inheritance the metaclass derives all the behavior of Class. But it also provides a place where class-specific behavior can be defined.

The metaclass hierarchy mirrors the class hierarchy. For example, if we have three levels of classes, there will also be three levels of metaclasses. The topmost metaclass will inherit from Class. But, of course, Class is an object, so it inherits from Object as well.[1]

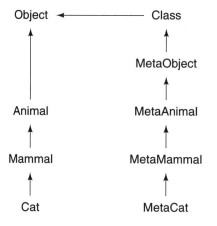

The object named MetaMammal in this diagram is also an object. What is its type? The answer is Meta. There are many strange loops at this level of the class

---

1. Even this diagram simplifies the class hierarchy somewhat, leaving out an additional level between Class and Object.

hierarchy. The following illustrates not the subclass relationships but the instance of relationship.

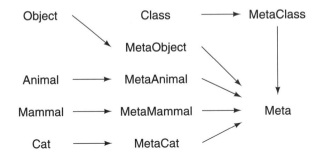

The class Meta is, oddly enough, an instance of itself. After looking at diagrams such as this, most Smalltalk programmers are glad that the class browser hides the existence of metaclasses from the programmer.

Summary ⊡

The term *reflection* refers to the ability of a running program to learn something about itself. Typically reflection facilities include the ability to take a run-time value and from the value determine its class, the ancestors of the class, the methods the class inherits, and so on. More advanced features include the ability to manipulate a method as an object—for example, invoking it with a given set of arguments. Other reflection facilities include the ability to dynamically load a class during execution or create a new class from a text description.

Reflection facilities form the basis for many component-based programming tools, since they allow a component to be dynamically loaded and queried regarding its abilities.

Further Reading ⊡

Reflection and introspection have long been part of dynamic languages such as Lisp. The standard reference for techniques in this language is [Kiczales 1991]. A more theoretical analysis of metaclasses in a language-independent framework is [Klas 1995].

Although reflection and metaclasses are not part of the basic C++ language, such facilities can be added by means of user-defined libraries. One such library is described in [Forman 1999].

A straightforward explanation of the reflection facilities in Java is given by [Flanagan 1997].

Self-Study Questions ▫

1. What does the ability of a program to reflect upon itself mean?
2. What is a class object?
3. What are some actions one can typically perform using a class object?
4. What are some actions one can typically perform using an object that represents a method?
5. What command is used to translate a string into a method in Smalltalk?
6. What action does a class loader perform in Java?
7. What is the type of the class Class in Smalltalk?

CHAPTER 26

Distributed Objects

We began this book by asserting that an object-oriented program should properly be envisioned as a community of agents, interacting with each other in order to achieve a shared objective.

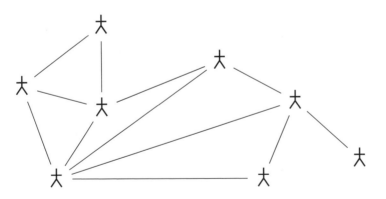

Nothing in this picture suggests that all these agents must exist in the same program, or even on the same computer. Much of what we have discussed in earlier chapters was concerned with limiting the connections between components. Thus, the object-oriented model lends itself quite naturally to the idea of *distributed computing*, where portions of a computing task are executed on one machine and other portions on a different machine.

Much of the excitement being generated around Java is due to the potential use of the language in just such applications. The language and the libraries it provides are particularly well suited to developing network applications—a process that

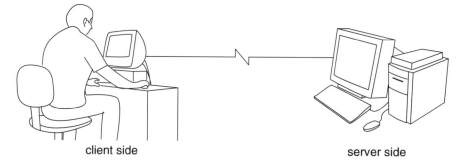

client side   server side

▫ Figure 26.1 —— Client and server side computing

deals with the task of connecting two or more computers so that they, and the
users working on them, can communicate and share resources.

A simple form of network programming is often described using the concepts
of client and server (see Figure 26.1). A *server* is an application that runs on one
computer, called the *host computer*, and provides both a means of connection
and useful information once a connection is established. Often we blur the lines
between the computer and the application, and we use the term *server* to mean
both the application and the host computer on which it runs. A *client* is an
application that runs on a different computer and seeks to establish a connection
to the server. Oftentimes there will be many clients for a single server.

Applets, such as those we examined in Chapter 21, are one form of client/server
network computing. An applet, you will recall, is a program that is stored
on a server computer but when requested is transmitted across the network
and executes on the client computer. However, applets are only a very simple
example of a much more powerful concept. In general, we would like to perform
computation on both the client and server sides of the network. In this chapter
we explore how this idea is realized in Java.

26.1 ▫ Addresses, Ports, and Sockets

In order to communicate with each other, computers must first be connected.
This connection can take various forms. Computers in a small area, such as a
single office, might be connected over a *local area network*, or LAN. Computers
connected over much longer distances, such as across a city or around the world,
are typically connected by a *wide area network*, or WAN. The best-known WAN
is the Internet, which is simply a loose connection of computers (really, a network
of networks) that have agreed to communicate with each other following certain
rules, or *protocols*.

For a computer to be able to select one application running on one computer out of the multitude of computers (tens of millions, in the case of the Internet) connected to a network, there must be an addressing scheme. On the Internet this address is known as an IP address and is usually written in the form of four numbers, each between 0 and 255, separated by dots. An example might be 100.12.11.13. Humans are not very good at remembering or dealing with numbers of this form. Thus, computer names can also be written in an alternative, and more human-friendly, representation.

A *domain name* address is another way to designate a specific computer. Like IP addresses, domain names are also written as a series of items separated by periods, although the connection between the two forms is not as direct as one might expect. Domain names denote a specific machine by means of a number of levels, the levels reading from more general on the right to more specific on the left. The computer on which this book is being written, for example, is addressed as oops.cs.orst.edu. This address can be read as follows: oops (the name of my machine) on the network for cs (the computer science department at my university) at the institution orst (Oregon State University), which is in the highest-level group edu (educational institutions in the United States).

The series of names can be imagined as being analogous to the way that a physical address is often described as a building address, street address, city name, and country name.

In order to exchange data, clients and servers need more than just an address. Many servers, for example, can be running simultaneously on the same computer and hence have the same IP address. Within a computer, the mechanism used to establish a rendezvous is termed a port. A *port* is a location where information can be exchanged between a client and a server.

One can think of the term as analogous to a shipping port, where goods come in from abroad and are picked up for delivery to the interior, and vice versa. Ports are designated by integer numbers. Typically, the values smaller than 1024 are reserved for predefined services (e-mail, file transfer, Web access), and user-defined ports have larger numbers.

The combination of IP address and port number is used to create an abstraction termed a *socket*. Again, one can think of this as an analogy to a connection, such as an electrical socket. A client can "plug into" the server, creating a connection along which information can flow, and can subsequently "disconnect," leaving the socket free for another use. As we will see in the programming examples, a socket provides the facilities for creating input and output streams, which allow data to be exchanged between the client and server.

Finally, files that reside on a specific computer are described using the now ubiquitous URL, or *universal resource locator*. A URL consists of a number of parts. Three of these are the protocol that indicates the communication method used to obtain the item (for example, ftp for file transfer, or http for Web pages), a domain name address, and a file name within the computer. A fourth part is an optional port number. The port number is necessary only when the default port for the particular protocol is, for some reason, not being used.

26.2 □ A Simple Client/Server Program

We will illustrate the basic ideas of client/server programming using a pair of simple programs. The server is shown in Figure 26.2. In addition to the classes found in java.io and java.net, we use the class Date found in java.util. The application is named DateServer.

The port number is arbitrarily chosen as 4291. In fact, any integer value larger than 1024 and not already in use on the server computer could have been selected.

The class ServerSocket is used to register the server with the port number on the underlying computer. Having registered itself, the server then sits and waits for a client.[1] The method accept will return when a client requests a connection. (An alternative form of accept allows the programmer to specify a time period for the wait so the program can time out if no client ever comes by.)

The constructor for the ServerSocket, the accept method, and the write method for the output writer can all generate an IOException. We can simplify the program by declaring this exception as part of the constructor interface and catching any such errors in the main method. By naming the exception in the method header for the constructor, any exceptions thrown by the library routines will pass through the constructor up to the calling procedure, where we catch them (in a try block) and simply print a message and halt.

The result returned by the accept message is a Socket, the connector that will allow a communication path to be established to the client. In particular, we can use the socket to create an OutputStream, which we here convert into an OutputStreamWriter. Having made a connection, the server then sends whatever information has been requested back to the client. In this case, we simply write the current date and time as yielded by the Date class.

We explicitly close the output stream, since the program will thereafter go back to waiting for another client. Closing the stream will flush any pending output and will free up certain system resources that are then available for use by this program or others. Oftentimes an explicit close will be omitted, since all such bookkeeping tasks will be performed automatically when a program terminates. However, if a program is finished with a resource and not yet ready to exit, as in this case, then it is considered good practice to explicitly release the resource.

---

1. Here the server is waiting in an infinite loop. On platforms where it is difficult to terminate programs running in the background, the reader may wish to replace the while loop with a finite loop, such as a for loop that will make three connections and then halt.

```java
import java.util.Date;
import java.net.*;
import java.io.*;

public class DateServer {
    static public void main (String [ ] args) {
        try {
            DateServer world = new DateServer();
        } catch (IOException e) {
            System.out.println("IO exception " + e);
        }
    }

    static final public int portNumber = 4291;

    public DateServer () throws IOException {
        ServerSocket server = new ServerSocket(portNumber);
        while (true) {
            System.out.println("Waiting for a client");
                // wait for a client
            Socket sock = server.accept();
            System.out.println("Got a client, send a message");
                // create an output stream
            OutputStreamWriter out =
                new OutputStreamWriter(sock.getOutputStream());
            String message =
                "Current date and time is " + new Date() + "\n";

                // write the message, then close the stream
            out.write(message);
            out.close();
        }
    }
}
```

▢ Figure 26.2 —— A simple server program

On the other side, we need a client. The DateClient code is shown in Figure 26.3. The client requests a socket to be created to the given port on a specific computer. In this simple example, we are assuming the client and server run on the same computer. The IP address of the computer on which an application is run can be accessed using the method InetAddress.getLocalHost(). A more general facility is

```
import java.io.*;
import java.net.*;

public class DateClient {
    public static void main (String [ ] args) {
        try {
            DateClient world = new DateClient();
        } catch (IOException e) {
            System.out.println("Received an IO exception " + e);
        }
    }

    static final public int portNumber = 4291;

    public DateClient () throws IOException {
            // open socket as a reader
        Socket sock =
            new Socket(InetAddress.getLocalHost(), portNumber);
        Reader isread =
            new InputStreamReader(sock.getInputStream());
        BufferedReader input = new BufferedReader(isread);
            // now read one line
        System.out.println("message is " + input.readLine());
    }
}
```

◻ Figure 26.3 ——The DateClient application

provided by InetAddress.getByName(domainName), which takes a string representation of a domain name and converts the name into an IP address.

Having created a socket, the socket can then be used to create an input stream, which we first convert to a Reader and then to a BufferedReader. The buffered reader provides a method to read an entire line of input, which we simply print out.

If we run both programs on the same computer, we will observe the expected outcome—namely, that the client will print the date and time given by the server.

26.3 ◻ Multiple Clients

There were many limitations to our first simple client/server system, but the two most important were that (1) it only provided communication one way, from the

```
import java.net.*;
import java.io.*;

public class Therapist {
    static public void main (String [ ] args) {
        try {
            Therapist world = new Therapist();
        } catch (IOException e) {
            System.out.println("Received an IO Exception" + e);
        }
    }

    static final public int portNumber = 5321;

    public Therapist () throws IOException {
        ServerSocket server = new ServerSocket(portNumber);
        while (true) {
            Socket sock = server.accept();
            // start new thread to handle session
            Thread session = new TherapySession
                (sock.getInputStream(), sock.getOutputStream());
            session.start();
        }
    }
}
```

▫ Figure 26.4 —— The Therapist application

server to the client, and (2) it only permitted one client for one server. In our second example program, we will address both of these points.

The Therapist program, Figure 26.4, is a rewriting of a classic and well-known computer game, originally called *Eliza* [Weizenbaum 1976]. The application simulates a Gestalt psychotherapist and conducts a sort of question-and-answer session with the user. An example session might be the following.

```
Hello.  Welcome to therapy. What is your name?
Tim.
Well, Tim what can we do for you today?
I am writing a book on Java.
Tell me more.
Do you know Java?
Why do you want to know?
```

```
Even my mother is learning how to program in Java.
Tell me more about your mother.
  .
  .
  .
```

The therapist application is very similar to the date server described earlier. One important difference is that when a socket is requested by a client, a new *thread* is created to service this request. This new thread then begins execution in parallel with the original task, which meanwhile completes the while loop and goes back to waiting for another client. In this fashion, many clients can be serviced simultaneously because each will be given his or her own thread of execution.

The servicing of the client is handled by an instance of TherapySession, shown in Figure 26.5. Note that the therapist passes both an input and output stream to the constructor for this class, permitting two-way communication between the client and the server. The class TherapySession is declared to be a subclass of Thread, which means that most of its processing will be performed by the run method invoked when the therapist starts the thread.

For the moment, we have omitted some of the code used in the execution of this thread so the overall structure can be seen more easily. In order to simplify input and output processing, the constructor for the class converts the input and output streams into buffered readers and writers.

The run method begins by writing a generic greeting. The flush method is needed to transfer the output across the network, since otherwise the buffering of the writer will wait until more output has been generated. The next line is assumed to be a one-word name. Another generic response is then given, and the program moves into the loop that is the heart of the application.

The infinite while loop simply reads a line of text from the user, then determines and writes a response. We will return to the issue of how the response is generated after discussing the client side code.

The client program is named TherapyClient (Figure 26.6), and again, it is very similar to the Date client. The program creates readers and writers to handle the socket input and output, and it then simply reads lines of text from the standard input and passes them across the network to the server, printing the response on the standard output.

Although the therapy session application clearly has no innate intelligence, people are frequently fooled into thinking otherwise. This effect is achieved by a clever selection of simple rules for responding to what the user writes. Figure 26.7 shows the code that embodies these rules. If the user asks a question (a condition discovered by checking the final character), then the program will answer with a question. Otherwise the line of text is converted into lowercase and broken into individual words.

```
import java.io.*;
import java.util.Vector;
import java.util.StringTokenizer;

public class TherapySession extends Thread {
  public TherapySession (InputStream ins, OutputStream outs) {
    Reader isread = new InputStreamReader(ins);
    in = new BufferedReader(isread);
    out = new OutputStreamWriter(outs);
  }

  private String name = "";
  private BufferedReader in;
  private Writer out;

  private String response (String text) {
      .
      .
      .
  }

  public void run () {
    try {
        // get name

      out.write("Hello.  Welcome to therapy. What is your name?\n");
      out.flush();
      name = in.readLine();
      out.write("Well " + name + " what can we do for you today?\n");
      out.flush();

        // now read and respond
      while (true) {
        String text = in.readLine();
        out.write(response(text) + "\n");
        out.flush();
      }
    } catch (IOException e) { stop(); }
  }
}
```

▫ Figure 26.5 —— The TherapySession class

```java
import java.io.*;
import java.net.*;

public class TherapyClient {
    public static void main (String [ ] args) {
        try {
            TherapyClient world = new TherapyClient();
        } catch (IOException e) {
            System.out.println("Received an IO exception " + e);
        }
    }

    static final public int portNumber = 5321;
    private BufferedReader input, term;
    private Writer output;

    public TherapyClient () throws IOException {
        // open standard input as buffered reader
        term = new BufferedReader(new InputStreamReader(System.in));

        // open socket as a reader and a writer
        Socket sock =
            new Socket(InetAddress.getLocalHost(), portNumber);
        Reader isread =
            new InputStreamReader(sock.getInputStream());
        input = new BufferedReader(isread);
        output = new OutputStreamWriter(sock.getOutputStream());

        // now read and print
        while (true) {
            // read and print something from therapist
            String line = input.readLine();
            System.out.println(line);
            // get our response
            line = term.readLine();
            if (line.equals("Quit"))
                break;
            output.write(line + "\n");
            output.flush();
        }
    }
}
```

▫ Figure 26.6 —— The TherapyClient class

```
private String response (String text) {
    // answer a question with a question
    if (text.endsWith("?"))
        return "Why do you want to know?";
    // break up line
    Vector words = new Vector();
    StringTokenizer breaker =
        new StringTokenizer(text.toLowerCase(), " .,?!");
    while (breaker.hasMoreElements())
        words.addElement(breaker.nextElement());
    // look for "I feel"
    if ((words.size() > 1) &&
        words.elementAt(0).equals("i") &&
        words.elementAt(1).equals("feel"))
        return "Why do you feel that way?";

    // look for relatives
    for (int i = 0; i < words.size(); i++) {
        String relative = (String) words.elementAt(i);
        if (isRelative(relative))
            return "Tell me more about your " + relative;
    }
    // nothing else, generic response
    return "Tell me more";
}

private boolean isRelative (String name) {
    return name.equals("mother") || name.equals("father")
        || name.equals("brother") || name.equals("sister")
        || name.equals("uncle");
}
```

□ Figure 26.7 —— The response generator

Once the line is broken into words, there are several simple rules that can be applied. If the user started a sentence with "I feel," then we can ask why they feel that way. Otherwise, we check every word to see if they mentioned a family member. If so, then we ask for more information on that relative. Finally, if nothing else has been applicable, we ask a general open-ended question. These are only a small sample of the rules that can be written—all to simulate intelligence when there is none.

26.4 ▫ Transmitting Objects over a Network

Objects can be transmitted over a network using the technique of *object serialization*. We illustrate this mechanism by presenting a portion of another client/server application. This application is an online pocket-change exchange calculator. The application will take a description of a collection of coins, either in British or American coinage, and calculate the equivalent in the other system.

To start, we need a class hierarchy to describe a collection of coins. This is provided by the three classes shown in Figure 26.8. The class PocketChange is an abstract class, parent to the two classes BritishCoins and AmericanCoins. Since both currencies share the concept of a penny, that is the only data field found in the parent class. Each subclass gives names for the various different coins used in that country. (Fifty-cent pieces and dollar coins have actually been minted in the United States, but they have never been popular.) This class description must be available on both the client and server sides of the network connection.

The class PocketChange has been declared as implementing the Serializable interface. This is all that is necessary to permit instances of the class to be written to and read from an object stream. It is not necessary to repeat the implements clause in the child classes BritishCoins and AmericanCoins, since they will inherit the serializable characteristic from their parent class PocketChange.

We give only a portion of the server program (Figure 26.9), leaving the completion of the server program and the development of a client application as an exercise for the reader. The ChangeMaker application waits for a client to request a connection. When a connection is made, the program reads a value from the input stream. Notice that the actual value read will be either an instance of AmericanCoins or an instance of BritishCoins, but the server has no idea which one. Instead, the server reads the value as an instance of the parent class PocketChange. Nevertheless, the *actual* value transferred will be an instance of one of the child classes.

Without knowing the exact class of the object that has been received, the server executes the message exchange, which is declared as abstract in the class PocketChange and is reimplemented in each child class. The method executed will depend on the dynamic type of the object received over the socket.

To calculate the correct amount, the value of the coins is first reduced to penny units and then multiplied by the current exchange rate. (A more sophisticated

```
import java.io.Serializable;

abstract public class PocketChange implements Serializable {
   public int penny = 0;
   abstract PocketChange exchange();
}

class BritishCoins extends PocketChange {
   public int twoPence = 0; // worth 2 pennies
   public int fivePence = 0; // worth 5 pennies
   public int tenPence = 0; // worth 10 pennies
   public int twentyPence = 0; // worth 20 pennies
   public int fiftyPence = 0; // worth 50 pennies
   public int pound = 0; // worth 100 pennies
   public int twoPound = 0; // worth 200 pennies

   public BritishCoins (int pence) { ... }

   public PocketChange exchange () { // convert to American
      int bPennies = bc.penny + 2 * bc.twoPence +
            5 * bc.fivePence + 10 * bc.tenPence +
            20 * bc.twentyPence + 50 * bc.fiftyPence +
            100 * bc.pound + 200 * bc.twoPound;
      int amPennies = (int) (bPennies
            * exchangeBPenniestoAPennies);
      return new AmericanCoins(amPennies);
   }
}

class AmericanCoins extends PocketChange {
   public int nickel = 0; // worth 5 pennies
   public int dime = 0; // worth 10 pennies
   public int quarter = 0; // worth 25 pennies

   public AmericanCoins (int cents) {
      quarter = cents / 25; cents %= 25;
      dime = cents / 10; cents %= 10;
      nickel = cents / 5; cents %= 5;
      penny = cents;
   }

   public PocketChange exchange () { ... } // convert to British
}
```

▢ Figure 26.8 —— The Coin class hierarchy

```
public class ChangeMaker {
    static final public int portNumber = 3347;
    static final public double exchangeBPenniestoAPennies = 1.615;

    public ChangeMaker () throws IOException {
        ServerSocket server = new ServerSocket(portNumber);
        while (true) {
            Socket sock = server.accept();
                // got a client, make the connections
            ObjectInputStream in =
                new ObjectInputStream(sock.getInputStream());
            ObjectOutputStream out =
                new ObjectOutputStream(sock.getOutputStream());

                // read the value
            PocketChange coins;
            try { coins = (PocketChange) in.readObject();
            } catch (ClassNotFoundException e) { continue; }
                // now convert the value
            coins = coins.exchange();
                // write out the result
            out.writeObject(coins);
            sock.close();
        }
    }
}
```

▫ Figure 26.9 ——— The ChangeMaker server application

program could, at this point, make another network connection to a server that
would yield the current exchange rate.) Having determined the American penny
equivalent to the British coins, a series of assignments are then used to convert
this quantity into quarters, dimes, nickels, and pennies.

Once the equivalent number of coins has been determined, the object representing the collection of coins is written to the output stream using the method
writeObject. On the client side this quantity will be read using a corresponding read-
Object method. The server then closes the socket and goes back to waiting for the
next connection.

26.5 ▫ Providing More Complexity

We have only scratched the surface of the techniques that can be used in network programming. We describe here some of the ways that further functionality can be added to our examples:

The *Remote Method Invocation* package (java.rmi) provides a framework for creating distributed applications (applications that run on two or more computers) in which the actual physical location of an object is transparent to the user. An object will support the same interface whether it is local to the machine or on a remote machine connected by a socket.

A common type of network application involves a server providing access to a database. The Java Database Connectivity (JDBC) library provides a simple and uniform interface that can be used to access a wide variety of different commercial database systems.

Servlets are an alternative to applets. While applets originate on the server computer but run on the client computer, servlets both originate and run on the server computer, and they only transmit their results to the client. This technique is useful, since programs running on the server are often permitted to perform tasks that are not allowed to be performed by applets. Just as the class Applet provides much of the mechanism for creating applets in a systematic and relatively easy fashion, the servlet library provides facilities for creating server software.

Summary ▫

Network programming involves applications running on two or more computers working in a cooperative fashion to solve a particular problem.

To work in tandem, applications must communicate. Computers establish connections by means of a series of different mechanisms. An *address* is used to designate a specific computer out of the many computers that may be connected to a network. A *port* is used to identify an individual application on a computer that is waiting to make a connection. Once the application is found, a *socket* is used to create the actual communication medium that links the two communicating applications.

The *streams* created by a socket can be used to transmit 8-bit byte values between the two communicating parties. By using the *stream* and *reader/writer* abstractions provided by the Java library, higher-level objects can also be transmitted easily across the network connection.

By processing requests in a separate thread of execution, a single server can be made to service many different clients simultaneously.

Further Reading ⊡

Flanagan [Flanagan 1997] provides a series of detailed examples to illustrate how network programming can be performed in Java. Simple examples illustrating RMI and servlets are also provided by [Campione 1999]. The techniques used to program servlets in Java are explained by Callaway [Callaway 1999].

Self-Study Questions ⊡

1. What is distributed computing?
2. Why does the object-oriented view of a program lend itself naturally to distributed computing?
3. Explain what is meant by the terms *client* and *server*.
4. Explain how applets represent one form of client/server computing.
5. How are different machines in a network addressed?
6. What is a port? What is the difference between a port and a socket?
7. In what way is a URL object similar to a Socket object?
8. What is the difference between a Socket object and an object of type Server-Socket?
9. What information is needed to form a socket?
10. How does a client create a connection with a server? How does a server create a connection with a client?
11. Having established a socket connection, how is communication between client and server effected?
12. What is the benefit of having the Therapist server create separate threads to handle communication with the client?
13. In the communication between the Therapist server and the client, why is it important for the writers to be flushed after a line of text has been output?
14. What Java facilities are required for transmitting objects over a network?

Exercises ⊡

1. Create an array of "fortune cookies," one-line comments offering advice or information. Then write a server program that will, when requested, return a randomly selected value from this list.
2. Many more rules can be added to the response generator for the therapist program. Examples include responding to "I want" or "I think" with a question that asks *why* the client wants or thinks that way (perhaps even including

the text of the material that follows the first two words), a randomly generated generic response if nothing else is appropriate, searching for keywords such as "computer," and making a response, such as "Computers can be so annoying, can't they?" Think of some more question-and-answer patterns, and implement them in your own version of the therapist.

3. Complete the ChangeMaker server, and write a client program that will interface with this server. Allow the user the ability to specify input as either American or British currency, using forms for the various numeric fields.

4. Unlike the Therapist program, the ChangeMaker does not service each client in a separate thread. Thus, each client must be completely serviced before the next client can be handled. Modify the ChangeMaker program to correct this so that servicing a client is performed in a separate thread and can be performed in parallel with the main program waiting for a new connection to be established.

CHAPTER 27

Implementation

It is not the intent of this book to provide a detailed introduction to programming language implementation. Nevertheless, a general understanding of the problems encountered in implementing object-oriented languages and the various ways to overcome them can, in many cases, help the reader better understand object-oriented techniques. In particular, this will help clarify the way in which object-oriented systems differ from more conventional systems. In this chapter, we provide an overview of some of the more important implementation techniques, as well as pointers to the relevant literature for the reader who desires further information.

27.1 ▫ Compilers and Interpreters

Broadly speaking, there are two major approaches to programming language implementation: compilers and interpreters. A *compiler* translates the user's program into native machine code for the target machine and is invoked as a separate process independent of execution. An *interpreter*, on the other hand, is present during execution, and it is the system that runs the user program.

As is true of most distinctions, while the endpoints are clear, there are large gray areas in the middle. There are compilers that compile interactively even during executing (at least during the debugging stages). These compilers gain some of the advantages of the interpreter while giving the execution-time advantage of the compiler technique. Similarly, some interpreters can translate into either an intermediate representation or native code.

Generally, a program that is translated by a compiler will execute faster than a program that is run under an interpreter. But the time between conception,

511

entering text, and execution in a compiled system may be longer than the corresponding time in an interpreter. Furthermore, when errors occur at run time, the compiler often has little more than the generated assembly language to offer as a marker to the probable error location. An interpreter will usually relate the error to the original text the user entered. Thus, there are advantages and disadvantages to both approaches.

Although some languages are usually compiled and others are usually interpreted, there is nothing intrinsic in a language that forces the implementor to always select one over the other. C++ is usually compiled, but there are C++ interpreters. On the other hand, Smalltalk is almost always interpreted, but experimental Smalltalk compilers have been produced.

27.2 ▫ The Receiver as Argument

In a compiled language, ultimately all methods are translated into functions that are, in many respects, just like any other function. The instructions for the function are rendered as a sequence of assembly language instructions that reside in a fixed location in memory, and when the function is executed, control is transferred to this location. As part of this transfer of control, an activation record[1] is created to hold the parameters and the local variables. So how does this code gain access to the instance data associated with the receiver?

To put the question in concrete terms, recall the class description of CardPile from the solitaire program.

```
class CardPile {
public:
    .
    .
    .
    bool addCard (Card * aCard);
    .
    .
    .
private:
    list<Card *> cards;
    const int x;
    const int y;
};
```

---

1. The activation record is a portion of the run-time stack set aside at procedure entry to hold parameters, local variables, and other information. Further details on the run-time environment of programs can be found in any compiler-construction textbook. See the section on further reading at the end of the chapter.

```
void CardPile::addCard (Card * aCard)
{
  card.push_front(aCard);
}
```

The compiler creates assembly language code for the method addCard. Seemingly, the only parameter is the playing card named aCard. How does this code gain access to the data field card?

The answer is that the receiver is in reality passed as a hidden first parameter. An invocation, like this

```
CardPile * aCardPile = ...;
Card * currentCard = ...;


aCardPile->addCard (currentCard);
```

is in reality translated as if it had been written like this.

```
addCard(aCardPile, currentCard);
```

At the other end, the code for the method is compiled as if it had been written as follows.

```
void addCard (CardPile * this, Card * aCard)
{
  this->card.push_front(aCard);
}
```

Notice how the pseudo-variable this has become a real first parameter. References to data fields or to methods within the class can be handled using this value.

27.3 ☐ Inherited Methods

The next problem we will consider is how it is possible for a method defined in a parent class to continue to function even when it is executed using an instance of a child class as receiver. This question arises both for differences in the receiver and differences in argument caused by the use of polymorphic variables as parameters. Indeed, as was noted in the previous section, the receiver for a message-passing expression *is* just a polymorphic argument.

To understand how unusual this is, note that in most other ways argument values can never be changed. It would not be possible for a procedure that is expecting an integer as an argument to work correctly when it is given a string.

The key insight that allows inherited methods to continue to operate is the way that child classes are represented in memory. In a compiled version of a program, data fields are not accessed by name but by a fixed offset relative to the beginning of an object. A child class will store the same fields at the same offsets. They may add new data fields, but these will be as *extensions* of the parent data fields.

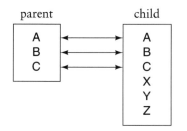

Since the code generated when the parent class is processed only requires that data fields be found at a known offset, the code will work regardless of whether it is dealing with an instance of the parent or an instance of the child.

27.3.1   The problem of multiple inheritance

One of the reasons why multiple inheritance is difficult to implement is precisely because a child class cannot store inherited data fields in exactly the same location as they are found in *both* parents. The child can mirror one parent or the other but not both at the same time.

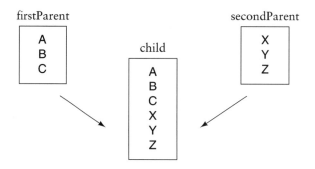

There are various solutions to this problem, but none results in a system that is as simple as that provided by single inheritance. The most common technique is that an object pointer is represented as a pair containing both the pointer to the base and an offset. However, the details concerning how this can be done are beyond the scope of this book.

27.3.2 The slicing problem

That a child class can only *extend* the data fields defined by a parent class nicely solves the problem of inherited methods. That is, it gives the compiler a way to generate code for procedure defined in a parent class so that it will nevertheless work on objects of a child class. But this same property introduces another problem.

As we discussed in earlier chapters, a *polymorphic variable* is one that is declared as representing one type but that in fact holds values from another type. In object-oriented languages the values usually must come from a subclass of the parent class.

When a compiler sets aside space in an activation record, it generally knows only the declared type for a variable, not the run-time type. The question is therefore how much memory should be allocated in the activation record. As we discussed in Chapter 12, most programming languages elect one of two solutions to this problem.

- The activation record holds only pointers, not values themselves.
- The activation record holds only the data fields declared in the parent, slicing off any data fields from the child class that will not fit.

There are merits to both alternatives, so we will not comment on which technique seems "better." However, as a programmer it is important that you understand the technique used by the system on which you work. C++ uses the slicing approach; Java and most other object-oriented languages use the pointer approach.

27.4 ▣ Overridden Methods

We have explained how inherited methods can execute even when presented with an instance of a child class, but what about the inverse? How is it possible that when an overridden method is invoked, the code that is executed will be that associated with the current value of the receiver, regardless of its declared type?

To put the question in concrete terms, recall that in our solitaire game the method addCard is redefined in the child class DiscardPile. A variable that is declared as maintaining a CardPile will, if it actually references a DiscardPile, execute the correct method.

```
CardPile * aCardPile = new DiscardPile();
Card * aCard = ...;

aCardPile->addCard (aCard); // will execute DiscardPile::addCard
```

Since the dynamic class can change during execution, there must be something stored in the variable that indicates the type of value it is currently maintaining.

This value is termed a *virtual method table pointer*. It is simply an additional data field, a hidden pointer that references an object called the *virtual method table*.

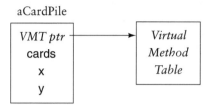

The virtual method table is a static data area constructed for each class. All instances of the same class will point to the same virtual method table. In some implementations the virtual method table may include a small amount of useful information, such as the class name or the size of instances of the class in bytes, but the most important part of the virtual method table is an array of pointers to functions.

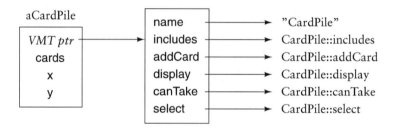

The offset to any particular method can be determined at compile time. Thus, an invocation of a virtual method is translated into an indirect access mediated through the virtual method table. The call

```
aCardPile->addCard (aCard);
```

becomes

```
aCardPile->VMTptr[3](aCardPile, aCard);
```

where VMTptr is the name of the hidden data field that references the virtual method table, and the offset of the addCard method is assumed here to be 3. (Note we have also passed the receiver as argument, as we described in Section 27.2.)

The next part of the solution to the problem of overridden functions deals with the layout of the virtual method table for a child class in relation to the table for the parent class. In short, overridden methods are placed at the same offsets in both but point to different functions.

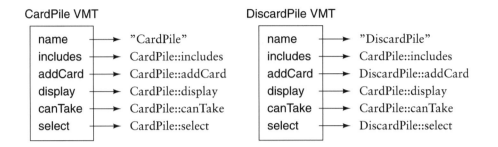

If a method is not overridden, the pointer in the virtual method table will be the same in the child as in the parent. If it is overridden, the location in the child will point to the child code, while the location in the parent will point to the parent code. New methods defined in the child but not found in the parent are tacked on to the end of the child's virtual method table. Thus, the table for the child is an extension of the parent, in much the same way that the data layout for the child is an extension of the data layout for the parent.

In this way the invocation of an overridden method can quickly and easily be resolved to the correct function. Notice that the overhead for a virtual method call is one level of indirection (the reference to the virtual method table) and one array index (the index into the table). On most machines this can be accomplished in one or two assembly language instructions.

27.4.1 Eliminating virtual calls and in-lining

Although the overhead of a virtual method invocation in comparison to a normal function call is small, in some instances (for example, inside of loops) even a small difference can be critical. If a compiler can determine at compile time the dynamic class of a receiver, then an invocation of a virtual method can be transformed into a normal procedure call, avoiding the overhead of the virtual method table lookup.

Most often this is accomplished through a technique termed data flow analysis. A careful trace is performed of all execution paths between the point a variable is given a value and the point it is used as a receiver. In many cases this analysis will reveal the exact type for the variable.

The elimination of virtual method calls is often combined with *method inlining*. Object-oriented programming tends to encourage the development of many small methods, often much smaller than the average function in an imperative language. If data flow analysis can link a message invocation to a specific method, and if the method is very small (for example, it may simply return a data field), then the body of the method can be expanded in-line at the point of call, thereby avoiding the overhead of the procedure call.

27.5 ▫ Name Encoding

Since methods are all known at compile time and cannot change at run time, the virtual tables are simply static data areas established by the compiler. These data areas consist of pointers to the appropriate methods. Because linkers and loaders resolve references on the basis of symbols, some mechanism must be provided to avoid name collisions when two or more methods have the same name. The typical scheme combines the names of the class and the method. Thus, the addCard method in class DiscardPile might internally become DicardPile::addCard. Usually, the user need never see this name unless forced to examine the assembly-language output of the compiler.

In languages such as C++ that allow methods to be further overloaded with disambiguation based on parameter type, even more complicated Gödel-like[2] encodings of the class name, method name, and argument types are required. For example, the three constructors of class Complex described in an earlier chapter might be known internally as Complex::Complex, Complex::Complex_float, and Complex::Complex_float_float, respectively. Such internal names, sometimes referred to as *mangled names*, can become very long. As we have seen, this internal name is not used during message passing but merely in the construction of the virtual tables and to make unique procedure names for the linker.

27.6 ▫ Dispatch Tables

Because languages such as C++ and Object Pascal are statically typed, they can determine at compile time the parent class type of any object-oriented expression. Thus, a virtual method table needs to be only large enough to accommodate those methods actually implemented by a class. In a dynamically typed language, such as Smalltalk or Objective-C, a virtual method table has to include *all* messages understood by any class, and this table needs to be repeated for every class. If an application has 20 classes, for example, and they each implement 10 methods on average, we need 20 tables, each consisting of 200 entries. The size requirements quickly become exorbitant, and a better technique is called for.

An alternative technique is to associate with every class a table that, unlike the virtual method table, consists of selector-method pairs. This is called a *dispatch table*. The selectors correspond only to those methods actually implemented in a

---

2. The term "Gödel-like" refers to the technique of encoding a large amount of information (such as an entire computer program) as a single quantity. The technique was first described by the German computer scientist Kurt Gödel in a paper in 1931 [Gödel 1931]. Its use in a linker was, to my knowledge, first described by Richard Hamlet [Hamlet 1976].

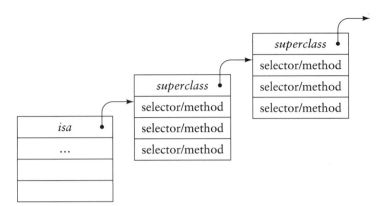

□ Figure 27.1 ——— An object and its dispatch table

class. Inherited methods are accessed through a pointer in this table, which points to the dispatch table associated with a superclass (see Figure 27.1).

As in a system using virtual method tables, when dispatch tables are used, every object carries with it an implicit (that is, not declared) pointer to the dispatch table associated with the class of the value it represents. This implicit pointer is known as the isa link (not to be confused with the is-a relation between classes). A message expression in Objective-C, such as the following expression from the eight-queens problem.

```
[neighbor checkrow: row column: column]
```

is translated by the Objective-C compiler[3] into

```
objc_msgSend(neighbor,"checkrow:column:", row, column)
```

The function objc_msgSend, called the *messaging function*, follows the isa link of the first argument to find the appropriate dispatch table. The messaging function then searches the dispatch table for an entry that matches the selector. If such an entry is found, the associated method is invoked. If no such method is found, the dispatch table of the superclass is searched. If the root class (class Object) is finally searched and no method is found, a run-time error is reported.

---

3. The Objective-C system is a translator that produces conventional C code. In addition, the string form of the selector is not actually used; instead, selectors are hashed into a numeric value.

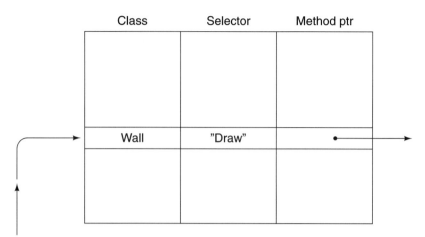

	Class	Selector	Method ptr
	Wall	"Draw"	•

obj_msgSend(Wall, "Draw")

▫ Figure 27.2 —— The messaging function checking the method cache

27.6.1   A method cache

Although for dynamically typed languages, the dispatch table is more economical in space than the virtual method table, the time overhead is considerably greater. Furthermore, this overhead is proportional to the depth of inheritance. Unless this penalty can be overcome, the latter point might lead developers to abandon inheritance, trading the loss in power for the gain in efficiency.

Fortunately, we can largely circumvent this execution time loss by means of a simple technique. We maintain a single systemwide *cache* of methods that have been recently accessed. This cache is indexed by a hash value defined on the method selectors. Each entry in the cache is a triple, consisting of a pointer to a class (the dispatch table itself can serve this purpose), a selector value, and a pointer to a method.

When the messaging function is asked to find a method to match to a selector class pair, it first searches the cache (see Figure 27.2). If the entry in the cache at the hash table location corresponds to the requested selector and class, the associated method can be executed directly. If not, the search process described earlier is performed. Following this search, immediately before executing the method the cache is updated, overwriting whatever entry it contained previously at the hash location given by the message selector. Note that the value stored for the class entry in the cache is the class where the search began, not the class in which the method was eventually discovered.

By appropriate selection of hash functions and cache sizes, one can achieve cache hit ratios in the range of 90 to 95 percent, which reduces the overhead involved in a messaging expression to slightly over twice that of a conventional procedure call. This figure compares favorably with the overhead incurred with the virtual method table technique.

27.7 □ Bytecode Interpreters

Interpreters are usually preferred over compilers if the amount of variation in a program is larger than can be accommodated easily in fixed code sequences. This variation can come from a number of sources. In a dynamically typed language, for example, we cannot predict at compile time the type of values that a variable can possess (although Objective-C is an example of a dynamically typed language that is nevertheless compiled). Another source of variation can occur if the user can redefine methods at run time.

A commonly used approach in interpreters is to translate the source program into a high-level "assembly language," often called a *bytecode* language (because typically each instruction can be encoded in a single byte). Figure 27.3 shows, for example, the bytecode instructions used in the Little Smalltalk system. The high-order four bits of the instruction are used to encode the opcode, and the low-order four bits are used to encode the operand number. If operand numbers larger

1111 xxxx	Special instruction xxxx
1110 xxxx	Unused
1101 xxxx	Send ternary message xxxx
1100 xxxx	Send arithmetic message xxxx
1011 xxxx	Send binary message xxxx
1010 xxxx	Send unary message xxxx
1001 xxxx	Send message to super
1000 xxxx	Send message xxxx
0111 xxxx	Pop into temporary variable xxxx
0110 xxxx	Pop into instance variable xxxx
0101 xxxx	Push system constant xxxx
0100 xxxx	Push class object number xxxx on stack
0011 xxxx	Push literal number xxxx on stack
0010 xxxx	Push argument xxxx on stack
0001 xxxx	Push instance variable xxxx on stack
0000 xxxx	Extended instruction with opcode xxxx

□ Figure 27.3 —— Bytecode values in the Little Smalltalk system

than 16 are needed, the extended instruction is used, and the entire following byte contains the operand value. A few instructions, such as "send message" and some of the special instructions, require additional bytes.

The heart of the interpreter is a loop that surrounds a large switch statement. The loop reads each successive bytecode, and the switch statement jumps to a code sequence that performs the appropriate action. We will avoid a discussion of the internal representation of a program (interested readers are referred to [Budd 1987]) and will concentrate solely on the processing of message passing.

```
while (timeslice-- > 0) {
  high = nextByte();   // get next bytecode
  low = high & 0x0F;   // strip off low nybble
  high >>= 4;          // shift left high nybble
  if (high == 0) {     //check extended form
    high = low;        // if so use low for opcode
    low = nextByte();  // get real operand
  }

  switch(high) {
    case PushInstance: ...
      .
      .
      .
    case PushArgument: ..
      .
      .
      .
  }
}
```

Just as objects in the compiled system presented earlier all contain a pointer to a virtual table, objects in the Smalltalk system all contain a pointer to their class. The difference is that, as we saw in Chapter 4, the class is itself an object. Among the fields maintained in the class object is a collection containing all the methods corresponding to messages that instances of the class will understand (Figure 27.4). Another field points to the superclass for the class.

When a message is to be sent, the interpreter must first locate the receiver for the message. By examining the class pointer for the receiver, it can find the object corresponding to the class of the receiver. It then searches the methods collection for a method that matches the name of the message being sent. If no such method is found, it follows the superclass chain, searching the classes in the superclass until either an appropriate method is found or the chain is exhausted. In the latter case, the interpreter reports an error. This is exactly the same sequence of steps as performed by the messaging function used in the dispatch table technique.

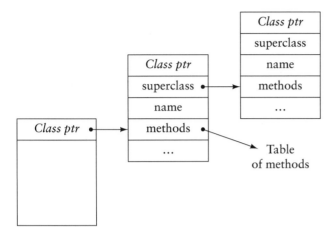

As with that technique, a cache can be used to speed up the process of method search.

Bytecode interpreters have recently been popularized through their use by Java systems. While the range of bytecodes used by Java is much more extensive than what has been described here, the key ideas remain the same.

27.8 ▫ Just-in-Time Compilation

The key criticism usually leveled against interpretive systems is that there execution time is typically much slower than that obtained from compilers. On the other hand, interpreters can be much more portable. Java is the language that has most recently trumpeted this advantage, claiming that Java bytecodes created on any machine can be executed on any other machine.

A scheme that tries to balance the benefits of both techniques is *just-in-time* compilation, or JIT. In a JIT system a program is first translated into a portable, high-level form—for example, Java bytecodes. When these bytecodes get loaded onto a specific machine, then at that instance, just before execution (the "just in time" of the name), the bytecodes are translated once again into machine code for the hardware on which execution is taking place.

The JIT technique gives the advantage of portability (the original bytecode form of the program can be moved to any machine) with the execution time performance of compiled code. There is a small time penalty that must be paid for translating the bytecodes into machine code, but normally the resulting machine code is saved so that if the same method is executed repeatedly, this translation cost is incurred only once and can be amortized over all the successive calls.

The major difficulty with JIT systems is that they are complicated systems to develop, particularly if they are combined with optimization techniques. But as the dramatic improvements in execution speeds of Java systems in the past few years has indicated, the benefits can be impressive.

Summary ▫

Regardless of whether an implementation is provided by a compiler or an interpreter, there are several fundamental problems that must be addressed. In this chapter we examined the following.

- Providing access to the receiver from within a method
- How an inherited method can continue to operate using an instance of a child class in place of an instance of the parent class
- How methods can be overridden and how a dynamic dispatch technique for a statically typed languages can select at run time the method that will match a polymorphic variable's dynamic class
- How unique names can be created for system software, such as linkers, that require this property
- How dynamic method lookup is performed in dynamically typed languages
- How bytecodes can be used as a flexible and portable internal representation of an object-oriented program
- How just-in-time compilation can provide the benefits of both portability and execution efficiency

Further Reading ▫

A good introduction to the problems of language implementation can be found in compiler construction textbooks, such as [Aho 1985, Fischer 1988].

For the reader interested in learning more about the implementation of object-oriented languages, Cox [Cox 1986] contains a detailed analysis of the time-space tradeoffs involved in various schemes. The implementation of multiple inheritance in C++ is sketched in [Ellis 1990], which is based on an earlier algorithm for Simula [Krogdahl 1985]. A detailed description of C++ implementation techniques is provided by Lippman [Lippman 1996].

The Smalltalk-80 interpreter is described in [Goldberg 1983]. [Krasner 1983] contains several papers that describe techniques for improving the efficiency of the Smalltalk-80 system. A simplified Smalltalk interpreter is detailed in [Budd 1987]. Kamin [Kamin 1990] presents a good general overview of the issues involved in the implementation of nontraditional languages.

Self-Study Questions ⊡

1. In broad terms, what are the differences between compilers and interpreters? What are some advantages of each technique?
2. When a method is translated into an ordinary function, what changes are necessary in order to provide access to the receiver?
3. What key feature of the memory layout of objects permits methods defined in a parent class to be used with instances of a child class?
4. Why is the simple approach to the inherited methods that is used by single inheritance languages not applicable when multiple inheritance is allowed?
5. Describe the run-time technique used to match the invocation of an overridden method to the correct method implementation.
6. What is a mangled name? Why is it necessary to create mangled names?
7. In what ways is a dispatch table different from a virtual method table? In what ways are they similar?
8. Explain how a message selector is matched to a method when the dispatch table technique is used.
9. What is a method cache? How does it speed up the task of message passing?
10. What is a bytecode?
11. Why are JIT systems described as "just-in-time"?

Exercises ⊡

1. Extend the dispatch table technique to permit multiple inheritance.
2. The Objective-C compiler permits optional declarations for object variables. Explain how a compiler might use such declarations to speed processing of messages involving such values. Consider what needs to occur on assignment and how messaging can be made more efficient.
3. Explain why methods that are not declared virtual in C++ can be invoked more efficiently than can virtual methods. How do you make measurements to determine whether the difference is significant?

4. Review the cache technique described in Section 27.6.1. Explain why the class stored in the cache is the one where the search for a method begins and not the one where the method is eventually found. Explain how the cache lookup algorithm would need to be changed if the latter value were used. Do you think the new algorithm would be faster or slower? Explain your answer.

5. Sketch the outline of a Smalltalk interpreter based on the bytecodes given in the text.

Source for the Eight-Queens Puzzle

This appendix gives the full programs for the eight-queens puzzle discussed in Chapter 6.

A.1 ▢ Eight-Queens in Apple Object Pascal

```
(*
   Eight-Queens Puzzle in Object Pascal
   Written by Tim Budd, Oregon State University, 1996
*)
Program EightQueen;

type
  Queen = object
    (* data fields *)
    row : integer;
    column : integer;
    neighbor : Queen;

      (* initialization *)
    procedure initialize (col : integer; ngh : Queen);
      (* operations *)
    function canAttack
      (testRow, testColumn : integer) : boolean;
    function findSolution : boolean;
    function advance : boolean;
```

```
    procedure print;
  end;
var
  neighbor, lastQueen : Queen;
  i : integer;

procedure Queen.initialize (col : integer; ngh : Queen);
begin
    (* initialize our column and neighbor values *)
  column := col;
  neighbor := ngh;

    (* start in row 1 *)
  row := 1;
end;


function Queen.canAttack
  (testRow, testColumn : integer) : boolean;
var
  can : boolean;
  columnDifference : integer;
begin
    (* first see if rows are equal *)
  can := (row = testRow);

    (* then test diagonals *)
  if not can then begin
    columnDifference := testColumn - column;
    if (row + columnDifference = testRow) or
      (row - columnDifference = testRow) then
        can := true;
    end;

    (* finally, test neighbors *)
  if (not can) and (neighbor <> nil) then
    can := neighbor.canAttack(testRow, testColumn);
  canAttack := can;
end;


function queen.findSolution : boolean;
var
  done : boolean;
```

```
begin
  done := false;
  findSolution := true;


    (* seek a valid position *)
  if neighbor <> nil then
    while not done and neighbor.canAttack(row, column) do
      if not self.advance then begin
        findSolution := false;
        done := true;
        end;
end;

function queen.advance : boolean;
begin
  advance := false;

    (* try next row *)
  if row < 8 then begin
    row := row + 1;
    advance := self.findSolution;
  end
  else begin

      (* cannot go further *)
      (* move neighbor to next solution *)
    if neighbor <> nil then
      if not neighbor.advance then
        advance := false
      else begin
        (* start again in row 1 *)
        row := 1;
        advance := self.findSolution;
      end;
  end;
end;

procedure queen.print;
begin
  if neighbor <> nil then
    neighbor.print;
```

```
      writeln('row ', row , ' column ', column);
   end;

begin
   neighbor := nil;
   for  i := 1 to 8 do begin
       (* create and initialize new queen *)
     new (lastqueen);
     lastQueen.initialize (i, neighbor);
     if not lastQueen.findSolution then
       writeln('no solution');
       (* newest queen is next queen neighbor *)
     neighbor := lastQueen;
   end;

   lastQueen.print;

   for i := 1 to 8 do begin
     neighbor := lastQueen.neighbor;
     dispose (lastQueen);
     lastQueen := neighbor;
   end;
end.
```

A.2 ⊡ Eight-Queens in C++

```
// Eight-Queens Puzzle in C++
// Written by Tim Budd, Oregon State University, 1996
//

# include <iostream>

class queen {
public:
    // constructor
  queen (int, queen *);

    // find and print solutions
  bool findSolution();
  bool advance();
  void print();
```

```
private:
    // data fields
  int row;
  const int column;
  queen * neighbor;

    // internal method
  bool canAttack (int, int);
};

queen::queen(int col, queen * ngh)
  : column(col), neighbor(ngh)
{
  row = 1;
}

bool queen::canAttack (int testRow, int testColumn)
{
    // test rows
  if (row == testRow)
    return true;

    // test diagonals
  int columnDifference = testColumn - column;
  if ((row + columnDifference == testRow) ||
    (row - columnDifference == testRow))
      return true;

    // try neighbor
  return neighbor && neighbor->canAttack(testRow, testColumn);
}

bool queen::findSolution()
{
    // test position against neighbors
  while (neighbor && neighbor->canAttack (row, column))
    if (! advance())
      return false;

      // found a solution
  return true;
}
```

```cpp
bool queen::advance()
{
  if (row < 8) {
    row++;
    return findSolution();
    }

  if (neighbor && ! neighbor->advance())
    return false;
  row = 1;
  return findSolution();
}
void queen::print()
{
  if (neighbor)
    neighbor->print();
  cout << "column " << column << " row " << row << '\n';
}

void main() {
  queen * lastQueen = 0;

  for (int i = 1; i <= 8; i++) {
    lastQueen = new queen(i, lastQueen);
    if (! lastQueen->findSolution())
      cout << "no solution\n";
    }

  lastQueen->print();
}
```

A.3 ▫ Eight-Queens in Java

```
//
// Eight-Queens Puzzle Written in Java
// Written by Tim Budd, January 1996
// revised for 1.3 event model July 2001
//

import java.awt.*;
import java.awt.event.*;
```

```
import javax.swing.*;

class Queen {
    // data fields
  private int row;
  private int column;
  private Queen neighbor;

    // constructor
  Queen (int c, Queen n) {
      // initialize data fields
    row = 1;
    column = c;
    neighbor = n;
    }

  public boolean findSolution() {
    while (neighbor != null && neighbor.canAttach(row, column))
      if (! advance())
        return false;
    return true;
    }

  public boolean advance() {
    if (row < 8) {
      row++;
      return findSolution();
      }
    if (neighbor != null) {
      if (! neighbor.advance())
        return false;
      if (! neighbor.findSolution())
        return false;
      }
    else
      return false;
    row = 1;
    return findSolution();

    }

    private boolean canAttach(int testRow, int testColumn) {
```

```
      int columnDifference = testColumn - column;
      if ((row == testRow) ||
        (row + columnDifference == testRow) ||
        (row - columnDifference == testRow))
          return true;
      if (neighbor != null)
        return neighbor.canAttach(testRow, testColumn);
      return false;
      }


  public void paint (Graphics g) {
      // first draw neighbor
      if (neighbor != null)
        neighbor.paint(g);
      // then draw ourself
      // x, y is upper left corner
      int x = (row - 1) * 50 + 10;
      int y = (column - 1) * 50 + 40;
      g.drawLine(x+5, y+45, x+45, y+45);
      g.drawLine(x+5, y+45, x+5, y+5);
      g.drawLine(x+45, y+45, x+45, y+5);
      g.drawLine(x+5, y+35, x+45, y+35);
      g.drawLine(x+5, y+5, x+15, y+20);
      g.drawLine(x+15, y+20, x+25, y+5);
      g.drawLine(x+25, y+5, x+35, y+20);
      g.drawLine(x+35, y+20, x+45, y+5);
      g.drawOval(x+20, y+20, 10, 10);
      }


  public void foo(Queen arg, Graphics g) {
      if (arg.row == 3)
        g.setColor(Color.red);
      }
  }


public class QueenSolver extends JFrame {

  public static void main(String [ ] args) {
    QueenSolver world = new QueenSolver();
    world.show();
    }
```

```java
private Queen lastQueen = null;

public QueenSolver() {
  setTitle("8 queens");
  setSize(600, 500);
  for (int i = 1; i <= 8; i++) {
    lastQueen = new Queen(i, lastQueen);
    lastQueen.findSolution();
    }
  addMouseListener(new MouseKeeper());
  addWindowListener(new CloseQuit());
  }

public void paint(Graphics g) {
  super.paint(g);
  // draw board
  for (int i = 0; i <= 8; i++) {
    g.drawLine(50 * i + 10, 40, 50*i + 10, 440);
    g.drawLine(10, 50 * i + 40, 410, 50*i + 40);
  }
  g.drawString("Click Mouse for Next Solution", 20, 470);
  // draw queens
  lastQueen.paint(g);
  }

private class CloseQuit extends WindowAdapter {
  public void windowClosing (WindowEvent e) {
    System.exit(0);
  }
}

private class MouseKeeper extends MouseAdapter {
  public void mousePressed (MouseEvent e) {
    lastQueen.advance();
    repaint();
  }
}
}
```

A.4 ▫ Eight-Queens in Objective-C

Note that both the classes Queen and SentinelQueen define implementation sections without prior interface definitions. This will produce a warning from the compiler but no error.

```
/*
  Eight-Queens Puzzle in Objective-C
  Written by Tim Budd, Oregon State University, 1996
*/


# include <stdio.h>
# include <objc/Object.h>


/*
  A sentinel queen sits
  to the left of the leftmost queen
*/

@implementation SentinelQueen : Object
- (int) advance
{
  /* do nothing */
  return 0;
}
- (int) findSolution
{
  /* do nothing */
  return 1;
}

- (void) print
{
  /* do nothing */
}

- (int) canAttack: (int) testRow column: (int) testColumn;
{
  /* cannot attack */
  return 0;
}
@end
```

```
@interface Queen : Object
{  /* data fields */
   int row;
   int column;
   id neighbor;
}

   /* methods */
- (void) initialize: (int) c neighbor: ngh;
- (int)  advance;
- (void) print;
- (int)  canAttack: (int) testRow column: (int) testColumn;
- (int)  findSolution;
@end

@implementation Queen : Object

- (void) initialize: (int) c neighbor: ngh
{
   /* set the constant fields */
   column = c;
   neighbor = ngh;
   row = 1;
}



- (int) advance
{
   /* first try next row */
   if (row < 8) {
     row = row + 1;
     return [ self findSolution ];
     }

   /* cannot go further, move neighbors */
   if ( ! [ neighbor advance ] )
     return 0;

   /* begin again in row 1 */
   row = 1;
   return [ self findSolution ];
```

```
}

- (void) print
{
  if (neighbor)
    [ neighbor print ];
  printf("column %d row %d\n", column, row);
}

- (int) canAttack: (int) testRow column: (int) testColumn
{ int columnDifference;

  /* can attack same row */
  if (row == testRow)
    return 1;

  columnDifference = testColumn - column;
  if ((row + columnDifference == testRow) ||
    (row - columnDifference == testRow))
      return 1;

  return [ neighbor canAttack:testRow column: testColumn ];
}

- (int) findSolution
{
  /* if neighbor can attack, then move on */
  while ( [ neighbor canAttack:row column: column ] )
    if ( ! [ self advance ] )
      return 0;
  /* otherwise we're safe for now */
  return 1;
}
@end

main() {
  id lastQueen, neighbor;
  int i;

  // create and initialize queens
  neighbor = [ SentinelQueen new ];
  for (i = 1; i <= 8; i++) {
```

```
    lastQueen = [ Queen new ];
    [ lastQueen initialize: i neighbor: neighbor ];
    [ lastQueen findSolution ];
    neighbor = lastQueen;
    }

// then print out solution
[ lastQueen print ];
}
```

A.5 □ Eight-Queens in Ruby

The version of eight-queens in Ruby was written by Mike Stok.

```
class Queen

  def initialColumn(column, neighbor)
    @column = column
    @neighbor = neighbor
    nil
  end

  def canAttack?(row, column)
    return true if row == @row

    cd = (column - @column).abs
    rd = (row - @row).abs
    return true if cd == rd
    @neighbor.canAttack?(row, column)
  end

  def testOrAdvance?
    if @neighbor.canAttack?(@row, @column)
      return next?
    end
    return true
  end

  def first?
    @row = 1
    return testOrAdvance? if @neighbor.first?
    return false
```

```
    end

    def next?
      if @row == 8
        return false unless @neighbor.next?
        @row = 0
      end
      @row += 1
      testOrAdvance?
    end

    def getState
      stateArray = @neighbor.getState
      stateArray << [@row, @column]
    end

  end

  class NullQueen

    def canAttack?(row, column)
      false
    end

    def first?
      true
    end

    def next?
      false
    end

    def getState
      Array.new
    end

  end

  # the program

  neighbor = NullQueen.new
  lastQueen = nil
```

```
1.upto(8) { |column|
  lastQueen = Queen.new
  lastQueen.initialColumn(column, neighbor)
  neighbor = lastQueen
}

if lastQueen.first?
  lastQueen.getState.each { |state|
    puts "row: #{state[0]} column: #{state[1]}"
  }
end
```

A.6 □ Eight-Queens in Smalltalk

The class SentinelQueen in the Smalltalk solution has no instance variables. It uses the following methods.

```
{advance}
  ↑ false
```

```
{canAttack:} row {column:} column
  ↑ false
```

```
{result}
  ↑ List new
```

The class Queen has three instance variables corresponding to the values of the row, column, and neighbor. It defines the following methods.

```
{setColumn:} aNumber {neighbor:} aQueen
    " initialize the data fields "
  column <- aNumber.
  neighbor <- aQueen.
    " find first solution "
  row <- 1.
```

```
{canAttack:} testRow {column:} testColumn | columnDifference |
  columnDifference <- testColumn - column.
  (((row = testRow) or:
    [ row + columnDifference = testRow]) or:
    [ row - columnDifference = testRow])
      ifTrue: [ ↑ true ].
```

```
↑ neighbor canAttack: testRow column: testColumn
```

{advance}
```
    " first try next row "
    (row < 8)
      ifTrue: [ row <- row + 1. ↑ self findSolution ].
      " cannot go further, move neighbor "
    (neighbor advance)
      ifFalse: [ ↑ false ].
    row <- 1.
    ↑ self findSolution
```

{findSolution}
```
    [ neighbor canAttack: row column: column ]
      whileTrue: [ self advance
        ifFalse: [ ↑ false ] ].
    ↑ true
```

{result}
```
    ↑ neighbor result; addLast: row
```

To find a solution, the following method is executed.

{run} | lastQueen |
```
    lastQueen <- SentinelQueen new.
    1 to: 8 do: [:i | lastQueen <- (Queen new)
      setColumn: i neighbor: lastQueen.
      lastQueen findSolution ].
    'got a result' print.
    lastQueen result do: [:x | x print. ' ' print ].
    Char newline print.
```

Source for the Billiards Game

This appendix lists the complete source for the billiards simulation described in Chapter 7.

B.1 ☐ The Version without Inheritance

```
unit GraphicsEx;

(*
        Billiards Simulation Program
        Written by Tim Budd, July 2001
*)

interface

uses
   Windows, Messages, SysUtils, Classes, Graphics,
     Controls, Forms, Dialogs, ExtCtrls, StdCtrls;

type
   TBall = class(TObject)
   public
      constructor create (ix, iy : Integer; iLink : TBall);
      procedure draw (canvas : TCanvas);
      function hasIntersected(aBall : Tball) : Boolean;
      procedure hitBy (aBall : TBall);
```

```
   procedure update;
   procedure setCenter (nx, ny : Integer);
   procedure setDirection (nd : Real);
private
   x, y : Integer;
   direction : Real;
   energy : Real;
   link : TBall;
end;


TWall = class(TObject)
public
   constructor create (ix, iy, iw, ih : Integer; cf : Real; ilink :
   TWall);
   procedure draw (canvas : TCanvas);
   function hasIntersected(aBall : Tball) : Boolean;
   procedure hitBy (aBall : TBall);
private
   x, y : Integer;
   height, width : Integer;
   convertFactor : Real;
   link : TWall;
end;


THole = class(TObject)
public
   constructor create (ix, iy : Integer; ilink : THole);
   procedure draw (canvas : TCanvas);
   function hasIntersected(aBall : TBall) : Boolean;
   procedure hitBy (aBall : TBall);
private
   x, y : Integer;
   link : THole;
end;


   (* following class description generated by Delphi IDE *)
TfrmGraphics = class(TForm)
   btnDrawExample: TButton;
   imgGraph: TImage;
   procedure DrawExample(Sender: TObject);
   procedure Initialize(Sender: TObject);
   procedure DoClick(Sender: TObject; Button: TMouseButton;
```

```
                Shift: TShiftState; X, Y: Integer);
    end;

var
   frmGraphics: TfrmGraphics;
   cueBall : TBall;
   listOfBalls : TBall;
   listOfWalls : TWall;
   listOfHoles : THole;
   saveRack : Integer;
   ballMoved : Boolean;

implementation

constructor TWall.create(ix, iy, iw, ih : Integer; cf : Real; ilink :
Twall);
begin
   x := ix;
   y := iy;
   height := ih;
   width := iw;
   convertFactor := cf;
   link := ilink;
end;

procedure TWall.draw(canvas: TCanvas);
begin
   with canvas do begin
      Brush.Style := bsSolid;
      Brush.Color := clBlack;
      fillRect(Rect(x, y, x + width, y + height));
   end;
end;

function TWall.hasIntersected(aBall : TBall) : Boolean;
begin
   if (aBall.x > x) and (aBall.x < x + width) and
      (aBall.y > y) and (aBall.y < y + height) then
      hasIntersected := true
   else
      hasIntersected := false;
end;
```

```pascal
procedure TWall.hitBy (aBall : TBall);
begin
     { bounce the ball off the wall }
   aBall.direction := convertFactor - aBall.direction;
end;

constructor TBall.create(ix, iy : Integer; iLink : TBall);
begin
   setCenter(ix, iy);
   setDirection(0.0);
   energy := 0.0;
   link := iLink;
end;

procedure TBall.setCenter(nx, ny : Integer);
begin
   x := nx;
   y := ny;
end;

procedure TBall.setDirection(nd : Real);
begin
   direction := nd;
end;

function TBall.hasIntersected(aBall : TBall) : Boolean;
var
   dx, dy : integer;
begin
   dx := aBall.x - x;
   if (dx < 0) then dx := - dx;
   dy := aBall.y - y;
   if (dy < 0) then dy := - dy;
   hasIntersected := (dx < 5) and (dy < 5);
end;

function hitAngle (dx, dy : real) : real;
const
   PI = 3.14159;
var
   na : real;
begin
```

```
    if (abs(dx) < 0.05) then
        na := PI / 2
    else
        na := arctan (abs(dy / dx));
    if (dx < 0) then
        na := PI - na;
    if (dy < 0) then
        na := - na;
    hitAngle := na;
end;

procedure TBall.update;
var
    hptr : THole;
    wptr : TWall;
    bptr : TBall;
    dx, dy : integer;
begin
    if energy > 0.5 then begin
        ballMoved := true;
            { decrease energy }
        energy := energy - 0.05;
            { move ball }
        dx := trunc(5.0 * cos(direction));
        dy := trunc(5.0 * sin(direction));
        x := x + dx;
        y := y + dy;

            { see if we hit a hole }
        hptr := listOfHoles;
        while (hptr <> nil) do
            if hptr.hasIntersected(self) then begin
                hptr.hitBy(self);
                hptr := nil;
            end
            else
                hptr := hptr.link;

            { see if we hit a wall }
        wptr := listOfWalls;
        while (wptr <> nil) do
            if wptr.hasIntersected(self) then begin
```

```
                wptr.hitBy(self);
                wptr := nil;
            end
            else
                wptr := wptr.link;

            { see if we hit a ball }
        bptr := listOfBalls;
        while (bptr <> nil) do
            if (bptr <> self) and bptr.hasIntersected(self) then begin
                bptr.hitBy(self);
                bptr := nil;
            end
            else
                bptr := bptr.link;
    end;
end;


procedure TBall.hitBy (aBall : TBall);
var
    da : real;
begin
        { cut the energy of the hitting ball in half }
    aBall.energy := aBall.energy / 2.0;

        { and add it to our own }
    energy := energy + aBall.energy;

        { set our new direction }
    direction := hitAngle(self.x - aBall.x, self.y - aBall.y);

        { and set the hitting balls direction }
    da := aBall.direction - direction;
    aBall.direction := aBall.direction + da;

        { continue our update }
    update;
end;


procedure TBall.draw(canvas : TCanvas);
begin
    with canvas do begin
```

```
      Brush.Style := bsSolid;
      if (self = cueBall) then
         Brush.Color := clWhite
      else
         Brush.Color := clBlack;
      Ellipse(x-5, y-5, x+5, y+5);
   end;
end;

constructor THole.create(ix, iy : Integer; ilink :
THole);
begin
   x := ix;
   y := iy;
   link := ilink;
end;

procedure THole.draw(canvas : TCanvas);
begin
   with canvas do begin
      Brush.Style := bsSolid;
      Brush.Color := clBlack;
      Ellipse(x-5, y-5, x+5, y+5);
   end;
end;

function THole.hasIntersected(aBall : TBall) : Boolean;
var
   dx, dy : integer;
begin
   dx := aBall.x - x;
   if (dx < 0) then dx := - dx;
   dy := aBall.y - y;
   if (dy < 0) then dy := - dy;
   hasIntersected := (dx < 5) and (dy < 5);
end;

procedure THole.hitBy (aBall : TBall);
begin
      { drain enery from ball }
   aBall.energy := 0.0;
```

```
     { move ball }
  if aBall = CueBall then
     aBall.setCenter(50, 100)
  else begin
     saveRack := saveRack + 1;
     aBall.setCenter (10 + saveRack * 15, 250);
  end;
end;


procedure TfrmGraphics.DrawExample(Sender: TObject);
var
  wptr : TWall;
  hptr : THole;
  bptr : TBall;
begin
  with imgGraph.Canvas do begin
  Brush.Color := clWhite;
  Brush.Style := bsSolid;
  FillRect(Rect(0, 0, 700, 700));
  end;
  wptr := listOfWalls;
  while (wptr <> nil) do begin
     wptr.draw(imgGraph.Canvas);
     wptr := wptr.link;
  end;
  hptr := listOfHoles;
  while (hptr <> nil) do begin
  hptr.draw(imgGraph.Canvas);
  hptr := hptr.link;
  end;

  bptr := listOfBalls;
  while (bptr <> nil) do begin
  bptr.draw(imgGraph.Canvas);
  bptr := bptr.link;
  end;
end;


procedure TfrmGraphics.Initialize(Sender: TObject);
var
  i, j : Integer;
begin
```

```
    (* first create all the walls *)
    listOfWalls := TWall.Create(10, 10, 290, 5, 0.0, nil);
    listOfWalls := TWall.Create(10, 200, 290, 5, 0.0, listOfWalls);
    listOfWalls := TWall.Create(10, 10, 5, 190, 3.14159, listOfWalls);
    listOfWalls := TWall.Create(300, 10, 5, 195, 3.14159, listOfWalls);
        (* now make the holes *)
    listOfHoles := THole.Create(15, 15, nil);
    listOfHoles := THole.Create(15, 200, listOfHoles);
    listOfHoles := THole.Create(300, 15, listOfHoles);
    listOfHoles := THole.Create(300, 200, listOfHoles);
      (* now make the balls *)
    cueBall := TBall.Create(50, 96, nil);
    listOfBalls := cueBall;
    for i := 1 to 5 do
    for j := 1 to i do
       listOfBalls := TBall.Create(190 + i * 8,
          100 + 16 * j - 8 * i, listOfBalls);
    saveRack := 0;
end;


procedure TfrmGraphics.DoClick(Sender: TObject; Button:
TMouseButton;
  Shift: TShiftState; X, Y: Integer);
var
   bptr : TBall;
begin
   cueBall.energy := 20.0;
   cueBall.setDirection(hitAngle(cueBall.x - x, cueBall.y - y));
      { then loop as long as called for }
   ballMoved := true;
   while ballMoved do begin
      ballMoved := false;
      bptr := listOfBalls;
      while bptr <> nil do begin
         bptr.update;
         bptr := bptr.link;
      end;
   end;
end;


end.
```

B.2 □ The Version with Inheritance

Only those sections of the program that differ from the original are presented.

```
type
  TBall = class;

  TGraphicalObject = class(TObject)
  public
        constructor Create(ix, iy : Integer; il : TGraphicalObject);
        procedure draw (canvas : TCanvas); virtual; abstract;
        function hasIntersected (aBall : TBall): Boolean; virtual;
              abstract;
        procedure hitBy (aBall : TBall); virtual; abstract;
        procedure update; virtual;
  private
        x, y : Integer;
        link : TGraphicalObject;
  end;


  TBall = class(TGraphicalObject)
  public
     constructor create (ix, iy : Integer; iLink : TGraphicalObject);
overload;
     procedure draw (canvas : TCanvas); override;
     function hasIntersected(aBall : TBall) : Boolean; override;
     procedure hitBy (aBall : TBall); override;
     procedure update;   override;
     procedure setCenter (nx, ny : Integer);
     procedure setDirection (nd : Real);
  private
        direction : Real;
        energy : Real;
  end;

  TCueBall = class(TBall)
  public
        procedure draw (canvas : TCanvas); override;
  end;

  TWall = class(TGraphicalObject)
  public
```

```
        constructor create (ix, iy, iw, ih : Integer;
            cf : Real; ilink : TGraphicalObject); overload;
        procedure draw (canvas : TCanvas); override;
        function hasIntersected(aBall : TBall) : Boolean; override;
        procedure hitBy (aBall : TBall); override;
    private
        height, width : Integer;
        convertFactor : Real;
    end;


    THole = class(TGraphicalObject)
    public
        constructor create
            (ix, iy : Integer; ilink : TGraphicalObject); overload;
        procedure draw (canvas : TCanvas);  override;
        function hasIntersected(aBall : TBall) : Boolean;  override;
        procedure hitBy (aBall : TBall); override;
    end;

constructor TGraphicalObject.Create
        (ix, iy : Integer; il : TGraphicalObject);
begin
        x := ix;
        y := iy;
        link := il;
end;


procedure TGraphicalObject.update ();
begin
        (* do nothing *)
end;


constructor TWall.Create(ix, iy, iw, ih : Integer; cf :
Real; ilink : TGraphicalObject);
begin
        inherited Create(ix, iy, ilink);
        height := ih;
        width := iw;
        convertFactor := cf;
end;


constructor TBall.Create(ix, iy : Integer; iLink :
```

```
TGraphicalObject);
begin
        inherited Create(ix, iy, iLink);
        setDirection(0.0);
        energy := 0.0;
end;


procedure TBall.update;
var
   hptr : TGraphicalObject;
   dx, dy : integer;
begin
   if energy > 0.5 then begin
      ballMoved := true;
         { decrease energy }
      energy := energy - 0.05;
         { move ball }
      dx := trunc(5.0 * cos(direction));
      dy := trunc(5.0 * sin(direction));
               x := x + dx;
               y := y + dy;

         { see if we hit an object }
      hptr := listOfObjects;
      while (hptr <> nil) do
         if (hptr <> self) and hptr.hasIntersected(self) then begin
            hptr.hitBy(self);
            hptr := nil;
         end
         else
            hptr := hptr.link;
   end;
end;


procedure TBall.hitBy (aBall : TBall);
var
procedure TBall.draw(canvas : TCanvas);
begin
        with canvas do begin
                Brush.Style := bsSolid;
                Brush.Color := clBlack;
                Ellipse(x-5, y-5, x+5, y+5);
```

```pascal
        end;
end;

procedure TCueBall.draw (canvas : TCanvas);
begin
        with canvas do begin
                Brush.Style := bsSolid;
                Brush.Color := clWhite;
                Ellipse(x-5, y-5, x+5, y+5);
        end;
end;

constructor THole.create(ix, iy : Integer; ilink :
TGraphicalObject);
begin
        inherited Create(ix, iy, ilink);
end;

procedure TfrmGraphics.DrawExample(Sender: TObject);
var
        gptr : TGraphicalObject;
begin
   with imgGraph.Canvas do begin
        Brush.Color := clWhite;
        Brush.Style := bsSolid;
        FillRect(Rect(0, 0, 700, 700));
   end;
   gptr := listOfObjects;
   while (gptr <> nil) do begin
        gptr.draw(imgGraph.Canvas);
        gptr := gptr.link;
   end;
end;

end.
```

Source for the Solitaire Game

This appendix contains the complete source for the solitaire game described in Chapter 9. This program is written in C# and uses the standard Windows run-time library.

```
namespace csSolitaire
{
    using System;
    using System.Drawing;
    using System.Collections;
    using System.ComponentModel;
    using System.WinForms;
    using System.Data;

public enum Suits { Spade, Diamond, Club, Heart };

//
//  PlayingCard
//

public class PlayingCard
{
  public PlayingCard (Suits sv, int rv)
    { s = sv; r = rv; faceUp = false; }

  public bool isFaceUp
```

```
  {
    get { return faceUp; }
  }

  public void flip ()
  {
    faceUp = ! faceUp;
  }

  public int rank
  {
    get { return r; }
  }

  public Suits suit
  {
    get { return s; }
  }

  public Color color
  {
    get
    {
      if ( suit == Suits.Heart || suit == Suits.Diamond )
        { return Color.Red; }
      return Color.Black;
    }
  }

  private bool faceUp;
  private int r;
  private Suits s;
}

//
//  CardView
//

public abstract class CardView
{
  public abstract void display (PlayingCard aCard, int x, int y);
```

```
  public static int Width = 50;
  public static int Height = 70;
}

//
//  CardPile
//

public class CardPile {
  public CardPile (int xl, int yl )
    { x = xl; y = yl; pile = new Stack(); }

  public PlayingCard top
    { get { return (PlayingCard) pile.Peek (); } }

  public bool isEmpty
    { get { return pile.Count == 0; }  }

  public PlayingCard pop
    { get { return (PlayingCard) pile.Pop (); } }

    // the following are sometimes overridden
  public virtual bool includes (int tx, int ty )
  {
    return( ( x <= tx ) && ( tx <= x + CardView.Width ) &&
        ( y <= ty ) && ( ty <= y + CardView.Height ) );
  }

  public virtual void select (int tx, int ty )
  {
    // do nothing-override
  }

  public virtual void addCard (PlayingCard aCard )
    { pile.Push(aCard); }

  public virtual void display (CardView cv)
  {
    if ( isEmpty ) {
      cv.display(null, x, y);
    } else {
      cv.display((PlayingCard) pile.Peek(), x, y );
```

```
    }
  }

  public virtual bool canTake (PlayingCard aCard)
    { return false; }

  protected int x, y; // coordinates of the card pile
  protected Stack pile; // card pile data
}

//
// SuitPile
//

public class SuitPile : CardPile
{
  public SuitPile (int x, int y) : base(x, y) {  }

  public override bool canTake (PlayingCard aCard ) {
    if( isEmpty )
      { return( aCard.rank == 0 ); }
    PlayingCard topCard = top;
    return( ( aCard.suit == topCard.suit ) &&
      ( aCard.rank == topCard.rank + 1 ) );
  }
}

//
// DeckPile
//

public class DeckPile : CardPile
{
  public DeckPile (int x, int y) : base(x, y) {
    // create the new deck
    // first put cards into a local array
    ArrayList aList = new ArrayList ();
    for( int i = 0; i <= 12; i++) {
      aList.Add(new PlayingCard(Suits.Heart, i));
      aList.Add(new PlayingCard(Suits.Diamond, i));
      aList.Add(new PlayingCard(Suits.Spade, i));
      aList.Add(new PlayingCard(Suits.Club, i));
```

```
    }
      // then pull them out randomly
    Random myRandom = new Random( );
    for(int count = 0; count < 52; count++) {
       int index = myRandom.Next(aList.Count);
       addCard( (PlayingCard) aList [index] );
       aList.RemoveAt(index);
    }
  }

  public override void select (int tx, int ty)
  {
    if ( isEmpty ) { return; }
    Game.discardPile().addCard( pop );
  }
}

//
// DiscardPile
//

public class DiscardPile : CardPile {
  public DiscardPile (int x, int y ) : base(x, y) { }

  public override void addCard (PlayingCard aCard) {
    if( ! aCard.isFaceUp )
      { aCard.flip(); }
    base.addCard( aCard );
  }

  public override void select (int tx, int ty) {
    if( isEmpty ) { return; }
    PlayingCard topCard = pop;
    for( int i = 0; i < 4; i++ ) {
      if( Game.suitPile(i).canTake( topCard ) ) {
        Game.suitPile(i).addCard( topCard );
        return;
      }
    }

    for( int i = 0; i < 7; i++ ) {
      if( Game.tableau(i).canTake( topCard ) ) {
```

```
          Game.tableau(i).addCard( topCard );
          return;
        }
      }
      // nobody can use it, put it back on our stack
      addCard(topCard);
    }
  }


  //
  // TablePile
  //

  public class TablePile : CardPile {
    public TablePile (int x, int y, int c) : base(x, y) {
      // initialize our pile of cards
      for(int i = 0; i < c; i++ ) {
        addCard(Game.deckPile().pop);
      }
      top.flip();
    }

    public override bool canTake (PlayingCard aCard ) {
      if( isEmpty ) { return(aCard.rank == 12); }
      PlayingCard topCard = top;
      return( ( aCard.color != topCard.color ) &&
        ( aCard.rank    == topCard.rank - 1 ) );
    }

    public override bool includes (int tx, int ty) {
      return( ( x <= tx ) && ( tx <= x + CardView.Width ) &&
        ( y <= ty ) );
    }

    public override void select (int tx, int ty) {
      if( isEmpty ) { return; }
      // if face down, then flip
      PlayingCard topCard = top;
      if( ! topCard.isFaceUp ) {
        topCard.flip();
        return;
      }
```

```
    // else see if any suit pile can take card
    topCard = pop;
    for(int i = 0; i < 4; i++ ) {
      if( Game.suitPile(i).canTake( topCard ) ) {
        Game.suitPile(i).addCard( topCard );
        return;
      }
    }
    // else see if any other table pile can take card
    for(int i = 0; i < 7; i++ ) {
      if( Game.tableau(i).canTake( topCard ) ) {
        Game.tableau(i).addCard( topCard );
        return;
      }
    }
    addCard( topCard );
  }

  public override void display (CardView cv) {
    Object [ ] cardArray = pile.ToArray();
    int size = pile.Count;
    int hs = CardView.Height / 2; // half size
    int ty = y;
    for (int i = pile.Count - 1; i >= 0; i--) {
      cv.display((PlayingCard) cardArray[i], x, ty);
      ty += hs;
    }
  }
}

//
// Game
//

public class Game {
  static Game () {
    allPiles = new CardPile[ 13 ];
    allPiles[0] = new DeckPile(335, 5 );
    allPiles[1] = new DiscardPile(268, 5 );
    for( int i = 0; i < 4; i++ ) {
      allPiles[2 + i] = new SuitPile(15 + 60 * i, 5 );
    }
```

```
    for( int i = 0; i < 7; i++ ) {
      allPiles[6 + i] = new TablePile(5 + 55 * i, 80, i + 1);
    }
  }

  public static void paint (CardView cv) {
    for( int i = 0; i < 13; i++ ) {
      allPiles[i].display(cv );
    }
  }

  public static void mouseDown (int x, int y) {
    for( int i = 0; i < 13; i++ ) {
      if( allPiles[i].includes( x, y ) ) {
        allPiles [i].select( x, y );
      }
    }
  }

  public static CardPile deckPile ()
    { return allPiles[0]; }

  public static CardPile discardPile ()
    { return allPiles[1]; }

  public static CardPile tableau (int index)
    { return allPiles[6+index]; }

  public static CardPile suitPile (int index)
    { return allPiles[2+index]; }

  private static CardPile[] allPiles;
}

//
//  WinFormsCardView
//

public class WinFormsCardView : CardView {
  public WinFormsCardView (Graphics aGraphicsObject) {
    g = aGraphicsObject;
  }
```

```
public override void display (PlayingCard aCard,int x,int y) {
  if  (aCard == null) {
    Pen myPen = new Pen(Color.Black,2);
    Brush myBrush = new SolidBrush (Color.White);
    g.FillRectangle(myBrush,x,y,CardView.Width,CardView.Height);
    g.DrawRectangle(myPen,x,y,CardView.Width,CardView.Height);
  } else {
    paintCard (aCard,x,y);
  }
}


private void paintCard (PlayingCard aCard,int x,int y) {
  String [] names = { "A","2","3","4","5",
    "6","7","8","9","10","J","Q","K" };

  Pen myPen = new Pen (Color.Black,2);
  Brush myBrush = new SolidBrush (Color.White);

  g.FillRectangle (myBrush,x,y,CardView.Width,CardView.Height);
  g.DrawRectangle(myPen,x,y,CardView.Width,CardView.Height);
  myPen.Dispose();
  myBrush.Dispose();

  // draw body of card with a new pen-color
  if (aCard.isFaceUp) {
    if (aCard.color == Color.Red) {
      myPen = new Pen  (Color.Red,1);
      myBrush = new SolidBrush (Color.Red);
    } else {
      myPen = new Pen  (Color.Blue,1);
      myBrush = new SolidBrush (Color.Blue);
    }
    g.DrawString (names[ aCard.rank ],
      new Font("Times New Roman",10),myBrush,x+3,y+7);
    if (aCard.suit == Suits.Heart) {
      g.DrawLine(myPen,x+25,y+30,x+35,y+20);
      g.DrawLine(myPen,x+35,y+20,x+45,y+30);
      g.DrawLine(myPen,x+45,y+30,x+25,y+60);
      g.DrawLine(myPen,x+25,y+60,x+5,y+30);
      g.DrawLine(myPen,x+5,y+30,x+15,y+20);
      g.DrawLine(myPen,x+15,y+20,x+25,y+30);
    } else if (aCard.suit == Suits.Spade) {
```

```
            g.DrawLine(myPen,x+25,y+20,x+40,y+50);
            g.DrawLine(myPen,x+40,y+50,x+10,y+50);
            g.DrawLine(myPen,x+10,y+50,x+25,y+20);
            g.DrawLine(myPen,x+23,y+45,x+20,y+60);
            g.DrawLine(myPen,x+20,y+60,x+30,y+60);
            g.DrawLine(myPen,x+30,y+60,x+27,y+45);
        } else if (aCard.suit == Suits.Diamond) {
            g.DrawLine(myPen,x+25,y+20,x+40,y+40);
            g.DrawLine(myPen,x+40,y+40,x+25,y+60);
            g.DrawLine(myPen,x+25,y+60,x+10,y+40);
            g.DrawLine(myPen,x+10,y+40,x+25,y+20);
        } else if (aCard.suit == Suits.Club) {
            g.DrawEllipse(myPen,x+20,y+25,10,10);
            g.DrawEllipse(myPen,x+25,y+35,10,10);
            g.DrawEllipse(myPen,x+15,y+35,10,10);
            g.DrawLine(myPen,x+23,y+45,x+20,y+55);
            g.DrawLine(myPen,x+20,y+55,x+30,y+55);
            g.DrawLine(myPen,x+30,y+55,x+27,y+45);
        }
    } else {    // face down
      myPen = new Pen (Color.Green,1);
      myBrush = new SolidBrush  (Color.Green);
      g.DrawLine(myPen,x+15,y+5,x+15,y+65);
      g.DrawLine(myPen,x+35,y+5,x+35,y+65);
      g.DrawLine(myPen,x+5,y+20,x+45,y+20);
      g.DrawLine(myPen,x+5,y+35,x+45,y+35);
      g.DrawLine(myPen,x+5,y+50,x+45,y+50);
    }
  }
  private Graphics g;
}


//
// Solitaire
//

public class Solitaire : System.WinForms.Form {
    // start of automatically generated code
        private System.ComponentModel.Container components;

        public Solitaire() {
            InitializeComponent();
```

```
        }

        public override void Dispose() {
            base.Dispose();
            components.Dispose();
        }

        private void InitializeComponent() {
        this.components = new System.ComponentModel.Container ();
        this.Text = "Solitaire";
        this.AutoScaleBaseSize = new System.Drawing.Size (5, 13);
        this.ClientSize = new System.Drawing.Size (392, 373);
    }
    // end of automatically generated code

  protected override void OnMouseDown( MouseEventArgs e ) {
    Game.mouseDown(e.X, e.Y);
    this.Invalidate();
    }

  protected override void OnPaint( PaintEventArgs pe ) {
    Graphics g = pe.Graphics;
    CardView cv = new WinFormsCardView( g );
    Game.paint(cv);
  }

  public static void Main(string[] args)
    { Application.Run(new Solitaire()); }
}

}
```

Glossary

Object-oriented programming techniques introduce many new ideas and terms that may not be familiar to the novice, even if he or she has had extensive experience with other programming languages. More problematic is that among the various object-oriented languages, several terms are often used for the same idea. Such terms are listed as synonyms in the following glossary. Also indicated are situations where a term is given a particular meaning in one language that is not the same for other languages.

abstract class   Syn. *deferred class*, *abstract superclass*. A class that is not used to make direct instances but rather is used only as a base from which other classes inherit. In C++, the term is often reserved for classes that contain at least one *pure virtual* method, whereas in Java the term refers to a class that is explicitly declared as abstract.

abstraction   A technique in problem solving in which details are grouped into a single common concept. This concept can then be viewed as a single entity and nonessential information ignored.

abstract method   (Java) A method that is explicitly declared as abstract. Such methods must be overridden by subclasses before an instance can be created.

accessor method   A method that is used to access the values of an instance variable. By restricting access through a function, the programmer can ensure that instance variables will be read but not modified (see *mutator*).

access specifier   (C++, Delphi Pascal) A keyword (private, protected, or public) that controls access to data members and methods within user-defined classes.

ad hoc polymorphism   Syn. *overloading*. A procedure or method identifier that denotes more than one procedure.

agent   Syn. *object*, *instance*. A nontechnical term sometimes used to describe an object in order to emphasize its independence from other objects and the fact that it is providing a service to other objects.

allocated class   Syn. *dynamic class*. See *static class*.

ancestor class   Syn. *base class*, *superclass*. (Object Pascal) A type from which an object type inherits. The type named in an object type definition statement is called the *immediate ancestor*.

ancestor type   See *ancestor class*.

argument signature   (C++) An internal encoding of a list of argument types; the argument signature is used to disambiguate overloaded function invocations, with that function body being selected that matches most closely the signature of the function call. See *parametric overloading*.

automatic storage management   A policy in which the underlying run-time system is responsible for the detection and reclamation of memory values no longer accessible and hence of no further use to the computation. Among the object-oriented languages discussed in this book, only Smalltalk and Java provide automatic storage management. See *garbage collection*.

automatic variable   A variable that is allocated space automatically when a procedure is entered. Contrast to a *dynamic variable*, which must have space allocated by the user.

base class   Syn. *ancestor class*, *superclass*, *parent class*. (C++) A class from which another class is derived.

binding   The process by which a name or an expression is associated with an attribute, such as a variable and the type of value the variable can hold.

binding time   The time at which a binding takes place. *Early* or *static binding* generally refers to binding performed at compile time, whereas *late* or *dynamic binding* refers to binding performed at run time. Dynamically bound languages, such as Smalltalk and Objective-C, do not bind a variable and the type of value the variable can hold at compile time. Message passing is a form of procedure calling with late binding.

block   (Smalltalk) An object that represents a sequence of statements to be executed at a later time. In this sense a block is similar to a nameless function. Blocks are values and can be passed as arguments or (less frequently) assigned to variables. A block executes its associated statements in response to the message value.

browser   A software tool used to examine the class hierarchy and methods associated with different classes. Originally developed as part of the Smalltalk programming environment, class browsers are now found in many programming environments. A different sort of browser is used to access information on the World Wide Web. More recent WWW browsers have included interpreters for the Java programming language, allowing Java programs to be very efficiently executed in during the reading of WWW pages.

cascaded message (Smalltalk) A shorthand way of sending multiple messages to a single receiver.

cast A unary expression that converts a value from one type to another.

child class Syn. *subclass*, *derived class*. (C++) A class defined as an extension of another class, which is called the *parent class*.

class Syn. *object type*. An abstract description of the data and behavior of a collection of similar objects. The representatives of the collection are called *instances* of the class.

Class (Smalltalk, Java) The class that maintains behavior related to class instance and subclass creation. See *metaclass*.

class description protocol The complete definition of all properties, features, and methods that are descriptive of any object that is an instance of a class.

class hierarchy A hierarchy formed by listing classes according to their class-subclass relationship. See *hierarchy*.

class method (C++) A method declared with the keyword static. Class methods are not permitted to access instance variables but can access only class variables. They can be invoked independently of receivers using explicit name qualification.

class object Syn. *factory object*. (Smalltalk) The single special object and instance of class Class that is associated with each class. New instances of the class are created by the message new being sent to this object.

class variable A variable shared by all instances of a class. (C++) A data member declared as static. (Smalltalk) A variable declared as a class variable in the class-construction message.

client-side computing In a network environment, a program that is executed on the client side rather than on the server side of the network. The Java programming language is intended to perform client-side computing and so is more efficient than programs that must wait for execution on the (generally more overloaded) server machine.

cohesion The degree to which components of a single software system (such as members of a single class) are tied together. Contrast with *coupling*.

collaborator   Two classes that depend on each other for the execution of their behaviors are said to be collaborators.

collection classes   See *container classes*.

composition   The technique of including user-defined object types as part of a newly defined object, as opposed to using inheritance.

constructor   A method used to create a new object. The constructor handles the dual tasks of allocating memory for the new object and ensuring that this memory is properly initialized. The programmer defines how this initialization is performed. In C++ and Java, a constructor is simply a method with the same name as the class in which it appears, while in Delphi Pascal a constructor is declared with a special keyword.

container classes   Classes used as data structures that can contain a number of elements. Examples include lists, sets, and tables. The STL provides a number of standard container classes for C++.

contravariance   A form of overriding in which an argument associated with a method in the child class is restricted to a less general category than the corresponding argument in the parent class. Contrast with *covariance*. Neither covariant nor contravariant overriding is common in object-oriented languages.

copy constructor   (C++) A constructor that takes as argument an instance of the class in which the constructor is being declared. The copy constructor is used to produce a copy, or clone, of the argument.

coupling   The degree to which separate software components are tied together. Contrast with *cohesion*.

covariance   A form of overriding in which an argument associated with a method in the child class is enlarged to a more general category than the corresponding argument in the parent class. Contrast with *contravariance*. Neither covariant nor contravariant overriding is common in object-oriented languages.

CRC card   An index card that documents the name, responsibilities, and collaborators for a class used during the process of system analysis and design.

data hiding   An encapsulation technique that seeks to abstract away the implementation details concerning what data values are maintained for an object to provide a particular service.

data member   (C++) See *instance variable*.

default constructor   (C++) A constructor with no arguments. Such a constructor is often used to initialize temporary variables.

deferred class See *abstract class*.

deferred method A method that defines an interface (that is, argument and result types) but not implementation. Implementation is provided by subclasses that override the deferred method, preserving the interface. See *pure virtual method*.

delegation An alternative to class-based organization. Using delegation, objects can defer the implementation of behavior to other objects, called *delegates*. This technique permits sharing of behavior without the necessity to introduce classes or inheritance.

derived class Syn. *descendant type, subclass, child class*. (C++) A class that is defined as an extension or a subclass of another class, which is called the base class.

descendant type Syn. *subclass, child class*. See *derived class*.

destructor (C++) A method that is invoked immediately before memory is released for an object. The destructor can perform any actions required for the management of the object. The name of the destructor is formed by a tilde (~) being prepended to the name of the class.

dispatch table (Objective-C) A table of method selectors and associated methods. Created when a class is compiled, the dispatch table is searched as part of the message-passing operation.

domain (Object Pascal) When used to refer to variables of object types, the set of object types that represent legal values for the variable. The domain consists of the declared type and all of the descendant types.

dynamic binding The binding of a name to an attribute that occurs at run time rather than compile time. See *binding time*.

dynamic class See *static class*.

dynamic type The type associated with the value currently being held by a variable, which need not be the same as the *static type* given by the declaration for the variable. In object-oriented languages the dynamic type is frequently restricted to being a subclass of the static type.

dynamically typed language A programming language in which types are associated with values, not variables, and variables can hold any type of value. Smalltalk is one example of a dynamically typed language.

dynamic variable A variable for which space must be allocated explicitly by the user. Contrast to an *automatic variable*, which has space allocated for it automatically when a procedure is entered.

early binding   See *binding time*.

ECOOP   The European Conference on Object-Oriented Programming, the major conference in Europe in which object-oriented techniques and tools are discussed.

encapsulation   The technique of hiding information within a structure, such as the hiding of instance data within a class.

exported name   An identifier (variable, type name, function, or method) available for use outside of the context in which it is defined. (Objective-C) A variable, type, function, or method that is global or is defined in an interface (*.h) file. (Object Pascal) A variable, type, function, or method defined within the interface section of a unit. (Java) A class that is declared as public within the package in which it is defined.

extends   (Java) A keyword used in forming a new class as a subclass of an existing class, or a new interface as an extension of an existing interface.

factory method   (Objective-C) A method recognized only by the class object for a class. Contrast to an *instance method*, which is recognized by instances of the class.

factory object   Syn. *class object*. (Objective-C) The unique object, associated with each class, used to create new instances of the class. Each factory object is an instance of class Class. New instances of the class are created by the message new being sent to this object.

final class   (Java) A class declared using the keyword final. This keyword indicates that the class cannot be used as a base class for inheritance.

finalizer   (Java) A method with the name finalize, no arguments, and no return type. This method will be invoked automatically by the run-time system prior to the object in which it is declared being recycled by garbage collection.

final method   (Java) A method declared using the keyword final. This keyword indicates that the method cannot be overridden in subclasses.

friend function   (C++) A function that is permitted access to the otherwise private or protected features of a class. Friend functions must be explicitly declared as such by the class that is protecting the features to which the friend is being given access. Friend classes and friend methods also can be defined.

function member   (C++) See *method*.

garbage collection   A memory management technique whereby the run-time system determines which memory values are no longer necessary to the running program and automatically recovers and recycles the memory for different use. Garbage collection is found in Smalltalk and Java.

generic method Syn. *virtual method*.

global variable A variable that potentially can be accessed in any portion of a program.

has-a relation The relation that asserts that instances of a class possess fields of a given type. See is-a relation.

heap-based memory allocation Memory allocation performed at run-time and not tied to procedure entry and exit. Contrast with *stack-based memory allocation*.

hierarchy An organizational structure with components ranked into levels of subordination according to some set of rules. In object-oriented programming the most common hierarchy is that formed by the class-subclass relationship.

hybrid language A language that incorporates features of more than one programming style. C++ and Object Pascal are hybrid languages, since they support both imperative and object-oriented programming. Smalltalk is a *pure* object-oriented language, since it supports only object-oriented programming.

immediate superclass The closest parent class from which a class inherits. The superclass relationship is a transitive closure of the immediate superclass relationship.

immutable value A value that is not permitted to change once it has been set. Variables that hold such values are sometimes called "single-assignment" variables. In C++ immutable values can be identified via the const keyword.

information hiding The principle that users of a software component (such as a class) need to know only the essential details of how to initialize and access the component and do not need to know the details of the implementation. By reducing the degree of interconnectedness between separate elements of a software system, the principle of information hiding helps in the development of reliable software.

inheritance The property of objects by which instances of a class can have access to data and method definitions contained in a previously defined class, without those definitions being restated. See *ancestor class*.

inheritance graph An abstract structure that illustrates the inheritance relationships with a collection of classes.

inherited (Object Pascal) A keyword used to activate the execution of an overridden procedure.

initialize   (Objective-C, Smalltalk) A special message sent to the class object before the class receives instances of any other message. Can be redefined as a factory method to set up the appropriate run-time environment before instances of a class are used.

in-line function   A function that can be expanded directly in-line at the location it is called, thereby avoiding the overhead associated with a function call. In-line functions can be defined by the directive in-line in C++ or the directive final in Java.

inner class   A class that is defined inside another class. An inner class is distinguished from a nested class in that an inner class maintains an implicit pointer to a specific surrounding object, whereas a nested class does not.

instance   Syn. *object*. (C++) A variable of a class type. (Object Pascal) A variable of an object type. (Smalltalk) A specific example of the general structure defined by a *class*.

instance method   Syn. *method*. (Objective-C) A method recognized by instances of a class. See *factory method*.

instance variable   An internal variable maintained by an instance. Instance variables represent the state of an object.

interaction diagram   A diagram that documents the sequence of messages that flow between objects participating in a scenario.

Internet   A worldwide collection of machines that have agreed to communicate with each other using a common protocol.

is-a relation   The relation that asserts that instances of a subclass must be more specialized forms of the superclass. Thus, instances of a subclass can be used where quantities of the superclass type are required. See *has-a relation*.

isa link   (Objective-C) An implicit pointer, contained in every object, that references to the dispatch table for the object. Since objects are characterized only by their behavior, this pointer in effect encodes the class of the object.

iterator   A class that is used mainly to provide access to the values being held in another class, usually a container class. The iterator provides a uniform framework for accessing values without compromising the encapsulation of the container.

late binding   See *binding time*.

Member   (Object Pascal) A system-provided Boolean function that can be used to determine whether the value (dynamic type) of a variable is a member of the specific object type.

member (C++) A general term for the attributes associated with instances of a class. Instance variables are called *data members* in C++; methods are called *procedure* or *function* members.

message Syn. *message selector, method designator, method selector, selector*. The textual string that identifies a requested action in a message-passing expression. During message passing, this string is used to find a matching method as part of the method-lookup process.

message expression (Objective-C) A Smalltalk-like expression enclosed in a pair of square brackets, [...]. The brackets are used to differentiate message-passing code from normal C code.

message passing The process of locating and executing a method in response to a message. See *method lookup*.

message selector Syn. *method designator, method selector, selector*. The textual string that identifies a message in a message-passing expression. During message passing, this string is used to find a matching method as part of the method-lookup process.

metaclass (Smalltalk) The class of a class object. For each class, there is an associated metaclass. The class object is typically the only instance of this metaclass. Metaclasses permit the specialization of class behavior. Without them, all classes would need to behave in the same way.

metaprogramming A style of programming that makes extensive use of meta-classes and in which the programming language itself can be used to control the semantics and meaning of different constructs. Smalltalk is one language that uses metaprogramming.

method A procedure or function associated with a class (or object type) and invoked in a message-passing style.

method declaration The part of a class declaration specific to an individual method.

method designator Syn. *message selector*. A method name identifier used as a procedure or function name in a message-passing expression. The method designator is used to search for the appropriate method during message sending. In general, you cannot determine from the program text which method a method designator will activate during execution.

method lookup The process of locating a method matching a particular message, generally performed as part of the message-passing operation. Usually, the run-time system finds the method by examining the class hierarchy for the receiver of the message, searching from bottom to top until a method is found with the same name as the message.

method selector   See *message selector.*

multiple inheritance   The feature that allows a subclass to inherit from more than one immediate superclass. Multiple inheritance is not supported by all object-oriented languages.

mutator method   A method that is used to modify the value of an instance variable. By requiring such modifications to be mediated through a function, a class can have greater control over how its internal state is being modified.

name mangling   The process of combining a method name with a textual description of its type signature and class name in order to create a unique internal name.

name space   (C++) A mechanism for restricting the accessibility of global names. Globals can be declared as being part of a specific name space and are only accessible to portions of a program that explicitly include that name space. See *scope.*

native method   (Java) A method that is implemented in another language, such as C or assembly language. See *primitive.*

nested class   A class definition that is given inside another class. (Allowed in Java, C++ and C#.) Unlike an inner class, a nested class does not automatically maintain a reference to a surrounding object.

object   See *instance.* (Object Pascal) A keyword used to indicate the definition of an object type.

object field designator   (Object Pascal) A (perhaps qualified) identifier that denotes the field within an object.

object hierarchy   Syn. *class hierarchy.* (Object Pascal) A group of object types all related through inheritance.

object-oriented programming   A style of design that is centered around the delegation of responsibilities to independent interacting agents and a style of programming characterized by the use of message passing and classes organized into one or more inheritance hierarchies.

object type   Syn. *class.* (Object Pascal) A data structure, similar to a Pascal record type definition, that can contain fields (methods) of procedures and functions as well as data fields.

OOPSLA The annual conference on Object-Oriented Programming Systems, Languages and Applications, sponsored by the Association for Computing Machinery.

overload Used to describe an identifier that denotes more than one object. Procedures, functions, methods, and operators can all be overloaded. A virtual method, or a method that is overridden, can also be said to be overloaded. See *parametric overloading*.

override The action that occurs when a method in a subclass with the same name as a method in a superclass takes precedence over the method in the superclass. Normally, during the process of binding a method to a message (see *message passing*), the overriding method will be the method selected. (Object Pascal) A keyword used to indicate that a method is to override the similarly named method in an ancestor type.

paradigm An illustrative model or example, which by extension provides a way of organizing information. The object-oriented paradigm emphasizes organization based on behaviors and responsibilities.

parametric overloading Overloading of function names in which two or more procedure bodies are known by the same name in a given context and are disambiguated by the type and number of parameters supplied with the procedure call. (Overloading of functions, methods, and operators can also occur.)

parameterized classes Classes in which some types are left unbound at the time of class definition. These bindings are filled in, resulting in qualified classes, before instances of the class are created.

parent class Syn. *superclass, ancestor class*. An immediate superclass of a class.

Parnas's principles Principles that describe the proper use of modules, originally developed by the computer scientist David Parnas.

persistent object An object that continues to exist outside of the execution time of programs that manipulate the object.

polymorphic Literally "many shapes." A feature of a variable that can take on values of several different types when used with functions that describe a function that has at least one polymorphic argument. The term is also used for a function name that denotes several different functions. See *pure polymorphism, ad hoc polymorphism*.

polymorphic variable   A variable that can hold many different types of values. Object-oriented languages often restrict the types of values to being subclasses of the declared type of the variable.

primitive   (Smalltalk) An operation that cannot be performed in the programming language and must be accomplished with the aid of the underlying run-time system.

private inheritance   (C++) Inheritance used for the purpose of implementation, which does not preserve the is-a relation and thus creates subclasses that are not subtypes. The inheriting class is permitted access to the features of the parent class, but instances of the child class cannot be assigned to variables declared as the parent class.

private method   A method that is not intended to be invoked from outside an object. More specifically, the receiver for the message that invokes a private method should always be the receiver for the method in which the invocation is taking place (see self). Contrast with public method. In Smalltalk private methods are established only by convention, whereas C++, Java, and Delphi Pascal can guarantee the behavior of private methods.

procedure call   The transfer of control from the current point in execution to the code associated with a procedure. Procedure calling differs from *message passing* in that the selection of code to be transferred to is decided at compile time (or link time) rather than run time.

protocol   See *class description protocol*.

prototype   (C++) A declaration for a function that lists the function name, return type, and argument types but does not provide the function definition (or body).

pseudo-variable   A variable that is never declared but can nevertheless be used within a method, although it cannot be directly modified (a pseudo-variable is therefore by definition read-only). The most common pseudo-variable is used to represent the receiver of a method. See *self*, *this*, and *super*.

public class   (Java) A class that is global and can be accessed from other packages. One public class may be declared in each compilation unit.

public method   A method that can be invoked at any time from outside an object.

pure polymorphism   A feature of a single function that can be executed by arguments of a variety of types. See *ad hoc polymorphism*.

pure virtual method   (C++) A *virtual method* without a body, created by the value 0 being assigned to the function in the class definition. Pure virtual methods provide specification for subclasses. See *deferred method*.

qualified name (C++) A name of a method or instance variable that indicates explicitly the class in which the method is located. In C++, the class name and method name are separated by two colons (class::method); in Java and Object Pascal, a period is used. Since the class of the method is named explicitly, a call on a qualified name can be performed by procedure calling in place of message passing.

rapid prototyping A style of software development in which less emphasis is placed on creation of a complete formal specification than on rapid construction of a prototype pilot system with the understanding that users will experiment with the initial system and suggest modifications or changes, probably leading to a complete redevelopment of a subsequent system. See *exploratory programming*.

receiver The object to which a message is sent. In Smalltalk and Objective-C, the receiver is indicated as the object to the left of the message selector. In C++ and Object Pascal, the receiver is the object to the left of the field qualifier (period). Within a method, the current receiver is indicated in various ways: In C++, the variable this is a pointer to the current receiver; in Objective-C, Object Pascal, and Smalltalk, the pseudo-variable self contains the current receiver.

redefinition The process of changing an inherited operation to provide different or extended behavior.

reference variable (C++) A variable declared by the address-of (&) modifier. The variable points to another value and is an alias for this value. Changes to the reference variable will be reflected in changes in the object to which the reference has been assigned.

refinement A style of overriding in which the inherited code is merged with the code defined in the child class.

renaming The process of changing the name for an inherited operation without changing its behavior. Contrast with *redefinition*.

replacement A style of overriding in which the inherited code is completely replaced by the code defined in the child class.

responsibility-driven design A design technique that emphasizes the identification and division of responsibilities within a collection of independent agents.

reverse polymorphism An attempt to undo an assignment to a polymorphic variable—that is, to take a value being held by a polymorphic variable and assign it to another variable that matches the dynamic type of the value, not the static type.

RTTI (C++) The *Run-Time Type Identification* system. A set of values and functions that permits the identification of the dynamic type of a variable, as well as other associated information.

scope When applied to a variable identifier, the (textual) portion of a program in which references to the identifier denote the particular variable.

selector See *message selector*.

self (Objective-C, Object Pascal, Smalltalk) When used inside a method, refers to the receiver for the message that caused the method to be invoked. See *this*.

shadowed name A name that matches another name in a surrounding scope; the new name effectively makes the surrounding name inaccessible. An example is a local variable with the same name as that of a global or instance variable. Within the procedure, the local variable will be attached to all references of the name, making references to the surrounding name difficult. In C++ and Java, access to such values can be provided by a fully qualified name.

single-assignment variable A variable the value of which is assigned once and cannot be redefined. (C++) Single-assignment variables can occur by use of either the const modifier or the definition of a reference variable (in the latter case, the reference is single assignment; the variable to which the reference points, on the other hand, can be modified repeatedly). A single-assignment variable can also be created by assigning a data member in a constructor and then not permitting any other method to modify the value.

slicing (C++) The process by which an argument of a derived type is passed to a parameter declared as a base type. In effect, the fields and methods of the derived type are sliced off from the base fields.

specification class An abstract superclass used only to define an interface. The actual implementation of the interface is left to subclasses.

stack-based memory allocation An implementation technique where memory is allocated for variables when the procedure in which the variables are declared is entered and freed when the procedure is exited. Stack-based allocation is very efficient, but it does not work if either the lifetime of values is not tied to procedure entry/exit or the size of values is not determined at compile time. Contrast with *heap-based memory allocation*.

static (C++ and Java) A declaration modifier that, when applied to global variables and functions, means that the variables are not accessible outside of the file in which they are declared. When applied to local variables, it means that they continue to exist even after the procedure in which they are declared has exited. When applied to class declaration fields, it indicates that the fields are shared by all instances of the class. (Object Pascal) A variable that is allocated space automatically when a procedure is entered. Contrast to dynamic variables, which must have space allocated by the user.

static method   A method that can be called by early binding. The method body can be determined uniquely at compile time, and thus no message passing is required to process a message to a static method.

static class   In statically typed object-oriented languages, such as C++ and Object Pascal, the declared class of a variable. It is legal, however, for the value of the variable to be an instance of either the static class or any class derived from the static class. The class of the value for the variable is known as the *dynamic class*.

static type   See *static class*.

statically typed language   A language in which every variable must have a declared type. Such languages are often, although not necessarily, strongly typed. Object-oriented languages may bend static type rules by permitting variables to hold any value that is a subtype (or subclass) of the declared type.

statically typed object   (Objective-C) A variable that is declared by class name, as opposed to simply being declared by the type id. Statically typing an object permits certain errors to be detected at compile time rather than at run time and permits certain optimizations.

strongly typed language   A language in which the type of any expression can be determined at compile time.

subclass   Syn. *descendant type*, *derived class*, *child class*. (Smalltalk) A class that inherits from another class.

subclass client   A class that uses the facilities of a superclass to implement its own functionality.

subclass coupling   The connection formed between a parent and child class. Subclass coupling is a very weak form of coupling, since instances of the subclass can be treated as though they were simply instances of the parent class. See *coupling* and *cohesion*.

substitutability, principle of   The principle that asserts one should be able to substitute an instance of a child class in a situation where an instance of the parent class is expected. The principle is valid if the two classes are subtypes of each other but not necessarily in general.

subtype   A type A is said to be a subtype of a type B if an instance of type A can be substituted for an instance of type B with no observable effect. For example, a sparse array class might be defined as a subtype of an array type. Subclasses need not be subtypes, nor must subtypes be subclasses.

super (Objective-C, Smalltalk, Java) When used inside a method, a synonym for *self*. However, when used as the receiver for a message, the search for an appropriate method will begin with the parent class of the class in which the current method is defined.

superclass Syn. *ancestor class*, *base class*. (Smalltalk) A class from which another class inherits attributes.

symbol (Smalltalk) A value that is characterized only by its unique value. Similar to an enumerated value in C or Pascal, with the exception that symbols can print themselves textually at run time.

this (C++) When used inside a method, a pointer to the receiver for the message that caused the method to be invoked. Note that the pointer must be dereferenced to obtain the value of the receiver—for example, to send further messages to the receiver. See *self*.

type signature See *argument signature*.

user client A class that uses the facilities provided by another distance object. See *subclass client*.

virtual method (C++) A method that can be called with late binding. The method body to be invoked cannot be determined at compile time, and thus a run-time search must be performed to determine which of several methods should be invoked in response to a message. See *pure virtual method*.

virtual method pointer (C++) A pointer, maintained by every object that uses virtual methods, that points to the virtual method table associated with the type of the value currently contained in the variable.

virtual method table (C++) A table of pointers to methods constructed for each class. All instances of the class point to this table.

void (C++, Java) A type name used to indicate a function returning no value—that is, a procedure.

World Wide Web A collection of machines on the Internet that have agreed to distribute information according to a common protocol. This information is usually accessed with a *browser*.

yo-yo problem Repeated movements up and down the class hierarchy may be required when the execution of a particular method invocation is traced.

References

[Abelson 1981] Harold Abelson and Andrea diSessa, *Turtle Geometry: The Computer as a Medium for Exploring Mathematics*, MIT Press, Cambridge, MA, 1981.

[Actor 1987] *Actor Language Manual*, The Whitewater Group, Inc., Evanston, IL, 1987.

[Aho 1985] Alfred V. Aho, Ravi Sethi, and Jeffrey D. Ullman, *Compilers: Principles, Techniques, and Tools*, Addison-Wesley, Reading, MA, 1985.

[Albahari 2001] Ben Albahari, Peter Drayton, and Brad Merrill, *C# Essentials*, O'Reilly, Cambridge, MA, 2001.

[Alexander 1977] Christopher Alexander, Sara Ishikawa, and Murray Silverstein, *A Pattern Language*, Oxford University Press, New York, 1977.

[Appel 1987] Andrew W. Appel, "Garbage Collection Can Be Faster Than Stack Allocation," *Information Processing Letters*, 25(4): 275–279, 1987.

[Alhir 1998] Sinan Si Alhir, *UML in a Nutshell*, O'Reilly, Cambridge, MA, 1998.

[Arnold 2000] Ken Arnold, James Gosling, and David Holmes, *The Java Programming Language*, 3rd Ed., Addison-Wesley, Reading, MA, 2000.

[Atkinson 1988] Malcolm P. Atkinson, Peter Buneman, and Ronald Morrison (Eds.), *Data Types and Persistence*, Springer-Verlag, New York, 1988.

[Beazley 2000] David M. Beazley, *Python Essential Reference*, New Riders Publishing, Indianapolis, IN, 2000.

[Beck 1989] Kent Beck and Ward Cunningham, "A Laboratory for Teaching Object-Oriented Thinking," *Proceedings of the 1989 OOPSLA—Conference on Object-Oriented Programming Systems, Languages and Applications*; Reprinted in *Sigplan Notices*, 24(10): 1–6, 1989.

[Bellin 1997] David Bellin and Susan Suchman Simone, *The CRC Card Book*, Addison-Wesley, Reading, MA, 1997.

[Berztiss 1990] Alfs Berztiss, *Programming with Generators*, Ellis Horwood, New York, 1990.

[Birtwistle 1979] Graham M. Birtwistle, Ole-Johan Dahl, Bjørn Myhrhaug, and Kristen Nygaard, *Simula Begin*, Studentlitteratur, Lund, Sweden, 1979.

[Böhm 1966] Corrado Böhm and Giuseppe Jacopini, "Flow Diagrams, Turing Machines and Languages with Only Two Formation Rules," *Communications of the ACM*, 9(5):366–371, May 1966.

[Booch 1999] Grady Booch, James Rumbaugh, and Ivar Jacobson, *The Unified Modeling Language User Guide*, Addison-Wesley, Reading, MA, 1999.

[Bracha 1990] Gilad Bracha and William Cook, "Mixin-Based Inheritance," *Proceedings of the 1990 OOPSLA—Conference on Object-Oriented Programming Systems, Languages and Applications*; Reprinted in *Sigplan Notices*, 25(10): 347–349, 1990.

[Brooks 1975] Frederick P. Brooks, Jr., *The Mythical Man-Month: Essays on Software Engineering*, Addison-Wesley, Reading, MA, 1975.

[Brooks 1987] Frederick P. Brooks, Jr., "No Silver Bullet: Essence and Accidents of Software Engineering," *IEEE Computer*, April 1987, pp. 10–19.

[Bruce 1994] Kim B. Bruce, "A Paradigmatic Object-Oriented Programming Language: Design, Static Typing and Semantics," *Journal of Functional Programming*, 4(1994), pp. 127–206.

[Budd 1987] Timothy A. Budd, *A Little Smalltalk*, Addison-Wesley, Reading, MA, 1987.

[Budd 1991] Timothy A. Budd, "Generalized Arithmetic in C++," *Journal of Object-Oriented Programming*, 3(6): 11–23, February 1991.

[Budd 1994] Timothy A. Budd, *Classic Data Structures in C++*, Addison-Wesley, Reading, MA, 1994.

[Budd 1998] Timothy A. Budd, *Data Structures in C++ Using the Standard Template Library*, Addison-Wesley, Reading, MA, 1994.

[Budd 1998b] Timothy A. Budd, *Understanding Object-Oriented Programming with Java*, Addison-Wesley, Reading, MA, 1998.

[Budd 1999] Timothy A. Budd, *C++ for Java Programmers*, Addison-Wesley, Reading, MA, 1999.

[Budd 2000] Timothy A. Budd, *Classic Data Structures in Java*, Addison-Wesley, Reading, MA, 2000.

[Callaway 1999] Dustin R. Callaway, *Inside Servlets*, Addison-Wesley, Reading, MA, 1999.

[Campione 1998] Mary Campione and Kathy Walrath, *The Java Tutorial*, Addison-Wesley, Reading, MA, 1998.

[Campione 1999] Mary Campione, Kathy Walrath, and Alison Huml, *The Java Tutorial Continued*, Addison-Wesley, Reading, MA, 1999.

[Cardelli 1985] Luca Cardelli and Peter Wegner, "On Understanding Types, Data Abstraction, and Polymorphism," *Computing Surveys*, 17(4): 471–523, 1985.

[Carroll 1995] Martin D. Carroll and Margaret A. Ellis, *Designing and Coding Reusable C++*, Addison-Wesley, Reading, MA, 1987.

[Castagna 1997] Giuseppe Castagna, *Object-Oriented Programming: A Unified Foundation*, Birkhäuser, Boston, 1997.

[Chan 2000] Patric Chan, *The Java Developers Almanac 2000*, Addison-Wesley, Reading, MA, 2000.

[Chirlian 1990] Paul M. Chirlian, *Programming in C++*, Merrill, Columbus, OH, 1990.

[Church 1936] Alonzo Church, "An Unsolvable Problem of Elementary Number Theory," *American Journal of Mathematics*, 58: 345–363, 1936.

[Cohen 1981] Jacques Cohen, "Garbage Collection of Linked Data Structures," *ACM Computing Surveys*, 13(3): 341–367, 1981.

[Cook 1988] Steven Cook, "Impressions of ECOOP'88," *Journal of Object-Oriented Programming*, 1(4), 1988.

[Cook 1990] William Cook, Walter Hill, and Peter Canning, "Inheritance Is Not Subtyping," Conference Record of the Seventeenth ACM Symposium on Principles of Programming Languages, pp. 125–135, ACM Press, January 1990.

[Coplien 1995] *Pattern Languages of Program Design*, edited by James A. Coplien and Douglas C. Schmidt, Addison-Wesley, Reading, MA, 1995.

[Cox 1986] Brad J. Cox, *Object-Oriented Programming: An Evolutionary Approach*, Addison-Wesley, Reading, MA, 1986.

[Cox 1990] Brad J. Cox, "Planning the Software Industrial Revolution," *IEEE Software*, 7(6): 25–35, November 1990.

[Craig 2000] Iain Craig, *The Interpretation of Object-Oriented Languages*, Springer-Verlag, London, 2000.

[Dahl 1966] Ole-Johan Dahl and Kristen Nygaard, "Simula, An Algol-Based Simulation Language," *Communications of the ACM*, 9(9): 671–678, September 1966.

[Danforth 1988]   Scott Danforth and Chris Tomlinson, "Type Theories and Object-Oriented Programming," *ACM Computing Surveys*, 20(1): 29–72, 1988.

[Deutsch 1989]   L. Peter Deutsch, "Design Reuse and Frameworks in the Smalltalk-80 System." In Ted J. Biggerstaff and Alan J. Perlis (Eds.), *Software Reusability, Volume II: Applications and Experience*, pp. 57–71, Addison-Wesley, Reading, MA, 1989.

[Dijkstra 1976]   Edsger W. Dijkstra, *A Discipline of Programming*, Prentice-Hall, Englewood Cliffs, NJ, 1976.

[Eckel 1989]   Bruce Eckel, *Using C++*, McGraw-Hill, New York, 1989.

[Ellis 1990]   Margaret A. Ellis and Bjarne Stroustrup, *The Annotated C++ Reference Manual*, Addison-Wesley, Reading, MA, 1990.

[Fairley 1985]   Richard Fairley, *Software Engineering Concepts*, McGraw-Hill, New York, 1985.

[Feldman 1997]   Michael B. Feldman, *Software Construction and Data Structures with Ada 95*, Addison-Wesley, Reading, MA, 1997.

[Felleisen 1998]   Matthias Felleisen and Daniel P. Friedman, *A Little Java, A Few Patterns*, MIT Press, Cambridge, MA, 1998.

[Fischer 1988]   Charles N. Fischer and Richard J. LeBlanc, Jr., *Crafting A Compiler*, Benjamin Cummings, Menlo Park, CA, 1988.

[Flanagan 1997]   David Flanagan, *Java Examples in a Nutshell*, O'Reilly, Cambridge, MA, 1997.

[Floyd 1979]   Robert W. Floyd, "The Paradigms of Programming," *Communications of the ACM*, 22(8): 455–460, August 1979.

[Forman 1999]   Ira R. Forman and Scott H. Danforth, *Putting Metaclasses to Work*, Addison-Wesley, Reading, MA, 1999.

[Gabriel 1996]   Richard P. Gabriel, *Patterns of Software*, Oxford University Press, New York, 1996.

[Gamma 1995]   Erich Gamma, Richard Helm, Ralph Johnson, and John Vlissides, *Design Patterns: Elements of Reusable Object-Oriented Software*, Addison-Wesley, Reading, MA, 1995.

[Gibbs 1994]   Wayt Gibbs, "Software's Chronic Crisis," *Scientific American*, 271(3): 86–95, September 1994.

[Gillett 1982]   Will D. Gillett and Seymour V. Pollack, *An Introduction to Engineered Software*, Holt, Rinehart & Winston, New York, 1982.

[Glass 1996]   Graham Glass and Brett Schuchert, *The STL Primer*, Prentice-Hall, Englewood Cliffs, NJ, 1996.

[Gödel 1931]   Kurt Gödel, "Über formal unentscheidbare Sätze der Principia Mathematica und verwandter Systeme," *Monatshefte für Mathematik und Physik*, 38: 173–198, 1931.

[Goldberg 1983]   Adele Goldberg and David Robson, *Smalltalk-80: The Language and Its Implementation*, Addison-Wesley, Reading, MA, 1983.

[Goldberg 1984]   Adele Goldberg, *Smalltalk-80: The Interactive Programming Environment*, Addison-Wesley, Reading, MA, 1983.

[Goldberg 1989]   Adele Goldberg and David Robson, *Smalltalk-80: The Language*, Addison-Wesley, Reading, MA, 1989.

[Goldberg 1995]   Adele Goldberg and Kenneth Rubin, *Succeeding with Objects*, Addison-Wesley, Reading, MA, 1995.

[Grand 1998]   Mark Grand, *Patterns in Java, Volume 1: A Catalog of Reusable Design Patterns Illustrated with UML*, Wiley, New York, 1998.

[Grand 1999]   Mark Grand, *Patterns in Java, Volume 2*, Wiley, New York, 1999.

[Gries 1981]   David Gries, *The Science of Programming*, Springer-Verlag, New York, 1981.

[Griswold 1983]   Ralph E. Griswold and Madge T. Griswold, *The Icon Programming Language*, Prentice-Hall, Englewood Cliffs, NJ, 1983.

[Gunnerson 2000]   Eric Gunnerson, *A Programmer's Introduction to C#*, APress, Berkeley, CA, 2000.

[Guzdial 2001]   Mark Guzdial, *Squeak: Object-Oriented Design with Multimedia Applications*, Prentice-Hall, Englewood Cliffs, NJ, 2001.

[Halbert 1987]   Daniel C. Halbert and Patrick D. O'Brien, "Using Types and Inheritance in Object-Oriented Programming," *IEEE Software*, 4(5): 71–79, 1987.

[Hamlet 1976]   Richard G. Hamlet, "High-level Binding with Low-Level Linkers," *Communications of the ACM*, 19: 642–644, November 1976.

[Hanson 1981]   David R. Hanson, "Is Block Structure Necessary?" *Software Practice & Experience*, 1(8): 853–866, 1981.

[Hebel 1990]   Kurt J. Hebel and Ralph E. Johnson, "Arithmetic and Double Dispatching in Smalltalk-80," *Journal of Object-Oriented Programming*, 2(6): 40–44, 1990.

[Henderson-Sellers 1992]   Brian Henderson-Sellers, *A Book of Object-Oriented Knowledge*, Prentice-Hall, Englewood Cliffs, NJ, 1992.

[Horowitz 1984]   Ellis Horowitz, *Fundamentals of Programming Languages*, Computer Science Press, Rockville, MD, 1984.

[Ingalls 1981] Daniel H. H. Ingalls, "Design Principles Behind Smalltalk," *Byte*, 6(8): 286–298, 1981.

[Ingalls 1986] Daniel H. H. Ingalls, "A Simple Technique for Handling Multiple Polymorphism," *Proceedings of the 1986* OOPSLA—*Conference on Object-Oriented Programming Systems, Languages and Applications*; Reprinted in *Sigplan Notices*, 21(11): 347–349, 1986.

[Jacobson 1994] Ivar Jacobson, *Object-Oriented Software Engineering: A Use Case Driven Approach*, Addison-Wesley, Reading, MA, 1994.

[Joyner 1999] Ian Joyner, *Objects Unencapsulated*, Prentice-Hall, Englewood Cliffs, NJ, 1999.

[Kaehler 1986] Ted Kaehler and Dave Patterson, *A Taste of Smalltalk*, W.W. Norton & Company, New York, 1986.

[Kamin 1990] Samuel N. Kamin, *Programming Languages: An Interpreter-Based Approach*, Addison-Wesley, Reading, MA, 1990.

[Kay 1977] Alan Kay, "Microelectronics and the Personal Computer," *Scientific American*, 237(3): 230–244, 1977.

[Kay 1993] Alan C. Kay, "The Early History of Smalltalk," The Second ACM SIGPLAN History of Programming Languages Conference (HOPL-II), *ACM SIGPLAN Notices* 28(3): 69–75, March 1993.

[Keene 1989] Sonya E. Keene, *Object-Oriented Programming in Common Lisp*, Addison-Wesley, Reading, MA, 1989.

[Keller 1990] Daniel Keller, "A Guide to Natural Naming," *Sigplan Notices*, 25(5): 95–102, May 1990.

[Kerman 2002] Mitchell C. Kerman, *Programming & Problem Solving with Delphi*, Addison-Wesley, Reading, MA, 2002.

[Kiczales 1991] Gregor Kiczales, Jim des Rivières, and Daniel G. Bobrow, *The Art of the Metaobject Protocol*, MIT Press, Cambridge, MA, 1991.

[Kim 1989] Won Kim and Frederick H. Lochovsky (Eds.), *Object-Oriented Concepts, Databases, and Applications*, Addison-Wesley, Reading, MA, 1989.

[Kirkerud 1989] Bjørn Kirkerud, *Object-Oriented Programming with Simula*, Addison-Wesley, Reading, MA, 1989.

[Klas 1995] Wolfgang Klas and Michael Schrefl, *Metaclasses and their Application*, Springer-Verlag, New York, 1995.

[Kleene 1936] Stephen C. Kleene, "λ-Definability and Recursiveness," *Duke Mathematical Journal*, 2: 340–353, 1936.

[Knolle 1989]   Nancy T. Knolle, "Why Object-Oriented User Interface Toolkits Are Better," *Journal of Object-Oriented Programming*, 2(4): 63–67, 1989.

[Koenig 1989a]   Andrew Koenig, "References in C++," *Journal of Object-Oriented Programming*, 1(6), 1989.

[Koenig 1989b]   Andrew Koenig, "Objects, Values, and Assignment," *Journal of Object-Oriented Programming*, 2(2): 37–38, 1989.

[Koenig 1989c]   Andrew Koenig, "What Are Friends For?," *Journal of Object-Oriented Programming*, 2(4): 53–54, 1989.

[Korienek 1993]   Gene Korienek and Tom Wrensch, *A Quick Trip to ObjectLand*, Prentice-Hall, Englewood Cliffs, NJ, 1993.

[Krasner 1983]   Glenn Krasner, *Smalltalk-80: Bits of History, Words of Advice*, Addison-Wesley, Reading, MA, 1983.

[Krogdahl 1985]   Stein Krogdahl, "Multiple Inheritance in Simula-Like Languages," *BIT*, 25: 318–326, 1985.

[Kuhn 1970]   Thomas S. Kuhn, *The Structure of Scientific Revolutions*, 2nd ed., University of Chicago Press, Chicago, 1970.

[Lakoff 1987]   George Lakoff, *Women, Fire, and Dangerous Things*, University of Chicago Press, Chicago, 1987.

[LaLonde 1990a]   Wilf LaLonde and John Pugh, "Integrating New Varieties of Numbers into the Class Library: Quaternions and Complex Numbers," *Journal of Object-Oriented Programming*, 2(5): 64–68, 1990.

[LaLonde 1990b]   Wilf LaLonde and John Pugh, *Inside Smalltalk*, Prentice-Hall, Englewood Cliffs, NJ, 1990.

[Lieberherr 1989a]   Karl J. Lieberherr and Ian M. Holland, "Assuring Good Style for Object-Oriented Programs," *IEEE Software*, 6(5): 38–48, 1989.

[Lieberherr 1989b]   Karl J. Lieberherr and Arthur J. Riel, "Contributions to Teaching Object-Oriented Design and Programming," *Proceedings of the 1989 OOPSLA—Conference on Object-Oriented Programming Systems, Languages and Applications*; Reprinted in *Sigplan Notices*, 24(10): 11–22, October 1989.

[Lieberman 1986]   Henry Lieberman, "Using Prototypical Objects to Implement Shared Behavior in Object-Oriented Systems," *Proceedings of the 1986 OOPSLA—Conference on Object-Oriented Programming Systems, Languages and Applications*; Reprinted in *Sigplan Notices*, 21(11): 214–223, 1986.

[Lippman 1996]   Stanley B. Lippman, *Inside the C++ Object Model*, Addison-Wesley, Reading, MA, 1996.

[Lischner 2000] Ray Lischner, *Delphi in a Nutshell*. O'Reilly, Cambridge, MA, 2000.

[Liskov 1977] Barbara Liskov, Alan Snyder, Russell Atkinson, and Craig Scaffert, "Abstraction Mechanisms in CLU," *Communications of the ACM*, 20(8): 564–567, August 1977.

[Liskov 1988] Barbara Liskov, "Data Abstraction and Hierarchy," *Sigplan Notices*, 23(5), 1988.

[Liskov 1986] Barbara Liskov and John Guttag, *Abstraction and Specification in Program Development*, McGraw-Hill, New York, 1986.

[Logan 1986] Robert K. Logan, *The Alphabet Effect*, St. Martin's Press, New York, 1986.

[MacLennan 1987] Bruce J. MacLennan, *Principles of Programming Languages*, Holt, Rinehart & Winston, New York, 1987.

[Madsen 1993] Ole Lehrmann Madsen, Birger Møller-Pedersen, and Kristen Nygaard, *Object-Oriented Programming in the BETA Programming Language*, Addison-Wesley, Reading, MA, 1993.

[Marcotty 1987] Michael Marcotty and Henry Ledgard, *The World of Programming Languages*, Springer-Verlag, New York, 1987.

[Markov 1951] Andrei Andreevich Markov, "The Theory of Algorithms" (in Russian), *Trudy Mathematicheskogo Instituta immeni V. A. Steklova*, 38: 176–189, 1951.

[McGregor 1992] John D. McGregor and David A. Sykes, *Object-Oriented Software Development: Engineering Software For Reuse*, International Thomson Computer Press, Albany, NY, 1992.

[Meyer 1988a] Bertrand Meyer, *Object-Oriented Software Construction*, Prentice-Hall International, London, 1988a.

[Meyer 1988b] Bertrand Meyer, "Harnessing Multiple Inheritance," *Journal of Object-Oriented Programming Languages*, 1(4): 48–51, 1988b.

[Meyer 1994] Bertrand Meyer, *Reusable Software*, Prentice-Hall, Englewood Cliffs, NJ, 1994.

[Meyers 1998] Scott Meyers, *Effective C++, 2nd Edition*, Addison-Wesley, Reading, MA, 1992.

[Micallef 1988] Josephine Micallef, "Encapsulation, Resuability and Extensibility in Object-Oriented Programming Languages," *Journal of Object-Oriented Programming Languages*, 1(1): 12–35, 1988.

[Milner 1990]   Robin Milner, Mads Tofte, and Robert Harper, *The Definition of Standard ML*, MIT Press, Cambridge, MA, 1990.

[Morehead 1949]   Albert H. Morehead and Geoffrey Mott-Smith, *The Complete Book of Solitaire and Patience Games*, Grosset & Dunlap, New York, 1949.

[Mössenböck 1993]   Hanspeter Mössenböck, *Object-Oriented Programming in Oberon-2*, Springer-Verlag, New York, 1993.

[Musser 1996]   David R. Musser and Atul Saini, *STL Tutorial and Reference Guide*, Addison-Wesley, Reading, MA, 1996.

[Nygaard 1981]   Kristen Nygaard and Ole-Johan Dahl, "The Development of the Simula Languages," in *History of Programming Languages*, Richard L. Wexelblat, Ed., Academic Press, New York, 1981.

[O'Brian 1989]   Stephen K. O'Brian, *Turbo Pascal 5.5: The Complete Reference*, McGraw-Hill, New York, 1989.

[Palsberg 1994]   Jens Palsberg and Michael I. Schwartzbach, *Object-Oriented Type Systems*. John Wiley & Sons, New York, 1994.

[Parnas 1972]   David L. Parnas, "On the Criteria to Be Used in Decomposing Systems into Modules," *Communications of the ACM*, 15(12): 1059–1062, 1972.

[Perry 1990]   Dewayne E. Perry and Gail E. Kaiser, "Adequate Testing and Object-Oriented Programming," *Journal of Object-Oriented Programming*, 2(5): 13–19, 1990.

[Pinson 1988]   Lewis J. Pinson and Richard S. Wiener, *An Introduction to Object-Oriented Programming and Smalltalk*, Addison-Wesley, Reading, MA, 1988.

[Pohl 1989]   Ira Pohl, *C++ for C Programmers*, Addison-Wesley, Reading, MA, 1989.

[Post 1936]   Emil L. Post, "Finite Combinatory Processes Formulation, I," *The Journal of Symbolic Logic*, 1: 103–105, 1936.

[Pree 1995]   Wolfgang Pree, *Design Patterns for Object-Oriented Software Development*, Addison-Wesley, Reading, MA, 1995.

[Pullum 1991]   Geoffrey K. Pullum, *The Great Eskimo Vocabulary Hoax*, The University of Chicago Press, Chicago, 1991.

[Raj 1991]   Rajendra K. Raj, Ewan D. Tempero, Henry M. Levy, Andrew P. Black, Norman C. Hutchinson, and Eric Jul, "Emerald: A General Purpose Programming Language," *Software-Practice & Experience* 21(1): 91–118, 1991.

[Rising 2000]   Linda Rising, *The Pattern Almanac 2000*, Addison-Wesley, Reading, MA, 2000.

[Rist 1995] Robert Rist and Robert Terwilliger, *Object-Oriented Programming in Eiffel*, Prentice-Hall, Englewood Cliffs, NJ, 1995.

[Rogers 1967] Hartley Rogers, Jr., *Theory of Recursive Functions and Effective Computability*, McGraw-Hill, New York, 1967.

[Rosenberg 1971] Jay F. Rosenberg and Charles Travis (Eds.), *Readings in the Philosophy of Language*, Prentice-Hall, Englewood Cliffs, NJ, 1971.

[Rumbaugh 1991] James Rumbaugh, Michael Blaha, William Premerlani, Frederick Eddy, and William Lorensen, *Object-Oriented Modeling and Design*, Prentice-Hall, Englewood Cliffs, NJ, 1991.

[Sakkinen 1988a] Markku Sakkinen, "On the Darker Side of C++," *ECOOP '88 Proceedings: European Conference on Object-Oriented Programming*, S. Gjessing and K. Nygaard, Eds., Springer-Verlag, New York, 1988.

[Sakkinen 1988b] Markku Sakkinen, "Comments on 'the Law of Demeter' and C++," *Sigplan Notices*, 23(12): 38–44, 1988.

[Sakkinen 1992] Markku Sakkinen, *Inheritance and Other Main Principles of C++ and Other Object-Oriented Languages*, Ph.D. thesis, University of Jyväskylä, Jyväskylä, Finland, 1992.

[Salus 1998] Peter H. Salus, Ed., *Handbook of Programming Languages*, Vol. 1: Object-Oriented Programming Languages, Macmillian Technical Publishing, 1998.

[Scott 2000] Michael L. Scott, *Programming Language Pragmatics*, Morgan Kaufmann Publishers, San Francisco, 2000.

[Sethi 1989] Ravi Sethi, *Programming Languages: Concepts and Constructs*, Addison-Wesley, Reading, MA, 1989.

[Schildt 1996] Herbert Schildt, *MFC Programming from the Ground Up*, McGraw-Hill, New York, 1996.

[Shammas 1996] Namir C. Shammas, *Object-Oriented Programming for Dummies*, IDG Books, Foster City, CA, 1996.

[Smith 1995] David N. Smith, *IBM Smalltalk: The Language*, Addison-Wesley, Reading, MA, 1995.

[Snyder 1986] Alan Snyder, "Encapsulation and Inheritance in Object-Oriented Programming Languages," *Proceedings of the 1986 OOPSLA—Conference on Object-Oriented Programming Systems, Languages and Applications*; Reprinted in *Sigplan Notices*, 21(11): 38–45, 1986.

[Stefik 1986] Mark Stefik and Daniel G. Bobrow, "Object-Oriented Programming: Themes and Variations," *AI Magazine*, 6(4): 40–62, 1986.

[Stein 1987] Lynn Andrea Stein, "Delegation Is Inheritance," *Proceedings of the 1987* OOPSLA—*Conference on Object-Oriented Programming Systems, Languages and Applications*; Reprinted in *Sigplan Notices*, 22(12): 138–146, 1987.

[Stevens 1981] W. Stevens, G. Myers, and L. Constantine, "Structured Design," *IBM Systems Journal*, 13(2), 1974. Reprinted in Edward Yourdon (Ed.), *Classics in Software Engineering*, Prentice-Hall, Englewood Cliffs, NJ, 1979.

[Stroustrup 1982] Bjarne Stroustrup, "Classes: An Abstract Data Type Facility for the C Language," *ACM Sigplan Notices*, 17(1): 42–51, January 1982.

[Stroustrup 1986] Bjarne Stroustrup, *The C++ Programming Language*, Addison-Wesley, Reading, MA, 1986.

[Stroustrup 1988] Bjarne Stroustrup, "What Is 'Object-Oriented Programming'?," *IEEE Software*, 5(3): 10–20, May 1988.

[Stroustrup 1994] Bjarne Stroustrup, *The Design and Evolution of* C++, Addison-Wesley, Reading, MA, 1994.

[Taenzer 1989] David Taenzer, Murthy Ganti, and Sunil Podar, "Object-Oriented Software Reuse: The Yoyo Problem," *Journal of Object-Oriented Programming*, 2(3): 30–35, 1989.

[Tesler 1985] Larry Tesler, "Object Pascal Report," Apple Computer, Santa Clara, CA, 1985.

[Thomas 2001] David Thomas, Andrew Hunt, *Programming Ruby*, Addison-Wesley, Reading, MA, 2001.

[Thompson 1996] Simon Thompson, *Haskell: The Craft of Functional Programming*, Addison-Wesley, Reading, MA, 1996.

[Tomlinson 1990] Chris Tomlinson, Mark Scheevel, and Won Kim, "Sharing and Organization Protocols in Object-Oriented Systems," *Journal of Object-Oriented Programming*, 2(4): 25–36, 1989.

[Turbo 1988] *Turbo Pascal 5.5 Object-Oriented Programming Guide*, Borland International, Scotts Valley, CA, 1988.

[Turing 1936] Alan Turing, "On Computable Numbers, with an Application to the Entscheidungsproblem," *Proceeds of the London Mathematical Society*, Series 2, 42: 230–265; and 43: 544–546, 1936.

[Ungar 1987] David Ungar and Randall B. Smith, "Self: The Power of Simplicity," *Proceedings of the 1987* OOPSLA—*Conference on Object-Oriented Programming Systems, Languages and Applications*; Reprinted in *Sigplan Notices*, 22(12): 227–242, 1987.

[Unger 1987]   J. Marshall Unger, *The Fifth Generation Fallacy*, Oxford University Press, New York, 1987.

[Usenix 1987]   *Proceedings of the C++ Workshop*, USENIX Association, Berkeley, CA, 1987.

[Vermeulen 2000]   Allan Vermeulen, Scott W. Wambler, Greg Bumgardner, Eldon Metz, Trevor Misfeldt, Jim Shur, and Patrick Thompson, *The Elements of Java Style*, Cambridge University Press, New York, 2000.

[Walrath 1999]   Kath Walrath and Mary Campione, *The JFC Swing Tutorial*, Addison-Wesley, Reading, MA, 1999.

[Webster 1989]   Bruce F. Webster, *The NeXT Book*, Addison-Wesley, Reading, MA, 1989.

[Wegner 1986]   Peter Wegner, "Classification in Object-Oriented Systems," *Sigplan Notices*, 21(10): 173–182, October 1986.

[Weinand 1988]   André Weinand, Erich Gamma, and Rudolf Marty, "ET++—An Object-Oriented Application Framework in C++," in *Proceedings of the 1988 OOPSLA—Conference on Object-Oriented Programming Systems, Languages and Applications*; Reprinted in *Sigplan Notices*, 23(10): 46–57, October 1988.

[Weiskamp 1990]   Keith Weiskamp and Bryan Flamig, *The Complete C++ Primer*, Academic Press, New York, 1990.

[Weizenbaum 1976]   Joseph Weizenbaum, *Computer Power and Human Reason*, W. H. Freeman and Company, San Francisco, 1976.

[Whorf 1956]   Benjamin Lee Whorf, *Language Thought & Reality*, MIT Press, Cambridge, MA, 1956.

[Wiener 1988]   Richard S. Wiener and Lewis J. Pinson, *An Introduction to Object-Oriented Programming and C++*, Addison-Wesley, Reading, MA, 1988.

[Wiener 1989]   Richard S. Wiener and Lewis J. Pinson, "A Practical Example of Multiple Inheritance in C++," *Sigplan Notices*, 24(9): 112–115, 1989.

[Wiener 1990]   Richard S. Wiener and Lewis J. Pinson, *The C++ Workbook*, Addison-Wesley, Reading, MA, 1990.

[Wikström 1987]   Åke Wikström, *Functional Programming Using Standard ML*, Prentice-Hall International, London, 1987.

[Wilson 1990]   David A. Wilson, Larry S. Rosenstein, and Dan Shafer, *Programming With MacApp*, Addison-Wesley, Reading, MA, 1990.

[Wirfs-Brock 1989a]   Allen Wirfs-Brock and Brian Wilkerson, "Variables Limit Reusability," *Journal of Object-Oriented Programming*, 2(1): 34–40, May 1990.

[Wirfs-Brock 1989b] Rebecca Wirfs-Brock and Brian Wilkerson, "Object-Oriented Design: A Responsibility-Driven Approach," *Proceedings of the 1989 OOPSLA—Conference on Object-Oriented Programming Systems, Languages and Applications*; Reprinted in *Sigplan Notices*, 24(10): 71–76, October 1989.

[Wirfs-Brock 1990] Rebecca Wirfs-Brock, Brian Wilkerson, and Lauren Wiener, *Designing Object-Oriented Software*, Prentice-Hall, Englewood Cliffs, NJ, 1990.

[Wulf 1972] William A. Wulf, "A Case Against the GOTO," *Proceedings of the Twenty-Fifth National ACM Conference*, 1972; Reprinted in Edward Yourdon (Ed.), *Classics in Software Engineering*, Prentice-Hall, Englewood Cliffs, NJ, 1979.

[Wulf 1973] William A. Wulf and Mary Shaw, "Global Variable Considered Harmful," *Sigplan Notices*, 8(2): 28–43, 1973.

Index